Labour in the Caribbean
From emancipation to independence

Edited by

Malcolm Cross and Gad Heuman

Ruth *Hutchinson*

2nd year CAS.

/

M
MACMILLAN CARIBBEAN

First published 1988

Published by *Macmillan Publishers Ltd*
London and Basingstoke
Associated companies and representatives in Accra,
Auckland, Delhi, Dublin, Gaborone, Hamburg, Harare,
Hong Kong, Kuala Lumpur, Lagos, Manzini, Melbourne,
Mexico City, Nairobi, New York, Singapore, Tokyo

ISBM 0−333−44729−8

Printed in Hong Kong

British Library Cataloguing in Publication Data
Labour in the Caribbean: from emancipation to
    independence. — (Warwick University
    Caribbean studies.)
    1. Labor and laboring classes — Caribbean
    Area — History   2. Labor and laboring
    classes — Political
    activity — History
    I. Cross, Malcolm   II. Heuman, Gad
    III. Series
    335'.009182'1   HX151
ISBN 0−333−44729−8

Cover based on a painting by Aubrey Williams presented to
The Centre for Caribbean Studies, University of Warwick.

Series Preface

The Centre for Caribbean Studies at the University of Warwick was founded in 1984 in order to stimulate academic interest and research in a region which, in spite of its creative vitality and geopolitical importance, has not received the academic recognition it deserves in its own right. In the past, the Caribbean has tended to be subsumed under either Commonwealth or Latin American Studies. The purpose of the Centre is to teach and research on the region (which includes those circum-Caribbean areas sharing similar traits with the islands) from a comparative, cross-cultural and inter-disciplinary perspective. It is intended that this Pan-Caribbean approach will be reflected in the publication each year of papers from the Centre's annual symposium as well as in other volumes. The essays in this book are a selection of those originally presented at the first two of these symposia.

The function of comparative study should be to stimulate the imagination, to pose new questions, to open up new perspectives, to assess the relative significance of the variables involved, and to formulate hypotheses. There are clearly difficulties in making comparisons across a region with such diverse characteristics as the Caribbean, fragmented by multiple colonial legacies and divided by differences in language, traditions and historical timing, but most Caribbean peoples are bound together by the common historical experience of slavery and most islands still have monoproductive economies and labour systems in which compulsion is discreetly veiled. This volume analyses the responses to that experience and to the imperatives of these economies. The variety of response, conditioned by pervasive colonial and metropolitan influences, both tangible and intangible, makes it difficult to generalize and hazardous to formulate general theories. Nevertheless, it is hoped that these essays will contribute towards a greater understanding of the complexities and variety of Caribbean labour history as well as stimulating further research on this unique region.

Prof. Alistair Hennessy
Series Editor

Warwick University Caribbean Studies

Andrew Sanders
The Powerless People — The Amerindians of the Corentyne River

Editors: Jean Besson and Janet Momsen
Land and Development in the Caribbean

Kelvin Singh
The Bloodstained Tombs — The Muharram Massacre in Trinidad 1884

David Nicholls
From Dessalines to Duvalier — Race, Colour and National Independence

Editors: Malcolm Cross and Gad Heuman
Labour in the Caribbean — From Emancipation to Independence

Harry Goulbourne
Teachers, Education and Politics in Jamaica, 1892-1972

Neil Price
Behind the Planter's Back — Lower Class Response to Marginality in Bequia Island, St Vincent

Douglas Hall
In Miserable Slavery — Thomas Thistlewood in Jamaica, 1750-86

To the memory of
Frank Cross (MC)
and
Lewis Weinstock (GH)

Acknowledgements

Eleven of the chapters in this book were originally prepared as papers for discussion at two symposia on 'Labour in the Caribbean' organised by the editors for the Centre for Caribbean Studies at the University of Warwick. We are grateful for financial assistance from the Centre and from the Nuffield Foundation. Three chapters have been added to rectify omissions in the original collection.

The manuscript was prepared in the Centre for Research in Ethnic Relations at the University of Warwick. We are pleased to acknowledge this support and, in particular, to thank Rose Goodwin and Ann Bromiley who worked so hard in helping us produce a final manuscript. We are indebted to Professor Sidney Mintz, whose participation in these symposia and whose writings have taught us so much on Caribbean labour. We are particularly grateful to him for contributing a foreword to this book.

Malcolm Cross
Gad Heuman
September, 1987

Contents

The Contributors

Michiel Baud is a member of the Department of Social History at the Erasmus University of Rotterdam (Holland). He teaches modern Latin American history, where he focuses on the transformation of Latin American agriculture in the period 1850–1930. He is writing his dissertation about the agrarian history of the Dominican Republic and has published various articles about related topics in Dominican journals.

O. Nigel Bolland is a Professor of Sociology at Colgate University. Formerly a Research Fellow at the Institute of Social and Economic Research, University of the West Indies, he received his Ph.D. from the University of Hull. Focusing on issues of colonialism and development, he has carried out extensive archival research on Belize and is the author of *The Formation of a Colonial Society: Belize, from Conquest to Crown Colony* (1977) and *Belize: A New Nation in Central America* (1986). He is currently working on a comparative study of the labour movement in the British West Indies in the 1930s and 1940s.

Malcolm Cross is Principal Research Fellow at the Centre for Research in Ethnic Relations at the University of Warwick. He has held lecturing posts at a number of universities, including the University of the West Indies. His books include *Urbanization in the Caribbean* (Cambridge University Press, 1979). He has recently edited a collection of essays on Caribbean migration to Britain and the Netherlands (*Lost Illusions: Caribbean Minorities in Britain and the Netherlands*, Tavistock, 1988) with Han Entzinger. He is currently working on the economic position of ethnic minorities in the U.K.

Rosario Espinal is a Dominican sociologist and a Faculty Fellow at the Kellogg Institute for International Studies, University of Notre Dame. Her work has concentrated on the study of political change in Latin America, primarily transitions from authoritarianism to democracy, the labour movement and the business class. She is co-author of *Democracia y Proyecto Socialdemócrata en República Dominicana* (1984), author of 'An Interpretation of the Democratic Transition in the Dominican Republic,' in G. Di Palma and L. Whitehead, eds., *The Central American Impasse* (1986), and of *Autoritarismo y Democracia en la Política Dominicana* (forthcoming). She is presently working on a comparative study of the process of democratic rule in Latin America.

Richard Hart   lawyer and historian, was active in the trade union movement in Jamaica from 1938 to the mid-1950s, secretary of the Caribbean Labour Congress (1946–52) and an Executive member of the Peoples National Party in Jamaica until its Marxist left wing was ousted in 1952. He edited *The Mirror* newspaper in Guyana (1964–5) and migrated to Britain in 1965. A 'life' member of NALGO, he is currently president of Caribbean Labour Solidarity. His published works include *Slaves Who Abolished Slavery* (2 vols. 1980, 1985) and *Rise & Organise: The Birth of the Workers and National Movements in Jamaica 1936–39* (1987).

Alistair Hennessy   is Professor of History and Director of the Centre for Caribbean Studies at the University of Warwick. He specialises in Cuban and Caribbean cultural history and is currently working on a study of West European-Cuban relations during the revolution.

Gad Heuman   is a member of the Department of History and the Centre for Caribbean Studies at the University of Warwick. Educated at Columbia College and Yale University, he is especially interested in the transition from slavery to freedom in the Caribbean. He is the author of *Between Black and White: Race, Politics, and the Free Coloureds in Jamaica, 1792–1865* (1981) and the editor of *Out of the House of Bondage: Runaways, Resistance and Marronage in Africa and the New World* (1986). He is presently working on a study of the Morant Bay Rebellion in Jamaica.

Harmannus Hoetink   is Professor of Caribbean and Latin American Sociology at the University of Utrecht. He is a past director of the Institute of Caribbean Studies at the University of Puerto Rico. During his twenty years in the Caribbean he also lived in Curaçao and the Dominican Republic. His books include, among others, *The Two Variants in Caribbean Race Relations* (1971), *Slavery and Race Relations in the Americas* (1973) and *The Dominican People 1850–1900* (1983, originally published in 1972 as *El Pueblo Dominicano: 1850–1900*).

Richard Lobdell   is a member of the Economics Department and Associate Dean of Arts at the University of Manitoba. Educated at the University of Kansas, the University of Wisconsin, and McGill University, he is particularly interested in late 19th and early 20th century West Indian economic history. He is the author of *Economic Structure and Demographic Performance in Jamaica, 1891–1935* (1987). He is currently working on a study of the life and thoughts of Sydney Olivier, and on British imperial policy in the West Indies after 1890.

Mats Lundahl is Professor of Development Economics at the Department of International Economics and Geography at the Stockholm School of Economics. He is the author of *Peasants and Poverty: A Study of Haiti* (1979), *Migration and Change in Rural Zambia* (1983), *The Haitian Economy: Man, Land and Markets* (1983), *Unequal Treatment, A Study in the Neo-classical Theory of Discrimination* (1984). He is also the editor of *Development Strategies and Basic Needs in Latin America* (1982). Presently, he is working on a historical study of foreign trade in Chile, on incentives for food production in Tanzania and on the customs union of southern Africa.

Andrés A. Ramos Mattei was a member of the Department of History and Chairperson of the Department of Puerto Rican & Hispanic Caribbean Studies at Rutgers University. Educated in the United States and England, he published *La hacienda azucarera: su crecimiento y crisis en Puerto Rico (siglo XIX)*, edited *Azúcar y esclavitud*, and was the author of numerous articles and essays, with two books in press. Until his untimely death in February 1988, he was doing research on plantation society of the earlier 20th century in Puerto Rico in the National Archives, Washington.

Janet Henshall Momsen was educated at Lady Margaret Hall, Oxford, McGill University and the London School of Economics and Political Science, and is now a Lecturer in Geography at the University of Newcastle upon Tyne. She was previously a Lecturer at the Universities of London and Leeds and a Visiting Professor at the University of Calgary and the Federal University of Rio de Janeiro. She is especially interested in the post-emancipation development of peasant agriculture in the Caribbean and the role of gender in development. She is author with R.P. Momsen Jr., of *A Geography of Brazilian Development* (1974) and co-editor of *The Geography of Gender in the Third World* (1987).

Paul Rich is visiting Lecturer in the Department of Politics, University of Bristol and Associate Fellow, Department of Politics, University of Warwick. He was educated at the Universities of Sussex, York and Warwick and has research interests in British imperial and South African history and the politics of race in Britain.

His publications include *White Power and the Liberal Conscience: Racial Segregation and South African Liberalism, 1921–1960 (1984)*, *Race and Empire in British Politics* (1986) and joint editor of *Race, Government and Politics in Britain* (1986). He is presently working on a study of British relations with South Africa since 1945.

Rebecca J. Scott   is Associate Professor in the Department of History of the University of Michigan, Ann Arbor, and Faculty Associate of the Centre for Afroamerican and African Studies. She received her Ph.D. at Princeton University in 1982, and has conducted research in Spain, Cuba, and Brazil. She is the author of *Slave Emancipation in Cuba: The Transition to Free Labour, 1860–1899* (Princeton University Press, 1985). She is currently working on a manuscript titled 'Giving Meaning to Freedom: Postemancipation Society in the Sugar Regions of Brazil, Cuba, and Louisiana.'

Mary Turner   is a member of the Department of History at Dalhousie University in Canada. Her publications include *Slaves and Missionaries, a study of the disintegration of Jamaican slave society 1784–1834* (1982). She is currently researching the processes on the estates and in England which undermined the slave labour system.

Foreword

Sidney Mintz

To some of us, 1992 is no more than a reference point in a remote future. But not so for Columbus's admirers, whose hearts quicken at the thought of what happened in an astonishing moment, now nearly five hundred years ago, to give meaning to the date:

> About one hour after this sighting the moon rose, and at 2 a.m. Friday, 12 October [1492], Rodrigo de Triana in *Pinta* cried, *"Tierra! Tierra!"*[1]

And land it was.

In the headlong rush to celebrate the quincentenary, however, some celebrants may have since forgotten that the New World began as little more than a detour, one which Columbus encountered unexpectedly, en route to somewhere else. He was trying to reach places already known to the West; he knew full well why he was looking for them; feathers and canoes and strange-looking people, however quaint, were not his goal. But the Americas were—have ever since been thought of as—his 'Discovery'.

Even before the magnitude of the Americas was grasped and Spain's obsession with precious metals had been transferred elsewhere, the search for other avenues to wealth had begun; and it began in the Antilles. All of the alternatives to gold and silver were linked to the land; at first, and for some time, 'the land' meant the Caribbean islands alone. The metallic resources of these lands were soon exhausted. Thereafter, and for ensuing centuries, the future of the Caribbean would be agricultural; its products would be plantation commodities; the capital that undergirded their production, the machinery that processed those products, and the markets they served, would be European. But the labour—that would be whatever could be obtained, from wherever, by whatever means, and as much of it as possible.

The first native Americans to be enslaved in the Antilles date from the first decade of the Conquest; the first enslaved Africans from 1503–1505. Nearly three hundred and fifty years later, the apprenticeship systems designed to ease the transition—for whom? —from slave to free labour were in place in many colonies. The importation of non-African labour to replace the slaves also dates from the nineteenth century. The labourers came from India, China, the Yucatan Peninsula, eventually from Indonesia and old French Indo-China and—in a few cases and in small numbers—from Europe and Africa as well. Caribbean planters did not discriminate against categories of labourer on grounds of their colour; in this regard alone, they appear to have been colour-blind.

In Cuba in 1886, approximately 375 years after the first enslaved Africans had been brought to the islands, Caribbean slavery came to an end. But contract labour—typified by unmistakeable, if concealed, doses of coercion—was still important as late as the 1930s; in fact, intra-Caribbean labour is still coerced.[2] And so the quincentenary can celebrate, *inter alia*, five centuries of Caribbean labour coercion.

But of course not only that. The history of resistance to European rule began with the Taino inhabitants of the Greater Antilles and the Island Carib of the smaller islands. It was continued by enslaved Africans, indentured Irish servants, contracted Chinese labourers, and contracted Indian labourers, both Muslim and Hindu. The zenith of such resistance is generally taken to have been the Haitian Revolution (1791–1804), and with reason. But Chinese labourers in Cuba and Indian labourers in British Guiana were struggling for more humane treatment and better work conditions, a century later. When we celebrate five centuries of oppression, then, we will also celebrate five hundred years of fighting back.

As in almost no other world region conquered and ruled for lengthy periods by the Europeans, the economic links between colony and metropolis, and the close fit of politics to eonomics in daily life, glitter like silver threads in the historical fabric. 'These Caribbean territories are not like those in Africa and Asia,' writes V.S. Naipaul:

> with their own internal reverences, that have been returned to them after a period of colonial rule. They are manufac-tured societies, labour camps, creations of empire...[3]

Naipaul is prepared to deny to Caribbean people much more; but on this score, at least, he is right. How these tiny islands became 'labour camps' is a story in its own right. Sugar cane was imported from the Canary Islands and planted in Santo Domingo in 1505; sugar was being made on the same island within a year. We are told that by 1516, the first *ingenio* (water-powered grinding mill) was operating; the following year, sugar was shipped to Seville. It was from that moment onward that the Caribbean islands became the 'manufactured societies, labour camps, creations of empire' of which Naipaul speaks. With their indigenous populations soon exterminated or genetically assimilated by the conquerors, these new colonies had to be repopulated from elsewhere. As the plantations were established the sugar mill machinery, the manacles, the clothing and even the food for the labourers were typically imported. The rhythms of work, because of the perishability of the sugarcane and the close links between field and factory this occasioned, were startlingly modern in their stress on time, and in their industrial discipline. In some measure, even before European industry had taken on its characteristic shape at home, the West Indian plantations were industrial enterprises, though most of their labourers through most of their history were frozen into the category of rural slaves. Slaves or no, these labourers were compelled to work in some ways that, were it not for slavery, would have been just as accurately described as the regimen of factory proletarians.

The strange contradictoriness of the colonial Caribbean was not lost upon those European thinkers who stayed at home and observed their colonies from afar. A succession of beautiful islands set in an emerald sea, each with its complement of toiling African slaves controlled and abused by a tiny minority of European masters, and each such master wholly dedicated to the sacredness of political as well as economic freedom — here was room for irony and bitter comedy, and it was not lost on the planters' countrymen. Montesquieu said it this way: '*Les peuples d'Europe ayant exterminé ceux de l'Amérique, ils ont dû mettre en esclavage ceux de l'Afrique, pour s'en servir a défricher tant de terres. Le sucre serait trop cher, si l'on ne faisait travailler la plante qui le produit par les esclaves.*'[4] Lemontey, in his anonymous spoof of the Société des Observateurs de l'Homme, made the same point differently. His hero is a Jamaican planter named Dominic Hangman, who wins a prize for having written the *worst* essay defending the slavery of women: 'The slavery of women is justified by reasons as good as those for the slavery of Negroes'. (De Gérando, 1969 [1800]). Voltaire, whose capacity to use social contradiction creatively was unmatched, looked at slavery through the eyes of Captain Candide, who meets a slave in Surinam:

As they drew near the town they came upon a Negro lying on the ground wearing only half his clothes, that is to say, a pair of blue cotton drawers; this poor man had no left leg and no right hand. 'Good heavens!' said Candide to him in Dutch, 'what are you doing there, my friend, in that horrible

state?' 'I am waiting for my master, the famous merchant
Monsieur Vanderdendur.' 'Was it Monsieur Vanderdendur,'
said Candide, 'who treated you this way?' 'Yes, sir,' said
the Negro, 'it is the custom. We are given a pair of cotton
drawers twice a year as clothing. When we work in the
sugar mills and the grindstone catches our fingers, they cut
off the hand; when we try to run away, they cut off a leg.
Both these things happened to me. This is the price paid
for the sugar you eat in Europe.'[6]

It is almost impossible to identify any important European thinker
between the middle of the seventeenth century and the middle of
the nineteenth who did not comment at some length and with strong
feelings on the issue of slavery, particularly in regard to the Caribbean
islands. This alone suggests how significant the 'labour question'
was, even if it was not commonly referred to in those terms. As
conceptions of individual liberty continued to evolve at home, the
European observers of the Caribbean spectacle used comedy, irony,
metaphor, logic, reason and indignation to dramatize the question:
why slavery? But the answer was not mysterious: slavery was perpetuated because it paid. If the victims could not prevent it, no one
else would, at least until it did not pay. For nearly four-fifths of the
Caribbean region's post-Columbian labour history, slavery remained
the most important means for relating labour to the land, and every
European thinker of note was aware of the monstrous contradiction
it represented. It is for this reason, among others, that the study of
Caribbean labour has so lengthy, honourable and contested a history.

Many writers have stressed the importance of the Antillean
colonies to the metropolises, but that story—and the debates that it
has generated—need no repetition here. But the ancient colonial
pedigrees, the genocide, the labour system based on coercion, and
the precocious industrialism—disguised by labels such as 'underdeveloped', 'non-Western', 'Third World' and 'agrarian'—these
need remembering. For the real significance of this odd region came
about with its initial consecration to the production of the first
overseas food commodities to which large European populations
would become inordinately attached: coffee and chocolate, together
with tobacco and rum, but especially sugar and molasses. The
tendency to write off such items by dubbing them 'dessert crops',
even in scholarly works thirty years ago, suggests how fundamental
has been the misunderstanding of the place of plantation foods in
the history of the West, and of the Caribbean in that history.[7] Even
the lively debates about the role of slavery and the plantations in the

accumulation of English capital at home seem somewhat irrelevant, in the light of the revolutionary transformation of the diet and nutrition of English workers between the end of the seventeenth and the start of the twentieth centuries. At its base, however, this was a labour issue, for the production of commodities in the Caribbean region depended upon the plantation and its labour force, and the consumers of those commodities soon became the factory workers of Europe.

As the editors point out, a number of original and imaginative scholars have dealt here with labour problems in specific historical and geographical contexts. The contributions vary widely in scope and chronology, as befits a work of this sort. But the particularity, if not the uniqueness, of the region always enters into their analyses. Comparisons with most parts of Africa, Asia and Latin America are not, in fact, very apt, in view of the Caribbean region's unusual past. In the light of that past, that increasing political freedom should have come only with declining economic significance is not particularly contradictory, for it merely provides a different reading of the term 'colonial'.

In these essays, the reader is afforded an authentic scholarly sense of Caribbean complexity and variety, without a single bongo drum or rum punch. There is no need here to say more of the essays themselves; the editors' introduction does this admirably. I believe that readers with serious Caribbean interests will find genuine enlightenment in these pages.

Notes

1 Samuel Eliot Morison and Mauricio Obregón, *The Caribbean as Columbus Saw It.* (Boston, Little Brown, 1964), p. 16.
2 See, for instance, Roger Plant, *Sugar and Modern Slavery.* (London Zed Books, 1987).
3 Vidia S. Naipaul, *The Overcrowded Barracoon and Other Articles.* (New York, Knopf, 1973) p. 254.
4 Charles de Secondat, Baron de Montesquieu, *De l'Esprit des Loix.* In André Masson, (ed.), *Oeuvres Complètes de Montesquieu,* Vol. I (Paris, Nagel, 1950), Livre XV, Ch. V, p. 330.
5 Cited in Joseph-Marie De Gérando, *The Observation of Savage Peoples.* (London, Routledge and Kegan Paul, 1969 [1800]) p. 49.
6 François Marie Arouet de Voltaire, *Candide.* In Ben Ray Redman, (ed.), *The Portable Voltaire.* (New York, Viking, 1962) pp. 281–2.
7 Sidney W. Mintz, *Sweetness and Power.* (New York, Viking, 1985).

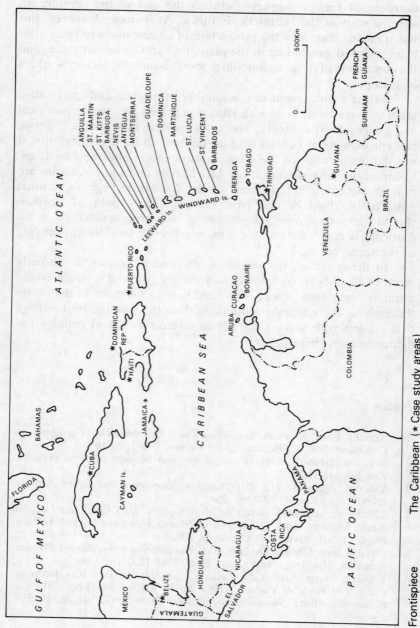

Frontispiece   The Caribbean (* Case study areas)

Introduction

Malcolm Cross and Gad Heuman

The perceptive visitor to Caribbean societies today is often struck by the everyday presence of their histories. An apparently seamless continuity binds the past to the present, and it does so primarily through the institutions of labour. Whereas the key features of other cultures can be captured through the actions of their ruling class, or through military interventions or through overseas adventures, in the Caribbean it is the bond of labour to land that stands both in the forefront and as the backdrop to their story.

In this sense, then, the history of the Caribbean can be defined as the history of labour. The first Europeans in the region in the fifteenth and sixteenth centuries exploited Amerindian labour and thereby decimated that population. Later, Europeans were imported to work as indentured labourers, and at least one contemporary observer, Richard Ligon, maintained that these whites were treated more harshly than the African slaves who succeeded them.[1] The history of slavery itself is in many ways identified with the Caribbean; African slavery existed in the area from the sixteenth century and continued until the end of the nineteenth. But the key relationship is that between production and labour. As Eric Williams put it 'sugar meant labour—at times that labour has been slave, at other times nominally free, at times, black, at other times white or brown or yellow'.[2]

Although this relationship of labour in general to the means of production figures so centrally in Caribbean history, relatively little attention has been paid to documenting it. Of course, at one level there are numerous studies of the forced labour that is to many the *Leitmotiv* of the New World. But the study of the Caribbean amply repays a broader vision, extending well beyond this extraordinary history. Slavery was by no means the only form of extracting labour power by coercion, nor Africans its only victims. Similarly, coercion was not the only repressive instrument. The force of law or the threat of destitution through increase in the labour supply have been used wherever capital and labour interact; yet in the Caribbean they

1

have a qualitatively different aspect. What this book tries to achieve, therefore, is something of this wider perspective. Our examples are drawn from across the centuries and from different cultural and colonial histories.

The most impressive body of writing on Caribbean history is on slavery itself. Historians, such as Francisco Scarano for Puerto Rico, Barry Higman for Jamaica and Franklin Knight for Cuba have concentrated on the affinity between sugar and slavery.[3] It has become clear that the historical experience of slavery in the Caribbean transcends linguistic and cultural divisions. Long ago Sidney Mintz pointed the way by comparing slavery in Jamaica and Puerto Rico, and this process needs to be continued. Mintz also highlighted its complex nature, with the development of a proto-peasantry arising out of slavery itself.[4] In some parts of the Caribbean slavery endured and co-existed with various forms of nominally free labour. Imported Chinese in Cuba and the *jornaleros* in Puerto Rico are only two from many examples. The process of emancipation has therefore been very complex, as Rebecca Scott has shown in the case of Cuba.[5] Elsewhere in the Caribbean, some ex-slaves were able to leave the estates and form the basis of free villages and settlements. Others had little choice but to remain on the plantations.[6] Nigel Bolland reminds us that the nature of political control in the aftermath of emancipation is thus crucial. The importation of labour —primarily from India—often served to make life even more difficult for the freedmen.[7]

The twentieth century literature has inevitably tended to concentrate on the rise of *organised* labour. Arthur Lewis's pioneering survey, first published by the Fabian Society in 1938, is subtitled 'the birth of a workers' movement'.[8] Other more detailed studies have followed in a similar vein, such as Ron Ramdin's recent history of trade unionism in Trinidad and Tobago.[9] Perhaps because of the chequered history of organised labour in countries experiencing long periods of dictatorship, studies of labour resistance and mobilisation have been less common. A notable exception is Ken Post's extraordinary volume on Jamaica which falls centrally in the 'heroic tradition'.[10] Notwithstanding the undoubted capacity of capital to resist and control labour demands, it is hard to equate his approach, however, with the fleeting successes and patchy progress that have been the hallmarks of Caribbean labour resistance. Labour internationalism, for example, has been as great an aspiration in the eyes of labour activists in the Caribbean as elsewhere but, aside from the progress made by the Caribbean Labour Congress in the late 1940s, it has not become a reality. This is true even within cultural and linguistic divisions, let alone between them.

One insight into why this is so can be gained from the anthropological studies of labour itself. The pioneering study here is Sidney Mintz's *Worker in the Cane*.[11] The life story of 'Don Taso' says much about the difficulties of capturing the energies of labour for political ends. It is not simply the extraordinary physical demands of planting, weeding and cutting cane as the permeability of Caribbean societies to external influences. Puerto Rico may be an extreme example but the dilution of labour through unrestricted movement to the US and elsewhere, coupled with the passifying influences of modern materialist culture, have done little to aid labour organisation. It is notable that Fidel Castro, in seeking to consolidate the 1959 Cuban revolution by promoting popular nationalism, spent many hours of speechmaking to both justifying the restriction on the return of Cuban migrants to the US and to limiting the invasion of North American culture.

In the first part of this introduction, we explore the aspects of Caribbean labour that are perhaps unique or found there in special forms. The object is to draw from the essays that follow some features that derive from these special histories. As Mintz has reminded us, the Caribbean colonies '. . .were, in fact, the oldest "industrial" colonies of the West outside Europe, manned almost entirely with introduced populations, and fitted to European needs with peculiar intensity and pervasiveness'.[12] The second section of this introduction raises more familiar themes in the study of labour. What has recently been called the 'new international labour studies' provides an agenda of great relevance for the Caribbean.[13] In the third section, we take a more dialectical stand. The labour relationship is so central that it is inevitably bound up with processes of historical change. But as with all social change, it frequently springs from unexpected sources and as the consequences of other intentions.

Unique aspects of Caribbean labour

The encounter with Europe was not, of course, everywhere the same and we start by looking at this diversity, while noting that even this wide range of experience has uniquely Caribbean properties. Moreover, a number of the essays in this book point to the growing significance of the United States which for more than a century has viewed the countries of the Caribbean as legitimate targets for intervention.

The effects of European powers on labour organisation may be seen both directly and indirectly. Although Richard Hart documents the *diversity* of experience in the Anglophone Caribbean from the 1890s, the equally striking similarities were clearly the result of indirect rule from Whitehall. Campaigns to establish freedom from tort for fledgling unions used arguments only freshly developed in the UK. It is true that here too the influence of North America was significant, since in the Jamaican case early unions were affiliates of the American Federation of Labour. However, there was nothing in the US connection which could match the supremely colonial practice of sending Royal Commissions to inquire into the economic and social wellbeing of these empire citizens. Between the Royal Commission of 1897 and that of 1938–39, there was a steady development of organised labour. In the earlier period, mostly skilled artisans were the sole spokesmen of labour but four decades later, the commissioners—who now included a senior representative of Britain's workers—were besieged by skilfully constructed evidence from well-organised unions.

There is also an important sense in which this period opened up the possibility for steady development towards internal self-government and eventual independence. The crisis of the sugar industry in the 1890s made it essential that other crops were grown. Since the planters had shown themselves unable to overcome the sweet memories of easy wealth, their inflexibility led to a reappraisal of the role of the peasantry. As Richard Lobdell argues, this broke the long established tradition that the interests of the coloniser were synonymous with the returns to the planters. From that time on, therefore, the previous tactics of new labour migration combined with oppressive use of law became more difficult to justify as the health of the colonies came to be defined more and more in terms of 'responsible' labour organisation. As both Lobdell and Rich remind us, however, no explanation of these great changes can be adequate without taking into account the role of individuals in London and the influence they brought to official thinking. The Colonial Office, while curiously detached from popular opinion, nonetheless reflected changes occurring with the rise of labour politics. It is true that the emergence of a stronger colonial voice led to some, like the Secretary of State Joseph Chamberlain (1895–1903), to reassert the importance of assuaging the interests of capital. Yet others, such as the early Fabian Sydney Olivier, were quite prepared to counter these views with forceful arguments in defence of organised labour and a free peasantry.

The indirect influence of Europe is very clear in some parts of the Hispanic Caribbean. While the actual numbers of British, French and Dutch *settlers* have always been tiny, this was not so in the case of Cuba and, to a lesser extent, the Dominican Republic. As Alistair Hennessy points out, the influence of free Spanish immigration in the Cuban case after 1902, together with the status of Spain itself as the poor man of Europe in this period, brought about an affinity between Cubans and Spaniards which is rare between coloniser and colonised. Thus there is little evidence here of nascent nationalism emerging out of colonial rejection as there is elsewhere. On the contrary, the emergence of revolutionary doctrines owes much to traditions of Spanish anarchism.

Nowhere is the importance of external influence greater than in the case of Puerto Rico after the US takeover in 1898. The Commonwealth of Puerto Rico is an exceptional case in some respects, but the significance of North America has risen generally in the area since that time. As far as labour was concerned the US presence brought with it a familiar paradox. On the one hand, the influence of the US constitution enabled a speedy transition to legal strikes and industrial action. On the other, the penetration of American capital following in the wake of political control led to an even stronger anti-labour stance by the administration that came after the military government.

The *introduction* of labour itself has special features in the Caribbean case. Coerced, induced or freely migrating labour leads to new societies but, in the process, it stamps them indelibly. Immigration can be a form of labour control. If slavery was the key institution in the establishment of Caribbean societies, then *new* labour was a crucial method used by capital to limit the dangers of emancipation and sometimes even of slavery itself. In discussing Jamaica, for example, Mary Turner points to the role of imported Africans to work on the estates. They were perceived as not having yet acquired the 'bad habits' of Jamaican-born slaves who were more familiar with the system. Thus it was Africans who formed significant proportions of the field slaves, the ones who did the most difficult work. After emancipation this pattern was repeated, but this time it was largely Indian indentured labour which was used. Indentured labour had the intended effect of limiting the bargaining power of the ex-slaves to keep wages below subsistence. The Hispanic Caribbean was not immune to this pattern of labour control; in Puerto Rico and the Dominican republic, *cocolos* (workers from the British West Indian islands) and labourers from Haiti were imported to work the estates and undermine the power of local labour. Although, as Harry Hoetink shows, there were also other factors at work, the importation of Haitian workers has continued to the present and their treatment has recently been likened to that of slavery.[14] The lesson of slavery was not, therefore, easily forgotten even when its logic had gone.

The 'industrial' aspect of Caribbean colonies and dependencies produced a third special feature, which was a rural industrialisation. Industrialisation in a market economy always produces its proletariat but *rural* proletariats seeking change have a particular problem. Plantation agriculture is hardly an ideal setting for labour organisation and in many places, trade unions had to await the coming of urban occupations on the waterfronts or in the factories. Lundahl makes the important point that the very size of the country and the dispersal of Haitian labour militated against effective organisation.

Yet rural organisation did occur amongst people who possessed some peasant-like features. Even before emancipation, slaves sought to organise and resist planter demands. Slaves withdrew their labour at crucial times and protested collectively at what they saw as unfair demands. Remarkably, they succeeded in sometimes having their white supervisory staff dismissed, and slaves were able on occasion to protect established work norms by advancing arguments of 'custom and practice'. More research will be needed to link the slave period with the aftermath of emancipation. In the case of Puerto Rico, for example, Andrés Ramos Mattei has shown that a rural proletariat was able to organise strike action at the end of the nineteenth century, using some methods which Jamaican slaves a century earlier could have recognised.

In any discussion of labour organisation, it is important to raise the problem of leadership. The working class in Caribbean societies has never lacked leaders of ability. They have, however, sometimes opposed rather than supported the aspirations of labour and on other occasions they have diverted the momentum of the masses to personal aggrandisement. This is hardly a unique phenomenon, but in parts of the Caribbean labour appears to have helped generate the conditions for popular dictatorships. There are dangers in assuming that organised labour is *always* conducive to progressive politics. The chapters by Rosario Espinal and Mats Lundahl make clear the range of examples that the Caribbean offers. In the former case the rise of the dictator Trujillo was achieved without working-class support. Labour laws were extensively used in the 1930s to control labour and only once during Trujillo's rule (1942–46) did a significant struggle emerge through the blanket of repression that was otherwise applied. After the dictator's fall, labour organisations flooded the country, and their very number and lack of co-ordination provided the ingredients for a sustained policy of divide and rule that followed. Organised labour tends to fare poorly, therefore, in those places where power becomes centralised and arbitrary, regardless of whose interests it was originally seized to promote.

The Haitian case is different, although many similarities exist. The unions emerged at a similar period but in Haiti they did so *before* the dictatorship became entrenched. Even before Duvalier, organised labour was defined as threatening to both the old mulatto élite and the new black middle class. The important point, however, is that worker militancy in removing Magloire in 1956 set the scene for a leader who was able to mobilise popular support by appealing to folk images and black nationalism. Following Duvalier's election the fortunes of organised labour changed; just a decade after a troubled birth the movement was killed off by systematic repression. In Lundahl's damning judgement, it achieved nothing for the Haitian masses.

The new international labour studies

The second section of this introduction raises more familiar themes in the study of labour. What have been the processes of proletarianisation, for example, and what forms have workers' struggles and resistance taken? A number of authors in the chapters that follow point to the severing of ties with plantations as a form of resistance. Mary Turner shows that familiar forms of protest, such as strikes, were possible even under slavery and she cites cases where industrial action by slaves sometimes led to the removal of white overseers. Michiel Baud also presents an analysis of forms of resistance but his example is the Dominican Republic in the crucial years around the turn of the century. What is particularly striking here is the importance he attaches to the *response* of peasants to capitalist expansion. Peasants, like all workers, are far from being automatons who simply respond to economic and political pressure. They struggle to develop and assert their view of events, and it is these interpretations which affect the *forms* of resistance to exploitation that peasants adopt. This leads in practice to a detached stance, which only changes when their very subsistence is undermined. The economic and cultural autonomy of the peasantry in the Dominican Republic may have precluded their taking a leading role in labour organisation, but they were neither eradicated by proletarianisation nor did they stand by passively as the tumult of capital penetration took place around them.

In Europe and North America the mobilisation of labour could easily be defined as an aspect of class struggle, but this is more problematic in countries with cross-cutting loyalties of ethnicity. Hennessy points, for example, to the oft-forgotten role of colour in Cuba. One effect of the American occupation was heightened racial discrimination which was exacerbated as Spanish migrants were settled as *colonos* on lands the Afro-Cubans thought were rightfully theirs. Similarly, a key feature of labour organisation in Trinidad and Guyana in the twentieth century is the salience of ethnicity, again exacerbated by the use of new labour migration as a device for weakening the wage-bargaining power of emancipated blacks.

Other divisions occurred within the working class and not just between peasants and proletarians. Turner notes the little researched divisions *within* the Jamaican slave population, with some slaves actually employing others, while Hart discusses the common features, throughout the Caribbean and elsewhere, of artisans and tradesmen leading the struggle to mobilise the proletariat. Except in countries like Haiti, where a subsistence economy has been the norm, labour organisation has benefited from the dominance of export economies. These inevitably generate core cities where the wealth of the country is funnelled through the ports. It is no accident that stevedores and dock workers have figured so prominently in the history of Caribbean labour.

No discussion of divisions within the working class and their salience for labour organisation would be complete without reference to the crucial significance of gender as a key dimension. Janet Momsen reminds us that the division of labour imposed during the slave period inevitably carried with it planter perceptions on the role of women. Plantations were unlikely to correct gender imbalances because of romantic notions on the importance of family life but became convinced that the central role of women in African production could be emulated in the Caribbean. As Momsen writes, it was not until the slave trade ended that the reproductive place of women came to assume an importance that matched their productive role. What we lack are similar detailed historical studies of the place women came to occupy in the labouring classes of the Hispanic Caribbean.

A third theme, where the story of Caribbean labour adds richly to labour studies in general, concerns the energies exerted by the interests of capital to utilise all possible devices for labour control. In every case considered in the chapters that follow, there are examples of legal coercion and alliances between capital and the forces of police or military control. As Scott notes in the Cuban case, the more interesting question is not *whether* these devices were employed but why, in some instances, there was an apparent reluctance to pursue this path of oppression. As she observes, the most probable answer is that, once again, new labour migration was preferred as a more certain and less damaging alternative. There is much in this theme for further research since labour dilution and intra-class competition emerge time and time again as a mechanism for labour control.

Finally, there is ample evidence, as a number of the following essays reveal, to indicate the importance of culture in shaping the form and content of labour movements. Indeed, the Caribbean has produced more than its share of popular philosophies on the role of labour itself in determining national evolution. Baud, for example, reminds us of the importance that peasant culture had in providing solidarity in times of extreme difficulty. Messianic cults arise in these settings to divert emotion and promise release. In Cuba and, of course, Haiti, it is impossible to ignore the relationship between messianic beliefs and labour movements. Often cult leaders were also labour leaders and even basically secular cultural forms, such as Garveyism, possess messianic properties of release from bondage and oppression.

Labour relations and historical change

In the third section of this introduction, we take a more dialectical stand. The labour relationship is so central that it is inevitably bound up with processes of historical change. But as with all social change, it frequently springs from unexpected sources and as the consequence of other intentions. The modernisation of the sugar industry, consequent upon the slump of the 1890s, set the conditions for the recovery of labour by modernising the relationship between capital and labour. However much the original plantations were enmeshed in a capitalist nexus, they were never completely capitalist in their organisation and day-to-day running. Payment by task, for example, is not the same as a piece-rate system. The latter is contained within an established working week, whereas tasks themselves determined working time. Similarly, payment in kind, through the allocation of provision grounds, or housing, or medical support, however rudimentary and inadequate, obscures the interaction between capital and labour. Wages paid to free labour for a set working week are the critical relationship of pure capitalism and with their arrival came organisations which could focus on that simple bond. The chapters by Malcolm Cross and by Nigel Bolland, both point to the effects of metropolitan capital in modernising the class system. In Trinidad and Guyana, which Cross compares, it is the successes of capital accumulation which produce the conditions for both bridging the ethnic divide and driving a thin but important wedge between the colonial administrators and the representatives of capital itself.

A second contradiction is no less crucial for being little studied. It concerns the role of the metropolis itself once the process of disengagement has commenced. It would be logical to assume that as the retreat from the colonial encounter gained momentum, the influence of the coloniser declined. In fact, the opposite is true in the development of Caribbean labour. The retreat from empire was in part the result of labour organisation at the core, and in the Anglophone Caribbean labour leaders from the metropolis became part of the advisory system. Their influence, and that of officials sympathetic to their goals, became critical just as traditional colonial values waned in importance. The Caribbean is a region of the world which is, paradoxically, both innovative and open to external influence. As Paul Rich implies, what we frequently ignore is the reverse flow of ideas and perceptions. While leading figures in Whitehall had an undoubted effect in the colonies, it is also true that an appreciation of Britain's imperial role helped stimulate Fabianism at home and a non-marxian commitment to labour internationalism.

Conclusion

The essays in this book thus point in a number of directions. They highlight the struggle of labour in the Caribbean to organise and resist exploitation. This was often very difficult, given the ingenuity of the planter class and the constraints of working in dispersed rural economies. At different times and in different places, anti-labour devices have included the use of truck systems on plantations, repressive legislation and, most notably, the importation of migrant workers. Yet the essays here show how labour has dealt with such coercive mechanisms. Even during slavery, labourers acted collectively. After emancipation, this process continued, resulting ultimately in the formation of more modern labour organisations. Themes of resistance and control permeate these essays, whether in Jamaica or Puerto Rico, the Dominican Republic or Haiti. It is our hope, therefore, that this book will help to stimulate more cross-cultural work on all aspects of Caribbean labour.

Fortunately, the essays here are suggestive about some of the directions for such future research. It is clear, for example, that labour acted collectively in the aftermath of emancipation. Many ex-slaves left the plantations, not always immediately and often under considerable pressure from planters. In *A History of the Guyanese Working People*, Walter Rodney discusses the types of collective action undertaken by ex-slaves and indentured labourers in British Guiana, but we know far less about what happened elsewhere in the Caribbean.[15] Furthermore, for those workers who remained on the estates, what kind of nascent organisations did they develop in the course of the nineteenth century?

The issues raised on gender and labour clearly need to be pursued more widely. Female slaves were crucial members of the field gangs, often forming the majority of this class of worker. But what roles did these women occupy after emancipation? Many women ceased working on the estates, but did they retreat to domesticity or, more likely, to a different work setting? Were 'Victorian values' applied to black women in the nineteenth century Caribbean and, if so, with what implications for life in the twentieth century?

The history of labour in the Caribbean is partly a history of oppression. But why, and under what circumstances, were different forms of labour control used? The importation of new workers was a common means of controlling local labour. But why was this option preferred over others when it was rarely cheap and often difficult to administer?

Resistance took many forms, but one of the most interesting was the use of cultural symbols to resist labour exploitation. The weapons of capital were not designed to deal with peasants who chose to celebrate feast days rather than work on the plantations. How did such cultural manifestations provide unity and purpose for resistance?

Finally, the drive towards decolonisation and independence was one in which labour played an important part. Yet how was it possible for dictators to emerge in the Dominican Republic and Haiti who used the power of labour while cynically disregarding its interests?

These are some of the issues we hope will be pursued in further work on Caribbean labour studies. This volume will have achieved its objective if it inspires such research.

Notes

1   Richard Ligon, *A True & Exact History of the Island of Barbados*, (London, Frank Cass, 1976; orig. pub. 1657), p. 43.
2   Eric Williams, *Capitalism and Slavery*, (New York, Capricorn Books, 1966; orig. pub. 1944), p. 29.
3   Francisco Scarano, *Sugar and Slavery in Puerto Rico: The Plantation Economy of Ponce, 1800–1850*, (Madison, The University of Wisconsin Press); B.W. Higman, *Slave Population and Economy in Jamaica, 1807–1834*, (Cambridge, Cambridge University Press, 1976) Franklin W. Knight, *Slave Society in Cuba During the Nineteenth Century*, (Madison, University of Wisconsin Press, 1979).
4   Sidney W. Mintz, 'Labor and Sugar in Puerto Rico and in Jamaica, 1800–1850,' *Comparative Studies in Society and History*, 1, 3, (March, 1959): pp. 273–280. See also his *Caribbean Transformations*, (Baltimore, The Johns Hopkins University Press, 1984; orig. pub., 1974).
5   Rebecca J. Scott, *Slave Emancipation in Cuba: The Transition to Free Labor, 1860–1899*, (Princeton, Princeton University Press, 1985).
6   Jean Besson, 'Land Tenure in the Free Villages of Trelawny, Jamaica: A Case Study in the Caribbean Peasant Response to Emancipation,' *Slavery and Abolition: A Journal of Comparative Studies*, 5, 1, (May, 1984): pp. 3–23. See also Douglas Hall, 'The Flight from the Estates Reconsidered: The British West Indies, 1838–42,' *Journal of Caribbean History*, 10 & 11 (1978): 7–24; Woodville K. Marshall, 'Commentary,' in Michael Craton, ed. 'Roots and Branches: Current Directions in Slave Studies,' *Historical Reflections*, 6, 1 (Summer, 1979), pp. 246–47.
7   O. Nigel Bolland, 'Systems of Domination After Slavery: The Control of Land and Labor in the British West Indies after 1838', *Comparative Studies in Society and History*, 23, 4 (October, 1981): pp. 591–619; but see also William A. Green, *British Slave Emancipation: The Sugar Colonies and the Great Experiment, 1830–1865*, (Oxford, Oxford University Press, 1976).
8   Arthur Lewis, *Labour in the West Indies: the Birth of a Workers Movement*, (London, New Beacon Books, 1977).
9   Ron Ramdin, *From Chattel Slave to Wage Earner: A History of Trade Unionism in Trinidad and Tobago*, (London, Martin Brian and O'Keeffe, 1982).
10   Ken Post, *Arise Ye Starvelings: The Jamaican Labour Rebellion and Its Aftermath*, (The Hague, Martinus Nijhoff, 1978).
11   Sidney W. Mintz, *Worker in the Cane: A Puerto Rican Life History*, (New York, W.W. Norton, 1974).
12   Sidney W. Mintz, 'The Caribbean as a Socio-cultural Area,' in Michael M. Horowitz (ed) *Peoples and Cultures of the Caribbean*, (New York, Natural History Press, 1971), p. 36.
13   Robin Cohen, 'Theorising International Labour,' in R. Boyd, R. Cohen and P.C.W. Gutkind (eds) *International Labour*, (Aldershot, Gower Press, 1987).
14   Maurice Lemoine, *Bitter Sugar*, (London, Zed Press, 1985).
15   Walter Rodney, *A History of the Guyanese Working People, 1881–1905*, (Baltimore, The Johns Hopkins University Press, 1981), chaps. 2, 5.

Section A

Reorganisation and Resistance

CHAPTER 1 | Chattel slaves into wage slaves: A Jamaican case study

Mary Turner

Slaves were distinguished from other categories of labour by being persons whose labour was denied exchange value. They faced as workers, however, fundamentally the same problems as serfs, or wage workers; they were forced to spend their lives expending labour over and above what was necessary for their own subsistence. Improvement in work conditions for all categories of workers meant improving rewards for labour extracted and cutting down on the coercive power(s) of the owners of the means of production. The question arises, therefore, whether these fundamental similarities in the nature of exploitation and in the goals of the exploited indicate some similarities in their methods of struggle?[1]

The structure of slave based sugar production in the British Caribbean suggests this possibility. The plantations were set up as specialised, export oriented, agro-manufacturing units of 200−600 workers, supervised by a skeleton staff of owners and their waged employees as an integral part of an economy characterised by wage labour. These specialised export crop production units developed as part and parcel of a commercial economy with internal and external market connections in which the slaves themselves were gradually integrated through the development of their provision grounds. These plots, allocated for subsistence to cut production costs, generated surpluses necessary to the development of the colonial economy and provided the body of slaves, as petty producers, with cash rewards. Skilled slaves, hired out as payment as the towns grew, became proxy wage earners. Supplying labour in response to direct physical coercion in societies characterised by wage labour and from workers involved in the cash economy, dictated struggles over the degree of coercion and the quantities of reward.

This chapter investigates, in relation to Jamaican sugar estate workers, the dynamics generated by this contradiction. It is based on estate papers for the parish of St Thomas in the East, one of the most important sugar producing parishes in Jamaica with a slave population, in 1832, of 23,000.[2] It shows that the forms of class struggle which characterised contract and wage sugar estate workers, such as group and collective verbal protests as well as appeals for mediation backed up by strike action, were adopted by slaves and contributed to undermining the slave labour based economy.

Early labour protest on the Blue Mountain and Grange Hill estates

The fundamental impetus which generated collective organisation among the slaves, these records suggest, was the struggle for survival. The provision ground system, usually regarded as in itself a mitigation of the slaves' work conditions, represented simply an alternative use of the slaves' labour by the owner who dictated that the slaves subsist on the labour power they used. In the early stages of estate development this system subjected the slaves to additional problems. Blue Mountain estate, for example, was developed for sugar in the latter half of the eighteenth century in a fertile interior valley by an influx of predominantly male Africans who increased the estate labour force from 170 to 350.[3] The demands for estate work were such that only some of the more privileged and longest settled slaves were able to establish provision grounds.

This situation surfaced in 1787 after Jamaica had been pounded by successive hurricanes and was suffering the effects of new trade restrictions with the United States. Consequent food shortages dictated that, in the Jamaica Assembly's own estimate, 15,000 slaves died.[4] Conditions at Blue Mountain contributed to this death toll. The 1786 hurricane destroyed the slaves' plantain walks; emergency supplies of potatoes and black-eye peas brought in from Kingston proved inadequate. As a result, the great gang could not carry out its routine. Moreover, cane holing, which was particularly strenuous work on the heavy soil of a valley bottom, was curtailed because the workers were beginning to 'drop off fast'.[5]

In these circumstances the planting attorney, William Sutherland, in charge of the estate between 1780–1804, discovered that the 'better sort' of slaves had established grounds and were using the 'poorer sort' to work them in return for a share of the produce. The system broke down when provisions were scarce and the 'poorer sort' required subsistence from the estate.[6] Sutherland's terminology clearly suggests that the 'better sort' were skilled and confidential slaves and the policy he pursued confirms this. He did not challenge the system directly. The fight for subsistence had created a slave village interest bloc which could not be simply disciplined out of existence. He proposed, rather, to provide the 'poorer sort' with the means to develop their grounds by supplying all their food for a year.[7]

No such arrangement was made. Substantial losses to the work force threatened if the provision ground problem was not resolved, but despite Sutherland's pleas that the 'odd slice' of salt pork saved lives, the owner refused to undertake the expense involved. When the same subsistence problem surfaced a decade later during a prolonged drought, Sutherland strongly recommended more drastic action, recruiting 'a small gang of about 15 or 16 Negroes...for the sole purpose of raising provisions'; in other words, workers should be withdrawn from sugar production to specialise in food production. Again, nothing was done; the workers were left to subsist themselves as best they could.[8]

The slave village interest bloc underpinned efforts to exert some control over work conditions and, in particular, to protest unjust and excessive use of coercion by overseers. Blue Mountain attorneys tried to minimise this problem by stocking the estate with new Africans; Jamaican born workers with 'bad habits' and 'connections outside the state', that is those familiar with local labour conditions and protest patterns, as well as experienced American slaves on sale after the revolution, were excluded.[9] Their method calls into question the rebellious qualities commonly attributed to 'wild Africans', but is, of course, consistent with industrial employers' preference for unorganised immigrant labour.

Despite these precautions Blue Mountain slaves effected the removal of two overseers between 1795 and 1800. In one case the action they took is not specified; in the paternalist language attorneys used, the overseer, William Grant, was described as having lost their (the slaves') affections. He had a 'peevish temper' and 'teasing methods' and his successor was recommended as a man of 'mild disposition'.[10] In this instance the slaves timed their protest well. The planters' fight against the Maroons, itself partly inspired by fear of revolutionary infection spreading from Haiti at the instigation of French agents, was in progress. Martial law, which drew overseers and bookkeepers away from the plantations was still in force and, when Grant was dismissed, had been extended for another month.[11] It was a moment which put a premium on management maintaining the 'affections' of the work force.

In the second instance, the attorney masked the slaves' success by delaying the overseer's departure until the crop was over so that his removal appeared to be part of the turnover customary for white estate personnel.[12] The overseer, his reputation as a good planter (i.e. maximum sugar producer) at risk in an excessively rainy crop season, extracted labour 'by harsh...bordering on cruel treatment of the Negroes, particularly the Pregnant Women'.[13] The pregnant women, despite the fact that they had most to lose by physical punishment, resisted work demands beyond their capabilities and won enough support among their fellows to make the overseer's position untenable.

The earliest and most developed form of labour protest in these records, however, took place at Grange Hill estate in 1770 during the attorneyship of Malcolm Laing (1759−78) who first developed Blue Mountain estate for sugar. The Grange Hill slaves' struggle was facilitated by two circumstances: the land was only marginally suitable for sugar so its anticipated profit margins were lower than at Blue Mountain and, more significantly, the estate slaves were intertwined with the wage work economy of Manchioneal, a port and market town where the demand for skilled workers and the ready sale of ground provisions demonstrated the cash value of labour.[14]

By 1770 the slaves, some 200 strong, had secured terms of service distinctly in advance of existing slave code provisions: they had Thursdays as well as Sundays to work their provision grounds[15] and estate artisans enjoyed material benefits which reflected their value as wage earners; benefits intended, presumably, to curb any ambition for free status. Carpenter Joe, for example, lived in Kingston at Laing's house for three months every year, perhaps at his own insistence,[16] either to be hired out or to earn something for himself. His services on the estate earned the same rations of meat, salt fish and rum as the white managers had.

An artisan, once valued at a rate comparable to white wage earners, naturally appealed in event of dispute with them, to the land owner's representative and, since an artisan was less replaceable than an overseer or a bookkeeper, such an appeal was likely to succeed. The Grange Hill records exemplify this process. Joe, in a dispute with the overseer, instantly appealed to the attorney who 'gave credit to the Carpenter' and sacked the overseer. The success of this grievance procedure naturally afforded 'a great triumph' and set a useful precedent to the whole work force.[17]

In February 1770 a new overseer, David Munro, an ex-soldier with a military man's view of slave labour, took charge. He considered 'the same Discipline and Subordination...proper to slaves, as is practised in the Army and Navy, and without which they can't be kept to their Duty...It is a well known Maxim that a relaxation of Discipline, has the same effect on Slaves which it has on Soldiers: inclining them to Dissolute Indulgence and Loose passions'.[18]

The slaves' response to Munro's methods was to strike; early in

September they took to the woods and sent four delegates 60 miles to Laing in Kingston to state their case. What ill usage sparked the strike does not emerge; Laing had a clearly articulated policy of listening to both sides of 'Negro Stories' and his reaction to the crisis suggests that it was not, in his experience, altogether unusual. He told the slaves to return to work, told the overseer to withhold any punishments and promised to investigate affairs in two weeks time when he had attended to business in Clarendon parish. In the upshot, Munro, the military style disciplinarian, was sacked.[19]

The struggle by slaves for work norms

In all these cases management, by judiciously responding to an immediate grievance, conceded very little and won a great deal. Laing, for example, by placating the work force before crop commenced in December, secured his income and reputation, and prevented another flight to the woods which risked the permanent loss of some slaves, the disruption of neighbouring estates and the threat of small scale rebellion. At the same time, the attorney impressed on propertyless whites respect for property in slaves. This class conflict was reflected also in the island courts; Laing himself took a white mason who shot one of the slaves in his charge to court 'as if the Man had perpetrated Murder'. Laing lost the case and the accused was awarded £5* for shooting a rebellious negro. As Grange Hill attorney, however, Laing had no intention of allowing Munro liberties with live investments and was perfectly prepared to give what the overseer termed 'glaring encouragement' to the slaves' 'contempt of Authority and of the White Colour'.[20]

Slave protests against the overseers' use of his coercive powers neatly exploited this class division and contributed to the turnover rate of white estate personnel. More significantly, this bargaining process secured the slaves material advantages which constituted informal contract terms, always disputed, but always likely to be reconfirmed and possibly improved upon. The bargaining process contributed, as Munro observed, to developing their political consciousness.

Island-wide developments fed and watered this consciousness in the early decades of the nineteenth century. The abolition of the slave trade in 1807 did not effect the transformation of the slave labour system the abolitionists hoped for, but it cut off the plantation owners' capacity to increase their effective labour force (i.e. workers aged 18–49) at will. The fixed labour force, with its own internally determined age structure, dwindled in numbers with the highest rates of loss on the sugar estates where the proportion of effective workers was reduced to some 40 per cent of the population by 1832.[21]

These circumstances generated new areas of struggle for the slave work force and contributed to important new gains. In the first place, efforts to rationalise the available labour power removed workers wholesale from marginal to more profitable properties.[22] This robbed the workers of property (houses and grounds) and of the burial plots which contained their history. Removals prompted widespread resistance and induced some careful managers to offer compensation — houses and grounds already prepared at the new location — but conflict and coercion were always anticipated.[23] Thousands of slaves were removed; some however, as one of the cases discussed below indicates, secured *de facto* occupation of their estate.

The overall labour shortage, however, in some ways improved the slaves' bargaining position. Coloured slaves claimed by custom a right to differentiated functions as skilled and domestic as opposed to field workers; estates short of blacks for field work advertised coloured slaves for exchange.[24] More significantly, a substantial proportion of slaves secured, like the Grange Hill workers, more time for the provision grounds. Their success was reflected in the 1816 Slave Code in which planters officially designated 26 days a year in addition to Sundays for provision ground cultivation. The slaves made it clear that they regarded the grounds and the time to work on them as a form of wages for their work on the estate. 'The slave thinks he has a right to those grounds on account of his labour on the property to which he belongs', one observer commented; at the same time, work on the grounds secured the slaves' foothold in the island's commercial economy and strengthened their bargaining position on the estate.[25]

The slaves' capacity to connect themselves to the island's commercial economy and to contribute to the export trade, exacerbated the tension between coerced labour and 'waged' labour. Consciousness was raised, struggles with management intensified and, as a result, slave workers were able to establish customary norms for estate work and respect for their expertise. As Robert Scott, proprietor and attorney (1802–26) for 4,000 slaves in the important sugar producing parish of Trelawny commented:

> They are excessively impatient of control, if you exact more from them than you ought to do, *they will not submit to it*, but they know very well what duty (i.e. informal

contract obligation) they have to do on a plantation and
if no more is exacted, they are very easily managed
and require no harsh treatment whatever.[26] (emphasis and
brackets added)

Labour bargaining and re-negotiation of informal contract terms
consequently took place whenever new overseers took charge.
Overseers expected to 'encounter opposition' rather than, as in the
cases reviewed, stir it up, and claimed that the whip was an essential
weapon in their initial struggle to determine terms of work, including
work loads.[27]

The establishment of work norms opened the way to demands
for task work, sharpening the division between masters' time and
slaves' time and led to forms of outright wage bargaining. The slaves
pressed for time, food or cash payments for work over and above
the production routine, such as the repair or extension of the
existing infrastructure, roads, buildings, fences, bridges and ditches.

Task work characterised coffee and pimento production in
Jamaica just as it characterised lowland rice cultivation in central
South Carolina because, as Philip Morgan argues, this was the most
efficient form of labour organisation.[28] Investigation may prove,
however, that the task work system reflected worker demands as
much as staple crop 'requirements'. Certainly, no later than the
1820s slaves were pressing for task work in sugar production, traditionally characterised by gang labour and team work. The method
seems to have been limited to cane holing, but it was suitable for
both planting and cutting as continental experience in low country
rice production demonstrated.[29] From management's point of view,
task work, while recognising work norms, also promoted productivity
and reduced jobbing costs; the danger for the slaves, as some slave
foremen realised, was that established work norms would be under-
cut.[30] Task work opened the way, however, to the demand for wages.

The slaves were always ready, as one observer put it, to work
for pay. The slaves paid each other wages; Sunday work on the
provision grounds, for example, could earn 1/8 per day plus breakfast.
Sunday work on an attorney's garden might earn 2/11 plus breakfast;
and cash payments were incorporated into task work deals. The
planters faced the uncomfortable realisation, articulated to the 1832
Commons Committee on Slavery, that they simply could not afford
to pay both wages and maintenance.[31] From their foothold in the
island's commercial economy, the slaves attacked directly the form
of exploitation to which they were subjected.

The political implications of the struggle to secure free time and cash rewards for estate work were clearly spelt out for the slaves by the free coloured and black population which more than quadrupled (10,000—46,000) between 1800 and 1834. Freedmen, traditionally urban based, jostling with the slaves at market, now appeared in little colonies adjacent to some plantations, on land rented from ruinate estates. They worked as small producers and traders, and, in some cases, established family connections with estate slaves.[32] They translated into material terms the slaves' vision of the future implicit in the provision grounds, and their campaign for full civil rights which succeeded in 1830, extended that vision to embrace citizen status, a hope also fostered by the Protestant missionaries and the abolition campaigners.

The planter class rallied to hold back the creeping tide of economic and political pressure undermining their economy by improving management techniques. *The Jamaica Planter's Guide* (1823), for example, explicitly advocated security of tenure for occupations usually dominated by coloured slaves (artisans and domestics) and dismissal of overseers who wantonly interfered with the authority of drivers and head men; it celebrated the expertise of sugar boilers and their crucial role in production and specified, as great gang requirements, good tools, rum rations in wet weather and shelter from persistent rain.[33]

Charles Lewsey and the challenge to white authority

The impact of these general circumstances and the limitations of good management techniques are well illustrated by developments at Grange Hill and Blue Mountain which were in the hands (1825—29) of a reforming attorney, Charles Lewsey, imported by the absentee owner from Barbados to make his Jamaican properties pay. Lewsey's correspondence, suffused with awareness of labour problems, contrasts sharply with that of Laing and Sutherland and suggests one measure, though refracted through Barbadian experience, of the shift in the balance of power between workers and owners since the end of the slave trade. The estate workers indicate the new spectrum of these relations: one work force bargaining within the parameters set by demands for sugar production while the other challenged those parameters.

The slave population at Blue Mountain in 1825 was just 176— about the size it was before sugar production developed; a reduction Lewsey unhesitatingly attributed to malnutrition and mismanagement after studying the estate records.[34] Cultivation was carried on with the assistance of jobbing gangs. The use of jobbers could mean that estate slaves had successfully transferred part of the work load to hired gangs; at Blue Mountain it was symptomatic, rather, of estate slaves working, in industrial terms 'at stretch', in planter terminology, being subjected to 'the pushing system'. The 'pushing system' served merchant rather than planter interests by pushing for maximum profit crop by crop, at the expense of the owners' reputedly long term profit interest.[35]

The slaves, nevertheless, had consolidated their village life and had their own social centre, a religious meeting-house with a regular priest, an elderly African, in charge. The priest is not characterised as an obeah man, perhaps because Lewsey did not wish to risk the effects of taking legal action against him, but may have been one of the syncretic sect leaders engendered by the Black Baptists (active since the 1780s) and the missions established in St Thomas in 1802. Whatever the case, the slaves made it clear to Lewsey that their religion was their own affair by resisting his efforts to make them good Anglicans; very few consented to be baptised even at the ceremony held for Lewsey's own infant daughter.[36]

On the estate, apparently under the leadership of Becky, the head driver, the slaves used a variety of methods to limit white authority and to assert their own expertise. They threatened strike action in response to manifestly unjust as well as cruel punishment. Conscious that the take-over period was a testing time for managers and workers, Lewsey, in good Barbadian fashion, set out to establish that he ran a tight ship; in pursuit of economy and efficiency he systematically attacked infringements of estate property rights and consequently curtailed traditional slave property rights. One such move sparked instant collective protest: he ordered the slaughter, without warning, of hogs found straying in the cane. Outraged property owners surrounded Lewsey, long discussions ensued, and though the slaves finally (in Lewsey's account) admitted they were wrong to let the hogs stray, the attorney was left in no doubt as to the injustice of his action.[37]

The slaves had their revenge; the head driver, Becky, made a mockery of Lewsey's efficiency campaign by demonstrating the incompetence of his assistant, overseer Parkinson, a trainee planter also from Barbados. Ordered to close up a drain trench that needed to be open, Becky defied the order. Parkinson compounded his error and called the second driver to take Becky to the stocks. Lewsey, who met the punishment detail on the way, instantly recognised 'all is done here with Mr Parkinson...The negroes find out he knows nothing'. Slave expertise had discredited white management; Lewsey raged privately that 'it was the overseer that ought to be put in the stocks'. Publicly, however, he tried to save face, told Becky he would 'beg Mr Parkinson for him' and put the trainee back on probation.[38]

Becky's exposure of Parkinson, nevertheless, undermined his authority. When he tried to solace himself by commanding new sexual favours and sent male slaves to solicit for him, they did not meet with instant success. Customarily, slave women sought alliances with white managers for there were immediate material benefits and the children were whitened. Parkinson, however, already had a resident 'housekeeper' and some male relatives of the girls solicited, concerned perhaps to assert their family's autonomy or to comment obliquely on Parkinson's career prospects with Lewsey, refused on their behalf. The three girls who were recruited were made a common laughing stock by field women next day. Parkinson, desperate to assert his authority, took advantage of Lewsey's absence in Vere and had the women flogged, 18 lashes on their naked shoulders.

The women, an important component in the first gang, sent a delegation to Mrs Lewsey and threatened to walk off the job to go to Vere and complain to Lewsey. Mrs Lewsey played mediator; she sent for Lewsey, and promised Parkinson would cease all punishments if the women returned to work. Lewsey, in contrast to Laing who, confronted by an actual strike could order the slaves back to work on the promise of an investigation two weeks later, was on the spot in 48 hours, heard all parties and immediately sent Parkinson off the estate.[39]

The intensity of the contract bargaining process at Blue Mountain permeates the correspondence and it is clear that agreement was reached chiefly because labour shortages forced Lewsey to rationalise production; this meant reduced work loads and improved work routines. The land laid out in sugar was 'beyond the strength' of the estate workers and jobbers were expensive: great gang work cost 2/1d., caneholing 2/6 per day per worker, or £7.10 an acre and their use tended to be cumulative, from clearing land, to cane holing, weeding and cutting.[40] Lewsey reduced the acreage in cane and organised sugar production to cut down on night work during crop. The Blue Mountain slaves became part of an experimental routine which attracted comment throughout the parish and was brought to the attention of the House of Commons Select Committee on Slavery in 1832. The mill was shut down for 6–8 hours every week night and from Saturday evening until Monday morning. This gave a 16–18 hour production day, worked in spells, but allowed for 6–8 hours sleep every night.[41]

The slaves at first regarded these innovations with suspicion and scepticism, suspecting that some new loss of privilege or property would make them pay for apparent improvement. As the new work routine continued, however, the reduced acreage to hole and weed and a reduced working day at the mill achieved co-operation. The benefits to management were measured when the 1826 crop was taken off. Like the crop of 1800, it was done in the face of heavy rains which fell from January through to July; 'not two days together have we had in those months fair'. The weather made extra work: the cattle pens became swamps and had to be moved seven or eight times. But, in marked contrast to 1800, the workers' health and spirits stayed good. They let Lewsey know they were trying their best; 'Let us put our shoulder to the wheel and break out a good crop for Massa'. Lewsey took the hint and put up an old steer (value £8cy) to fatten for the harvest home. Almost lyrical with success, he wrote, 'It is truly gratifying to see we can make such an improvement (in the quality of sugar) in the same copper and with the same people'. All this was achieved without a single case of insubordination or a single complaint 'presenting itself for some months'.[42]

The benefits to the slaves were described by the head driver. Lewsey, characteristically, asked him if the cane cutters did more work after they had a night's rest.

> He said that the Negroes did not require to be *Drove* that frequently *before time* when the officer had to look for the people in the morning they would find 5 or 6 absent, or Gone to some cane piece to sleep, that those that had *Heart* to take the Flogging would come up and receive it and go to work and those that had none would *Run*.

The results had been bad sugar, bad returns and 'disgraceful depopulation on this estate'.[43]

The slaves at Blue Mountain, as sugar workers, had something to gain from improved contract terms; at Grange Hill they had everything to lose. Grange Hill slaves had successfully cut down on estate work and devoted themselves to provision ground production and marketing. On their grounds they employed, for payment in cash or kind, slaves from other estates and runaways and took the produce to market on the estate mules. Manchioneal was no longer their main outlet; they travelled thirty miles to Morant Bay and shipped from there to the Kingston market.[44]

It is not clear how all the slaves fitted into this system; certainly some enjoyed a higher than average standard of living. Slaves usually owned a few chickens, a hog and sometimes a goat, but only headmen had mules to ride. At Grange Hill slaves commonly owned donkeys with a market value of £8cy.[45] Sugar production was marginalised; the 'Engine ground the Cane juice and the Coppers Stewed the same into what they call Sugar'. Local jobbing gangs did most of the work, not because the estate slaves were subjected to the 'pushing system', but because they had minimized their work loads and 'enjoyed a Life of Idleness'.[46]

Lewsey initially held his predecessor ('a sinecurist') responsible for this state of affairs but experience taught that his real enemy was John Reay, the head driver. Reay had a reputation in the parish as a man of good character—a court case was settled in his favour on that account—and his support among the Grange Hill work force made him, virtually, ruler of the estate. Lewsey's efforts to tighten discipline and improve production met with collective non-co-operation. His threat to sell the slaves if runaways were found on the provision grounds was met by silence or possibly of disbelief since slave prices were low. The promise of cash rewards ($1 a head) and the threat of the work house for Reay if he was not the first to inform on culprits, produced no results.[47] The threat to rent out their provision lands and supply them with corn instead (the practice in Vere parish) provoked, however, a strong verbal response; drivers and people in a grand chorus, nicely calculated for the ear of a man himself devoted to their owners' service, begged for forgiveness, and promised to work their lands. Led by the drivers they pleaded with special fervour that Lewsey not 'write and inform *Master* of their bad conduct'.[48]

The chorus of assurance expressed primarily, as Lewsey rapidly discovered, the collective determination to defend the status quo. Lewsey resorted to physical punishment of individuals; slaves identified as 'trouble makers' were weeded out periodically and sent to 'cool' in the work house. The punishment of individuals did not provoke any overt retaliation from the slaves and no work stoppages or grievance meetings ensued. Management hopes of 'redeeming this property from ruin' were sustained.[49] But such punishments did not alter the power structure on the estate; Lewsey's threats against Reay intensified—he promised to destroy him by sending him from one work house to another through the island, 'unless an immediate emendation takes place in the conduct of the people'—but he never judged it appropriate to do so. The only slave to lose office, in fact, was the woman driver of the productively least important third gang. Mary Tait was 'broke from her Office' for 'winking at the Idleness of those under her charge and for not paying attention to the children and reporting the dirt eaters to the Overseer and the

Head Man'.[50] Lewsey made no attempt, either, to move the slaves collectively to Blue Mountain. Although desirable in economic terms, this threatened resistance at Grange Hill and disruption at Blue Mountain. Transfers were individual and voluntary and on this basis ten young men, prime workers, moved to Blue Mountain.[51]

The processes which undermined productivity and with it white authority, are illustrated by the case of Mr Fry the bookkeeper. Sent with a driver and the head watchman to clear a yam piece, he left at least half the yams in the ground 'and those the pick Yams of the whole piece', the overseer reported that 'they took good care not to dig one good one for me'. This 'neglect of duty' by the bookkeeper, together with similar instances, and an old grievance against his 'shameful conduct in attempting mauling a female in the Hot House' secured his dismissal.

The bookkeeper's 'neglect of duty' may have been just that; the circumstances suggest, however, that the level of disaffection among the slaves made it more politic to leave a job half done than coerce them to complete it. Mr Fry did not make an issue of the yam digging and neither, in fact, did the overseer; he sacked Mr Fry, but makes no mention of punishing the slaves.[52] The bookkeeper and the overseer seem to have agreed that, given the state of labour relations on the estate, disciplinary action was not appropriate.

The slaves won this round in the struggle; Lewsey reluctantly concluded he could never promote at Grange Hill 'the Great Work of Reform' achieved at Blue Mountain. Surrounded by 'A set of subjects which meet me on every Quarter with Low Cunning and Vile Cant' efficient sugar production was out of the question; he could only 'extinguish it' as a sugar estate.[53] The property was turned to pasture and livestock, which complemented the slaves' provision ground production and rationalised the economic transformation they had effected.

Conclusion

The slaves at Blue Mountain and Grange Hill demonstrate that the methods of struggle customarily identified with contract and wage workers were first developed by slave workers cognisant of the crucial value of labour power. Collective withdrawal of labour, the presentation of grievances and the use by owners and managers of mediation were methods developed by 1770. Group action by slaves with particular grievances was also used, notably by women, and secured positive results. Skilled and confidential slaves pioneered these processes and the head men on both estates emerge as instigators and, by inference, organisers of group and collective action.

The immediate cause of action was physical coercion: the whip used to extract more intensive, or longer hours of labour or to exert arbitrary authority. The protests recorded were directed against the slaves' immediate oppressors, a realistic objective given the sharp class difference between owners and their representatives and their hirelings. It is clear, however, that the slaves also fought to command their own labour and their own produce, including a 50 per cent share in the estate yam piece. The records reflect primarily, the *results* of these struggles which were facilitated by long term trends— the diminution in the labour force and the expansion of the internal market. The *methods* used can also be inferred—1770 style strike action together with informal 'deals' and 'understandings' between head men and overseers. The problems presented by 'managing' slaves practically dictated that overseers were either strict disciplinarians (like Munro), or time servers. In either case, their transience assisted the modification of work loads and increased rewards. The attorneys themselves were no more than occasional visitors whose self interest, like Laing's, was often best served by acceding to the slaves' demands—a pattern sufficiently common by the 1820s for attorneys to attempt to conceal from the slaves their key role in overseer dismissals.[54]

The Blue Mountain and Grange Hill experience suggests more than one parallel with nineteenth century Russian serf bargaining procedures. Many serfs were also owned by absentees, supervised by stewards (attorneys) and managed by bailiffs (overseers). Deterioration of work conditions, excessive work demands, excessive punishments, removal of livestock, and seduction of women, also prompted grievance procedures. In this case, written petitions to a higher authority—the owners, a local official (magistrate) or even the Tsar—were carried by delegates who risked flogging. Complaints often focused on the bailiff and, if nothing was done, the serfs went on strike until a special land court composed of local officials (a form of Council of Protection) reviewed the complaint. The end result, which affected the fortunes of several hundreds of thousands of workers on vast estates, was frequently armed resistance and military confrontation.[55]

The slaves use of strike action and their long tradition of bargaining for informal contract terms places in a new perspective the role played by strike action in slave rebellions (e.g. the 1831 Jamaica rebellion) and invites revision and re-assessment of small scale events currently labelled 'rebellion'. Small scale outbreaks may represent spontaneous reactions to the failure of mediation processes.

The struggle of the Jamaican slaves also places in context their astonishing performance as apprentices. The Apprenticeship scheme, implemented in August 1834, incited the workers to bring to bear on a published contract all the skills they had acquired in making, maintaining and developing informal contract terms. The new contract, which established the working week at 40½ hours a week and also rolled back customary allowances to the levels sanctioned by the slave code, resulted in island-wide class confrontations. For several months Jamaica teetered on the verge of some form of general strike. The crisis was only resolved when, with crop season looming, 'all the prominent attorneys' and all the big sugar producers conceded the old allowances for the shorter working week.[56] The part-time wage slaves' first task, under the new contract, was to consolidate the gains they had made as chattel slaves.

The records also demonstrate the crucial role, in these developments, of the slaves' connection with the world of wage labour outside the plantation. The differences between Grange Hill and Blue Mountain derive to a large extent from the fact that Grange Hill slaves were closely inter-twined with that economy no later than 1770. Their access to cash returns for labour on their provision grounds exacerbated the tension between coerced labour on the estate and exchange-valued labour on the grounds. In the last decade of slavery these workers were able to carry this struggle a significant step further and take the estate out of sugar production. Grange Hill represents, perhaps, one extreme of a spectrum with Blue Mountain, a profitable sugar property where workers still bargained for terms as sugar producers, at the other.

By 1832 Jamaica's gross domestic product was worth £5.5 million sterling of which exports from the plantation sector represented just under 50 per cent (£2.2 million). The slaves' contribution to the economic pie 'outside the canefields' has been calculated at £1.5 million and included almost complete dominance of food production for local consumption (£847,000 of £900,000) as well as contributing arrowroot and ginger, for example, to the export trade. No less than 27 per cent of Jamaica's total agricultural output came from the slaves' provision grounds and was the product of waged labour. The slaves in Jamaica were bursting the bonds of the coerced labour economy by the same processes which undermined the serf economy in western Europe.[57]

The slave labour system, instituted by capitalists to foment rapid capital accumulation, was undermined by the slaves' participation in the capitalist economy they were intended simply to serve. This development reached its apogee in the 1831 rebel slaves' demand, reinforced by the destruction of a million pounds worth of their owners' crops and property, for wages. In the context created by the re-formation in 1832 of Britain's own ruling class, the Jamaican slaves' militancy destroyed slave labour as a separate category throughout the British Empire and forced acknowledgement of their right to wages for their work.

Notes

* £1 sterling = £4 cy

1 Slave labour is more usually considered a 'peculiar institution': E. Foner for example, in *Nothing But Freedom*, (Baton Rouge, University of Louisiana Press 1983) writes of the slave plantation as generating 'a distinct system of social relations as well as its own characteristic class system and political economy' (p. 9). This analysis was presented in April 1986 at the Association of Caribbean Historians' Conference, Nassau, Bahamas. While any shortcomings remain my own I am indebted to friends and colleagues for encouragement and advice, including Nigel Bolland, Paul Bugwin, Stanley Engerman, Gad Heuman, Barry Higman, Woodville Marshall, Sidney Mintz and Robert Shenton.

2 Fitzherbert Papers 239M/E, Derbyshire Country Record Office, Matlock, Derbyshire; Barry Higman, *Slave Population and Economy in Jamaica 1807–1834*, (Cambridge 1976) p. 53, Table 6: 123, Table 24.

3 Fitzherbert Papers 239M/E 17766, William Sutherland (planting attorney) to Jacques and Fisher (mercantile attorneys) 24 Nov. 1783; hereafter referred to as 239M/E.

4 Hurricanes struck Feb., Oct., 1780: Aug. 1781: Oct. 1786. Richard S. Dunn, 'The crisis of Subsistence in the British West Indies during and after the American Revolution', *William and Mary Quarterly*, 33: Oct. 1976, pp. 625, 632.

5 239M/E, 17787, 17803, Sutherland to Jacques and Fisher, 29 Aug. 1785; 9 April 1787.

6 239M/E 17803, *ibid*. 9 April 1787.

7 *Ibid.*, Great Britain, Parliamentary papers, (Commons) *Report from the Select Committee on the Extinction of Slavery Throughout the British Dominions*, (no. 721) 1831–2, 20: Q: 6398, William Shand (hereafter cited as P.P. (Commons) (no. 721), 1831–2, 20) corn took 4, yams 8, and plantains 11 months to mature.

8 239M/E 17843 Sutherland to Sir William Philip Perrin (absentee owner), 14 Jan. 1798. Some sugar estates (e.g. Worthy Park) resolved the subsistence problem by importing Jamaican food, (yams, cocos, plantains) from specialised provision grounds. It is not clear, however, that the slaves' conditions there were significantly better than at Blue Mountain. Michael Craton and James Walvin, *A Jamaican Plantation: The History of Worthy Park, 1670–1970*, (London, 1970): p. 135.

9   239M/E 16972−3, Jacques and Fisher to Perrin, 24 April 1783; 17766, Sutherland to Jacques and Fisher, 24 Nov. 1783; 17143, Jacques to Perrin, 28 Feb. 1794.
10 239M/E, 17177, Jacques to Perrin, 7 Sept. 1795.
11 239M/E, 17177, 17179, Jacques to Perrin, 7 Sept., 6 Oct., 1795.
12 239M/E, 17322, Jacques, Laing and Ewing to Perrin, 26 July 1800; Craton and Walvin, *A Jamaican Plantation*, p. 145.
13 239M/E, 17323, Jacques, Laing and Ewing to Perrin, 26 July 1800.
14 239M/E, 17084, Jacques and Fisher to Perrin, 12 April 1785; 17733, James Blaw (overseer) to Perrin, 7 Feb. 1775.
15 239M/E, 17717, David Munro (overseer) to Mrs. Frances Perrin, narrative account.
16 Charles B. Drew, 'David Ross and the Oxford Iron Works: a study in Industrial Slavery in the early nineteenth century', *William and Mary Quarterly*, 31: April 1974, p. 205. c.f. case of Billy Bacon, skilled slave who insisted on being hired out in Richmond; his owner had to employ a white miller to replace him.
17 239M/E, 17717, Munro, narrative account.
18 *Ibid*.
19 239M/E, 17711, Malcolm Laing (planting attorney) to Munro, 11 Sept. 1770. U.S. planters recognised that disciplinarian overseers had the greatest difficulties in managing slaves. Wm. K. Scarborough, *The Overseer*, Baton Rouge, Louisiana State University Press, 1966, pp. 79−80.
20 239M/E, 17717, Munro, narrative account.
21 Higman, *op. cit.*, p. 128, Table 25; p. 206.
22 *Ibid*. pp. 224−5.
23 P.P. (Commons) (no. 721), 1831−2, 20: Q. 25, W. Taylor; Q. 513, J.B. Wildman.
24 Higman, *op. cit.*, pp. 208−9.
25 P.P. (Commons) (no. 721), 1831−2, 20: Q. 1406, 1495, Rev. P. Duncan.
26 *Ibid*. Q. 5283, Robert Scott.
27 *Ibid*. Q. 510−11, William Taylor.
28 Higman, *op. cit.*, pp. 23, 29, 220; Philip S. Morgan, 'Work and Culture: The task system and the World of Low Country Blacks 1700−1880', *William and Mary Quarterly*, 39, Oct. 1982, pp. 563−99.
29 *Ibid*. p. 583.
30 P.P. (Commons) (no. 721), 1831−2, 20: Q. 63, 90, William Taylor.
31 *Ibid*. Q. 89, 90, 111, 570, William Taylor.
32 *Ibid*. Q. 129, William Taylor.
33 T. Roughley, *The Jamaica Planter's Guide*, (London, 1823), pp. 82, 97, 101−2, 340−1.
34 239M/E, 21021, Lewsey to Fitzherbert, 9 May 1826.
35 239M/E, 21032, Lewsey to Fitzherbert, 2 July 1826.
36 239M/E, 20992, Lewsey to Fitzherbert, 9 Aug. 1825.
37 239M/E, 20985, 20987, Lewsey to Fitzherbert, 12 June, 18 July 1825.
38 239M/E, 20985, Lewsey to Fitzherbert, 12 June 1825.
39 239M/E, 20993, Lewsey to Fitzherbert, 25 July 1825.
40 Higman, *op. cit.*, p. 238, Table A1, 1.
41 239M/E 21021, Lewsey to Fitzherbert, 9 May 1826; P.P. (Commons) (no. 721), 1831−2, 20: Q. 563, William Taylor.

42 239M/E, 21032, 21021 Lewsey to Fitzherbert, 9 May, 2 July, 1826;
    Higman, *op. cit.*, p. 237.
43 239M/E, 21021, Lewsey to Fitzherbert, 9 May 1826.
44 239M/E, 20986, Lewsey to Fitzherbert, 18 July 1825.
45 Higman, *op. cit.*, p. 238.
46 239M/E, 20139, Lewsey to Fitzherbert, 22 Aug. 1826.
47 239M/E, 20985, 20986, 20987 Lewsey to Fitzherbert, 12 June, 8, 18
    July 1825.
48 239M/E, 20986, Lewsey to Fitzherbert, 8 July 1825.
49 239M/E, 21004, Lewsey to Fitzherbert, 28 Feb. 1826.
50 239M/E, 21039, Lewsey to Fitzherbert, 22 Aug. 1826.
51 230M/E, 21021, Lewsey to Fitzherbert, 9 May 1826.
52 239M/E, 21004, William Duncan (overseer) to Lewsey, 28 Feb. 1826.
53 239M/E, 21039, Lewsey to Fitzherbert, 22 Aug. 1826.
54 P.P. (Commons) (no. 721), 1831−2, 20: Q. 6510, William Shand.
55 Peter Kolchin, 'The Process of Confrontation; Patterns of resistance
    to Bondage in 19th Century Russia and the United States', *Journal
    of Social History*, vol. 11, 1977−78, pp. 459−463.
56 W.L. Burn, *Emancipation and Apprenticeship*, London 1970, pp.
    176−177.
57 M. Craton, ed., *Roots and Branches*, Toronto 1979, S.W. Mintz,
    'Slavery and the Rise of Peasantries', p. 231 quoting A.J.G. Knox,
    'Opportunities and Opposition, The Rise of Jamaica's Black Peasantry
    and the Nature of Planter Resistance', *Canadian Review of Sociology
    and Anthropology*, 14, 1977, p. 386. c.f. Robert Brenner, 'Agrarian
    Class Structure and Economic Development in Preindustrial Europe',
    Past and Present, no. 70, Feb. 1976, pp. 30−75.

CHAPTER 2

The rise of a sugar proletariat labour force and the emergence of strikes in the Puerto Rican sugar industry: 1873–1905

Andrés A Ramos Mattei

Technology and the rise of a sugar proletariat labour force in Puerto Rico: 1873–1905

The abolition of slavery and the beginning of fundamental technical innovations fostered the rise and eventual formation of a free labour force for the Puerto Rican sugar industry. The development of this free labour force began chronologically after 1873. It rapidly accelerated to completion after 1898 when Spain lost the island to the United States as a result of the Spanish-American war.

By the end of the nineteenth century, Puerto Rico had a population of nearly a million inhabitants. The island depended upon an agricultural export economy based on such crops as sugar, coffee, and tobacco. Thus, it should be born in mind that the labour force being referred to in this chapter is one resident in rural areas and in an agricultural setting.

After 1873, the sugar industry underwent a process of change culminating in the establishment of the central factory system of production. The central, with its fully mechanised factory for the making of sugar, eventually replaced the traditional hacienda system of sugar production. Many sugar units adopted partial mechanisation since their owners could not afford the cost of complete mechanisation. But by so doing, they were able to increase production in the short run and momentarily meet competition.

In the technologically most advanced units, the labour force exhibited several characteristics, all leading to its identification as a rural proletariat class. First of all, labourers were landless. They were basically dependent upon their ability to work to derive an income on which to subsist. Sugar plantations provided housing for workers, with low monthly rentals or free of charge, in plots of land usually within the confines of the units. These houses could be clustered together or dispersed, according to the quality of land available. Row houses, divided into single rooms, were also provided for seasonal workers during the cane-cutting season.

Labourers received a daily salary based upon a six day week. However, they were not paid in cash but in tokens coined by each sugar unit. These tokens, or *fichas*, came in several denominations up to a peso. They bore the name of the sugar unit, the owner's name, and sometimes showed the date of coinage. More importantly, they could only be spent in the plantation store. Because wages were so low, averaging 50 centavos a day for field labourers, practically all income earned went towards buying food and primary necessities in the plantation stores.[1]

Even though the above characteristics applied to sugar workers in the most advanced units by 1898, especially in central factories, one should make an important distinction between agricultural field workers and those working at the factory. The fact that the latter worked in the factory elevated them to a higher place in the sugar labour hierarchy. The plantations developed various means which visibly differentiated the factory from the field labourers. Factory workers, for example, received higher salaries due to their skills in running the factory machinery. Moreover, they were provided with housing superior to field labourers. Their homes were not only separated from those of field workers but also clustered near the sugar mill. Even living closer to the mill became a status symbol for the factory workers.

Although bearing in mind these differences, this chapter is concerned primarily with the field labourers. They made up the bulk of the labour force in the sugar units. The larger numbers represented an undifferentiated category of cane-cutters during the crop season and performers of many non-skilled tasks outside of it.

Sugar strikes during the 1880s

Along with the Caribbean region, Puerto Rico experienced a severe socio-economic crisis in the final fifteen years of the nineteenth century. It is within this framework that collective protests during that period should be understood. The crisis can be seen in different ways and from various angles. The apparent prosperity of coffee exports has been a main contributing factor in ignoring the profound economic crisis of this period. Coffee had guaranteed markets in both Cuba and Spain, but around this fictitious situation, the whole economy practically collapsed.

The sugar industry was brought down during this period under the weight of declining prices and a demand for a better quality sugar. The traditional hacienda system could not extricate the industry from its predicament. The central factory system of production became the universally recognised panacea which would solve the sugar industry's problems. Yet although there were some centrals established during the latter part of the nineteeth century, this system did not prevail as the means for bringing the sugar industry out of stagnation.

There were many problems. The main ones were lack of capital with which to buy machinery and land; lack of working capital with which to operate the harvest season and pay the labourers; lack of stable commercial relations with foreign markets, particularly the United States; and an erratic, often capricious tariff system. To these, of course, may be added the uncertainty of fluctuating prices in the principal markets.

In the last fifteen years of the nineteenth century, Spain engaged the United States in a losing battle for control of its colonial markets in the Caribbean. By that time, the United States was the principal seller of foodstuffs and other commodities to both Cuba and Puerto Rico. Trying to curtail this situation, Spanish authorities decreed a 25 per cent increase in the prevailing tariff paid by United States goods.[2] The measure was self-serving in more ways than one. Spain could not hope to substitute United States imports in both islands. It had carried on for too long the practice of importing American wheat flour and sending it back to Cuba and Puerto Rico as if it were Castilian flour. The tariff increase protected this costly monopoly.[3]

The result was a sudden, steep rise in the price of basic commodities. This affected the dire situation of thousands of labourers who depended on a meagre diet of rice, beans, and salted fish and whose salaries of about 50 centavos a day were not raised. The situation was even worse for those agricultural sugar workers whose jobs were disappearing as more haciendas closed because of the sugar crisis. These displaced labourers were in a desperate position. Even those who still held on to jobs had to face the problem that sugar was a seasonal industry. Not all could find jobs in the six months period following the harvest. Thus the demise of the hacienda system brought about impoverishment for the agricultural working class.

The impact of the rise of the cost of living in 1890, therefore, was felt more deeply by sugar workers. It should not come as a surprise that from that date onwards strikes are recorded which reflect the desperate conditions in which workers found themselves. There were, at the beginning, isolated instances such as the case of labourers at Hacienda Belle Sitio in Río Piedras who struck for higher wages in May 1891. Its owner, Geronimo Landrau, reported to municipal authorities that 29 labourers refused to continue working for wages less than 62.5 centavos a day. Landrau argued that he could not pay even this meagre increase from the prevailing 50 centavos rate. He blamed low sugar prices as his main source of financial troubles.[4]

Collective protests took place again in January 1895 at the beginning of the cane cutting season. Workers went on strike in seven of the most developed sugar plantations in Ponce, a town on the southern coast.[5] The agricultural field labourers were protesting at the sudden rise in prices for basic commodities sold in plantation stores. These had unexpectedly been doubled at the outset of the harvesting season. The field workers were demanding a higher salary or a return to the previous price levels.[6]

The extraordinary thing about these strikes was the sympathy they enjoyed among various sectors of the propertied class, including plantation owners themselves. Actually, the strikes served to dramatise the predicament of the island's economy to the colonial government. Perhaps this is one basic reason why Spanish authorities did not attempt to dissolve the strikes or arrest the participants.

Behind these strikes loomed the announced intention by the colonial government to carry out a monetary reform, starting with the introduction of a new specie, coined especially for Puerto Rico: the silver provincial peso. Rumour had it that Spain intended exchanging the circulating coin, the Mexican silver peso, at a 50 per cent discount. That rate of exchange would have been in line with the value of silver in the international money markets. However, it would conveniently ignore that Spanish authorities had imposed the Mexican peso with a full circulating value of 100 centavos. The announced exchange was to take place sometime in early 1895. Merchants, however, did not wait and simply doubled the price of their goods, which were sold among others to plantation store owners. Sugar proprietors in turn had no choice but to do the same at the outset of the sugar season.

Thus, planters could not openly favour the strikes; however, the strikes were very useful in dramatising the predicament that planters and large segments of society were in as the cost of living doubled instantly. And this should be taken quite literally since practically all of the labourers' salaries went for food and other basic commodities. Spain buckled under the pressure, especially as it was facing the serious problems which would soon erupt into the Cuban second war of independence. It approved a rate of exchange of 95 cents to a Mexican silver peso, and prices returned to their previous levels.

The only other collective protest recorded before the end of Spanish domination took place on the eve of the American invasion of the island, in April 1898.[7] The strikes were concentrated in the area of Carolina and Loiza, towns adjacent to the capital, San Juan. For example, about 300 field labourers at British owned Central Canovanas went on strike demanding an increase in wages. Commerce by then had come to a virtual standstill due to the impending war, and foodstuffs had not only become scarce but more expensive. Partly due to the fact that they had to carry on the harvest and finish as soon as possible and partly because of the need for social stability in the face of war, workers obtained an increase to 75 centavos in their daily wages shortly after the stike began.[8]

Around the middle of April 1898, further news of strikes was received by municipal authorities in Carolina. There, workers struck at *Central Buena Vista*, owned by the Spanish commercial house of Sobrinos de Ezquiga. They were demanding a salary increase to 1.05 pesos. Authorities were very much alarmed at this news for they already had knowledge of the strike at Canovanas. They feared that the strikes would spread to nearby *Central Progreso*, another British-owned sugar enterprise. As a result, the entire area from Carolina to Loiza would be on strike.[9]

Military government under the United States: 1898–1900

The plight of the Puerto Rican sugar labourers was not abated by American domination of the island.[10] On the contrary, the economy further declined in the period of military occupation. This situation came about because of several factors. First of all, the war and then military rule literally paralysed the economy. The island lost its traditional markets for coffee and tobacco: Cuba and Spain. On the other hand, sugar did not gain duty-free access to the United States market until 1901.

During the military period, American currency was introduced into the island. The rate of exchange was fixed by a United States presidential decree of one peso equal to 60 cents US. Meanwhile, military authorities surveyed 'public' opinion as to what the eventual rate should be and whether United States currency should supersede the existing one.

All propertied interests in the island wanted to adopt the American currency. The rate of exchange, however, was another matter. Bankers, merchants, and money lenders all favoured a rate as deflated as possible, reflecting the fact that they had lent in pesos and were concerned about how many dollars they would now get back. Landowners, and in particular sugar planters, wanted just the opposite since their desire was to repay their loans with as inflated a currency as possible. The currency problem had disastrous effects on the working class. First of all, merchants and retailers began the practice of charging merchandise as if the dollar and peso were of equal value. This practice did not affect large segments of the population until the substitution of the provincial money ordered by the Foraker Act of 1900. Enforced at the prevailing rate, it augmented the cost of living by 40 per cent. Worst of all, however, the economy gradually came to a standstill as banks and merchants refused to continue lending money to planters until the matter of fixing a final value to the currency was cleared up.[11]

This critical situation led, among other things, to the partial failure of the 1899 and 1900 agricultural harvests. Such was the hardship that the military governor decreed a moratorium on loan payments throughout the island in February 1899. The effect was disastrous since planters could not obtain additional working capital to operate their sugar units for the rest of the harvest season. Nature compounded the woes of the economy with a tropical hurricane in August 1899. It destroyed the coffee crop and did extensive damage in the sugar cane districts of the coastal plain.

Under these conditions, the propertied class in the island could only hope for an alleviation of their difficulties through duty-free access to the American market and the adoption of United States currency. These two measures would create an attractive atmosphere for both American and local capital.

For the sugar agricultural labourers the case was far different. Up to then, their meagre salaries had been barely enough to provide food for themselves and their families. Little if anything was left after satisfying material needs. They could keep up with the rising cost of living only by increasing their salaries. They also demanded to be paid an equivalent amount of American currency as they had previously received in silver pesos. So desperate was the situation that, contrary to prevailing views, many strikes in the sugar plantations occurred during the American military occupation.

The military government was only six weeks old when strikes broke out in several plantations of Ponce and in the nearby town of Juana Diaz. Field labourers at Hacienda Fortuna and Boca Chica in Juana Diaz and Union in Ponce struck at the end of November 1898. They were asking for better working conditions and one dollar US for a day's work.[12] Shortly after, the island press began carrying reports that planters were recruiting field labourers from other parts of the island. Furthermore, planters, among others, took recourse to importing contracted labourers from the nearby British West India islands of Tortola, Antigua, Nevis, and St Kitts.[13]

During the month of December a rash of fires took place in the cane fields of several plantations in Ponce. Again Haciendas Fortuna and Union figured prominently. Several of the most important plantations of the region, such as Potala, were subjected to sporadic fires in their cane fields.[14] In the following months, field labourers went on strike in areas such as Guayama on the southeastern coast, and Manati in the north.[15] Workers were now demanding an eight hour day with wages fluctuating between 75 cents and one dollar US.

The military governor made it clear that strikes were perfectly legal, contrary to the express prohibition in the Spanish criminal code of 1879. As a matter of fact, one military governor, Guy V. Henry, even decreed the eight hour day for island-wide workers.[16] This led, no doubt, to the practice of bringing strike breakers from depressed parts of the island and to the importation of British contracted labourers, known as *cocolos*, to break the strikes. With these measures, planters hoped to control collective protests, debilitate strikes, and maintain wages at their present levels. Labourers retaliated by, among other things, setting fire to cane fields and going on strike in individual plantations.

The general sugar strike of 1905

For the crop season of 1905, sugar field workers were again involved in collective demonstrations and went on strike in the various cane growing regions but particularly in the southern part of the island. This time, however, the strike did not take place on individual plantations isolated from each other. Thousands of workers went on strike due to the organising efforts of the *Federación Libre de Trabajadores*.

The Federation had been founded during the military administration in June 1898. It reflected American policy towards organised labour. Authorities felt it was more convenient to allow the labour movement to develop under its constant supervision and control.[17] In 1901, the Federation became affiliated to the American Federation of Labor (AFL). With its reformist and pure economic goals, the AFL was the perfect check for the Puerto Rican labour movement.[18] In allying itself to the AFL, the Federation was looking for the strength it did not have. It was hoping that financial aid could be obtained whenever workers were on strike. Thus, strikes would be given at least a chance of success as workers would be provided with aid received from the AFL.[19]

The 1905 sugar strike was the first experiment of a long discussed tactic within the *Federación Libre*: a general, island-wide strike. However, instead of the Federation leading events, initially there were numerous strikes in which the organisation was not involved. These strikes took place mainly on the north coast. Again labourers in the Loiza area figured prominently in these protests. They alleged that sugar prices had risen to $5.00 per hundredweight and were therefore demanding a salary increase accordingly.[20] By the end of January there were at least 2,000 field labourers on strike in the Río Grande area, adjacent to Loiza. In another coastal town of the north, Arecibo, there were also about 3,000 labourers on strike. The latter averaged only 30 to 40 cents for a day's work.[21]

In light of the seriousness of the strikes, the public authorities decided to intervene. The Government acted as a mediator between planters and workers. By early February, sugar proprietors announced their willingness to increase salaries by 20 per cent from their present levels, which meant wages could rise to a maximum of 75 cents a day.[22]

However, things were different in Arecibo. Sugar owners began to bring in contracted labourers from the surrounding highlands. This situation led to violence and police attacks against the striking workers. So serious were the events in Arecibo that a full investigation was sought in the House of Delegates, the local legislature. Unfortunately, it never took place.[23]

Even so, strikes continued to occur unabated. On 7 February, labourers at *Central Carmen* in Vega Alta struck.[24] A week later, on the other hand, it was reported that strikes in the Loiza area had ceased.[25] Meanwhile, the Federation was making plans for the general strike in the southern region. Ponce became the main headquarters of the Federation leaders. From there, they fanned out as far as Guanica to the west and Guayama to the east. This was no accident as the largest sugar central factories in the island operated in both these places. In fact, the stike was directed initially against the 'sugar trust' in Guanica where South Porto Rico Sugar Company managed the largest sugar factory in the island, Guanica Centrals.

The Federation argued for better wages and improved working conditions for field labourers. It pointed out the recent prosperity of the sugar industry, and demanded a base salary of 75 cents for a nine hour day. At that time, the average wage fluctuated between 35 and 50 cents for at least a twelve hour day.[26] The Federation wrote letters to planters, explaining the workers' demands and announcing that the workers were being represented by them in negotiating collective contracts. This set the stage for a long series of strikes during the month of April 1905.

Initially, planters threatened to import contract labourers from the British Leeward islands but this never took place. As in Arecibo, many planters chose to bring in cane cutting labourers from the highlands. South Porto Rico Sugar Company not only contracted highland labourers but provided them with housing. The Company thus tended to isolate workers from the strikers. Things were not that simple as police had to protect strike breakers day and night. Aside from this, highland workers were not skilled at cutting cane.[27]

The police force took a decidedly anti-labour stance. In the town of Yauco, for example, the local police prohibited workers' meetings or public demonstrations. The official in charge threatened to break any public meeting with club-wielding policemen. In Guayama, police forbade passers-by even to stop in front of the Federation offices in that town.[28] Unfortunately, the strikes ended in riots, deaths, and many wounded participants. On 16 April, a mass meeting took place in the town square of Ponce. Over 8,000 workers gathered that day. Using a disturbance caused by a drunken participant as an excuse, local mounted police charged into the crowd without warning, brandishing swords and shooting at will.[25]

Soon afterwards the Federation leaders had a meeting with the American civil governor. They argued for their constitutional rights, such as free speech and the right to assemble. The governor simply ignored these arguments. Instead, he insisted over and over again that workers were responsible for the disturbances at meetings and that he had ordered police to disperse workers' meetings.[30] With colonial authorities so clearly on the side of sugar proprietors' interests, the strikes gradually began to fizzle out. Nevertheless, sporadic strikes continued to take place. Several plantations belonging to *Central Fortuna* in Juana Diaz were still on strike on 28 April.[31] Two days later, workers struck at *Central Fajardo* on the east coast. There, they were earning about 40 cents a day.[32]

Meanwhile, the Federation called for a mass meeting in Ponce where about 5,000 sugar labourers gathered in the town square. There, on 1 May, it announced that an average increase of 30 per cent in wages had been won as a result of the strikes.[33] However, the Federation glossed over the fact that it failed in its main objective: becoming the representative of sugar agricultural labourers in collective bargaining with sugar proprietors.

Conclusion

The formation of a sugar proletariat labour force in Puerto Rico unfolded in the last three decades of the nineteenth century. North American domination of Puerto Rico after 1898 accelerated this process. The internal growth of the sugar units of production fostered the rise of an undifferentiated mass of sugar field workers, cutting cane during the crop season. This rural proletariat labour force can be characterised as landless, even homeless, since plantations provided them with living quarters, and tied to individual units through a symbolic salary spent in the plantation store.

This particular relationship led to the first recorded strikes in the sugar industry by the 1890s. Common problems such as meagre salaries, exorbitant increments in the cost of acquiring basic foodstuffs, and increases in the cost of living all led sugar labourers to use the strike as the only means available to obtain their rights.

Strikes were legalised after the American occupation of the island in 1898. By 1905, the first ever recorded, coordinated strike took place in the southern part of the island. It was under the auspices of the *Federación Libre de Trabajadores*. By then, however, the local police were placed at the side of sugar proprietors who destroyed the general strike.

Notes

1   For a fuller discussion, see for example, Sidney W. Mintz, 'The Rural Proletariat and the Problem of Rural Proletarian Consciousness' *Journal of Peasant Studies*, 1, 3, (1974).
2   Lidio Cruz Monclova, *Historia de Puerto Rico (siglo XIX)*, (Río Piedras, Editorial Universitaris, 1970) Tomo III, Primera parte, p. 333.
3   *Ibid*.
4   Document published in *Anales de Investigación Histórica*, IX, 1–2 (enero-diciembre de 1982) pp. 72–73.
5   *La Correspondencia*, 24 to 28 January 1895.
6   *Ibid.* 26 January 1895.
7   Such was the plight of sugar workers by then that a newspaper article expressed relief at the end of the mourning period for the death of

Juan Serralles, owner of several plantations in Ponce who died in Barcelona in late 1897. When work was again continued, the article stated: 'Los vecinode Coto han visto reanudarse los trabajos y el hambre ya no los amenaza'. *El País*, 1 October 1897.

8   *La Correspondencia*, 17 April 1898.

9   AGPR, Carolina, Caja I–GG, 1898.

10   As late as March 1900, it was reported plantations on the eastern coast could only hire half the normal labour force required. 'They (the planters) are awaiting for Congress to do something'. *San Juan News*, 29 March 1900.

11   On the eve of the American invasion, newspaper articles complained of regional droughts, minor crop failures, scarcity of commodities, and increased prices of foodstuffs. Work on sugar plantations could be had for only two or three days at the most. See: *La Correspondencia*, 9 May and 22 June 1898.

12   *La Democracia*, 30 November 1898.

13   *La Correspondencia*, 19 November 1898.

14   *La Democracia*, 2 and 6 December 1898.

15   *Ibid.* 18 January 1899.

16   Ingualdad Iglesias de Pagán, *El obrerismo en Puerto Rico*, (Palencia, Ediciones Juan Ponce de León, 1973) p. 87.

17   *Ibid.* pp. 71–73.

18   Gervasic García and Angel Quintero, *Desafío y solidaridad: breve historia del movimiento obrero en Puerto Rico*, (Río Piedras, Ediciones Huracán, 1982) p. 40.

19   *Ibid.* p. 36.

20   *El Boletín Mercantil*, 24 January 1905.

21   *Ibid.* 30 January 1905. See also Rafael Alonso Torres, *Cuarenta años de lucha proletaris*, (San Juan: Imprenta Baldrich, 1939) p. 335. This author states that the most important central sugar factories in Arecibo, Los Caños and Cambalache, had to stop grinding cane due to the strike.

22   *El Boletín Mercantil*, 2 and 3 February 1905.

23   *Unión Obrera*, 12 February 1905.

24   *El Boletín Mercantil*, 13 February 1905.

25   *Ibid.* 16 February 1905.

26   *Unión Obrera*, 26 March 1905. See also Santiago, Iglesias Pantin, *Luchas emancipadoras*, (San Juan: Imprenta Venezuela, 1929) p. 345 where he states that sugar labourers in French-owned Central Fortuna, near Ponce, made 40 cents for a 14 hour day.

27   *Unión Obrera*, 15 May 1905.

28   *Ibid.* 16 April 1905.

29   See *El Boletín Mercantil*, 17 April 1905 or *Unión Obrera*, 23 April 1905. Also, consult Jesus M. Balsac, *Apuntes históricos*, (Mayaguez: Imprenta Moutaluo, 1906), p. 44. He states that in Mayaguez money donations were collected for striking workers in Ponce. Furthermore, a mass demonstration was organised to protest police brutality in the 16 April incidents at the Ponce public square.

30   *Unión Obrera*, 23 April 1905.

31   *El Boletín Mercantil*, 28 April 1905.

32   *Unión Obrera*, 30 April 1905.

33   *Ibid.* 7 May 1905.

CHAPTER 3

Origin and development of the working class in the English-speaking Caribbean area 1897–1937

Richard Hart

The first wave of working class activity

Labour organisation in the English-speaking Caribbean area developed in three main waves or stages, the first of which lasted from the late 1890s to the beginning of World War I. The first instances of the organisation of workers for the improvement of wages and working conditions occurred in Trinidad and Jamaica, but their organisational forms were very different.*

In Jamaica, the Carpenters, Bricklayers & Painters Union,[1] popularly known as the Artisans' Union, was organised in 1898. It endeavoured to regulate rates of pay for artisans and sought to improve their skills through the establishment of a trade school and the regulation of apprenticeship. The union advocated the establishment of a government technical school, but made no political proposals of a more general nature. In 1901 officers of the Artisans' Union assisted in the formation of a Tailors and Shoemakers' Union. Neither union lasted for more than a few years. The first organisation of teachers, which subsequently became the Jamaica Union of Teachers, had been formed in 1895, but being under establishment auspices it could not properly be described as a trade union at that time.

In 1907 two other groups of skilled workers in Jamaica, the printers and the cigar makers, formed trade unions. Both were organised as 'chapters' or 'locals' of North American unions affiliated to the American Federation of Labour (AFL). In 1908 both unions called members out on strike, with disastrous consequences. They lacked the resources and experience to conduct major strikes so soon after their formation and the defeats they suffered led to their disintegration.[2]

There is also mention of another AFL affiliate in Jamaica in 1907 called the Jamaica Trades & Labour Union but nothing is known of the categories of workers it sought to organise. However, W.G. Hinchcliffe, a master carpenter who had been the Secretary of the Artisans' Union, was involved in this organisation. Some years later, in a statement reported in a local newspaper, he said that it had ceased to function in 1909 because its most 'zealous' members 'through circumstances had to emigrate, some to Haiti, and some to Colon. Others to Port Limon'.[3] There is no record of the survival of any of these early Jamaican unions into the second decade of the twentieth century.

The first organisation seeking to represent the workers in Trinidad made its appearance in 1897. This was the Trinidad Workingmen's Association (TWA). Though it relied heavily on the same stratum of skilled tradesmen as the early trade unions in Jamaica, the TWA differed from the latter in two important respects. Firstly, its organisers sought to include all the different trades and occupations of workers within one organisation, including unskilled workers employed on the railway and at the waterfront. An unsuccessful waterfront workers' strike in 1902 is said to have adversely affected its membership.[4] Secondly, the TWA served the functions of both a trade union and a political organisation, seeking to appeal to and obtain the support of other social strata in addition to the working class. Indeed, the initiative for its formation may have come from persons of petty bourgeois origin. Its first President, Walter Mills, is described as a druggist which, in the context, probably means that he owned a small chemist shop. His successor, Alfred Richards, was also a druggist. Another prominent foundation member was Sidney deBourg, sometimes described as a 'cocoa proprietor' and identified in a 1906 list of committee members as a 'commission agent'.

The TWA's political proposals articulated the demands of a considerably broader constituency than the working class. In 1897 it was advocating, among other things:

 a) a reduction of taxes, especially on foodstuffs and agricultural implements;
 b) better transportation facilities;
 c) the establishment of minor industries;
 d) a savings bank;
 e) the further opening up and availability of unused government owned land.[5]

In 1906 it was making proposals for constitutional reform and petitioning the British government for 'a purely elective Municipal Council for the City of Port of Spain and some measure of reform of the Legislative Council'.[6] In 1913 it proposed that 'representative institutions should precede federation'.[7] Another interesting difference of orientation is the fact that whereas the Jamaican trade unions of the first decade of the twentieth century were organised

within affiliates of the North American trade union federation, the
AFL, the TWA in 1906 sought affiliation to the British Labour
Party. In the event, their application was unsuccessful, Ramsay
Macdonald rejecting it on the ground that the Labour Party's constitution did not provide for external affiliations. The British party
nevertheless agreed to raise a number of questions affecting Trinidad
in the House of Commons and the member who undertook the
responsibility for doing this was laughingly referred to by his colleagues as 'the member for Trinidad'.[8]

Whether the British Labour Party influenced the political philosophy of Trinidadians is open to question, but when a Labour MP
visited Trinidad in 1912, a local newspaper warned him that the
TWA was made up of 'irresponsible elements' who would stop at
'nothing short of a socialist state'![9]

Though the TWA outlasted the trade unions which had come
into existence in Jamaica during this first wave or stage of working-
class organisational activity, it appears to have ceased to function
or, if it did continue to exist, operated at a very low level of activity
during the first three years of the 1914–18 war. What appears to
have contributed to its decline was a split in the ranks of its leadership
between those whose focus of attention was on the trade union side
of its activities and those whose orientation was mainly towards the
achievement of political reforms. This came to a head in 1914. The
former faction was initially headed by deBourg and included James
Braithwaite, a stevedore, who subsequently succeeded him. The
latter faction was led by the President, Alfred Richards.[10] Though
the presence of deBourg in the former rather than the latter faction
may seem strange given his occupation, it does appear to have been
in character. DeBourg had long enjoyed a reputation as a radical,
having advocated, in the Constitutional Reform Committee as far
back as 1892, the widening of the franchise so as to give poor
peasants the vote.[11]

But perhaps a more important reason than the factional split,
for the decline and possibly the demise of the TWA, was war-time
restrictions and the war-time atmosphere. When World War I started,
propaganda suggesting that war-time sacrifices were needed in the
common interest was very persuasive. This was not the climate in
which progressive or radical ideas could thrive.

In Guyana (then called British Guiana) too there were initiatives
by artisans towards the end of the nineteenth century. E.A. Trotz, a
carpenter, and others presented a petition to the West Indian Royal
Commission of 1897, signed by 200 carpenters, masons, engineers,
bricklayers, builders, porters and carters. The petition stressed the

decrease of employment opportunities, which the petitioners attributed to the decline in the sugar industry and the amalgamation of many sugar estates. They also complained of high indirect taxation on essential food imports.[12]

Earlier, in 1888, a Bakers' Association had been formed which was 'described as being on a footing similar to that of other Benefit Societies'. And in 1890 Trotz had assisted in the formation of a Guianese Patriotic Club and Mechanics Union although, as Walter Rodney records, 'no details have come to hand on this last named venture'.[13] Neither organisation appears to have survived into the twentieth century. There had been unrest among several groups of urban workers in 1890. In that year there were strikes of lightermen, stevedores, coopers and bakers and the press referred to 'an epidemic of strikes'.[14]

The most militant initiative, however, came not from the skilled tradesmen but from the poorest and most depressed and exploited sections of the working class—the indentured and former indentured plantation labourers. Indentured labourers had had clashes with the police in the early 1870s. This had been followed by a period of calm which lasted into the early 1880s. In 1884 the Immigration Report recorded that there had been only five minor stoppages, but a further period of militancy had begun soon afterwards. Three had been 31 'strikes and disturbances' in 1886, 15 in 1887 and 42 in 1888.[15] Unrest and dissatisfaction had again manifested itself on the sugar estates in the mid-1890s. In 1896 a notoriously trigger happy police officer ordered his men to fire upon workers at Plantation Non Pareil who were endeavouring to prevent the arrest of persons alleged to be the promoters of their grievances. Five were killed, including Jungali who was one of their leaders, and fifty-nine wounded.[16]

There were more strikes of plantation labourers in the early years of the twentieth century—in 1903, 1904 and 1905. In May 1903 an indentured gang at Plantation Friends in Berbice struck work in support of a demand for an increase in their task rates from $1.00 to $1.44. Management offered an increase of 20 cents but refused to compromise at the workers' revised demand of $1.28. When some of the workers were charged before the court in New Amsterdam with having threatened the manager, a crowd assembled in front of the court house. The Riot Act was then read and the police opened fire, killing six and seriously wounding seven. Six workers were sentenced to one year's imprisonment and two others to six months. A key leadership role in this dispute is said to have been played by Salamea, an indentured Indian woman.[17]

The working class upheaval in 1905, though spontaneous, unorganised and devoid of revolutionary objectives, was, nevertheless, revolutionary in its dimensions. Both urban and rural workers were in motion and, on many of the sugar plantations, the predominantly Indo-Guyanese field workers and the predominantly Afro-Guyanese factory workers were acting in concert.

In May there was a strike of field workers on plantation Lusignan which demonstrated their increasing determination to resist the traditional overbearing oppressiveness of the supervisory staff. It was sparked off by the overseer assaulting an indentured worker. One hundred and fifty-six strikers then set out, armed with cutlasses, shovels and sticks, to march all the way to the capital to lay their complaints before Crosby, the Immigration Agent General. However, after such a militant start, the demonstration collapsed when the marchers were intercepted and disarmed by the police at Kitty and five of their number were arrested.[18]

Unrest and dissatisfaction continued to rise as the year progressed. On Tuesday, 28 November the young stevedores on Sandbach's wharf in Georgetown led the way in refusing to work unless the so-called 'special rate' of 16 cents per hour, received on the previous Sunday for a special job, became the regular rate. On the following day some 300 stevedores paraded along the waterfront carrying a banner reading: '16 cents an hour or no work'.[19]

At mid-day on 29 November the African porters at the Ruimveldt factory struck. The employers countered by endeavouring to get Indian workers to take over their jobs, playing one race off against the other. But the strikers were prepared to resist any such attempt by force and no takers could be found among the Indians. On hearing news of the strike the field workers also came out on strike, led by the cane-cutter George Henry. By the next day all work on the plantation was at a stand still. The police, under the command of the same officer who had ordered his men to shoot the workers at Non Pareil in 1896,[20] fired into a crowd of strikers. Four were killed and others wounded. Among those who died was the strike leader, Robert Chapman. George Henry was arrested and subsequently sentenced to six months imprisonment and flogging.[21]

That same night there was rioting in Georgetown. Ruimveldt Plantation was very close to the capital and the spark which ignited the already tense situation appears to have been the sight of four wounded strikers being carried through the streets of the city in an open cart on their way to hospital. Far from intimidating the crowds who witnessed it, the sight evoked an angry and sympathetic reaction. Shops were looted and some property was damaged or destroyed.

On 1 December the waterfront workers' strike continued, as did the rioting in the city. On that day too, the factory workers at Plantation Diamond on the east bank of the Demerara River stopped work. Over the next three days most of the plantations on East Bank, Demerara, and some in other areas, became strike bound. On Plantation Versailles the African and Indian workers came out together. Nowhere did the employers or the government succeed in dividing the strikers along racial lines.

Some employers believed that concessions should be made to the workers, but Governor Hodgson[22] would have none of that. He threatened plantation owners on West Bank, Demerara, who had offered wage increases, that unless they withdrew their offers he would withdraw from their estates the protection of the armed forces. This caused even the *Chronicle*, which could usually be relied on to support the government and call for law and order, to describe him as a partisan of the planters.

The strikes of 1905 in Guyana were eventually suppressed, with the active assistance of the British armed forces transported to the colony on two British warships soon after the disturbances began. These troops were used to police the plantations for a month following the upsurge of strikes and rioting, and the workers derived little or no immediate advantage from their struggles. But although the planters and the government had emerged victorious, the colonial establishment had been severely shaken by the discovery that it could not rely for support on any social strata within the society outside the numerically insignificant plantocracy and wealthy mercantile community.

One of the most remarkable features of the events of 1905 was the extent to which the middle classes and persons in clerical occupations were alienated from the establishment and failed to support the government, as had been expected of them. Indeed, several prominent public figures of middle class origin openly supported the workers cause; an outstanding case being A.A. Thorne, the founder and headmaster of a private secondary school. In his perceptive analysis, published posthumously, Walter Rodney has disclosed that this was, in part, a reflection of the extent to which the middle classes and the native intelligentsia generally had been excluded by the colonial establishment from participation in the political processes.[23]

The establishment's isolation was vividly illustrated, during the short period before the arrival of the British warships, by the failure to respond to the call to duty of 100 of those eligible for service in the militia, the force on which the government had thought it could rely in times of emergency to supplement the police. One militia sergeant, a school master named William Dathorne, not only refused to report for duty but was accused of harassing those who did — an accusation resulting in his subsequent prosecution. So doubtful was the prospect of recruiting infantry volunteers that the government was forced to confine its recruitment to a small number of white residents on horseback.[24]

In 1906 there was another strike on the Georgetown waterfront but on this occasion it had been carefully and secretly organised. The stevedore, Hubert Critchlow, who was later to become widely known as the country's foremost trade union leader, was one of the conspirators. The strike, which took the wharf owners by surprise, was initially effective. But the employers, taking advantage of the fact that the strikers had decided to stay away from the wharves to avoid clashes with the police, were able to introduce strike-breakers and break the strike.[25]

The cumulative effect of this defeat of the waterfront workers in 1906 and their lack of achievement in the previous year, coupled with the ruthless and bloody suppression of the recent strikes and demonstrations of the sugar workers at the nearby Ruimveldt Plantation, had a demoralising effect on the workers in the capital. According to the trade union historian, Ashton Chase, they were reduced to 'a state of passivity for about ten years'[26] In the rural areas further away from Georgetown, however, strikes continued to occur. Match factory workers at Vreed-en-Hoop were on strike for a week in March 1908. Nor did a single year pass from 1908 to 1913 in which sugar workers somewhere in the colony were not on strike.

Strikes occurred on Plantations Friends, Wales (West Bank, Demerara), Marionville (Leguan Island) and La Bonne Intention (East Coast, Demerara) in 1908, at Plantations Wales, Leonora (West Coast, Demerara) and Peter's Hall (East Bank, Demerara) in 1909, at Friends again in 1910 and in 1911, 1912 and 1913 at Plantations Lusignan and Uitvlugt (West Coast, Demerara), Diamond (East Bank, Demerara) and Blairmont (West Coast, Berbice).[27] But all this represented only spontaneous unrest and activity. No working class organisations resulted from it. And in Guyana, as in Trinidad and Jamaica, a period of calm set in with the outbreak of World War I.

Summarising this first stage or wave of working class activity in the English-speaking Caribbean area we find the skilled tradesmen of Jamaica had created several separate trade unions which, after a short period of activity and a couple of pioneering strikes, had all become defunct. In Trinidad a much broader and all embracing organisation had flourished for a time and made some impact, but had ceased to function actively, or perhaps not at all, by the beginning of the war. In Guyana a much more numerous contingent of workers had militantly entered the struggle but had, at least in the capital, been beaten back and had been unable to create any lasting organisations. No organisations of a trade union nature had made their appearance in the smaller islands.

The second wave: 1917—30

The tide of working class unrest and organisational activity began to rise for the second time in 1917. It flowed in the next few years but once more began to ebb away in the mid-1920s. An important source of discontent was the rapid increase in the prices of imported items of popular consumption during the course of the war, against a background of little or no increase in the level of wages. These price increases were accompanied by a dramatic fall in the quantities imported.

With the prices of Guyanese imports in 1914 as his base figure of 100, Peter Fraser has shown that by 1916 the price of flour had risen to 131, salted fish to 141, salted beef to 101 and cotton manufactures to 200. By 1918 these prices stood respectively at 227, 228, 229 and 400—representing a very appreciable increase in the cost of living. Over the same period imports into Guyana of flour, salted beef and cotton manufactures had fallen to approximately two-thirds of the 1914 level and imports of salted fish by over 39 per cent.[28] A similar situation was occurring throughout the English-speaking Caribbean area.

A secondary source of disillusionment was the news of the racial discrimination black soldiers serving overseas were suffering which, by the beginning of 1917, was filtering through to the Caribbean colonies. On their return home after the war the bitterly disillusioned soldiers swelled the ranks of the discontented. Failure to provide the demobilised servicemen with sufficient land or financial assistance to re-establish themselves in their homelands led to protests and disorders, particularly in Jamaica and Trinidad.[29]

As early as the end of 1916 there were signs of working class dissatisfaction in Guyana. On 7 December a 'petition' advocating wage increases and a reducton of the working day from 11½ to 10 hours, supported by 585 signatures, was presented to the legislature, the 'Court of Policy'. But it was from the Chamber of Commerce, not the legislature, that a reply was received, suggesting that only a minority of the workers were dissatisfied and that the grievances alleged were exaggerated. In the weeks that followed interest in and support for the petition mounted and at the beginning of 1917 the Chamber of Commerce met with representatives of the petitioners. But the waterfront workers rejected the new rates and hours of work proposed by the Chamber and on 6 January came out on strike.

This was followed by strikes of Georgetown Railway workers and of Sea Wall Defence Workers at Lusignan and Clonbrook on 10 January. The waterfront workers' strike lasted six days, There was also a strike in New Amsterdam and a strike of factory workers on a sugar plantation in Berbice. Other petitions were received from clerks, nurses and messengers in government departments. By 20 January all the strikes had ended and some modest improvements had been obtained, though the Sea Wall Defence workers got nothing. On 31 January the Governor, in a letter to the Colonial Office, stated: 'In view of the undoubted increase of prices due to the war, I fear the labour unrest in the Colony cannot yet be regarded as at an end'.[30]

In the latter part of 1917 Hubert Critchlow, still working as a stevedore in Georgetown, and others began to campaign once more for wage increases, using again the locally well known device of the petition. Teams of workers were organised to collect signatures and tremendous popular enthusiasm was generated. On 28 October, 1917 the petition was presented to the Chamber of Commerce; meanwhile the campaign in support of the demand for wage increases continued. The employers, alarmed at the growing popular unrest, authorised the Chamber to negotiate with the petitioners. In December an increase of 10 per cent was agreed. As a result of this victory Critchlow emerged as the recognised leader of the workers and early in 1918 set about organising a second petition, this time for an 8-hour day.

As a campaign gathered momentum the principal employers, led by Bookers, the giant British firm with interests in sugar plantations, wharves and commerce monopolising the greater part of the country's economy, decided that Critchlow must be stopped. He was dismissed from his job as a stevedore and barred from further employment on the waterfront. But the workers became more determined and Critchlow's popularity became greater than ever. The campaign reached its climax in a massive demonstration which marched to Government House in Georgetown. There the Governor (unlike his counterpart in Trinidad who had refused to see Braithwaite) received a delegation led by Critchlow. From this meeting

Critchlow emerged to announce the formation of a trade union, the British Guiana Labour Union. The union held its founding conference early in the New Year. By the end of 1919 it had enrolled 7000 members and, with the aid of a mortgage, had acquired its own headquarters.[31]

One of the earliest manifestations of rising unrest in Jamaica was a spontaneous strike at the Kingston Ice Factory in 1917 which resulted in the imprisonment of several of the strikers.[32] In October of that year the cigar makers again went on strike, this time successfully. Their leader was A. Bain-Alves who had been a member of the union which had collapsed after an unsuccessful strike in 1908. A new union of cigar makers was now formed.[33] In 1918 there was a further eruption of strikes in Kingston, the first of these being a strike of employees of the fire brigade in April. Between April and June longshoremen on the Kingston wharves, coal heavers at the Palisadoes Coaling Station and sanitation workers came out on strike.

Bain-Alves was active in the organisation of trade unions of longshoremen and of banana carriers and coal heavers. In the following years he assisted other categories of workers, including match factory workers and hotel employees, to organise trade unions and these he grouped together in a Jamaican Federation of Labour under his presidency.[34] In the following year the name of W.G. Hinchcliffe, the veteran of the 1898 Artisans Union, was also mentioned in a local newspaper as endeavouring to organise workers in the building trades.[35]

There was also unrest among sugar workers in Jamaica at this time. At the beginning of July 1918 the strike wave spread from Kingston to some of the rural areas. There was a strike at Amity Hall sugar plantation in Vere on 1 July which closed down the factory. Three workers were shot and killed on 3 July when they attempted to prevent the boilers being restarted. Other strikes occurred at Golden Grove and at Annotto Bay. These strikes led to the appointment by the Government of a Conciliation Board.[36] But no attempt appears to have been made to organise a trade union of sugar or agricultural workers at this time.

In 1919 the workers employed at the Jamaica Government Railway went on strike and the management had to concede all their demands. Arising out of the strike these workers formed an organisation called the Workingmen's Co-operative Association. This, in the words of one of their leaders, was 'a union under cover'. The name was chosen because they were aware that at that time trade unions were illegal in the British Caribbean colonies. The tide of militancy in 1919 also affected categories of employees on whose loyalty the establishment had always felt it could rely. Many policemen, teachers and civil servants were also on strike. The policemen's grievances were speedily rectified.[37]

Though there was no contact at the popular level between the widely separated colonies of Jamaica, Trinidad and Guyana at that time, the lines of communication of each colony being northerly to the metropolis rather than laterally to each other, the wave of unrest affected all parts of the English-speaking Caribbean area at the same time. The first manifestations in Trinidad occurred in the oilfields at Fyzabad and Point Fortin, where the workers went on strike in February 1917 but were intimidated into returning to work.[38] In the same month there was a strike of workers employed by the asphalt company at the pitch lake, in the course of which there was a serious fire. In addition to the usual involvement of the police against the strikers, troops were also called in. Five of the strike leaders were arrested, two of whom were sentenced to imprisonment for two years, the others for one year, all with hard labour.[39]

It seems unlikely that these strikes were organised by the Trinidad Workingmen's Association, though certainly, at around this time, steps were being taken by the trade union orientated faction of the leadership of the TWA to revive it. It has been suggested that it was not until March 1919, after a period of indecision, that the TWA adopted a policy of active support for strikes.[40] Be that as it may, the revived organisation was at this time concerned more with trade union activities than the formulation of political demands. In May 1919 the TWA negotiated for the asphalt workers a wage increase of 33⅓ per cent, a reduction of the working day by one hour, an increase in overtime rates of 150 per cent and promises of better housing with land for vegetable plots.[41]

In November, 1919 the TWA made demands for wage increases on behalf of the waterfront workers. The shipping agents described this as 'a piece of impudence on the part of those who had no authority from the men to make such representations', and refused to discuss the matter.[42] On 15 November the waterfront workers went on strike. The extensive support of the public for the strikers was displayed on 1 December when thousands turned out to join the strikers in a march through the streets of Port of Spain which brought all business to a stand-still. Alarmed at the success of the strike and the extent of public support for it, the colonial government at first adopted a conciliatory attitude. A formula was found which enabled the TWA representatives, in a single sitting with the employers, to negotiate a pay increase of 25 per cent, facilitating the settlement of the strike on 3 December.[43]

In the meanwhile, however, the Governor had appealed to the imperial government for armed reinforcements. The first of these arrived in two British warships on the very day the strike was settled and immediately the Governor discarded his conciliatory mask. A campaign of harassment and persecution of the workers' leaders and intimidation of the working class was instituted. Braithwaite and other leaders were sent to prison and others were fined in prosecutions before the courts. Several prominent members and supporters of the TWA who had been born outside Trinidad, including the ageing deBourg who had lived in the island for very many years, were deported.[44] During this period however, despite the persecution, the membership of the organisation continued to rise. By the end of 1919 it had 6000 members. In mid-January 1920 its leaders were reported to have estimated the membership at 10,000.[45]

There was labour unrest too in both the Leeward and Windward Islands before the end of the war. From St Lucia, in February 1917, the Administrator sent a telegram to the Colonial Office reporting several strikes. He reported that local merchants had increased wages by 15 per cent in consequence of a strike of coal carriers, that stevedores had obtained on average increases of 25 per cent; and he recommended that there be increases for public employees also. He also reported strikes in the rural areas.[46]

In some of the islands, possibly because of the fact that there was no enabling trade union legislation, the first popular organisations to make their appearance took the form of benevolent societies. This is how it was in St Kitts-Nevis in 1917 after one reported attempt to form a trade union had not materialised.[47] In his unpublished manuscript 'Working Class Struggles of a Half Century', the veteran Kittician journalist and trade unionist, Joseph N. France, records that at that time some workers desired to form a union but were conscious of the fact that this would have been illegal and did not dare to go beyond what was permissible under the Leeward Islands Friendly Societies Act. Some idea of the absolute domination exercised by the employers during this period may be gleaned from what happened to some workers in the St Kitts district of St Pauls when, in 1918, they refused to continue working at the prevailing rates. They were arrested and sentenced to imprisonment for having committed the offence referred to locally as 'bridge (breach) of Contract'.

In 1917 the St Kitts-Nevis Universal Benevolent Association was formed and registered under the Friendly Societies Act. But it is interesting to note that one of its sponsors, a small shopkeeper named J.A. Nathan, had become familiar with trade unionism during a period of residence in the USA. J. Matthew Sebastian, the president, started a newspaper called *The Union Messenger* in 1921 which was printed and published by the Society.[48]

In Antigua there was a strike in March 1918. This resulted from an attempt to reduce the rate per ton paid to the workers for cutting cane. Workers knew that higher wages were paid in St Croix in the nearby US Virgin Islands. During the strike canefields were burned and some planters were attacked. The tension and dissatisfaction in the rural areas spread to the capital St John, where the police fired into an allegedly rioting crowd, killing two.[49]

The militant upsurge of working class activity in the English-speaking Caribbean area should not, however, be viewed in isolation from world events. There had indeed been an upsurge of working class unrest in 1917 in many parts of the world. But although revolutionary upheavals occurred in many other countries in the immediate post-war years, it was only in Russia that the workers had the organisation and determination to maintain working class power. By the mid-1920s the revolutionary upsurge had subsided everywhere else.

A parallel subsidence occurred in the British Caribbean colonies. In Jamaica, when the railway drivers and firemen came out on strike for three weeks in 1923 there was no organisation to support them, nor were they able to create one.[50] The railway management had already succeeded in destroying the Workingmen's Co-operative Association by the simple expedient of exerting pressure on the leaders. Some had been transferred to rural stations remote from the Kingston workshops, others were forced out of the service.[51] One by one the unions which A. Bains-Alves had assisted in organising also became defunct.

There was a short-lived revival of trade union organisational activity in Jamaica at the end of the 1920s which petered out in the early 1930s. Encouraged by two organisations based in the USA—the Trade Union Unity League and the Negro Labour Congress—an organisation called the Jamaica Workers and Labourers Association (JWLA) or the Jamaica Trades and Labour Union (these may have been alternative names for the same organisation or two parallel organisations) was formed in or about 1929. S.M. DeLeon played a leading part and Otto Huiswood, the Surinam born Communist who was 'field organiser' of the Negro Labour Congress, was in Jamaica helping with organisational work. For a time Marcus Garvey, who had returned to Jamaica after his deportation from the USA, co-operated with the JWLA. In April 1930 he presided at a meeting of a committee, the purpose of which was 'to pave the way for labour unions'. At the end of the same month Garvey addressed a JWLA meeting at the Edelweiss Park headquarters of his Universal Negro Improvement Association. But Garvey was opposed to Huiswood because he was a Communist and this co-operation does not appear to have lasted very long.[52]

In Trinidad the post-war history of working class activity, though no doubt affected by the world-wide rise and decline of revolutionary unrest, was strongly influenced by peculiarly local factors. As has been mentioned above, the TWA was originally designed to perform both trade union and political functions. Its revival at the end of World War I had been under the influence of the working class, trade union orientated, faction of the leadership. But in 1919 there returned to Trinidad, from overseas service with the British armed forces, a remarkable man of upper middle class origins whose personal influence was to be a significant factor in the future development of the TWA.

Arthur Cipriani, though Trinidad born, was of Corsican descent. Being white, he had secured an officer's commission in the Army. But, unlike other white or pass-white officers of West Indian origin, he had been deeply concerned about the racial discrimination suffered by the black soldiers serving overseas, and had fearlessly championed their cause. When he returned to Trinidad in the wake of many of the demobilised soldiers, his reputation had preceded him and he was already tremendously popular. Soon after his return, though exactly when is not clear, he joined the TWA and was offered and accepted the presidency. But Selwyn Ryan concludes that 'Cipriani does not appear to have been of any major significance during the disturbances'.[53]

The organisation Cipriani joined was an already functioning one and it seems probable that for some time after, he assumed the titular leadership, as the decisive voices in policy and decision making were still those of the working class leaders Braithwaite, Phillips and Bishop. It may be significant that it was the veteran deBourg, not Cipriani, who was sent to represent the TWA at the conference of the B G Labour Union in Guyana in 1920 (from which, incidentally, he was not permitted to re-enter Trinidad)[54] and that it was Bishop who represented the TWA at the British Labour Party conference in August 1921.[55] Indeed, Wendy Charles has reached the conclusion that it was 'between 1924 and 1928' that 'Cipriani gained control of the TWA'. This, she says was 'the decisive turning point in the development of the organisation'.[56]

Cipriani's reputation, social status and dynamic personality were all tremendous assets to the TWA. Its membership and influence grew rapidly. Its industrial and occupational branches continued to perform their trade union functions, but Cipriani's bias was towards reformist politics rather than working class struggles. And he was particularly uneasy about the fact that in Trinidad, unlike Jamaica and Guyana, trade unionism was still illegal in the 1920s. As his control over the organisation increased he discouraged the trade union side of its activities and concentrated its attention on the achievement of political reforms. In particular he was responsible for creating considerable illusions as to what could be achieved by winning the elected seats in the colonial legislature introduced under the recent constitutional reforms. These illusions were all the more remarkable when it is remembered that the elected members, who in any case were elected on a restricted franchise which excluded the majority of the workers, were to be in a minority in the legislature.

In the 1925 elections the TWA won three of the five elected seats and Cipriani entered the Legislative Council. After failing to obtain the enactment of legislation legalising trade unions, his reluctance to allow the TWA branches to engage in trade union activities appears to have grown stronger.[57] The late pioneer trade unionist Quintin O'Connor made numerous unsuccessful attempts, on behalf of the Clerks branch of the TWA, to get Cipriani's policy on this matter over-ruled.[58] Thus, although some industrial and occupational branches of the TWA, notably those at the waterfront and the railway which were functioning as trade unions, disapproved of what was happening, the trade union activities of the TWA declined under Cipriani's leadership.

The organisation became almost entirely a reformist political party. Even when, in 1932, trade union legislation was enacted in Trinidad and Tobago along the same lines as that existing in Jamaica, Cipriani still refused to allow the TWA to register as a trade union. This was because the statute did not give trade unions the immunities in tort and breach of contract and the right to picket contained in the English legislation of 1871.[59] When, in 1934, Cipriani changed its name to the 'Trinidad Labour Party', this merely confirmed a change of function that had long since been achieved in practice.

In Barbados too the placid war-time situation was disturbed in the immediate post-war years, but the first expressions of dissatisfaction appear to have come from the newly emerging intelligentsia. There does not appear to have been at this time any evidence of working class organisational activity. Initially the expressions of dissatisfaction took the form of demands for mildly progressive political reforms, articulated in the articles of C.W. Wickham in *The Herald* newspaper. Wickham, who returned from war-time military service in the Middle East in 1919, is said to have been inspired by the example of Captain Cipriani. His newspaper soon became the inspiration of a new intellectual ferment.[60] But it was not until the return to Barbados of Dr C.D. O'Neale in 1924 that these popular expressions of the need for changes in the prevailing system and standards of value were given organisational expression.

O'Neale was about 45 years of age when he returned home. He had obtained his qualifications in Edinburgh and practised medicine in the north of England for many years. Active in local government, he had represented the British Labour Party on the Sunderland Council.[61] He is said to have been influenced by Keir Hardie and to have 'learned his Socialism from the Fabian Society'.[62] In October 1924 he and others launched a political organisation called the Democratic League.

In April 1927 the longshoremen in Bridgetown went on strike and O'Neale, who had volunteered his services to the strikers, wrote seeking a conference with their employers to negotiate their demands. Rejecting his request, the latter informed him that the relationship between employer and employee was a private matter. At the time the workers do not appear to have been sufficiently militant to take the issue of their right to representation further. Subsequently, O'Neale formed the Workingmen's Association, an organisation designed to serve the workers as a trade bargaining agent, with additional educational and credit provision functions.[63] But it would appear that the Association did not succeed in mobilising the workers for sustained trade union activity. The attempt to organise them had come too late to take advantage of the wave of militancy which had swept through the Caribbean colonies in the wake of World War I. The Barbados Workingmen's Association had been formed at a time when, elsewhere in the region, the trade union movement was defunct or on the decline.

In Guyana the B G Labour Union suffered its first decline for a purely local reason, before the world-wide tide of revolutionary working class activity had begun to ebb. Soon after the end of its first year of existence as a registered trade union, a bid was made by a group of prominent middle-class people, with a reformist political rather than a working-class trade unionist orientation, to oust Critchlow and take over the union. The attempt was defeated but the struggle for leadership had a destructive effect on the newly formed organisation and the workers' confidence in it declined. By March 1923, unable to meet the mortgage payments, the union lost its headquarters. Its bank balance was down to $7.18 and its membership had declined to 205. But it survived none the less and slowly recovered. Its membership in 1924 was 1,129.[64]

The post-war militancy of Guyanese workers was still very apparent in 1924 and, once the leadership crisis had been resolved, this was a positive factor in the recovery of the B G Labour Union. In March of that year the union was demanding increases in the daily pay of stevedores from $1.60 to $2.00 and truckers from 84 cents to $1.20,[65] and increases in overtime rates. Other categories of workers were also demanding increases and the union had petitioned the government for legislation introducing a minimum wage. Though it had not succeeded in organising field workers on the sugar plantations, the union had also put forward a demand for 'East Indians to be paid on an equal basis with other labouring people of other races in the Colony'.[66]

On 31 March the Union called the waterfront workers out on strike, introducing for the first time an organised picket line. On the second day of the strike there was a mammoth workers demonstration in Georgetown which several hundred sugar workers journeyed to the city to join. The demonstrators forced the closing of saw mills and drove strike-breakers off the wharves. They also closed down the city's sewage works, the electricity company and the railway. Such was the militancy of the demonstration that in some streets upper-class residential premises were entered and domestic servants required to cease work.

It would appear, however, that after his recent experience with the challenge to his leadership, Critchlow, whose popularity was once more on the ascendancy, had lost some of his earlier confidence in the tenacity of the workers. Misguidedly placing confidence in the Governor, the union leadership began to apply the brakes on the workers' militancy, advising them to return to work before they had received guarantees that any of their demands would be met. The Chamber of Commerce, representing the employers, stretched out the negotiations with the Union until the militancy had subsided and then announced that the employers could not afford any increases of pay. Critchlow's appeal to the Governor at the beginning of April, to compel the employers to arbitrate on the workers' demands, was promptly rejected.[67] Nor did the report made on 29 April, by a Commission of Inquiry appointed by the government, bring any appreciable benefits to the workers.

The failure of the B G Labour Union to achieve substantial wage increases in 1924 greatly discouraged the urban workers and led to a slowing down in the recovery of the union. The strikes of the sugar plantation workers on the East Bank of the Demerara River, which commenced on 2 April, had been more militantly pursued. The workers had closed the factory at Plantation Diamond, but had had no organisation to represent them. A military force consisting of infantry and artillery, and policemen armed with rifles and machine guns, was sent to the area. But although the intimidated factory workers resumed work, the field workers stayed out.

On 2 April a procession had set out for Georgetown to enlist the support of Critchlow, but the marchers were dispersed at Providence before they could reach the city. On the following day a large demonstration of about 4,000 from various plantations on the East Bank was barred at Ruimveldt from proceeding. Though an offer was made to allow one or two representatives to proceed alone to the city, this was rejected and the crowd tried to break through the police guard. Meanwhile, the services of the president of the East Indian Association, which had disclaimed all reponsibility for the strike, and a pandit, were employed at Ruimveldt in an unsuccessful attempt to persuade the people to disperse. The police then fired on the demonstrators, killing 12 and seriously wounding 15. Unable to advance in the face of gunfire, the workers retreated and dispersed. The demonstrators had been mainly, but not exclusively, East Indians. Chase records that 'certain Barbadian labourers from Diamond reported to be members of the B G Labour Union were said to be the ring leaders of the crowd at Ruimveldt'.[68]

The militancy shown by the workers of Guyana in 1924 inevitably receded as feelings of frustration rose resulting from their failure to achieve significant results. The recovery of the B G Labour Union was undoubtedly retarded by the leadership's failure to pursue the urban workers' demands more vigorously. Likewise the union's prospects of extending its influence to the sugar workers were entirely frustrated. Nevertheless, the B G Labour Union did survive throughout the remaining years of the decade, avoiding the eclipse which affected, in one way or another, the workers' organisations in Jamaica and Trinidad.

Throughout the 1920s the B G Labour Union was the only workers' organisation in Guyana. The various categories of workers were served by different sections of the union. But it did not succeed in organising the country's most numerous category of workers—the workers on the sugar plantations. Its greatest strength remained on the waterfront. In 1931 a rival organisation, the B G Workers League, was formed, though at no time during the 1930s did its membership rise above about 500. It did eventually succeed in organising sugar factory workers on some plantations, but never the field workers who comprised the bulk of the labour force, and it never achieved the numerical strength or influence of the B G Labour Union.[69] Guyana was the only British colony in the Caribbean area in which, when the third wave or stage of working class organisational activity commenced in the second half of the 1930s, there was an already functioning trade union of manual workers.

The first World War had created a temporary boom in sugar prices but, after the war, prices slumped again. This had led to a number of the less efficient sugar producers in the Caribbean colonies going out of business. In Jamaica some sugar plantations went over to banana cultivation. In response to a demand which had been steadily growing since the 1880s, especially after the replacement of sailing ships by steam-ships, exports of bananas had been rapidly increasing. Other sugar plantations were swallowed up in the process of concentration which was occurring in the sugar industry. Between 1920 and 1930 the number of sugar factories in Jamaica was reduced from 66 to 39 while the average annual output per factory rose from 561 to 1,572 tons.[70] Higher yields were also being obtained from a smaller acreage due to the introduction of new varieties of cane. But, generally speaking, the 1920s was a bleak decade for the sugar industry in all the British colonies, a situation made worse by the fact that beet sugar production was on the increase in Europe and the British government had embarked upon a policy of subsidising its growth.[71]

The rapid and continuing increase in banana exports had helped to cushion the damaging effects on the Jamaican economy of the decline in sugar; Jamaica had indeed become the world's largest producer of bananas. Oil exports from Trinidad and, to a lesser extent, bauxite exports from Guyana had had a similar effect in those territories. But these were the only bouyant features of the generally depressed and declining economies of the British colonies in the Caribbean area during the 1920s. Imports of sugar into Britain and Canada from the empire did enjoy a tariff preference over sugars imported from non-empire sources, but the sugar producers complained that this was not enough to make sugar production profitable. In 1929 the open market price of sugar was £8.25 per ton and the tariff concession in Britain was worth £3.15 making a total of £12. But the sugar producers claimed that their cost of production, excluding freight and insurance, was £12.7.6. They admitted that they were receiving a good price for their by-product, rum, but claimed that even after taking the revenue from rum into account they were losing £1.7.6. per ton and making no allowances for depreciation.[72]

In response to this urgent plea for assistance, the British government in 1929 appointed a commission of inquiry. As a result of its investigations and recommendations the British government in 1930 agreed to an over-all rescue operation involving better guaranteed prices, quotes and other concessions and subsidies derived from increased local taxation. Further measures of assistance were introduced two years later. Thus was the profitability of British Caribbean cane sugar production once more restored.[73]

Economic distress in the 1930s

By the mid-1930s the giant British sugar refining firm of Tate & Lyle had begun to acquire sugar plantations in Jamaica and Trinidad. Whether these acquisitions were a consequence of the fact that sugar production in the colonies of the Caribbean areas had once more become profitable or whether, conversely, the desire to invest had come first and the company had then used its influence to persuade the British government to assist the industry, is not clear. Further research will be required to determine the sequence of these events. But, be that as it may, the advent of Tate & Lyle expedited the process of modernisation and consolidation.

Tate & Lyle's Jamaican subsidiary, the West Indies Sugar Company, built a giant new central mill at Frome in Western Jamaica which replaced five smaller factories. Later they built an even larger sugar factory in Vere, on the south-central plain. But although sugar production,[74] and the prospect of profits, dramatically improved from the second half of the decade of the 1930s, there was no corresponding increase in the wages of the unorganised sugar workers. Meanwhile banana exports, which had helped to keep the Jamaican economy going during the lean years of the sugar industry, had, by the mid-1930s, collapsed under the effects of devastating plant diseases. From this collapse the banana industry of Jamaica has never fully recovered.

Agriculture could not absorb the rapidly increasing populations and from the mid-1920s onwards the Latin American avenue of escape had been blocked. As the report of the West India Royal Commission, appointed in 1938, recorded: 'For some ten years or more the emigration outlets that previously existed have been virtually closed'.[75] The US economic crisis at the end of 1929, which by 1930 was affecting the whole capitalist world, also had its depressing effect on conditions in the Caribbean. By the mid-1930s poverty and unemployment in the English-speaking Caribbean area had reached alarming and explosive proportions.

Wages in Jamaica which, with the possible exception of Trinidad, were above those in the eastern Caribbean colonies, will serve to illustrate the general poverty. In November 1938 G.H. Scott, the Unemployment and Wage Rates Officer recently appointed by the Jamaican Government, presented to the West India Royal Commission a memorandum containing his estimates of average daily wages of artisans and labourers in the years 1932 and 1937 and in the year 1938 before and after the labour uprising of that year. This memorandum showed that the daily pay of male labourers in the capital Kingston remained at three shillings (3/-) until after the disturbances and then rose to three shillings and ninepence (3/9). The corresponding rates for women labourers were one shilling and three pence (1/3) in public employment and one shilling and sixpence (1/6) in private employment, both rising after the disturbances to one shilling and ten pence halfpenny (1/10½). In the rural parishes the male daily rate was two shillings and four pence (2/4) in public employment and one shilling and ninepence (1/9) in private employment, rising after the uprising to two shillings and ten pence (2/10) in public employment. Corresponding women's rates were one shilling and a penny (1/1) rising to one shilling and four pence (1/4) in public employment, and eleven pence (11[d]) in private employment. Most artisans earned seven shillings per day in the capital and considerably less in rural areas, and they appear to have obtained no immediate improvement in 1938.[76]

No census statistics are available for the 1930s, but Table 3.1 shows the weekly earnings of Jamaicans as recorded in the census taken there on 12 December 1942. It must, however, be borne in mind that wages recorded in the December 1942 census would have

Table 3.1 All wage earners in Jamaica for week ending 12 December 1943.[77]

	Numbers	Percentage	
Under 6 shillings	54,947	28.3	
6/- to 10/-	46,583	24.0	
10/- to £1	49,952	25.7	90.4
£1 to £2	24,027	12.4	
£2 to £3	9,110	4.7	
£3 to £4	4,063	2.1	
£4 to £5	1,980	1.0	
£5 to £10	2,912	1.5	
£10 to £15	381	0.2	
£15 to £20	174	0.09	
Over £20	129	0.07	

included increases obtained as a direct result of the working class upheaval in 1938, described on page 63.

Low as these earnings were, an equally revealing indication of poverty was the high level of unemployment, which had become characteristic of these colonies by the mid-1930s. Table 3.2 shows the level recorded in Jamaica in the same census:

Table 3.2   Gainfully occupied and unemployed in Jamaica—12 December 1942

		Numbers	Percentage
Employers in agriculture	18,993		
Other	1,775	20,768	3.7
Own account workers		153,274	27.6
The working class			
In employment		242,069	
Unemployed — unemployed who have worked	88,981		
— aged 15–24 and never worked but seeking work	50,528	139,509	68.7
			100.0
Unemployed as percentage of working class			36.5
Unemployed as a percentage of the gainfully occupied and unemployed			25.1

Detailed statistics such as these were not at that time available for the other British colonies in the area. However, in a report based on sample surveys prepared for the Barbados Government some 13 years later,[78] George Cumper estimated out of crop unemployment in Barbados at 24 per cent of the labour force. By way of comparison he stated that the corresponding figure disclosed by the Jamaican census was 'an unemployment rate (among wage earners only) of 30 per cent' and that 'a sample survey of Antigua in July 1950 found 25 per cent of the labour force to be unemployed'.

It is not clear how Cumper arrived at his 30 per cent figure for Jamaica. If he included the 50,528 persons aged 15–24 who had not obtained their first job, the unemployed percentage of the total number of workers would have been 36.5; if excluded 23.3. Though the Cumper report introduced considerable mystification into the concept of unemployment in Barbados, its tables showed the total number of workers out of crop in 1954—55 to have been 111,000 of whom 32,700 were unemployed and 5,100 sick and disabled. On these figures the unemployed percentage of the total would be 29.4.

All things considered, the 1930s was a decade of severe distress for the working class masses in the English-speaking Caribbean area and for the peasants too in the colonies where peasantries existed. The distorted and vulnerable export-import economies of the colonies, having experienced over the centuries little or no diversification, could provide no alternative opportunities for employment. A factor which contributed to the ability of the employers to keep wages from rising appreciably during the early 1930s was the absence of trade unions. The B G Labour Union in Guyana was the only important organisation of manual workers in existence. Furthermore, the use of the armed forces in suppressing expressions of popular dissatisfaction was still fresh in the memories of many workers.

The third wave: The labour rebellions of the 1930s

What appeared on the surface was a picture of general working class subservience and docility. Surveying the scene, colonial officials, representatives of the big foreign owned enterprises and the local employers and upper middle classes generally felt confident and secure. Those who interpreted the situation differently, like the visiting professor W.M. Macmillan, whose book *Warning from the West Indies*[79] was first published in Britain in February 1936, were dismissed as alarmists or trouble-makers. Sullen resentment and dissatisfaction were, nevertheless, swelling among the working people and the unemployed in all the British colonies of the Caribbean area. By the middle years of the decade the situation was like a cauldron of liquid coming to the boil, with isolated early warning here and there disturbing the apparently placid surface.

The earliest warnings came from Trinidad where there was a small demonstration of unemployed workers in Port of Spain in 1933. In the following year came a large demonstration of some 400—500 unemployed workers which led to the appointment by the legislature of a committee of enquiry.[80] Earlier that same year there had been spontaneous strikes and demonstrations of short duration on several Trinidad sugar plantations. Other early warnings came in

1935, from Guyana where there were strikes and disturbances on several sugar plantations[81] and from Jamaica where there were strikes of port workers in several out-port towns and among banana loaders on Kingston wharves.[82]

From 1935 onwards a wave of militant working-class protest began to swell across the Caribbean area, as major social upheavals occurred in one British colony after another. The first of these explosions took place on the island of St Kitts, an island entirely devoted to the production of sugar. Though an organisation called the Workers' League had been formed there in 1932, it was still legally impossible for it to act as a trade union. The social upheaval which occurred three years later was spontaneous and unorganised.

The trouble began on 28 January, 1935 when cane cutters refused to permit the reaping of the new crop to start at Shadwell plantation, on the outskirts of the capital Basseterre. The employers had offered work at 8 pence (16 cents) per ton, the rate which cane cutters had been forced to accept under protest in the previous year. This the workers now refused to agree to and the news of their refusal spread quickly to the adjoining plantations. Workers at the island's sugar factory also came out on strike, demanding a wage increase. Their wages had actually been reduced by one penny in the shilling in 1930 and subsequently by a further penny.

Workers on other plantations also refused to start the crop. At Lodge estate the owner-manager threatened the workers with a gun but when, instead of submitting or running away as expected, they disarmed him and broke the gun in two, they found that it was not loaded. This fact appears to have saved him from being harmed. At Estbridge estate, however, a party of armed police succeeded in arresting some of the strikers.

A new spirit of determination now spread throughout the length and breadth of the island as groups of workers went from plantation to plantation calling for a general strike. On Tuesday, 29 January, the workers everywhere were in a militant mood. Processions of workers were moving around the island on foot and no work was allowed to start. That afternoon, at Buckley's plantation, two to three hundred strikers, carrying sticks, entered the estate yard. Armed with guns, the manager and the overseer ordered the workers to leave but they were in no mood for retreat. Stones were thrown and the manager, either before or after the stone throwing fired into the crowd injuring three or four workers.

An armed party of police arrived under a former British army major, but the workers refused to obey his order to disperse. Instead, they demanded that the manager be arrested. At about 6.0 p.m. a contingent from the local military force arrived, by which time the crowd had increased to four to five hundred. The Riot Act was read and when this had no effect the armed men fired into the crowd. John Allen and James Archibald, both labourers, and Joseph Samuel, a factory watchman, were killed and eight others were wounded. According to the official report, fifty-five shots were fired. The report alleged that stones had been thrown at the armed forces.

Next day a British warship arrived and marines were landed. For several weeks thereafter unarmed workers were terrorised and intimidated by the police and soldiers. Thirty-nine strikers were arrested and sentences of imprisonment ranging from two to five years were imposed on six of them.[83] Thus was the militant upsurge contained for the time being. But the fact that the workers on such a small island, so vulnerable to economic pressures from their employers, should have dared to offer a militant challenge to the plantocracy and the colonial government, was of tremendous significance. A new spirit or working class determination was now in evidence.

The events in St Kitts signalled the commencement of the third upsurge of working class protest and organisational activity in the British colonies of the Caribbean area. Later that same year there was an eruption in St Vincent, though the spark which ignited the social conflagration there was not primarily a strike. The riot that occurred in St Vincent represented a protest against rising retail prices, including prices of articles of popular consumption, occasioned by the imposition of increased customs duties. These had been introduced in a situation of static and extremely low wages, threatening a further reduction in an already desperately low standard of living.

St Vincent shared a colonial governor with the other 'Windward' islands. In October the Governor arrived to attend a meeting of the local legislature. The Legislative Council at that time consisted of a majority of colonial officials and persons nominated by the Governor who represented the principal business and financial interests, and a minority of members elected on a franchise restricted by property and income qualifications to about 10 per cent of the adult population. On 15 October the Governor, in a move designed to increase government revenues at the expense of the ordinary consumers, introduced his new taxation proposals. It was also proposed to maintain the high local tariff on sugar which had previously been imposed to assist the sugar producers at the consumers' expense. The legislature was scheduled to meet again on 21 October to approve the Governor's proposals and, during the intervening week, there was mounting popular opposition as more and more people realised that there would be an appreciable increase in the cost of living.

On the morning of 21 October, an angry crowd of workers gathered in the capital, Kingstown, at the chemist's shop of George McIntosh, a popular member of the Town Council. They wanted him to present their grievances to the Governor.[48] It is doubtful whether there was any clear consensus as to what their demands should be, withdrawal of the proposed tax increases and sugar tariff or increased wages to meet the increased cost of living or perhaps both. But McIntosh is alleged to have stressed that to avoid oppression people have to fight for their rights.[85] He wrote an urgent letter to the Governor, seeking an interview on the people's behalf, which he then took to the building where the Legislative Council was in session. At about mid-day, while McIntosh was seated in the public gallery of the Legislative Council awaiting a response from the Governor to whom his letter had been handed, a large crowd armed with sticks, stones, cutlasses and other implements, assembled in front of the building.

McIntosh emerged from the building to say that the Governor had replied that he would be willing to receive a delegation later that afternoon at 5.0 p.m. This immediately aroused suspicions that the Governor was only buying time and intended to leave the island before that hour. The demonstration became increasingly militant and some workers forced their way into the building.[86] Among the remarks shouted the following were heard: 'We can't stand any more duties on food or clothing'; 'We have no work...'; 'We are hungry'; 'Something will happen in this town today if we are not satisfied'. Such was the alarm created that the Governor adjourned the session of the legislature.[87]

As the Governor and other officials emerged from the chamber and the former tried to restore calm, several incidents occurred. The Attorney General, who had drafted the taxation measures, was cuffed by a man who claimed that he had kicked him. The Governor was pushed and struck and is alleged to have received several cuts. Some of the Court House windows were smashed and the motor cars of several officials were destroyed or damaged. A crowd broke into the prison and released the ten prisoners there. The business premises of F.A. Corea, a member of the Legislative Council who was also the island's largest merchant and plantation owner, were ransacked.

The tables were turned when a large force of armed policemen arrived and the Governor personally took command of their operations. The Riot Act was read and the crowd at Corea's store was fired on. One person was killed and several others injured. Meanwhile the riot had spread beyond the city to Georgetown, twenty-one miles to the south, and Chateaubelair the same distance to the north. All telephone wires were cut and several bridges were destroyed. Armed police and 'volunteers' were posted to guard the cable and wireless station and the electricity plant.

At midnight on 21 October a British warship arrived. Military personnel known as 'Volunteers' were also brought in from other islands. On 22 October a state of emergency was proclaimed. Though the uprising was suppressed in the capital by the end of the first day, disorders in the rural areas continued for the next two days. Many plantation workers were involved. The police met particularly strong resistance at Byera's Hill, Campden Park and Stubbs. In these areas demands were made for land, for better wages and for better living conditions. Such was the level of unrest that the state of emergency was maintained for three weeks.[88]

In Kingstown the working-class leader who had emerged from the spontaneous uprising to play the principal agitational role in the demonstrations was Sheriff Lewis, previously known as Pablo but later nick-named 'Selassie' because of his advocacy of the cause of Ethiopia at the time of the Italian invasion of that country. Also mentioned as playing a leading role was a woman named Bertha Mutt, nick-named 'Mother Selassie'.[89] But the lime-light soon shifted to McIntosh who, despite his attempts to encourge 'law and order', was arrested on a charge of treason felony on 23 November. The weakness of the charge against McIntosh was revealed in the case presented against him at the preliminary examination before a stipendiary magistrate which lasted for five days. The magistrate, in dismissing the case, commented that all except one of the many witnesses called by the prosecution had given evidence which established the absence of guilt of the accused.[90] The effect of the prosecution was that McIntosh emerged as unchallengeably the most popular leader of the working class.

At the end of 1935 there was a strike of coal loaders in the neighbouring island of St Lucia. With recent events in St Kitts and St Vincent very much in mind the Governor mobilised the local military force and called upon the British government for reinforcements. A warship was quickly on the scene and marines patrolled the streets of Castries while for several nights the ship's searchlights played upon the city. The show of force was extended also to the rural areas. Faced with this massive intimidation the workers returned to work to await the report of an official commision of inquiry set up to consider their demands. The commission, however, felt sufficiently secure to reject the workers' claim for increased pay.[91]

These events in the Leeward and Windward islands were followed by a social upheaval in the island of Barbados. Clement Payne, who could be described as the person responsible for the disturbance which occurred there in 1937, had been born to Barbadian parents resident at the time of his birth in Trinidad. His parents had returned to their native land when their son was only four years old and it is doubtful whether he had ever become aware that he had not been born in Barbados. In later years he himself had migrated to Trinidad where his political awareness was no doubt aroused. He later claimed to have been an associate of Uriah Butler, the charismatic Grenadian who in the 1930s had been an active member of the Trinidad Workingmen's Association and had, along with others, broken with Cipriani in 1936.

In March 1937, at the age of 33, Payne returned to Barbados. To the immigration officer on duty he declared that he had been born in Barbados. Shortly after his arrival he began holding street meetings, announcing his intention of forming a trade union. On 1 May, 1937 he distributed the first ever May Day celebration leaflets in Barbados. Arrangements he had made to rent a hall for meetings were frustrated when the proprietor discovered his purpose, but his public meetings at Golden Square in Bridgetown began to attract large working-class audiences. Others who joined Payne in his efforts to arouse support for launching a trade union were Fitz Archibald Chase, Olrick Grant, Mortimer Skeete, Israel Lovell and Darnley Alleyne.

Alarmed at the agitational effect of Payne's speeches, the Governor decided to act. The first move was to prosecute him for making a false declaration as to his place of birth. But although Payne's father testified that he had been brought back to Barbados at the age of four and might not have known where he was born, and Payne said that he had always thought himself to be a Bardadian, he was fined £10 with the alternative of three months imprisonment at hard labour. The fine of £10 was far beyond Payne's own ability to pay. He appealed and was granted bail. On the next day he led a march to Government House, demanding to see the Governor. The crowd refused to disperse when ordered to do so by the police. Payne was then arrested and taken into custody along with several others. He was refused a renewal of bail pending the hearing of his appeal three days later and, whilst in custody, was served with a deportation order.

Payne's supporters took up a collection to fight his legal battles and if necessary pay the fine. He had been unrepresented at the original hearing, having been unable to find the fee requested by Grantley Adams, the lawyer he had hoped would represent him. But by the time of the appeal enough money had been raised to secure Adams' services. Some 5000 of Payne's supporters assembled outside the Court.

Payne's appeal, heard by the Court on 26 July, was successful. It could not be seriously contended by the prosecution that his declaration of birth in Barbados had been made in the knowledge that it was false or with an intent to deceive. But he was not released from custody. Instead the Governor had the police smuggle him on to a ship bound for Trinidad and deported him in pursuance of the deportation order. In Trinidad the police were waiting for him and he was arrested for having forbidden literature in his possession.[92]

When it became known in Bridgetown that Payne had been deported, there was an angry popular reaction. On the night of 27 July a large crowd assembled in the Lower Green and Golden Square which was addressed by Payne's closest associates. Next morning there was widespread rioting and disorder in the city. *The History of the Barbados Workers' Union* records: 'Shop windows were smashed, cars were pushed into the sea, passers-by were attacked; police patrols, caught unarmed and unawares, fled beneath a hail of bottles and stones...During the next two days the "trouble" spread to the rural parishes where a few lawless souls stoned cars on the highways while the bolder spirits among the hungry poor took advantage of the general fear and confusion to break into shops and to raid the sweet potato fields in isolated incidents of spontaneous opportunism. Shops remained closed, work came to a standstill in town and country alike...'[93]

Three weeks before these disturbances a strike at the Central Foundry had commenced and the workers were still out on strike at the time of Payne's deportation. On 28 July the lightermen, whose importance can only be appreciated when it is remembered that no deep water piers had yet been constructed in Barbados, came out on strike. They resumed work on 4 August when their demands were met. Other sporadic strikes and threats of strikes occurred in numerous work places. The Government however acted ruthlessly to suppress the widespread unrest and intimidate the workers. Firearms were used on several occasions, the final toll being 14 dead, 47 injured and more than 500 arrested.

Payne's closest associates received sentences of imprisonment on charges of inciting to riot. Grant and Skeete were each sentenced to ten years imprisonment, Lovell and Alleyne to 5 years. The atmosphere was well illustrated by the sentencing of Chase to nine months imprisonment. The words he was alleged to have uttered on 27 July, for which he was arrested and charged for inciting to riot, were: 'tonight will be a funny day'![94]

On Payne's behalf Grantley Adams challenged, unsuccessfully, the validity of the deportation order. His request that Payne be allowed to return to give evidence on the question of his domicile was adamantly rejected by the Governor. Rejected also was Payne's request in the following year to be allowed to return to give evidence to the West Indies Royal Commission.[95] But having so valiantly assisted in excavating the foundations for a trade union movement in Barbados and been denied the opportunity to assist in laying them, his services were not entirely lost to the Caribbean workers' cause. In Trinidad he became a founding member and organiser for the Federated Workers' Trade Union, which he served for several years. He was also a member of the radical political group known as the Negro Welfare and Cultural Association. On 7 April, 1947, he collapsed while addressing a meeting and died shortly afterwards.

The situation to which Payne had returned in Trinidad in July 1937 was tense. A strike in the oilfields in June, when the police attempted to arrest Uriah Butler, the strike leader, had developed into widespread rioting with loss of life and destruction of property. In the following year a working-class uprising in Jamaica escalated far beyond sporadic rioting into an all-island general strike. Widespread strikes and demonstrations followed in Guyana in 1938 and 1939. Out of the womb of these events, affecting the entire English-speaking Caribbean area, the modern labour and trade union movements were born.

The law and the trade unions

Prior to 1918 trade unions were illegal in all the British colonies of the Caribbean area. There was the English common law proscription against activity in restraint of trade, from which trade unions had been exempted by statute in Britain in 1871 but not in the colonies. There were, in addition, local statutes in force which made participation in such combinations a criminal offence. Law 15 of 1839 in Jamaica is a good example. The preamble to that statute stated:

> ...all combinations for fixing the wages of labour and for regulating and controlling the mode of carrying on manufacture, trade or business, or the cultivation of any planta-

tion...are injurious to trade and commerce, dangerous to the tranquility of the country and especially prejudicial to the interest of all who are concerned in them...[97]

Legislation of this kind, initially designed to prevent the slaves emancipated in the 1830s from combining as free men to obtain better wages, was still in force.

So far as the writer is aware, no prosecutions were instituted against the organisers of the unions of skilled workers formed in Jamaica during the first stage or wave of working-class activity. It is worth considering why this should have been so. Certainly the Gleaner Company, the largest printer affected by the 1908 strike, was aware of the legal position. The fact that the printers' union was illegal would not have escaped the notice of the astute lawyer, Lewis Ashenheim, who was a Director of the company. Nevertheless, the reason given by the managing director for refusing to recognise the union was that it was affiliated to the American, rather than the British, trade union movement.[98] He did not resort to the argument that it was illegal. The explanation may be that, at that early period, the employers were confident that they could easily defeat this attempt of their employees to organise, and saw nothing to be gained by drawing attention to the fact that what was lawful for white workers in England was unlawful for black workers in the colonies.

The workers, however, appear to have been aware of their vulnerable legal position. On their behalf, in 1909, S.A.G. (Sandy) Cox, a progressive elected member of the Jamaican legislature, asked the governor to introduce trade union legislation along the lines of legislation existing in Britain. The governor referred the request to the Colonial Office, where it was placed before the Secretary of State with the following revealing memorandum from a senior civil servant:

this movement is apparently being engineered by the 'American Federation of Labour' and if it is successful, will mean that any unions formed in Jamaica will be controlled by the American organisation, thus leading to a further development of the Americanisation of Jamaica, which we are trying to hinder in other directions. Setting aside any questions of its merits as a matter between employer and employed, I think it is on this ground a dangerous movement which we should not help forward if we can avoid it.[99]

This cunning civil servant then went on to point out that if Mr Cox were reminded that he could raise the matter himself in the legislature, the proposal would be killed there if he did so. The author of the memorandum was relying on the reactionary composition of the legislature, to a majority of whose members, as he explained, the proposal would 'probably be objectionable...on other grounds'. The Secretary of State accepted this advice. It is interesting to note that the Governor of Jamaica at the time, with whose unprotesting co-operation this proposal for trade union legislation was killed, was Sydney Olivier, the well known Fabian socialist!

When the second wave of militant working-class activity broke upon the English-speaking Caribbean area, trade union activity was still illegal. There were no local equivalents of the legal recognition conceded by statute to trade unions in Britain in 1871. But the second wave was far more widespread and militant than the first had been and before long the British Government decided that the time had come to make concessions. On 25 October, 1919 a trade union law was enacted in Jamaica. The legislation did not confer upon the unions and workers engaged in industrial disputes immunity from liability for tort or breach of contract. Nor did it legalise peaceful picketing. But it was, at least, a gesture that trade unionism would be tolerated. In June 1921 similar legislation was enacted in Guyana.

In Trinidad, unlike Jamaica and Guyana, there was no corresponding legalisation of trade union activity. Indeed, the policy of the government there moved towards repression rather than token liberalisation. The Habitual Idlers Ordinance of 1918, designed to discourage indentured labourers whose terms had expired from leaving the plantations, provided that any male, who could not prove that he had worked for four hours per day during the preceding three days, could be sent to a government labour camp or be contracted out by the government to private employers. The Strikes and Lockouts Ordinance, the first statute enacted in 1920 after the display of working-class militancy in November and December of the previous year, was a temporary measure which prohibited strikes and provided for arbitration to settle disputes between employers and employees. When this ordinance expired in June 1920 it was replaced by the Industrial Court Ordinance (No. 26 of 1920) designed to achieve the same purpose on a more permanent basis.

A particularly repressive statute was the Seditious Acts and Publications Ordinance (No. 10 of 1920) which, in addition to banning a number of publications, created the criminal offence of 'disaffection' against the King, the Government of Trinidad and Tobago or any other British possession and the colony's Executive and Legislative Councils. Offenders could be sentenced to imprisonment for up to two years and/or fined up to £1000.[100]

A point which requires further elucidation is the reason why the government of Trinidad and Tobago failed to follow the example of Jamaica and Guyana in introducing trade union enabling legislation at this time, and set off so persistently in exactly the opposite direction. Is this divergence to be understood entirely in terms of the personal inclinations of the respective governors and the tendency of the Colonial Office to trust the man on the spot? Or could the development of the commercial production of oil in Trinidad and the fact that in 1910 Winston Churchill, First Lord of the Admiralty, had begun to convert the ships of the British Navy from coal to oil burning,[101] have had something to do with it? Further research into the official correspondence of the period may yet provide the answer.

One of the planks of the Trinidad Workingmen's Association in the 1925 election in Trinidad and Tobago had been a demand for legislation making trade unions lawful. As has been mentioned, the TWA's leader, Captain Cipriani, had discouraged the organisation from fulfilling its trade union functions precisely because these were illegal. But although the TWA, even on the restricted franchise, had won three of the five elected seats in Trinidad, the Colonial Office could still not be persuaded to instruct the colonial governor to introduce trade union enabling legislation until 1932. Even then, the legislation followed the Jamaican Trade Union law of 1919 in failing to authorise peaceful picketing. Cipriani appealed on this point to the Secretary of State for the Colonies, but the decision was against variation of the legislation.

Meanwhile a trade union Bill had, on T.A. Marryshow's insistence, been introduced in the Grenada Legislative Council in 1933. Learning of Cipriani's appeal to the Secretary of State, Marryshow secured a decision to delay final passage of the Bill until information could be obtained as to the decision on the Trinidad and Tobago legislation. When this had been received the Grenada Law was enacted in the same form, without the legalisation of picketing.[102] Not until after the third wave of social upheavals had swept across the region in the late 1930s did trade unions become lawful in all parts of the English-speaking Caribbean area.

Notes

*An earlier version of this chapter was published by the Community Education Trust.

1 George Eaton, 'Trade Union Development in Jamaica' in *Caribbean Quarterly*, Vol 8, Nos 1 & 2 citing *Daily Gleaner*, Aug 8, 10 (1908); R Lobdell, 'Jamaican Labor 1838–1938' (unpublished), Univ. of Wisconsin, USA, 1968, p. 38.

2 *Jamaica Times*, Nov 25, 28 (1908) *Jamaica Guardian*, Dec 1, 16, 22 (1908) (for copies of which the writer is indebted to Robert Hill); the writer's interviews with A.J. McGlashan, a foundation member of this printers union, Feb 1958.

3 Eaton, *loc.cit.*

4 Selwyn Ryan, 'Rise and Fall of the Barefooted Man' in *Trinidad & Tobago Index*, (Winter 1966), No. 3, p. 5.

5 B. Samaroo, 'The Trinidad Workingmen's Association and the Origins of Popular Protest in a Crown Colony' in *Social & Economic Studies*, Vol 21, No 2 (June 1972) pp. 205−22; W.F. Elkins, 'Black Power in the Caribbean; the Beginnings of the Nationalist Movement' (unpublished MS which the author kindly sent to the writer); Selwyn Ryan, *loc. cit.* p.5.

6 PRO: CO 295/436 enclosed in Clifford to Elgin, 24 April 1906—cited by Samaroo *loc. cit.*

7 *The Mirror*, 17 April, 1913—quoted by Samaroo, *loc. cit.*

8 B. Simpson-Holley, 'Members for Trinidad' in *Journal of Caribbean History*, Vol 6, (May 1973).

9 Wendy Charles, *Early Labour Organisation in Trinidad and the Colonial Context of the Butler Riots*, (St Augustine, Trinidad, Univ. of the WI., Dept. of Sociology, 1978).

10 Samaroo, 'Constitutional and Political Developments in Trinidad, 1898−1925, (unpublished thesis), Univ. of London, 1969.

11 Elkins, *op. cit.*

12 Walter Rodney, *A History of the Guyanese Working People, 1881− 1905*, (London, Heineman Educ. Books, 1981), p. 104.

13 *Ibid*. p. 163.

14 *Ibid*. pp. 164−5.

15 *Ibid*. p. 154 citing D.W. Comins, *Note on Emigration from India to British Guiana*, (Calcutta, 1893) p. 96.

16 Rodney, *op. cit.* p. 158.

17 *Ibid*. pp. 157, 159.

18 Ashton Chase, *A History of Trade Unionism in Guyana 1900−1961*, (Georgetown, New Guyana Co., 1964), pp. 31−2, 20−2, 25−6.

19 *Ibid*. p. 38.

20 This sanguinary policeman, Major deRinzy, made every attempt to break the strike, sending his men into the 'logies' to force the workers out to work, but without success. He personally ordered that Chapman be shot in the legs, which led to his bleeding to death.

21 Rodney, *op.cit.* pp. 191, 209−10; Chase, *op. cit.* pp. 25−6.

22 Sir Frederick Hodgson was the same man who, as Governor of the Gold Coast during the Ashanti War, had outraged that African people by demanding that they produce their sacred golden stool (embodying the spirits of their ancestors) for him to sit on!

23 In his remarkable account and analysis of these events, Walter Rodney (who himself was to suffer a martyr's death in 1980 before his book was published) put the events of 1905 in their true perspective. He also recorded the valuable contribution to the historical process of those workers who, without prior organisation or preparation, were able to respond to the situation and emerge as leaders of the unorganised strikers, in some cases at the cost of their lives.

24 Rodney, *op. cit.* pp. 190, 220; Chase, *op. cit.* pp. 20−7.
25 Chase, *op. cit.* pp. 36−7.
26 *Ibid.* p. 38.
27 *Ibid.* pp. 39−42.
28 Peter Fraser, 'Some Effects of the First World War on the British West Indies', London Univ. Inst. of Comm. Studies seminar paper presented March 1981.
29 Elkins, *op. cit.*
30 Fraser, 'Some Effects...', pp. 4−5.
31 Chase, *op. cit.* p. 53.
32 Information from Edward Reid, ex-soldier and Kingston electrician.
33 Lobdell, *op. cit.* citing *Daily Chronicle* 12 Oct., *Jamaica Times*, 20 Oct., 1917.
34 Eaton, *loc. cit.* Lobdell, *op. cit.* pp. 35−41 citing *Daily Gleaner*, 27 June, 23 Aug, 22 & 28 Oct, 1918, *Jamaica Times*, 14 June, 23 Aug., 1919; interviews with A.J. McGlashan.
35 Lobdell, *op. cit.* p. 39 citing *Jamaica Times*, 19 April, 17 May, 1919.
36 Fraser, 'Some Effects...' p. 6.
37 Interview, 14 Nov, 1950, with P.A. Aiken, one of the leaders of the Railway Workers' strike.
38 Samaroo, *loc. cit.* p. 211; Fraser, 'Some Effects...' p. 5.
39 Samaroo, *loc. cit.* p. 213 citing *Port of Spain Gazette*, 29 March, 1917.
40 *Ibid.* p. 213.
41 *Ibid.* p. 213 citing *Trinidad Guardian*, 27 May 1919.
42 *Ibid.* citing *Trinidad Guardian 14 Nov., 1919*.
43 *Ibid.* pp. 213−4 and citing *Trinidad Guardian* 4 Dec., 1919.
44 *Ibid.* p. 215 and citing PRO: CO 295/526—Chancellor to Milner 27 Jan., 1920; Charles, *op. cit.* p. 10.
45 Ryan, *loc. cit.* Elkins, *op. cit.*
46 Fraser, 'Some Effects...' p.6.
47 Fraser (*ibid.* p. 6) mentions allegations by the officer administering the Government that one Arlington Newton was behind attempts to form a trades union in St Kitts in 1917, and a strike in Antigua in March 1918.
48 Joseph N. France, 'Working Class Struggles of a Half Century,' unpublished MS consisting in part of selected contemporary weekly articles in *The Union Messenger*. The writer is indebted to J.E. (Fidel) O'Flaherty for making this MS available.
49 Fraser, 'Some Effects...' p. 6.
50 Information from Railway Driver A.G. (?) Myers, c. 1942−3.
51 Information from Cyril Ivey, a 1919 strike leader, later Vice-Pres., Jamaica Govt. Railway Employees' Union in 1942, and from P.A. Aiken.
52 *Daily Gleaner*, 4 April and 12 May, 1930; *The Blackman*, 12 April, 1930.
53 Ryan, *loc. cit.* p. 8.
54 Elkins, *op. cit.*
55 Charles, *op. cit.* pp. 11−12.
56 *Ibid.* p. 13.
57 *Ibid.* p. 13; Ryan, *loc. cit.* p. 9.
58 Lennox Pierre, *Quintin O'Connor*, Port of Spain, n.d.

59 Ryan, *loc. cit.* p. 10.
60 F.A. Hoyos, *Barbados, a History from the Amerindians to Independence*, (London, Macmillan, 1978), pp. 196–7.
61 Keith Hunte, 'Duncan O'Neale: Apostle of Freedom', in *New World Quarterly*, Vol. 3, Nos. 1–2 (1966), pp. 84–6.
62 Hoyos, *op. cit.* p. 198.
63 Hunte, *loc. cit.* p. 85.
64 Chase, *op. cit.* pp. 51–3, 56, 59.
65 The eastern Caribbean and Guyanese dollar at that time was tied to the £ sterling, the cent being the equivalent of a half-penny, the dollar being worth 4 shillings 2 pence.
66 Chase, *op. cit.*
67 *Ibid.* pp. 66–70.
68 *Ibid.* 71–2.
69 *Ibid.* pp. 80–2. For a time after 1941 the B G Workers League membership topped 1000.
70 G. Eisner, *Jamaica 1830–1930*, (University of Manchester Press, Manchester 1961), p. 203.
71 Noel Deerr, *The History of Sugar*, (2 vols), Chapman & Hall, London, 1949, p. 481.
72 *Report of the Sugar Industry Commission, Jamaica, 1944–5*, Govt. Printer, Kingston, 1945, pp. 5–7.
73 *Ibid.* pp. 7–14.
74 Deerr, *op. cit.* p. 199.
75 *Report of the West India Royal Commission*, HMSO, London, 1945, p. 10.
76 P.R.O., CO 950/152 — Royal Comm. Evidence file No. J. 2–6.
77 *Census of Jamaica, 1942*, Kingston, 1943.
78 G. Cumper, 'History of the Barbados Labour Market' (mimeographed report).
79 W.M. Macmillan, *Warning from the West Indies*, (London, 1936, 2nd edit. Penguin Books, London, 1938).
80 Govt. of Trinidad & Tobago Council Paper no. 109 of 1934.
81 Chase, *op. cit.* p. 79.
82 Lobdell, *op. cit.* p. 45.
83 France, *op. cit.* pp. 92–100. The men sentenced were John Palmer and Simeon Prince (5 years), Albert Sutton and James Liburd (3 years), Thomas Fergus (2 years 6 months) and Thomas Saddler (2 years) — all with hard labour.
84 Verbatim report of the Magistrate's examination of George McIntosh, a *Port of Spain Gazette* publication, n.d. Trinidad.
85 Ralph Gonsalves, 'The Role of Labour in the Political Process of St Vincent (1935–1970)', Univ. of the W.I.Kingston, Ja., 1971 (unpublished M.Sc. thesis).
86 *Port of Spain Gazette* report of examination.
87 Gonsalves, *op. cit.* p. 23 citing *The Times*, Kingston, 24 Oct., 1935.
88 *Ibid.* pp. 23–28, citing: *The Times*, Oct 24; *The Investigator*, 29 Oct., 2 & 7 Nov., 1935; and an interview with an eye-witness.
89 *Ibid.* pp. 26–77 and citing K. John & O.Peters, '1935 Revisited' in *Flambeau*, No 8, (Kingston Study Group, Kingstown, Sept 1967).
90 *Port of Spain Gazette* report of examination.

91 W. Arthur Lewis, *Labour in the West Indies*, (Fabian Society, London, 1939; new ed. (S, Craig, ed.); New Beacon Books, London & Port of Spain, 1977), pp. 21—22.

92 Francis Mark, *The History of the Barbados Workers Union*, (Bridgetown, B'dos Workers' Union, n.d.) pp. 1—5.

93 *Ibid*. pp. 5—6.

94 *Ibid*. p. 7.

95 *Ibid*. p. 8.

96 For a detailed account of the labour rebellion in Jamaica in 1938 see R. Hart, *Rise and Organise: the Birth of the Workers' and National Movements in Jamaica 1936—39*, (London, Karia Press, 1987).

97 R. Gonsalves, 'The Trade Union Movement in Jamaica' in C. Stone and A. Brown (eds.), *Essays in Power and Change in Jamaica*, (Kingston, Jamaica Publishing House, 1977), p. 91.

98 Interviews with A.J. McGlashan.

99 P.R.O., CO 137/674—memo initialled G.G. The writer is indebted to Richard Lobdell for identifying the author of this memo as G. Grindle, senior adviser and later private secretary to the Permanent Under Secretary for the Colonies.

100 Charles, *op. cit.* pp. 10—12.

101 NACLA, 'Oil in the Caribbean: Focus on Trinidad', *Latin America and Empire Report*, Part 2, (San Fernando, Oilfield Workers' Trade Union, 1976).

102 P.R.O., CO 104/52—Grenada Leg. Co. Minutes, 15 Nov. and 29 Dec., 1933.

CHAPTER 4 | Labour control in Cuba after emancipation

Rebecca J. Scott

Slave emancipation in Cuba was a complex, prolonged process that began in 1868 and ended in 1886.[1] It arose from the crisis of supply following the cutting off of the contraband transatlantic slave trade, from the need of the Spanish government to respond to domestic and international pressures, from the desire of Cuban separatists to enlist the support of slaves and free blacks, from the initiatives of slaves themselves, and, finally, from the eventual, if grudging, willingness of Cuban planters to relinquish the institution called slavery if appropriate controls over labour could be found to replace it. Cuban emancipation in its first stages involved a legal commitment to gradual abolition—children and the elderly were freed in 1870—in response to an anticolonial insurgency, and a breakdown of slavery in regions under insurgent control. Spanish-controlled areas of the island generally clung to slavery, however, until 1880, when parliament decreed abolition and the establishment of the *patronato*, or 'apprenticeship', designed to prolong control over those who had been slaves. I have discussed elsewhere the social and political interactions of slaves and masters during this process; here I shall address the question of the restructuring of labour arrangements after emancipation.[2]

Cuba was, from the point of view of the production of export crops, a post-emancipation success story. Operating in an environment of falling sugar prices but growing US demand, Cuban producers increased the island's production from 657,000 tons of sugar in 1886 (the year of final abolition), to just over one million tons in 1892.[3] The mechanism whereby this rapid expansion took place, however, was a large-scale reorganisation of the entire process of production, at severe cost to substantial sectors of the society. The mechanised or semi-mechanised *ingenio* gave way to the highly mechanised *central* surrounded by satellite cane farms called *colonias*, pushing many former planters out of processing and into cane-growing, while drawing smallholders and tenants into the sugar economy as *colonos*, producers of cane for the central mills. This transformation is well know, having been analysed and denounced decades ago in Ramiro Guerra's *Azúcar y Población en las Antillas*.[4] The fate of the former slaves, however, is less well understood. Many became landless agricultural labourers on sugar estates, while some apparently succeeded in withdrawing to a degree from the orbit of the plantation. The process varied widely from region to region: the province of Matanzas retained a large portion of its former slaves as wage labourers, while the eastern province of Santiago de Cuba witnessed the growth of a substantial peasant population.[5] Wages for rural workers apparently declined steadily between 1870 and 1902, and the purchasing power of those wages was often undermined by the extensive use of company stores.[6]

For the purposes of this discussion, I would like to pose three major questions about the reorganisation of labour in Cuba. I have chosen these questions both because they are central to understanding post-emancipation Cuban society, and because they lend themselves to examination in the light of comparative evidence, and are thus particularly appropriate in a study addressing such issues throughout the Caribbean. The first concerns the link between central mills and abolition, the second addresses the racial composition of the *colono* class, the third deals with the issue of legal coercion of former slaves.

The link between central mills and abolition

What is the relationship between the growth of the central and its associated *colonias*, on the one hand, and the aboliton of slavery on the other? It has been argued by some scholars, Manuel Moreno Fraginals among them, that abolition was largely brought about by the collapse of an internally contradictory slave-based organisation of production and a need on the part of Cuban producers for rapid modernisation to regain profitability.[7] I remain unconvinced that such a mechanism can be shown to have brought about Cuban abolition.[8] However, if technological contradictions and a need for modernisation did not impel the movement towards abolition as such, rapid technological innovation none the less followed immediately in the wake of abolition. The question then becomes the following: was there a necessary connection between freeing labour from the constraints of slavery and establishing the capital-intensive central, with its decentralised network of supply? In the Cuban case the timing of emancipation coincides with other factors which stimulated the growth of centrals, such as the cheapening of the steel rails necessary to establish a network of transportation linking fields and mill, and the growth of the North American consumer market. But can we find in other sugar-growing societies evidence either (1) that such centrals could be established with slave labour, or (2) that emancipation alone did not facilitate their growth? Alternatively, does the pattern of disappearance of slavery and appearance of central recur under different market conditions? In the latter case, we should examine the nature of the links between the two, in terms of actual patterns of labour, availability of capital, and adoption of new technology.

The case of the French Antilles would seem to be especially relevant to such a comparison. Centrals were built there before the end of slavery, although extensive construction of such units came after emancipation (and, indeed, after the post-emancipation depression).[9] In Louisiana, by contrast, there was a substantial lag between emancipation, which took place in the mid-1860s, and the construction of central mills, which began haltingly in the 1870s and continued during the last decades of the century.[10] In this context, Cuba stands out for the virtual simultaneity of the transition to free labour and the transition to central mills. Further comparative study may reveal the extent to which this should be attributed to particular features of abolition in the Cuban case, and to what extent it simply reflects a coincidence of domestic juridical change with the availability of specific technologies and market opportunities internationally.

The racial composition of the colono class

One result of the development of the system of central mills was the rapid emergence of a large new social and economic stratum in Cuban society: the *colonos*. These cane-growers, generally tenants on the land of larger estates but sometimes owners of their own land, became an intermediate group, sharing some of the risks and benefits of the sugar boom with millowners, while acting as employees either of wage workers or of family labour. Analysing and describing their role in both the production process and the social hierarchy of the island is a crucial part of the task of interpreting Cuba at the turn of the century.

In theory, some former slaves could have moved into this group. In practice, very few seem to have done so. The occupation of *colono* quickly became disproportionately white. Far more cane farms were operated by whites than blacks, and by 1899 the farms with 'coloured' owners or renters comprised less then 4.5 per cent of the total land of plantations dedicated to the growing or processing of cane.[11] (Indeed, many of these 'coloured' owners and renters were in all likelihood the descendants of pre-emancipation free persons of colour rather than of recently freed slaves.) The *colonato* originated both as an institution to hold former slaves to the land and as an institution to draw new white workers into sugar, but its first function seems to have been quickly superseded by its second.

How does one explain this pattern? Did Cuban planters exercise active discrimination, punishing their former slaves as some Brazilian coffee planters punished theirs, by denying employment or leases of land?[12] Or was it that former slaves lacked capital, and preferred in any case to work in crops other than sugar? Clearly there was an ideological dimension to the process; many Cuban planters had long *believed* white families to be the most appropriate tenants. But what were the mechanisms by which former slaves came to be largely excluded from this category?

A substantial literature has discussed the way in which share-cropping came to seem the appropriate form of post-emancipation labour control in much of the southern United States. The institution is now frequently portrayed as one that represented a compromise between planters' desire for supervised gang labour and freedmen's desire for landownership.[13] In Cuba, however, there is little evidence of such a compromise. To be sure, the *colonato* is not precisely comparable to sharecropping; but it shares some of the same characteristics. Like sharecropping, it is a form of tenancy that transfers a substantial portion of the risk to the tenant, while maintaining much of the legal control over land and crop in the hands of the owner. Yet it did not become a predominant mechanism for controlling ex-slaves.

Comparison with other sugar-producing regions where there was less white immigration may be illuminating. In the case of Louisiana, planters moved towards cash wages, initially backed up by contracts, with their former slaves. When the advent of central factories made a form of sharecropping possible, they extended the option only to whites. Over time, however, a few Louisiana blacks did manage to gain a foothold as tenants and owners when the land of insolvent plantations came onto the market, and they were able to sell cane to the central mills.[14] In Jamaica, by contrast, it seems that when the land of abandoned estates came within the reach of former slaves they only rarely produced cane destined to be milled into sugar for the export market.[15] There was no lack of militancy among the former slaves of Lousiana and Cuba, but élites there do not appear to have adopted a strategy of compromise on the issue of landholding in order to defuse potential conflict. Comparative investigation of the question of race and tenancy in sugar areas affords an opportunity to examine the relative importance of differing planter ideologies and levels of technological development, and the accompanying forms of conflict between freedmen and former masters.

Legal coercion of former slaves

In some post-emancipation societies, explicit legal measures were taken to compel former slaves to work on plantations. In Cuba, such measures were discussed repeatedly but in the end were not implemented during the late 1880s and the 1890s. Neither Cuban planters nor the colonial government showed any inherent reluctance to exercise coercion against workers when they felt it appropriate; what explains their diffidence in this case? One can invoke as explanations the precarious political situation, and the threat of separatism from an alienated Afro-Cuban population. Or one can note the large number of freed slaves and the relatively few options available to them in any case.

Mere geography and population density cannot fully explain this phenomenon, though one could argue that the large volume of immigration served in effect as a kind of mechanical substitute for direct coercion by exercising a downward pressure on wages. Whatever the actual balance of land and labour, planters repeatedly asserted that they faced a labour shortage. Why did they not follow the lead of other ruling groups and engage in direct legal coercion of available labour? Some countervailing forces seem to have been at work, and the colonial government was not insensitive to them. A comment by the Consejo de Administratión during the debate on proposed vagrancy legislation is illuminating: The people of colour should not be alienated, they argued, for 'It is important to the nation to maintain them tranquil, loyal, and submissive to the laws...'[16]

To explain this absence of racially-specific repression, and of legislation explicitly designed to compel rural workers to labour in the export sector, a comparative perspective may again be useful.[17] Do we find a similar reluctance in comparably delicate political situations elsewhere? An examination of varieties of anti-vagrancy legislation and their actual enforcement in other Caribbean contexts should be revealing. The Puerto Rican *libreta* system of work registration disappeared along with slavery, for example, while the French

Antilles saw the imposition of a system of work passes after emancipation.[18] It remains to be seen what mix of political, economic, and demographic factors can most effectively explain so wide a variety of outcomes. Moreover, this question affords an opportunity to trace in a concrete way the links between political control and labour systems, examining the circumstances under which the state is willing and able to oblige planters by providing them with direct means of coercion over their labour force, in contrast to those circumstances under which such assistance is deemed either unnecessary or unwise.

This brings us to the larger question of the link between emancipation and popular, political mobilisation. The dramatic political denouément in the Cuban case — a vigorous, and ultimately successful, anti-colonial rebellion in which a wide range of social groups participated — is virtually unprecedented. Emancipation in Cuba, it seems, had helped to break down some of the crucial barriers to anti-colonial mobilisation across racial and ethnic lines, while the reorganisation of production had inadvertently opened the way for an effective attack on the economic basis of colonial society.[19]

Perhaps, then, if we can begin to sort out some of the essential relationships linking the growth of central factories, the ordering of labour, and the creation of new classes in a range of sugar-producing societies, we wil have taken important steps towards explaining the varied political sequels to slavery as well.

Notes

1 I would like to thank Sidney Mintz and Peter Railton for their comments on this essay, and Joseph Reidy and Thomas Holt for copies of their unpublished work on emancipation.
2 See Rebecca J. Scott, 'Gradual Abolition and the Dynamics of Slave Emancipation in Cuba, 1868–1886', *Hispanic American Historical Review*, 63 (August 1983), pp. 449–477.
3 Production figures are from Manuel Moreno Fraginals, *El ingenio: complejo económico social cubano del azúcar*, (Havana, Editorial de Ciencias Sociales, 1978), 3, pp. 37–38.
4 Ramiro Guerra y Sánchez, *Azúcar y Población en las Antillas*, (Havana, Cultural, 1944; reprint ed. Havana, Editorial de Ciencias Sociales, 1976).
5 See chapters 9–11 of Rebecca J. Scott, *Slave Emancipation in Cuba: The Transition to Free Labor, 1860–1899*, (Princeton, Princeton University Press, 1985).
6 See Victor S. Clark, 'Labor Conditions in Cuba', *Bulletin of the Department of Labor*, 14, (July 1902), pp. 682–3. On company stores, see Manuel Moreno Fraginals, 'El token azucarero cubano', in his *La*

historia como arma y otros estudios sobre esclavos, ingenios y plantaciones, (Barcelona, Editorial Crítica, 1983), pp. 145—161.

7   See his essay, 'Plantations in the Caribbean: The Cases of Cuba, Puerto Rico, and the Dominican Republic in the Late Nineteenth Century', in Manuel Moreno Fraginals, Frank Moya Pons, and Stanley Engerman, (eds.), *Between Slavery and Free Labor: The Spanish-Speaking Caribbean in the Nineteenth Century*, (Baltimore, The Johns Hopkins University Press, 1985).

8   See my argument in 'Explaining Abolition: Contradiction, Adaptation, and Challenge in Cuban Slave Society, 1860—1886', *Comparative Studies in Society and History*, 26 (January 1984), pp. 83—111.

9   See Christian Schnakenbourg, 'From Sugar Estate to Central Factory: The Industrial Revolution in the Caribbean (1840—1905)', in Bill Albert and Adrian Graves, (eds.) *Crisis and Change in the International Sugar Economy: 1860—1914*, (Norwich, ISC Press, 1984), pp. 83—93.

10   See Joseph P. Reidy, 'Sugar and Freedom: Emancipation in Louisiana's Sugar Parishes', presented at the American Historical Association Annual Meetings, December, 1980, and Reidy, 'The Development of Central Factories and the Rise of Tenancy in Louisiana's Sugar Economy, 1880—1910', prepared for the Social Science History Association Annual Meeting, November, 1982.

11   U.S. War Department, *Report on the Census of Cuba, 1899*, (Washington, Government Printing Office, 1900), p. 560. 'Colored', in this context, refers to those categorized by the census as Negro, 'mixed', or Asian.

12   See Warren Dean, *Rio Claro: A Brazilian Plantation System, 1820—1920*, (Stanford, Stanford University Press, 1976), pp. 172—174.

13   See for example Eric Foner, *Nothing but Freedom: Emancipation and its Legacy*, (Baton Rouge, Louisiana State University Press, 1983); Leon Litwack, *Been in the Storm So Long: The Aftermath of Slavery*, (New York, Random House, 1979); Roger L. Ransom and Richard Sutch, *One Kind of Freedom: The Economic Consequences of Emancipation*, (Cambridge, England, Cambridge University Press, 1977); and Harold Woodman, 'Sequel to Slavery: The New History View the Postbellum South', *Journal of Southern History*, 43, (November 1977), pp. 523—54.

14   See Reidy, 'Sugar and Freedom', and 'The Development of Central Factories'.

15   See Thomas Holt, 'The Problem of Freedom: The Political Economy of Jamaica after Slavery', unpublished, and Douglas Hall, *Free Jamaica 1838—1865: An Economic History*, 1838—1865 (New Haven, Yale University Press, 1959.)

16   See 'Medios de estirpar la vagancia' in Archivo Histórico Nacional, Madrid, Seccion de Ultramar, legajo 4952, expediente 345.

17   For an interesting debate on the role of coercion in post-emancipation labour relations in the US south, see Jonathan Wiener, 'Class Structure and Economic Development in the American South, 1865—1955', *The American Historical Review*, 84 (October 1979), pp. 970—992, and comments by Robert Higgs, Harold D. Woodman, and Jonathan Wiener in the same issue, pp. 993—1006.

18 See Andrés A. Ramos Mattei, *Azúcar y esclavitud*, (San Juan, Puerto Rico, Universidad de Puerto Rico, 1982), and Schnakenbourg, 'From Sugar Estate to Central Factory', p. 85.
19 For a further development of this argument, see Rebecca J. Scott, 'Class Relations in Sugar and Political Mobilization in Cuba', in *Cuba Studies/Estudios Cubanos*, 15, (Winter 1985), pp. 15−28.

CHAPTER 5 | The rise and fall of the Haitian labour movement

Mats Lundahl

The story of organised labour in Haiti so far has been a short and unhappy one. Trade unions have had a role to play only during the short period between the 1946 elections that made Dumarsais Estimé president and 1963, when François Duvalier dissolved the organised labour movement. The budding unions were destroyed before they had really accomplished anything. In the present chapter we will deal with the rise and fall of the Haitian labour movement. We will try to find out why and how the movement surfaced in 1946, what role it played during the subsequent decade-and-a-half, how it was silenced and why the movement failed.

Trade unions did not exist in Haiti before the turn of the century. An author writing in 1892 stressed that the word 'strike' was unknown in the country.[1] Eleven years later 46 shoe workers founded a *Syndicat des Cordonniers Haïtiens*.[2] In 1922, during the American occupation, an attempt was made to organise construction workers. After the foundation of the *Parti Communiste d'Haïti* in 1934, some 'worker cells' were set up in the Port-au-Prince slums, and in 1937 a more ambitious attempt was made to constitute a drivers' union which was broken up by the Ministry of the Interior.[3] Then in 1946, unions started to appear by the dozen which were to play a particular role for about a decade-and-a-half. Let us begin by attempting to explain why the union movement came into existence in the mid-1940s. To do so, however, we need a somewhat longer historical perspective, interpreted within a particular analytical framework.

In his book *Exit, Voice, and Loyalty*[4] Albert Hirschman makes the observation that slack is continuously being generated in all types of organisations, even those with a well-designed institutional set-up. There is a tendency for organisations to decline over time in terms of quality. However, Hirschman also notes that such decay will call forth countervailing mechanisms that strive to restore quality. These mechanisms are of two kinds: 'exit' and 'voice'. 'Exit' is a fairly clear-cut term. It means that somebody who is disappointed with an organisation puts an end to his involvement with that particular organisation, either by transferring his loyalty to a rival organisation or by leaving the field in question altogether. 'Voice', in turn is a broad concept: 'any attempt at all to change, rather than to escape from, an objectionable state of affairs...'[5]

Trade unions can be viewed as a voice mechanism, especially when their 'political' role is taken into account, and if we want to find out why the labour movement made its appearance in 1946, we must know something about the role of exit and voice in Haitian history and how the trade union movement fits into this tradition.

Exit and voice in Haitian history

Throughout the colonial period, *marronage* was the dominant mechanism among the slaves for expressing discontent with the quality of government.[6] Thousands of slaves ran away from the plantations, taking one of three escape routes. The first led to the Spanish side of the island, where treatment was comparatively milder and where the Saint-Domingue slaves often stood a good chance of being manumitted. The second led into the wilderness of the mountains where the fugitives attempted to hide from the French authorities, subsisting on agriculture and/or quick raids on the plantations. The third route was into the towns where, with luck, the maroons could pass for *affranchis*.

The alternative to *marronage* was open rebellion — a very strong 'voice' option. Slave uprisings took place in 1679, 1691, 1697, 1703, 1719, 1734 and 1751.[7] 'If ever slaves had reason to rebel, the Negroes of Saint-Domingue did', writes James Leyburn,[8] but uprisings were exceptions. *Marronage* was the rule. This form of protest was used both as 'exit' (*grand marronage*, where the runaway slave did not intend to return, staying away as long as he could) and 'voice' (*petit marronage*, where he came back after a few days or weeks).

Petit marronage was by far the most common form of popular protest in Saint-Domingue. It is not difficult to understand why when the alternatives are considered. For several reasons rebellion was very difficult. The slaves could offer little resistance to the *colons* because they were unorganized and split, came from too many African tribes, those from the same tribe being spread out across different plantations, and were prevented from leaving the plantations unless authorised to do so. In addition, the French had superior forces at their disposal. Looking at it from the point of view of the individual slave, his personal incentives for becoming involved in an uprising were few. The probability that rebellion would be successful was extremely low, whereas the fate that he would suffer if the rebellion failed would be a harsh one—in the extreme, capital punishment.[9] By the same token *grand marronage* could have serious consequences for the slaves. Therefore, it constituted an exception. Its main function rather was to lend credibility to *petit marronage*, by posing the threat of permanent escape, thus making the milder voice option more efficient.

The powerful, highly atypical, voice outburst of 1791 and the ensuing wars of liberation ended French rule in Haiti. The masses were put back on the plantations to work in a *corvée* system under military supervision and stern discipline. To this, they responded by 'exit'. The 'exit' tradition was very much reinforced among the Haitian masses during the course of the nineteenth century. 'The peasants have had more than 180 years of experience in sorting out their local affairs so as to minimise government intervention', write Brian Weinstein and Aaron Segal in their recent handbook on Haiti.[10] Once the forced labour system had crumbled, the peasants generally tried to stay clear of the government. Most of the time, this was not too difficult. The population had declined by an estimated 150,000 from 1791 to 1805[11] and that in practice meant that an agricultural frontier had been established where land was in infinitely elastic supply.[12] Thus, obtaining the means of subsistence was comparatively easy until the agricultural frontier was closed during the last quarter of the century.[13] In addition, the grip of the administration in Port-au-Prince grew successively weaker.[14] Thus, among the masses, 'exit' was sovereign. The peasants voted with their feet.[15]

At the same time, however, another tradition was begun: a perverted variety of 'voice'. After the fall of Boyer in 1843, a predatory state started to develop in Haiti.[16] In this setting, politics turned into a game between small cliques contending for power. Each clique defined political success mainly in terms of the spoils that the sitting government conferred on that particular clique. If the spoils were not large enough and the balance of forces was sufficiently favourable, an attempt to overthrow the sitting government was made. Over a hundred more or less violent attempts have been identified for the period between 1843 and 1915.[17]

The nineteenth-century pattern came to an abrupt end as the United States marines moved in and occupied Haiti in 1915.[18] During the occupation, a new pattern of response emerged. Now, 'voice' took over almost completely. In the first place, the Marines were forced to crush what remained of the old cliques and of the *caco* armies that these cliques used for obtaining political power.[19] In 1918, new hostilities flared up. This time, the cause was that the peasants had been forced to work in road gangs under circumstances that reminded them too much of slavery. An uprising, under Charlemagne Péralte, took place which was not completely subdued until 1920.

From this point on, 'voice' took on a less violent character. The Americans had destroyed the *cacos* and were in the process of substituting an American-controlled constabulary for the old army — what was to become the *Garde d'Haïti*. The scales had been tipped too much in favour of the occupation forces in matters of violence. Instead, the mass media were used, when censorship did not prohibit it, to spread anti-American propaganda.

The occupation ended in 1934, but the decision to end it was a product of events that took place in 1929. At this time, Haitian discontent with the Americans had been mounting for several years, to the point where it only took a few incidents to provoke a nationwide reaction. President Hoover then appointed a commission which was sent to Haiti to evaluate the occupation, and the decision was taken to end it.

The American occupation thus constituted a break with the nineteenth-century tradition. During the occupation, 'voice' was rehabilitated while 'exit' lost its importance more or less completely. In the first place, 'exit' had become much more difficult than before, since the agricultural frontier had been closed. The emigration during the occupation was primarily an economic phenomenon.[20] Besides, with both Cuba and the Dominican Republic under American control, 'exit' to those countries did not take the Haitians outside American rule. Thus, the control established by the Americans in Haiti was more efficient than that of the domestic governments had been during the nineteenth century. There was no scope for 'exit'.

'Voice' was the natural choice in a second way as well. The occupation constituted an invasion by a foreign power. Such events of course tend to put at least a temporary end to old dissensions, and Haiti was no exception. The Haitians united against a common enemy. Finally, 'voice' stood a better chance of being efficient with American rule than with the nineteenth-century domestic cliques. The United States was a democracy with periodic elections, and the Haitian occupation was therefore made an issue in internal American politics. During the internal Haitian fights preceding the occupation, no similar 'audience' existed. The politicians were not at all intent on lending an ear to complaints regarding government quality. 'Voice' was an instrument used only in the clique fights over the presidency.

Paving the way

After the occupation, 'voice' was firmly entrenched in Haitian political life. The first step towards an organized labour movement had been taken. During the 1930s, two more steps were made. The first was ideological. Two important currents of ideas that were to play important roles in the 1946 events began to make themselves felt. Both took a critical stand with respect to the existing distribution of economic power in Haitian society.

One of these defined skin colour as the key to the problem. With Stenio Vincent as president, the mulatto élite was back in power and was to remain there until 1946. During the nineteenth century, Haitian culture had largely been identified with the French heritage. During the American occupation, this idea had been called into question by an 'ethnological' movement which started to seek Haiti's roots in the Africa of the masses instead of in the France of the élite. A closely connected phenomenon was the new literary movement which drew its inspiration from similar sources.[21] Together, they constituted the beginning of *négritude*.

In the 1930s, the new strands of thought were picked up and turned into a political ideology by such black middle-class based groups as *Les Griots*, including the young François Duvalier, who stressed Africa and voodoo in the Haitian culture and interpreted the country's history largely as a struggle between a mulatto minority and a black majority.[22] In terms of practical politics, the *noiristes* challenged the ruling élite, on an allegedly mass-based platform, the real power base being the urban middle class.

The second current was socialist and analysed Haitian history in materialist terms, stressing economic factors. The importance of colour was played down and questions of ownership of the means of production were put at the centre. According to the socialists, the class struggle did not proceed along colour lines. The existing economic structures would have to be broken up and collectivist solutions should be substituted for them. The socialist groups did not constitute any mass-based movement either. Their ideologies were *Lesefrüchte*, not a result of real life experiences. 'Very few of them, for example, were prepared to involve themselves in the embryonic labour movement, preferring to write poems about the suffering of the masses', writes David Nicholls.[23] Nevertheless, socialist ideas had come to Haiti, and in 1934 Jacques Roumain founded the *Parti Communiste d'Haïti* which was immediately outlawed.[24]

The new ideological currents did not have any immediate impact. In 1930, Stenio Vincent had been elected president, on his resistance to the American occupation. However, this confidence was quickly lost. Little by little Vincent converted the presidency into a dictatorship. A new constitution was passed in 1935 which extended the term of the president, legally due to expire in 1936, by five more years.[25] In 1939, the constitution was to be changed again. Vincent planned to succeed himself a second time. However, he failed to obtain United States support for such a move, and had to step down in 1941.

In this process, Vincent had kept a close eye on the opposition. The country had been put under a constitutional state of siege. The press had been controlled. Mail was censored. Free speech and public assembly did not exist.[26] Still, the 'voice' tradition that had emerged during the occupation was not dead. It was subdued, but ready to spring into action when the circumstances permitted, as 1946 would show. 'Voice' had now obtained a 'legitimate' character and both *noiristes* and socialists catered for the masses and insisted on the importance of the masses in their political messages, at least in terms of rhetoric.

The third step towards a labour movement was a demographic and economic one. Before 1920, in-migration to Port-au-Prince had been negligible, but as the 1950 census would in time reveal, almost half the population of the capital that year was born outside the city.[27] A movement away from the countryside had started in the 1920s and accelerated during the next two decades. The principal recipient of this exodus was Port-au-Prince. Towards the end of the 1940s there were an estimated 55,000 workers in the capital.[28] A base for the labour movement which had previously been lacking was by then established.

Political flux: The unions emerge

In 1941, Elie Lescot was elected president by the Senate and the Chamber of Deputies for a period of five years.[29] Lescot followed the same path as Vincent had. He immediately made use of the army and police. Military courts were authorised to deal with all kinds of offences, including civilian ones. Immediately after Pearl Harbour, Lescot declared war on the Axis and a state of siege inside

Haiti. Soon after, constitutional rights were suspended for the duration of the war and Lescot obtained the power to issue decrees regulating whatever measures the situation was deemed to require.

The latter included silencing all 'voice': newspapers, magazines, deputies, the clergy, etc. The president ruled the country without advice and with the tacit consent of the *Garde d'Haïti*. He demanded and obtained legislation for complete control over the budget, and in 1944, had the 1935 constitution changed to extend his term from five to seven years and to enable him to fill vacancies in the Senate and the Chamber of Deputies without elections. No elections were to be held until the end of the war.

Lescot made himself unpopular in other ways as well. In 1941 and 1942, the Catholic church launched an 'anti-superstition' campaign against voodoo with the support of the government, a campaign which provoked a lot of resistance from the peasants.[30] In addition, Lescot sponsored a joint Haitian-American agricultural project that 'looked like madness to those who knew agricultural conditions in Haiti'.[31] This venture, the *Société Haïtiano-Américaine de Dévelopment Agricole* (SHADA), was to develop the agricultural resources of Haiti. In particular an indigenous vine rubber, the *cryptostegia*, was to be grown on a large scale to sustain American war efforts. The project fell flat. No rubber was ever exported, but some 40,000 peasant families were evicted from their lands in order to make room for the rubber plantations.

Both the anti-voodoo campaign and the *cryptostegia* programme dealt severe blows to the president's popularity among the peasants. Other disturbing features upset the black middle class:

> Lescot had no political finesse. During his Presidency the privileged position of the élite became more pronounced and drew increasing resentment. Inept members of the upper class held choice government jobs, while the social barriers kept ambitious blacks from making progress on merit.

All these factors interacted to create a strong opposition to Lescot's rule. 'Voice' was reactivated. In 1944, there was an abortive plot in the *Garde*. The following year, a student newspaper demanded freedom of the press, for which it was silenced. However, another more potent newspaper, *La Ruche*, under the direction of René Depestre and Théodore Baker, continued this stand with the result that when the first issue of 1946 was published the editors were jailed. This immediately triggered a student strike. The *Garde* was called in to silence the students. Within a few days, the *Parti*

Démocratique Populaire de la Jeunesse Haïtienne, led by Depestre, Baker and Jacques Stéphen Alexis, demanded the release of political prisoners, freedom of the press and immediate elections. Following these events, a wave of strikes was begun by government employees, teachers and shopkeepers. The turmoil spread to provincial towns. Lescot's cabinet resigned. Finally, the *Garde* decided that Haiti had seen enough of the President, and an army junta consisting of Colonel Franck Lavaud, Major Antoine Levelt and Major Paul Magloire took over.

The fall of Lescot was the beginning of intensive political activity. The 1946 events marked the strongest leftist current hitherto seen in Haitian politics. Not even the more conservatively oriented politicians could afford to neglect the masses completely. A popular movement was taking shape which was to influence the course of election politics in 1946.

This development was not only due to the three reasons already indicated. Two more factors have to be added. Firstly, the political situation was not a stable one. The *Garde* could probably have decided matters unilaterally, but chose not to intervene in the process.[32] In this way, with the strongest force in a 'neutral' role, a 'new' situation was created in Haitian politics. This situation had much in common with the one described by Andre Gunder Frank where a temporary reduction of the power of the metropolis allows the satellite to develop.[33] In 1946, with the *Garde* remaining passive, politics could be influenced by a much larger segment of the population than had traditionally been the case in Haiti.

Parties and labour unions, sometimes hard to distinguish from each other, began to be formed *en masse*. A number of the parties had an outspoken Marxist or socialist character. The most important of these was the *Front Révolutionnaire Haïtien* (FRH), which was a federation of several radical groups, notably the *Parti Communiste d'Haïti*, which was now reformed, and the *Parti Socialist Populaire*, a mulatto party that concentrated on the fight against American imperialism. In addition, there were a number of smaller socialist parties, some of which participated in the FRH, and two popular front movements, also of a Marxist/socialist character.

Secondly, there was Daniel Fignolé, a young ex-mathematics teacher and labour union leader who had founded the *Mouvement Ouvrier Paysan* (MOP). The ideology of the MOP represented a curious mixture of socialist ideas and those of the *négritude* theoreticians. The movement was populist, anti-élite, and much of what was professed was demagogic. Whatever ideological influences Fignolé claimed the foremost asset of the MOP was its leader's charisma and his inspiration of the moment. Fignolé was a marvellous Creole speaker, the political idol of the masses in the capital, eminently capable of whipping his *rouleau compresseur* street crowd into action at any time and without notice.[34]

Undoubtedly, Fignolé's charismatic person constitutes the fifth and final important explanation why the labour movement came to the forefront of political action in 1946. The MOP, which was to continue to play an important role in Haitian politics for a decade to come, controlled a number of labour unions, the most important being those of HASCO, the American-owned sugar company (led by Fignolé himself), the Port-au-Prince dock workers and the Bata shoe factory, but its major strength lay in Fignolé's hold over the masses. The effective base of the MOP was thus much wider than that which the unions were able to provide themselves.

Three other federations were started at the same time. The *Féderation des Travailleurs Haïtiens* (FTH), under Edris Saint-Amand, with a Marxist outlook, which had its strongholds among railroad, electricity and printing workers. The *Union Nationale des Ouvriers Haïtiens*, which was associated with the American AFL-CIO movement, organised workers in the tobacco and tanning industries, in customs and in the bakeries. Finally, there were a number of 'independent' unions: drivers, transport and construction workers, and those employed in commerce.[35]

The total size of the membership of the trade unions is difficult to establish. Jean-Jacques Doubout and Ulrick Joly list 28 different unions in 1946, and two more in 1949,[36] but few of these unions worked in large companies.[37] David Nicholls is probably correct when suggesting that the figure did not reach 10,000.[38] This should be compared to the labour force figure of 55,000 for the capital a couple of years later, since the vast majority of unions operated in the Port-au-Prince area. However, due to the popular appeal of the MOP, the unions 'were able to exert influence out of all proportion to their size'.[39]

The trade unions quickly started to make their presence felt. The first strike, in February 1946, was organised by Jacques Stéphen Alexis, then head of the leather workers' union. Other strikes followed, at the HASCO (organised by Fignolé and the MOP), the docks, the railroad, the electrical plant, Plantation Dauphin and SHADA, and the MOP attempted a general strike.[40] These strikes aimed at, and also to some extent secured, recognition of unions and improvement of wages and working conditions, but there were political overtones as well, not least in the attempt to launch a general strike. The FTH worked in close collaboration with the two communist parties, mainly the *Parti Communiste d'Haïti* (PCH) and, to a lesser degree, the *Parti Socialist Populaire* (PSP), and Fignolé used the MOP to stir up political action.

In May, there were elections for the Senate and the Chamber of Deputies. The results for the socialists were not as satisfactory as the left-wing parties had hoped for. In particular, Fignolé was defeated. For a while, politics continued in a flux, with riots and street action. The National Assembly started to draft a new constitution, under pressure from mob elements, until the *Garde* threw the troublemakers out. The draft carried a heavy leftist imprint,[41] but in August the Assembly finally decided to go back to the 1932 constitution, the one which had been discarded by Vincent.

This paved the way for presidential elections, which were scheduled for 16 August. The votes were to be cast by the two chambers of the National Assembly. Four main candidates presented themselves: Edgar Néré Numa, Bignon Pierre-Louis, Dumarsais Estimé and Démosthenès Calixte. Numa, who was a fairly conservative candidate, was surprisingly enough backed by the PSP. The reason for this alliance was that the PSP leaders felt that the time had not yet come to have a socialist government, but it is also clear that the party did not expect Numa to be much more than a nominal leader. Numa also had the support of some more conservative groups, and according to Bernard Diederich and Al Burt, that of the American embassy as well.[42] Pierre-Louis' main support came from a couple of Port-au-Prince journals. Estimé was the candidate of most of the *Front Révolutionnaire Haïtien*, especially its non-Marxist groups, the *noiristes*, the business community and the *Garde*. Calixte, finally, ran because Fignolé was too young to become president and hence had chosen to associate himself with the ex-commander of the *Garde*. After two ballots, Estimé had secured the necessary majority in the National Assembly, and was sworn in as president.

The 1946 'Revolution'[43]

The labour movement had entered the political arena. What did it achieve by so doing? Estimé attempted to co-opt his adversaries by giving them posts in the new cabinet.[44] Fignolé got the education portfolio and George Rigaud of the PSP commerce. The PCH also backed Estimé, issuing a statement which argued that the new government would be in favour of the working class. For a while, it seemed that this was effectively the case. It cannot be denied that Estimé made an effort to break up Haiti's rigid class structure. Ever since the beginning of independence, the country had been divided into a tiny mainly light-skinned, élite and a mass of peasants. However, in the 1930s, a black middle class had started to emerge and Estimé championed the interests of this class. Many of his administrative cadres were recruited from this segment of the population.

In his inaugural speech, the new president put considerable emphasis on social issues and support for the masses:

> Let us begin with the country's financial liberation, the masses' education, rational organisation of our agriculture. Progressive systems, such as the co-operative, will be encouraged, because the soil has to enrich the cultivators and not the middlemen. We will protect the craftsmen, the wage earner. Never will the...labour unions...be oppressed, for they support the hard-working against the whim of the patronate.[45]

The school system was reorganised and a literacy campaign was begun. The enrolment rate in public primary schools increased by 45 per cent.[46] The freedom of the press was proclaimed and political parties were permitted. Overt criticism of the government could take place. The trade unions quickly took advantage of this to publish a large number of journals, magazines and information bulletins.

Estimé created a *Bureau du Travail* to deal with labour issues. 'One of the main objectives of this office was to stop the exploitation of workers by contractors, to iron out conflicts between patronate and syndicate', writes Jean-Pierre Gingras.[47] The daily minimum wage increased from 1.50 to 3.50 gourdes. François Duvalier became Under-secretary of State for Labour in 1948 and Minister of Public Health and Labour the following year. 'Contemporaries recall no particular programme he pushed, and said he simply seemed to be sitting out the job', write Diederich and Burt.[48] In April 1949, a labour congress was held in Port-au-Prince, which according to Doubout and Joly was part of an effort to obtain stronger trade union backing for the government.[49] The only result was a 585-page volume of proceedings without much substantive content.[50]

In the political propaganda, not least during the Duvalier period, the 1946 events have been hailed as a social 'revolution'. But this view is a highly exaggerated one. We have already seen that Estimé presented a programme at the outset with some emphasis on social justice, but it would soon be apparent that his presidency was not a revolutionary one. The masses never gained any control in spite of a fairly intense participation in politics. The year 1946 instead constituted the triumph of the black middle class and of those black political theoreticians who interpreted history in terms of skin colour. The socialists found themselves without much influence, and so did the labour unions.

Against this background, it comes as no surprise that Estimé gradually generated discontent and opposition against his regime. There were a couple of corruption scandals on the debit side of his political account. In 1935 a banana boom had begun in Haiti, thanks to a monopoly conferred on the US Standard Fruit Company. Lescot had started to break up this monopoly, by giving concessions to competing companies as well. In 1946, Estimé gave it the death blow, selling concessions left and right. This killed the banana business within a couple of years. There was also the bicentennial exposition to celebrate the foundation of Port-au-Prince, a venture which, unaccountably, cost three times as much as calculated.[51]

In addition to this, Estimé opted for political repression. During the first two years of his presidency there was 'a minimum of impatiently tolerated democratic liberties'.[52] Thereafter, however, Estimé started to silence 'voice'. The effort to co-opt his adversaries failed. Fignolé put party politics first and did not hesitate to attack his fellow ministers when this suited his purposes. Rigaud in particular came under fire and left the government. Soon, Fignolé himself left as well. Both the PSP and the MOP thus joined the opposition which thereby gained two highly vocal groups. In 1947, a law against communism, outlawing the PCH, was passed. The trade unions were attacked as well. Splinter unions were created and some union leaders were bought off by the government to weaken the force of their organisations.

Events reached a climax when Estimé proposed to succeed himself in office. A constitutional amendment to this end was proposed in 1949. Towards the end of the year, the labour unions called a general strike. This centred on the university so Duvalier, as Minister of Public Health and Labour, proceeded to close the Faculty of Medicine to silence student unions. Other union leaders were arrested and police intervened to break up strikes. Newspapers were closed. The PSP, the FTH and the MOP were dissolved by the government. Fignolé had to seek refuge in the Argentine embassy. Finally, in 1950, after sending a street mob into the Senate to intimidate reluctant members of the legislature to endorse his candidate, Estimé saw his term abruptly ended. The *Garde*, which held the ultimate monopoly of violence, decided that it was time for him to leave. The same junta as four years earlier took over.

Magloire[53]

The junta immediately dissolved the legislature and appointed a commission to work on a new constitution. The document produced introduced a novelty in Haitian politics: the president was to be elected directly by the people at the same time as the senators and deputies. Every adult male was allowed to vote. Elections took place on 8 October, 1950. The main candidate was Paul Magloire. His reputation was excellent, having been a member of the junta that disposed of both Lescot and Estimé. Magloire preached national unity during his election campaign, both between blacks and mulattoes and between economic classes. He had the backing of the *Garde*, the élite, the church, the business community, the American embassy, Fignolé and the MOP, as well as some of the Marxists. The other candidate was Fénélon Alphonse, an Estimé follower, who hardly bothered to campaign at all. Most Estimé sympathizers boycotted the elections. Under these circumstances, only one result was possible. Maglorie obtained 99 per cent of the votes cast.

In his inauguration speech, the new president promised to remain the first servant of the people, to give everybody an equal opportunity in government, to help the peasants and to reject oppression. Freedom of the press was declared and national reconciliation was again stressed.

National unity, however, obtained only on the surface. There could be no doubt that with Magloire the old élite was back in power, in spite of the fact that Magloire was black. Nicholls labels the call for national unity 'a mask behind which the élite together with a number of opportunist black politicians were able to return to power', a modern variety of the *politique de doublure*.[54]

Intolerance started to show during Magloire's first year in power. The military junta had already issued a decree prohibiting voodoo, and in 1951 Magloire banned both the MOP and the PSP for alleged preparations of sabotage against foreign investment and closed their newspapers down. Fignolé's position as first deputy of Port-au-Prince was of no consequence. This had only been a co-optation move.

The labour unions achieved very little. They had surfaced during the period following the fall of Estimé, but were nowhere close to their old strength. Doubout and Joly list a mere seven unions, most importantly, the drivers, HASCO, the port administration in the capital, Bata, and the electrical company. In addition to these unions some of the 'independent' and UNOH unions had survived Estimé. A national labour federation had been encouraged by the president, but it was quickly made clear that 'active' unions would not be tolerated. The right to strike existed only theoretically, for when strikes were later actually attempted, the participants were jailed. Some of the leaders were simply bought off by the government and thus made quiescent. The official propaganda continued to stress harmony between labour and capital. May Day was turned into a manifestation of the concord between the two. The government had obtained control over the labour movement. The result was that Magloire's presidency witnessed very little union struggle.

However, the resistance to Magloire was mounting. In 1952, Fignolé launched a new party, the *Grand Parti National Démocrate*, which built on the MOP and which professed to be 'anti-communist and anti-totalitarian'.[56] Discontent was brewing elsewhere as well. The middle class felt forgotten. Magloire was leaning mainly on the *Garde* and on his business connections. Corruption became ever more visible:

> In the absence of either a broadened political base and equitable distribution of the new wealth, or the inculcation through oratorical means of a sense of meaningful participation or sacrifice for an ongoing national enterprise, discontent was bound to arise. The gap between the emerging city proletariat and salariat and their leaders seemed to them to be widening; a sense of relative deprivation accompanied the new prosperity, as it nearly always does. The bribery and corruption which had regularly been prominent in Haiti flourished...It was widely known that contracts and concessions to foreigners or Haitians would be granted only in exchange for appropriate individual rewards (sometimes partnership) to the ministers, military officers, and others who occupied positions of influence. Magloire also controlled the soap, sisal, and cement monopolies. As many previous occupants had demonstrated, succession to the presidency implied a license to make money.[57]

In 1954, it became increasingly apparent that Magloire did not intend to adhere to the constitution any more than his predecessors had done. The drivers, the best organised union, attempted a strike, protesting against certain taxes that had been levied on them. The police answered by arresting union leaders and other activists and the union was broken up.[58] In January, the president had denounced what he perceived as a plot against him. In December 1953, Fignolé and a few others had founded the *Lique de Défense des Libertés Publiques*. The connection was obvious. Thus, Fignolé's new paper,

Haíti Démocratique, was closed. The editor, some employees, Fignolé and a number of other politicians were arrested and accused of plotting against the government, fomenting strikes and spreading political propaganda.

In April, an amnesty was granted, but this did not mean that the regime discontinued its authoritarian ways. Schools under suspicion of being centres of subversion were closed, together with the Faculty of Medicine, whose student body was dissolved. The press was kept in a strait jacket. In 1955, Fignolé, 'the most popular political figure ever known in Port-au-Prince', lost his seat in the Chamber of Deputies by 4,000 votes to 40.[59]

In 1956, real political turmoil broke out. The controversy was about when Magloire's term was due to end. In May, secondary school students went on strike in Cayes, Jacmel and the capital, and took to the streets. Anti-Magloire pamphlets appeared and the students clashed with the police. A state of siege was proclaimed in Port-au-Prince and the two provincial towns. A student newspaper, *Le Souverain*, called for a return to the 1946 'revolution'. In November, bombs started to explode in markets and other public places, apparently placed by the agents of François Duvalier who had by then entered the race for the presidency. Younger officers inside the *Garde* showed discontent with slow promotion. One night Daniel Fignolé was ambushed on his way out of the capital but managed to escape.

Duvalier denied all knowledge of the continuing spate of bombings. In December, Magloire prohibited political meetings, broadcasts and publications and arrested almost 150 political foes. This led to a general strike. 'Ninety per cent of Port-au-Prince closed down. Stores and shops shuttered their doors, lawyers refused to take cases, labourers would not work'.[60] This was the end of Magloire's presidency. On 12 December, the *Garde* saw to it that he had to leave the country.

The 1957 elections[61]

Once Magloire had been ousted, Haiti entered a period of political turmoil which was to last until the elections in September 1957. During this period, five different provisional governments failed in their attempts to ensure an orderly transition until a new president could be elected. Below the surface a lot of politicking, involving the trade unions, was going on and time after time it came to open clashes between the contending factions. Politically, Haiti had reached a depth which it had not seen since 1915.

During this tumultuous period, a large number of presidential candidates came and went, but only four can be regarded as 'serious': Louis Déjoie, Clément Jumelle, Daniel Fignolé and François Duvalier. Déjoie was a mulatto landowner from the south, with interests in the essential oil business, who had strong backing from many important quarters:

> The social élite was incarnate in Déjoie. The majority of the commercial sector supported him; many high-ranking officers of the army were among his followers; his peasant clientele in the south remained devoted to the boss who had provided their livelihood; the French clergy leaned to some extent in his favour; and the US Embassy was strongly believed to regard him as a favourite son.[62]

Clément Jumelle, who was black, had been the personally chosen successor of Magloire, a fact which was to hinder his candidacy considerably, particularly since Jumelle had served as Minister of Finance and the country was left with a practically empty treasury when Magloire departed. He ran on a programme of 'better understanding' between the Haitians and on a professed willingness to narrow economic gaps between different classes, being in this respect a product of the 1946 'revolution' of Estimé, whom he had also served as Minister of Labour.

Fignolé still maintained his magic command over the masses and had gained a decade of experience and maturity since 1946. The MOP was back in political business, as strong as ever among the masses of the capital, including the lower ranks of the army, but lacking support elsewhere.[63] Fignolé was the only genuinely popular candidate of the four.

Finally, there was François Duvalier. He had refused to join the Magloire government and had gone into hiding instead. The programme he presented was vague, pointing to Magloire as an oppressor and to Estimé as a precursor in the area of social reform, which Duvalier himself was to continue. Economic improvements and national unity were two other recurrent themes.[64] He was well supported:

> Duvalier's chances were good in terms of the traditional requirements for success. Among the forces he could hope to command were a consortium of the political veterans and businessmen of 1946, who constituted the Old Estiméan Guard; a devoted group of young intellectuals of the School of Ethnology who hoped to shape a new society according to their standard-bearers ideals; support among the urban

middle classes and peasant masses all over the country, aroused by the vigorous appeal of Estime's ideas; strong devotion among a military nucleus which had suffered the Magloire regime without supporting or benefiting from it; support from a strong sector of the native Catholic clergy as well as from the Protestants; and an intelligence network among the *houngans* and traditional rural leaders throughout the countryside.[65]

Together with Déjoie he was to be the main candidate.

The first provisional head of state was Nemours Pierre-Louis, head of the Haitian Supreme Court, who committed the mistake of leaving Jumelle and Déjoie without a place in the provisional cabinet. Pierre-Louis quickly came under fire, not only from the followers of the two presidential candidates but also from the left-wing *Parti du Peuple Haïtien* (PPH), which advocated going back to Estimé's 'revolutionary' programme. The PPH started to form terror commandos, implementing 'popular justice', which meant hunting down alleged Magloire supporters in government and public agencies, and planting bombs. The party was also pursuing Jumelle because of the empty public treasury.

Pierre-Louis did not last long. Strikes started to be called. The fall of Magloire had given new life to the existing trade unions and new ones came into existence: hotel, bar and restaurant employees, carpenters, construction workers, mechanics, cement workers, labourers in soft drink factories. White collar workers reorganised as well. The primary and secondary school teachers closed their ranks. A union was formed among the employees of the *Banque Nationale*.[66] On 1 February 1957, a general strike was called, after Déjoie, Duvalier and Fignolé had demanded the resignation of the president on account of the Jumelle issue. The capital was paralysed, and in a few days' time Pierre-Louis gave up.

Next in turn was Franck Sylvain, originally an independent candidate for the presidency who, however, stood no chance. Sylvain pursued the Jumelle issue very actively, in order to remove him from the contention. He even went to the point of issuing an order for his arrest. Déjoie and Fignolé started to put pressure on the new president, accusing him of setting up the elections for an easy Duvalier victory. Meanwhile, riots and disorders continued in various parts of the country. The employees of HASCO and the *Banque Nationale* went on strike but not, it appears, for political reasons. Still, this added to the disorder, and the *Banque* had to close in mid-March. On 1 April, another general strike was called. The same day a bomb factory was discovered. A bomb exploded. Duvalier and his followers, including President Sylvain, were blamed. Before that, Sylvain had been removed by the army.

The military now set up a collegial government which was to include representatives of all the presidential candidates. The effort, however, failed: 'With elections reset for 16 June, candidates popped in and out of hiding, their representatives flounced in and out of council sessions, arrests multiplied'.[67]

Déjoie and Fignolé called yet another general strike when General Leon Cantave, commander of the *Garde*, pushed for army rule. Meanwhile Duvalier and Jumelle supporters were busy building road blocks and setting off riots. Anti-government demonstrations broke out in the capital and the situation threatened to get completely out of hand when the provisional government (mainly the Déjoie representatives) attempted to substitute Colonel Pierre Armand for Cantave. The two army factions opened fire on each other.

While this was going on, Fignolé joined forces with Jumelle and Duvalier. When the cease-fire was called, he was made provisional president, and General Antonio Kébreau took over as commander of the *Garde*. After a mere nineteen days, Kébreau sent Fignolé out of the country. Only three candidates were left. Fignolist leaders were jailed. The *rouleau compresseur* immediately started to move. Section after section of the capital was darkened, and buildings were set on fire. The army took charge and moved in on the Fignolé supporters with machine guns.

A military junta directed by Kébreau set elections for 22 September. In the meantime Kébreau saw to it that all Déjoie, Jumelle and Fignolé supporters in the *garde* were replaced by officers backing Duvalier. Strikes were now outlawed. A state of siege was used to control press and radio. With the army behind him the balance gradually tipped in favour of Duvalier, and two days before the elections Jumelle gave up and withdrew his candidacy. As expected, Duvalier won, with almost 680,000 votes, Déjoie receiving 267,000, with all seats in the Senate going to Duvalier.[68]

Death of the labour movement

During the 1957 elections, the trade unions played a particular role. It was, however, mainly a political one. With the exception of the HASCO/*Banque* strike, the strike activities were political, launched and directed by the contenders for the presidency who used unions and strikes only as one among many weapons. After the elections, however, union attention was focused on labour issues instead.

During the first years of Duvalier's government, the unions

were able to develop their activities in relative peace. At his first press conference after the elections, the new president stated that he considered it a duty to free the Haitian citizens politically and economically by setting up an economic democracy. This was the only way, he envisaged, to ensure a fair distribution of national wealth to all classes.[69] On his inauguration, he stressed the heritage of 1946 and asserted that this ideology should be reinforced and that civil rights should be guaranteed.[70]

For a while these promises appeared to be kept as far as the trade unions were concerned. While the president was busy eradicating other opposition groups[71] the unions could work. During the 1950s, the feeble industrial base of the country had improved somewhat. Some new companies employing more than a hundred workers had arrived, for example Reynolds (bauxite), Desren (copper), *Ciment d'Haïti*, Safico (Textiles) and the Cayes sugar mill. Around 1960, industrial employment amounted to some 63,000 people and approximately 11,000 individuals were working in construction.[72]

In December 1957, 14 different unions agreed on the foundation of a *Comité Intersyndical*. During the next five months this organisation prepared a demonstration for May Day which was to be independent of the government. The Ministry of Labour expressed its opposition but it was at last agreed that in the morning the workers were to take part in the government organised celebrations and have the union demonstrations in the afternoon. After the morning's activities, however, Duvalier went on the air, prohibiting the unions from holding their own celebrations.[73] In the afternoon, bombs were exploding in the capital. In his May Day message to his fellow citizens, Duvalier celebrated the 'reaffirmation' of the presence of the working class and the 'triumph of the peasant and the worker', hailing the day as the point of departure for a united front to 'consecrate the unity of employers and employees.'[74]

One month after these events union leaders met again. The *Comité* was rebaptised *L'Intersyndicale*, and this new organisation was legalised in December by the Ministry of Labour. Soon, however, it split when dissenters founded the *Fédération Haïtienne des Syndicats Chrétiens* in collaboration with the Catholic church. At this time, the unions concentrated on activities connected with union rights, wages and working conditions, employing strikes, agitation and discussions with the Ministry of Labour.[75]

The president himself was involved in one of these discussions, when *Ciment d'Haïti* had dismissed Heyne Desmangles, the leader of the union in the company, who was also the founder of the FHSC. Duvalier chose to use the occasion to warn the unionists:

> The country...is undergoing an acute crisis. Capital is
> fleeing the country for more hospitable shores. We ought
> to do everything to try to keep this capital. All popular
> movements will be repressed with utmost rigor. The re-
> pression will be total, inflexible and inexorable.[76]

Curbing the unions was important. In the elections Duvalier had
strong support in the countryside and in the provincial towns. Déjoie
had won his native Cayes, Jacmel and Port-de-Paix but also Port-au-
Prince with Pétionville,[77] the centre of political power outside election
time.[78] Since the masses in the capital were fignolists or communists
and hence constituted a threat to Duvalier, their main voice — the
unions — had to be silenced. Otherwise, extra-parliamentary methods
and street politics could easily come back on stage.

Little by little, the repression of the unions was stepped up.
Another of the union leaders at the *Ciment d'Haïti*, Gerard Pierre-
Charles, had already left the country. He was soon followed by
Pierre Delmont from HASCO, one of Fignolé's followers. Nathanael
Michel, leader of the old UNOH, was arrested. The union of *Banque
Nationale* employees was dissolved, without resistance. 'Its leaders
had been tactically cut off from the rank and file by a government
body of promotion, infiltration, and corruption'.[79] In his 1959 May
Day message, Duvalier stressed that he wanted that day to be the
point of departure for the battle of production and conservation and
increase of resources so that the peasant and the worker could be
assured 'a more equitable and more human distribution of income'.[80]

The message was exclusively for the gallery. Soon the primary
and secondary school teachers' unions were dissolved as well.
The latter union, in particular, had resisted the new government.
'Its leaders, firm in their opinions but weak in their means of
struggle, had underestimated certain forces by openly challenging the
government.[81] The president of the secondary school teachers was
jailed. The schools were 'duvalierised'.

On May Day 1960, Duvalier had the following to say:

> The fidelity to the patient and laborious effort of our
> peasant masses; the enlightened conscience of the coopera-
> tion between capital and wage earners; the combination of
> their actions in the national production perspective, renewed
> in the ardour of this day, fortify me and remake in me,
> more beautiful, all the betrayed hopes. In this I put new
> motives for faith and hope.[82]

Reality was somewhat different. In August, more union leaders
were arrested, among others Rodolphe Moïse, leader of the *Union*

Paysanne de Kenscoff. In November the *Union Intersyndicate d'Haïti* (ex-Intersyndicale) supported a student strike, demanded that jailed students be released, as well as Moïse, who was still in prison, and that the university be reopened. The only result was that more unionists were jailed. Others had to leave the country. On May Day 1961, the president spoke about the current policy with which the government attempted to 'introduce a more human note' and again stressed that 'prosperity is common riches and that the labour force and capital are complementary in the production of economic goods and a maximum national income'.[83]

The same philosophy is seen in the *Code du Travail François Duvalier*, which was promulgated in October.[84] Its first paragraph states that 'The object of the Labour code shall be—to harmonise the relations between capital and labour...'[85] The *Code* explicitly defends the right to organise: 'The right of workers to combine in defence of their lawful interests shall be guaranteed and protected by the State... All the workers...in a given occupation or in similar or allied occupations, in the same or in different undertakings, may combine freely for the defence of their common interests without prior authorisation...'[86] On May Day 1962, Duvalier referred to the Code as 'the fruit of your battles.' Employers and employees were given 'the instrument that fixes the conditions for pacific and harmonic coexistence...'[87]

The *Code* was mere window dressing to please international opinion. Still, the unions managed to continue their activities for some time: propaganda, strikes, negotiations, with concentration on professional issues, frequently achieved positive results.[88] The UIH claimed some thirty-three unions with a total membership of 22,000, the FHSC consisted of another ten unions, and the *Force Ouvriére Paysanne* consisted of about as many unions as the FHSC.[89]

However, the days of the labour movement were numbered. In 1963, Duvalier did not make a May Day speech. Instead, he waited until the end of the year to settle accounts. At that time, the UIH was involved in a conflict with the tobacco company *Comme il Faut* and called for a one-hour general strike of all the unions belonging to the UIH. The strike was carried out. The following day, 17 December, ten UIH leaders were arrested and a government decree dissolving the UIH, on the pretext of communist activities, was read out on the radio. A few weeks later the FHSC was also dissolved. The FOP was taken over by the Duvalierists. Henceforth, only token unions, backing the government, were allowed to exist.

By 1965, Duvalier, had collected all the threads of power into his own hands. There were no longer any groups in Haiti that could threaten him. In 1969, he held a second national labour congress in Port-au-Prince.[90] In his message to this congress he stressed the ambitions of the government in the labour field:

> The Duvalierist Revolution, as you know, is a social strengthening movement. How could we hope to realise our aims if we do not have in our hands a positive and objective image of...this labour class to whom we finally ought to give the means for obtaining a more legitimate share of the national product.[91]

Gérard Pierre-Charles, writing the same year, gives a somewhat different summary of labour relations under Duvalier:

> Politically, the workers, like the rest of the population, are terrorised. They know that there does not exist any possibility whatsoever for legal union struggle. Only the most advanced minority have discovered the possibility and existence of a clandestine struggle which goes beyond economic demands and have joined that.[92]

Only unions like the *Syndicat des Chauffeurs-Guides* union, backed by Duvalier, from which many of the *tonton macoutes* were recruited, and which provided strong support for the sitting government, could continue to exist.[93]

This situation has continued up to the present day. Occasionally, efforts have been made to build independent unions, but these have met with repression. In 1980, a *Centrale Autonome des Travailleurs Haïtiens* was constituted out of 24 unions, but the *tonton macoutes* quickly clamped down on the leaders and Yves-Antoine Richard, Secretary General of the CATH, was expelled from the country.[94] Strikes have broken out from time to time, but, after some success in improving working conditions in the early 1970s, have regularly been suppressed.[95] 'Regarding docility, labour militancy is still unknown in Haiti', write Joseph Grunwald, Leslie Delatour and Karl Voltaire in a recent survey of assembly industry production. In a sample of 51 firms, they found that more than three-quarters of the workers did not have any idea of what a trade union was and that in none of the firms were the workers organised.[96]

Why the unions failed

We started this chapter by pointing to 'voice' (*petit marronage*) as the dominant mode of response to the deterioration of government quality during the colonial period. During the nineteenth century 'voice' degenerated into politicking and 'exit' was used by the masses. From the American occupation up to the mid-1960s, 'voice' was rehabilitated. With the two Duvaliers, we are again back to 'exit'. For those who were not content with Papa Doc's regime, exile was the only altenative to keeping quiet. Under Jean-Claude 'voice' was attempted during the alleged liberalisation, up to 1980. Parties and trade unions were formed and the press began to publish articles that were critical of the government.[97] Thereafter, 'voice' has been silenced. Again, 'exit' is the dominant mode of response.[98]

The labour movement never really achieved anything for the masses. So far it has only been a temporary parenthesis in Haitian history, both in political terms and in terms of its influence on wages, working conditions, etc. The final question, then, is why did the labour movement fail? Two sets of factors explain this failure: those connected with the labour movement itself and those having to do with the character of the Haitian state.

Beginning with the former, the base for the union movement was very narrow. The vast majority of the Haitians are peasants, not urban workers. A figure of 55,000—65,000 industrial workers in an active population of 1.7 million or more[99] is very little. Undoubtedly a labour movement in order to be strong would have to include the peasantry as well, but this poses formidable difficulties. The peasants as a rule do not live in concentrated settlements but are dispersed across sometimes fairly large areas. This makes it difficult to organise rural communities in Haiti, not least since progressive 'natural' leaders are lacking.[100] In addition, the vast majority of peasants have access to land. Haiti does not present the situation which is typical for Latin America as a whole, where landownership is concentrated in the hands of a tiny minority and large groups of people in the countryside are landless. It is the latter category which is easiest to unionise.

Even if we limit our attention to urban areas, there have been severe problems of organisation. The weak industrial base has created an unemployment problem, above all in the capital. In 1950 registered unemployment amounted to 40,200 people whereas in 1971 the figure was 245,700. Most of this increase took place in the capital.[101] This means that during the period under consideration the bargaining position of urban workers probably did not improve, even discounting the political difficulties that the unions were facing.

On top of this, the labour movement was politically heterogeneous.[102] As we have seen, in the 1940s there were four different groupings of unions, split between the MOP and socialists of various shades. At the beginning of the 1960s, there were three different factions. Hirschman points out that 'competitive political systems have a considerable capacity to divert what might otherwise be a revolutionary swell into tame discontent with the governing party. Although this capacity may normally be an asset, one can surely conceive of circumstances under which it would turn into a liability'.[103] The Haitian labour movement provides an excellent example of this. Had the different federations been able to unite and present a common stand against the government instead of being drawn into the split and splinter politics of different parties, organisations and individuals, they would have stood a better chance of reaching at least some of their goals.

Turning to the character of the state, the most immediate explanation for the failure of the labour movement is that the passivity of the group possessing a comparative advantage in violence ceased after the 1957 elections. Duvalier took over the *Garde,* got rid of the higher officers, substituting his own men for them. In addition, he created the *tonton macoutes,* who owed allegiance to nobody but the president. With this he had a formidable repression apparatus at his disposal. In *Exit, Voice and Loyalty,* Hirschman writes: '. . . in comparison to the exit option, voice is costly and conditioned on the influence and bargaining power customers and members can bring to bear within the firm from which they buy or on the organisations to which they belong'.[104] In the case of Haiti under Papa Doc, 'voice' costs most of the time were prohibitively high, since 'voice' was met with an inordinate amount of violence.

After 1971, when Jean-Claude assumed power, violence was no longer as open as in the 1960s. Instead, voice was curbed by more subtle means: 'Like Mao's "Let a Hundred Flowers Bloom" campaign in China in 1957, the Haitian government occasionally tolerated minor criticisms in publications of limited circulation. It used these outbursts in print to identify potential opposition circles, and to provide outlets for grievances'.[105] Commonly, those protesting were exiled. Thus, 'voice' tended to lead to 'exit' instead of to improved government quality. For the powerholders, this was a much cheaper alternative than the one of maintaining a large apparatus of repression.

It is also possible to take a long-term perspective. Historically, Haiti has been governed by a long series of kleptocrats and the postwar situation does not constitute any exception to this rule. To understand the behaviour of Haitain rulers, one has to think in terms of a predatory state, not in contractual terms.[106] Hirschman stresses that 'voice' is most efficient in restoring quality when it is backed by the threat of 'exit'.[107] In Haiti, however, the predatory character of the state precludes this mechanism from working. We have a 'market failure' in the sense of Dennis Young, i.e. 'exit' does not bring about any restoration of government quality.[108] On the contrary, the state *welcomes* 'exit' by individuals who otherwise would have been employing 'voice' inside the country. The predatory state does not need those who 'exit', since it has no development ambitions. As Nicholls points out, there is only a small class of people who are interested in 'foreign aid, foreign trade, and foreign investment...the urban and suburban bourgeoisie', and this is not because they want the economy to develop, but 'to maintain their privileged position'.[109] Those controlling the state, on the other hand, care very little. Insofar as their aim is to enrich themselves, it is much easier to redistribute income in their own favour, even though this may retard growth and development severely, than to encourage growth of the national product and pocket only the proportion of this increase that legitimately accrues to them.[110]

Another facet of the predatory state is that government quality in Haiti has the characteristics of a 'connoisseur good'. Those who have benefited from government undertakings have mainly been the upper crust of society, and after 1946, to some extent the black middle class. On the other hand, government pressures have little impact on the life of the masses. In particular, the peasants do not expect any benefits from the government, and the same to a large extent goes for the urban workers. Since the government has done nothing for them, their 'consumer surplus' from government activities has been low. Therefore, their incentive to employ both 'voice' and 'exit' has been low as well. They have been predisposed to passivity. Rocking the boat could easily lead to a deterioration of government quality as the masses view it, instead of to an improvement. This was true in particular during the presidency of Papa Doc, when 'voice' was often met with extremely strong repression.

Finally, a slightly more subtle point: during Estimé's and François Duvalier's presidencies, Haiti experienced more upward social mobility than it had since at least the mid-nineteenth century. This, although desirable in itself, may have contributed to subduing 'voice': 'In societies which inhibit passage from one social stratum to another, resort to the 'voice' option is automatically strengthened: everybody has a strong motivation to defend the quality of life at his own station'.[111] When suddenly in a society where social mobility has been minimal for a century, the opportunity to advance socially presents itself, the chances are high that attention will be focused on competitive social climbing instead of on co-operation in order to improve the lot of a particular social class as a whole. This was probably the case with the members of the black middle class. With more social rigidity Haiti would possibly have seen more and stronger white-collar unions.

Ultimately, the success or failure in Haiti of an organised labour movement, and more importantly, of 'voice' in general, depends on the actions of government. During the period under consideration in the present essay, Haiti has been characterised by the existence of a political low level equilibrium trap. In particular since 1957, 'voice' has proved inefficient when it comes to restoring the quality of government, for repression has been resorted to when 'voice' has made its appearance. Even modest calls for reform have failed.

The fate of the labour movement constitutes an excellent example of this failure. Active trade unions threatened to upset the power structure that Duvalier was in the process of creating at the beginning of the 1960s. At least that was how Duvalier himself perceived the situation. This killed the labour movement. The main lesson to be drawn from the fate of the trade unions is not one which is specific for the labour movement. In the present perspective of 'exit' and 'voice', the unions are interesting mainly as an example of the workings of a more general process. As we have already pointed out, the labour movement so far has only been an historical parenthesis, but this parenthesis, when interpreted in terms of 'voice', can serve to identify some of the political structures that contribute to keeping Haiti underdeveloped.

According to Hirschman, '...once voice is recognised as a mechanism with considerable usefulness for maintaining performance, institutions can be designed in such a way that the cost of the individual and collective action would be decreased.'[112] In Haiti, unfortunately, the opposite has been true. Organisations have been designed so as to *maximise* the costs for individuals and collectives of using 'voice'.

This was the case under Papa Doc, but Jean-Claude's government was also much more intent on controlling 'voice' than on limiting 'exit'.[113] There were good reasons for this. Less 'exit' combined with less severe repression could increase the potential for 'voice' inside the country. Hence, the Haitian government has had a positive interest in facilitating 'exit'. If the interest of the dissenters is focused on 'exit', attention is being diverted from what the government is doing.

Hirschman points out that political power has very much in common with a market monopoly 'in that it permits the powerholder to indulge either his brutality or his flaccidity.'[114] Papa Doc did the former. It appears his son opted for the latter: 'an important and too little noticed type of monopoly-tyranny: a limited type, an oppression of the weak by the incompetent and an exploitation of the poor by the lazy which is the more durable and stifling as it is both *unambitious and escapable.*'[115] Those who hold power in this way have a strong incentive for shipping off people who otherwise could resort to 'voice', instead of keeping them in the country and resorting to strong repression. In this way, however, it is easy to end up in a cumulative sequence *à la* Gunnar Myrdal, where those who care most for government quality — the 'quality makers' — tend to leave the country first. This makes government quality deteriorate even further, more people leave when their tolerance has been exceeded, again the quality deteriorates, etc.

'Exit' thus does not constitute any solution to the problem of government quality in Haiti, other than for the sitting government itself. In the worst case, it makes the political situation worse. The economy may also be affected negatively. Those who are in the best position to 'exit' are those with alternatives abroad, i.e. mainly those with a good education. Thus, in the first round 'exit' will tend to be selective, in that it will create a brain drain. As I have demonstrated elsewhere,[116] a brain drain, however, tends to have the consequence that unskilled labour and industrial capital leave the country as well and hence to what is known as 'demodernisation', with falling industrial output and a falling share of industry in total employment. That is, had not 'exit' had to bear the entire burden of political protest, industrialisation would presumably have proceeded far quicker in Haiti than has actually been the case.

Acknowledgements

The research was supported by a grant from the Jan Wallander Foundation. This is gratefully acknowledged. I have benefited from the comments by David Nicholls on a draft version.

Notes

1 Joseph Jérémie, quoted by Jean-Jacques Doubout and Ulrick Joly, *Notes sur le développement du mouvement syndical en Haïti*, (n.p., 1974), p. 11 and David Nicholls, *From Dessalines to Duvalier: Race, Colour and National Independence in Haiti*, (Cambridge, 1979), note, p. 310.
2 Jacques B. Brutus, 'Aperçu historique du mouvement syndical en Haïti', *Rond Point*, No. 7, (1963), p. 2, Georges M. Fortuné, *Haïti, Una nación al servicio del 5%*, (Guarenas, 1976), p. 23, Nicholls, *From Dessalines*, p. 218.

3 Doubout and Joly, *Notes*, p.11.
4 Albert O. Hirschman, *Exit, Voice, and Loyalty, Responses to Decline in Firms, Organisations, and States*, (Cambridge, Mass., 1970). Cf. also Albert O. Hirschman, *Essays in Trespassing. Economics to Politics and Beyond*, (Cambridge, 1981).
5 Hirschman, *Exit*, p. 30.
6 For discussions of *marronage*, see e.g. Yvan Debbasch, 'Le marronage: Essai sur la désertion de l'esclave antillais', *L'Année Sociologique*, 3, (1961, 1962), Gabriel Debien, 'Le marronage aux Antilles Françaises au XVIIe siècle', *Caribbean Studies*, 6, (1966), *Les esclaves aux Antilles Françaises (XVIIe-XVIIIe siècles)*, (Basse Terre and Fort-de-France, 1974) and Jean Fouchard, *Les marrons de la Liberté*, (Paris, 1972).
7 Robert Debs Heinl, Jr. and Nancy Gordon Heinl, *Written in Blood. The Story of the Haitian people 1492–1971*, (Boston, 1978), pp. 27–28.
8 James G. Leyburn, *The Haitian People*, Second edition (New Haven and London, 1966), p. 22.
9 Cf. the theory of revolution advanced in Gordon Tullock, *The Social Dilemma. The Economics of War and Revolution*, (Blacksburg, Va., 1974), Chapter 7.
10 Brian Weinstein and Aaron Segal, *Haiti. Political Failures, Cultural Successes*, (New York, 1984), p. 3.
11 Mats Lundahl, *Peasants and Poverty; A Study of Haiti*, (London and New York, 1979), p. 272.
12 Cf. the situation analysed in Bent Hansen, 'Colonial Economic Development with Unlimited Supply of Land', *Economic Development and Cultural Change*, 27, (1979).
13 Gerald F. Murray, 'The Evolution of Haitian Peasant Land Tenure: A Case Study in Agrarian Adaptation to Population Growth', (unpublished Ph. D. thesis, Cornell University, 1977), p. 410.
14 Cf. Lundahl, *Peasants and Poverty*, Chapter 7.
15 The situation very much resembled the one described by Charles Tiebout, 'A Pure Theory of Local Expenditures', *Journal of Political Economy*, 64, (1956), where citizens choose between different 'menus' of local government expenditure patterns by moving to the community which is considered to be closest to the optimal mixture.
16 This is analysed in some detail in Mats Lundahl, 'Government and Inefficiency in the Haitian Economy: The Nineteenth-Century Legacy', in Michael B. Connolly and John H. McDermott (eds.), *The Economics of the Caribbean Basin*, (New York, 1985).
17 Heinl and Heinl, *Written in Blood*, p. 404. For an analysis of these, see Lundahl, 'Government and Inefficiency'.
18 Some standard works on the occupation are Emily Greene Balch (ed.), *Occupied Haiti*, (New York, 1927); Paul H. Douglas, 'The American Occupation of Haiti', *Political Science Quarterly*, 42, (1927); Arthur C. Millspaugh, *Haiti under American Control*, (Boston, 1931), Robert Melvyn Spector, 'W. Cameron Forbes and the Hoover Commissions to Haiti', (unpublished Ph.D thesis, Boston University, 1961); Suzy Castor, *La ocupación norteamericana de Haïti y sus consecuencias (1915–1934)*, (Mexico, 1971); Hans Schmidt, *The United States Occupation of Haiti, 1915–1934*, (New Brunswick, N.J. 1971) and Brenda Gayle Plummer, 'Black and White in the Caribbean: Haitian-

American Relations, 1902—1934', (unpublished Ph.D. thesis, Cornell University, 1981). Cf. also Heinl and Heinl, *Written in Blood*, Chapter 12.

19 *Cacos* were peasant mercenary troups.

20 Cf. Mats Lundahl, 'A note on Haitian Migration to Cuba, 1890—1934', *Cuban Studies*, 12, (1982) and Mats Lundahl and Rosemary Vargas, 'Haitian Migration to the Dominican Republic', in Mats Lundahl, *The Haitian Economy: Man, Land and Markets*, (London and Canberra, 1984).

21 For this, see e.g. Nicholls, *From Dessalines*, pp. 152—64 and J. Michael Dash, *Literature and Ideology in Haiti 1915—1961*, (London and Basingstoke, 1981).

22 Cf. e.g. Lorimer Denis and François Duvalier, *Le problème des classes à travers l'histoire d'Haïti*, (Port-au-Prince, 1948) for an interpretation of Haitian history in these terms.

23 Nicholls, *From Dessalines*, p. 166.

24 For more details regarding *noiristes* and socialists, see *ibid.* pp. 165—76 and Dash, *Literature and Ideology*.

25 Robert I. Rotberg and Christopher K. Clague, *Haiti. The Politics of Squalor*, (Boston, 1971), pp. 154—55.

26 Heinl and Heinl, *Written in Blood*, p. 533.

27 Lundahl, *Peasants and Poverty*, p. 629.

28 Marcel Daumec, 'Statistique de travail', in République d'Haïti, Department du Travail et Bien-être Social, *Actes du Premier Congrès National du Travail. Ier mai 1949*, (Port-au-Prince, n.d.), p. 81.

29 See e.g. Rotberg and Clague, *Haiti*, pp. 167—70; Heinl and Heinl, *Written in Blood*, pp. 536—45; Nicholls, *From Dessalines*, pp. 166—67, 181—83; Jacques Barros, *Haïti de 1804 à nos jours. Tome II*, (Paris, 1984), pp. 551—54, for details.

30 O. Ernest Moore, *Haiti: Its Stagnant Society and Shackled Economy: A Survey*, (New York, 1972), pp. 64—65.

31 Bernard Diederich and Al Burt, *Papa Doc. Haiti and Its Dictator*, (Harmondsworth, 1972), p. 52.

32 Because of this, Heinl and Heinl, *Written in Blood*, p. 550, call 1946 'the Garde's finest hour'. To what extent the junta was able to manipulate the electors is not clear. Some authors maintain that the elections were staged so that Estimé could win. See e.g. Gérard Pierre-Charles, *Haïti: la crisis uninterrumpida 1930—1975*, (n.p., n.d.), p. 28.

33 Andre Gunder Frank, *Capitalism and Underdevelopment in Latin America. Historical Studies of Chile and Brazil*, Revised edition (New York, 1969), p. 11.

34 The secretary general of the MOP was François Duvalier.

35 Doubout and Joly, *Notes*, pp. 14—15.

36 *Ibid.*

37 *Op. cit.* p. 16.

38 Nicholls, *From Dessalines*, p. 189.

39 *Ibid.*

40 Doubout and Joly, *Notes*, p. 21.

41 '...a long-winded Jacobin-Marxist tirade.' Heinl and Heinl, *Written in Blood*, p. 549.

42 Diederich and Burt, *Papa Doc*, p. 59.
43 For discussions of the Estimé government, see e.g. Jean-Pierre O. Gingras, *Duvalier, Caribbean Cyclone. The History of Haiti and Its Present Government*, (New York, 1967), Chapter 8; Rotberg and Clague, *Haiti*, pp. 170—75; Heinl and Heinl, *Written in Blood*, pp. 550—62.
44 Cf. Hirschman, *Essays*, p. 241. Voice is easily subject to being bought off by those in power.
45 Quoted by Gingras, *Duvalier*, p. 81.
46 Lundahl, *Peasants and Poverty*, p. 472.
47 Gingras, *Duvalier*, p. 82.
48 Diederich and Burt, *Papa Doc*, p. 61.
49 Doubout and Joly, *Notes*, p. 18.
50 République d'Haïti, Department du Travail et du Bien-être Social, *Actes du Premier Congrès National du Travail. 1er mai 1949*, (Port-au-Prince, n.d.).
51 Lundahl, *Peasants and Poverty*, p. 341.
52 Barros, *Haïti*, p. 556.
53 The Magloire government is discussed e.g. in Gingras, *Duvalier*, Chapter 9; Rotberg and Clague, *Haiti*, pp. 175—86; Diederich and Burt, *Papa Doc*, pp. 64—79; Moore, *Haiti*, Chapter 7; and Heinl and Heinl, *Written in Blood*, pp. 562—74.
54 Nicholls, *From Dessalines*, p. 192. *Politique de doublure* meant that a black president was controlled by the mulatto élite. This was common during the second half of the nineteenth century.
55 Doubout and Joly, *Notes*, p. 28.
56 Nicholls, *From Dessalines*, p. 193.
57 Rotberg and Clague, *Haiti*, p. 183.
58 Colbert Bonhomme, *Révolution et contre-révolution en Haïti de 1946 à 1957*, (Port-au-Prince, 1957), pp. 89—90, Doubout and Joly, *Notes*, p. 30.
59 Diederich and Burt, *Papa Doc*, p. 74.
60 *Ibid.* p. 78.
61 For details regarding the 1957 elections, see e.g. Bonhomme, *Révolution*; Rotberg and Clague, *Haiti*, pp. 186—96; Diederich and Burt, *Papa Doc*, Chapters 8 and 1; Maurepas Auguste, *Genèse d'une république héréditaire. 25 mai 1957 en Haïti*, (Paris, 1974) and Heinl and Heinl, *Written in Blood*, pp. 575—84.
62 Leslie Manigat, *Haiti of the Sixties. Object of International Concern*, (Washington, D.C., 1964), p. 43.
63 *Ibid.* p. 44.
64 For details see Mats Lundahl, 'Papa Doc: Innovator in the Predatory State', *Scandia*, 50, (1984), pp. 46—49.
65 Manigat, *Haiti*, pp. 46—47.
66 Doubout and Joly, *Notes*, pp. 31—32.
67 Heinl and Heinl, *Written in Blood*, p. 578.
68 Nicholls, *From Dessalines*, p. 209.
69 Gingras, *Duvalier*, p. 99.
70 Francois Duvalier, *Oeuvres essentielles, Volume III. La révolution au pouvoir (Première partie)*, (Port-au-Prince, 1967), p. 13.
71 A summary is given in Lundhal, *Papa Doc*.

72 Willem Brand, *Impressions of Haiti*, (The Hague, 1965), p. 37. The figure for industry is lower than the one for 1950, but this is presumably due to the fact that the number of artisans had dropped, 'as it is generally admitted that employment in industrial enterprises has somewhat risen.' (*Ibid*).

73 Doubout and Joly, *Notes*, pp. 36–38.

74 Duvalier, *Oeuvres III*, pp. 61–64.

75 Doubout and Joly, *Notes*, p. 43, list a number of concrete instances.

76 Quoted by *ibid*. pp. 43–44. Joly was present, as president of the *Intersyndicale*.

77 Nicholls, *From Dessalines*, p. 209.

78 Cf. David Nicholls, 'Past and Present in Haitian Politics', in Charles R. Foster and Albert Valdman (eds.), *Haiti—Today and Tomorrow. An Interdisciplinary Study*, (Lanham, Md., 1984). p. 257.

79 Manigat, *Haiti*, p. 57.

80 Duvalier, *Oeuvres III*, p. 157.

81 Manigat, *Haiti*, p. 56.

82 Duvalier, *Oeuvres III*, p. 229.

83 *Ibid*. p. 259.

84 Labour and Welfare Department, *François Duvalier Labour Code*, (Port-au-Prince, 1961).

85 *Ibid*. p. 1.

86 *Ibid*. p. 48 (paragraphs 260, 263).

87 Duvalier, *Oeuvres III*, p. 36.

88 See Doubout and Joly, *Notes*, pp. 62–66, for details.

89 Nicholls, *From Dessalines*, p. 218. Cf. Pierre Dejean, 'Panorama actual du syndicalisme Haïtien', *Rond Point*, No. 7, (1963), for details. As Nicholls remarks, in the international perspective these were low figures, among the lowest in Latin America.

90 This congress produced two volumes of proceedings République d'Haïti, Secrétairerie d'Etat des Affaires Sociales, *Actes du Deuxième Congrès National du Travail, 21–30 avril 1969*, (Port-au-Prince, 1969), only slightly more interesting than the 1949 one.

91 François Duvalier, 'Addresse de Son Excellence le Docteur François Duvalier, Président à Vie de la République, à l' occasion du Deuxième Congrès National du Travail', in République d'Haïti, *Actes du Deuxième*, Vol, 1, p. 53.

92 Gérard Pierre-Charles, *Radiografia de una dictadura—Haïti bajo el régimen del doctor Duvalier*, (Mexico, 1969), p. 84.

93 Weinstein and Segal, *Haiti*, pp. 75–76.

94 *Ibid*. p. 75.

95 For some examples, see Gérard Lehmann, *Babydocratie et presse écrite en Haïti. Considérations sur le regne de l'illustre Héritier du Père de la Nouvelle Haïti de décembre 1980 à juillet 1981*, (Odense, n.d.), pp. 196–201. In 1976, the journalist Gasner Raymond, working for *Le Petit Samedi Soir*, was murdered after having reported on a strike at *Ciment d'Haïti*.

96 Joseph Grunwald, Leslie Delatour and Karl Voltaire, 'Offshore Assembly in Haiti', in Charles R. Foster and Albert Valdman (eds.) *Haiti—Today and Tomorrow. An Interdisciplinary Study*, (Lanham, Md., 1984), p. 238.

97 See e.g. Weinstein and Segal, *Haiti*, pp. 43–44, 70–79; Nicholls, 'Past and Present'; Joseph Ph. Antoio et al., *Haïti Briser les chaines*, (Lausanne, 1984), *passim*, for some details.

98 Exit from Haiti is eloquently summarised in the map entitled *La diaspora* in George Anglade, Rafael Emilio Yunén and Audetter Denis, *Hispaniola: lecturas sobre un mapa mural/Les lectures d'une carte murale*, (Montréal, 1982).

99 Brand, *Impressions,* p. 44; Lundahl, *Peasants and Poverty*, p. 634.

100 Lundahl, *Peasants and Poverty*, pp. 597–98.

101 *Ibid*. p. 633.

102 This is a recurrent theme in Doubout and Joly, *Notes*.

103 Hirschman, *Exit*, p. 28.

104 *Ibid*. p. 40.

105 Weinstein and Segal, *Haiti,* p. 76 Cf. Hirschman, *Exit*, p. 124: '... voice can become mere "blowing off steam" as it is being emasculated by the institutionalisation and domestication of dissent...'

106 Cf. Douglas C. North, *Structure and Change in Economic History*, (New York and London, 1981), Chapter 3, for a general discussion, and Lundahl, 'Government and Inefficiency', for an analysis of Haiti.

107 Hirschman, *Exit*, p. 82.

108 Dennis R. Young, 'Consolidation or Diversity: Choices in the Structure of Urban Governance', *American Economic Review*, 66, (1976).

109 Nicholls, 'Past and Pressent', p. 256.

110 See Lundahl, 'Government and Inefficiency', for a discussion of this.

111 Hirschman, *Exit*, p. 53.

112 *Ibid*. p. 42.

113 Weinstein and Segal, *Haiti*, p. 77.

114 Hirschman, *Exit*, p. 58.

115 *Ibid*. p. 59. For Baby Doc, see Nicholls, 'Past and Present', pp. 262–64; Weinstein and Segal, *Haiti*, pp. 77–79, 140–47.

116 Mats Lundahl, 'Brain Drain, Illegal Migration and Capital Exports from Less Developed Countries: A Neoclassical Approach', *Economics Letters*, 17, (1985).

CHAPTER 6

The struggle for autonomy: Peasant resistance to capitalism in the Dominican Republic, 1870–1924

Michiel Baud

Expressions of peasant protest in the Third World have attracted a great deal of attention in modern social sciences. The literature is immense and many theories have been constructed in order to analyse and explain peasant rebelliousness. Although there is always a certain simplicity and arbitrariness in rough distinctions, we could divide these theories as having a 'structuralist' and an 'anthropological' tendency. In the first, emphasis is placed on the structural changes in the social and economic situation of the modern Third World countries. These structural changes, which had profound consequences on peasant livelihoods, are considered to constitute the final determining factor in the analysis of peasant protest.[1] The second approach gives a central place to the peasant society itself and the perception of reality by its members. It rejects the attempts to establish a fixed set of 'objective' parameters which aim at explaining forms of peasant protest.[2] For instance, Scott, one of the most avowed exponents of this line of thought, writes: 'The problem of exploitation and rebellion is...not just a problem of calories and income, but is a question of peasant conceptions of social injustices, of rights and obligations of reciprocity'.[3]

Both approaches have their analytic and heuristic value. The former, because it allows us to compare a social phenomenon such as peasant protest in different historical regional contexts and gives insights into the macro-economic determinants of social change. The second, because it leads us to a real social history in which the lives and perceptions of the historical actors — the peasant men and women — obtain a central place.

In this sense, a combination of these two approaches could be very fertile. It could lead us to the core of social change in Third World agriculture. Were the processes of change not precisely formed by the interplay of the changing social and economic structures on national and international level and the various and diverse reactions of the local populations? Was it not the strained relation between augmenting state involvement and a more insistent presence of capitalist enterprises with local power structures and societies, which shaped the processes of change, which are so significant for nineteenth and twentieth century history? A history which combines these two approaches can help us to explain the similarities and differences in the socio-economic structures which resulted from the interplay of the expanding capitalist world economy with local modes of production. It allows us to confront a grassroots perspective with an analysis of the structural changes in the larger society.[4]

Although it should be emphasised that it was not necessarily, or even normally, only the peasants who were affected by these processes of change, it is nevertheless unmistakable that the peasant population in general bore the main brunt of their negative consequences. Scott and Kerkvliet rightly emphasise, that it is not for some form of innate conservatism, but 'because the commercialisation of agriculture so frequently works *against* the interests of most peasants that one generally finds the peasantry in the role of defending traditional rights...'[5]

It would, however, be a mistake to assume that the reactions of the peasantry to the consequences of capitalist penetration in agriculture automatically meant open or even violent conflict. Michael Adas, writing about precolonial Southeast Asia, has stated: 'Too long our attention has continued to be focused on movements involving direct, often violent, confrontations between the wielders of power and dissident groups'. In contrast, he focuses attention on what he calls 'avoidance protest', 'by which dissatisfied groups seek to attenuate their hardships and express their discontent through flight, sectarian withdrawal, or other activities that minimise challenges to or clashes with those whom they view as their oppressor'.[6] This plea equally holds true for Latin American historiography, which has shown a marked preference for the study of well documented cases of open rebellion. This can lead to a serious distortion of the social history of the peasantry. We should only remember Scott's dictum: 'There is good reason...for holding that rebellion is one of the least likely consequences of exploitation'.[7]

It will become clear that the Dominican peasantry[8] resorted only very hesitantly to violence and did its very best to avoid open conflict as long as possible. Peasant protest in the Dominican Republic before 1930 consisted in general in pulling away from the market, diminishing cash crop production, outmigration or supporting political factions which were perceived as supporting their interests. Actually, it was only when their subsistence economy was endangered, that open resistance ensued. This was generally a matter of access to land, the 'central part of household autonomy',[9] but could also concern rights to water or other essential elements of the peasant economy.

In this chapter I want to sketch a number of ways in which the peasant population in the Dominican Republic reacted to the unfavourable consequences of capitalist development. Because of the scarcity of sources, this endeavour must necessarily have a tentative character. Future research will hopefully be able to throw more light on the world view and perceptions of the peasant population and the composition and social background of the organised peasant movements.

The northern tobacco sector[10]

The northern valley of the Dominican Republic, called the Cibao, developed initially as the most dynamic and prosperous part of the young Republic (independent since 1844). It was separated from the southern parts by a practically impassable mountain range. The cultivation of tobacco, which originated in the last period of Spanish colonialism, sustained a relatively large peasant population and a growing class of urban merchants operating from Puerto Plata and Santiago.

Peasant families were growing their tobacco in a rather unsophisticated way. Land existed in abundant supply and was cleared by slash-and-burn techniques. All the work was done by family labour. A great part of the peasant family's energy was devoted to the cultivation of foodcrops. Whenever more labour was needed than the family could provide, the peasants resorted to a system of mutual co-operation, the *Junta gratuita* or *Junta de vecinos*. In spite of the primitive technology, the Cibao peasantry should not be automatically connected with poverty and submission. The peasant families were descendants of the Spanish colonists, creolised and isolated, but also enterprising and self-conscious.[11]

Their agricultural activities were only one element of a peasant culture, in which agriculture, handicrafts, religious and social obligations were closely interwined. The Cibao did not have a class of large landowners, who monopolised the land and other economic resources. The peasant families were thoroughly linked to the cash-economy and the world market, and as such liable to exploitation, but easy access to land and a solid subsistence base were sufficient to safeguard a considerable autonomy.

The decentralised structure of the tobacco cultivation impeded direct relations between the export houses and the producers.

Therefore the supply of the tobacco depended on a highly diversified and complex network of middlemen, called *corredores*. The *corredores* lived in the countryside and collected the tobacco in the regions where they wielded their influence. They often possessed a strong social, political and economic position in the local peasant communities. They owned shops, gave credit, acted as *compadres* and led armed bands. Living within an economy in which tobacco cultivation formed the only regular source of money income, the peasants were, for their outside contacts, dependent on these *corredores*, who acted as social and economic brokers and were the only source of credit and political support. In spite of the clear elements of a patronage-relation between the peasants and these local strong men, the latter had little claim to higher status and their role was not institutionalised or culturally sanctioned. In this respect, they can be described as *Caciques*.[12] They doubtlessly belonged to the rural society, but at the same time formed the bridge between countryside and city.

The organisation of the tobacco trade reflected itself also in the political realm. The urban mercantile class was on top. In close co-operation with the powerful foreign mercantile houses, on which they were utterly dependent, they were actively engaged in regional and national politics. Using their influence over the *corredores*, they secured a kind of local clientele, which supported them politically and militarily. These vertical loyalties formed the backbone of the so called 'blue' party, which dominated late nineteenth century Cibao politics.

The second half of the nineteenth century saw a ferocious struggle between the northern tobacco élite and the southern landowning cattle breeders. It was only during the long dictatorship of the 'blue' general 'Lilis' Heureaux (1882–1899) that the continuous civil war was (temporarily) terminated. Under his supervision the central state managed for the first time to exercise some practical control over the country.[13] This was made possible, among other things, by the financial support Heureaux received from the recently emerged sugar plantations in the south.

The tobacco crisis after 1879

Recently Eric Wolf has again emphasised the crucial importance of the late nineteenth century crisis of 1873–1894 for the realignment of many Third World economies.[14] The Dominican Republic constitutes an excellent example of this statement. On top of the already slumping tobacco prices on the world market, came the integration of the two Hanseatic cities, Hamburg and Bremen, in the unified Germany. This limited the access of the Dominican tobacco to the German market and accelerated the pricefall in the Dominican Republic. The urban merchants, who were directly dependent on the German market, were the first to feel the effects of this crisis. They experienced considerable financial difficulties and between 1879 and 1884 the number of commercial houses in Santiago decreased from twenty-five to six.[15]

The Dominican merchants tried to cope with the crisis by squeezing the peasant producers as much as possible. The newspapers became filled with complaints about the stupidity and carelessness of the peasant population. These opinions, which concurred with the traditional contempt the urban middle classes held for the *campesino*, served in this period above all as an excuse to push the prices paid to the producers to their lowest level. Since they had a complete monopoly over the tobacco trade, they succeeded and the prices fell in the following manner:

1849	14—20	pesos per quintal (46 kilos)
1872	9	pesos per quintal
1887	4	pesos per quintal
1912	3.50[16]	pesos per quintal

The success of this strategy partly depended on the increasing role of the state in the control over peasant production. The repressive apparatus which became quite sophisticated during the Heureaux administration, was instrumental in pushing the price below production costs. In this manner the peasants bore the main burden of the tobacco crisis.

The reactions of the peasants to these deteriorating market conditions were diverse. In general they were comparable with reactions of peasants in other parts of Latin America.[17] The first reaction to falling tobacco prices was bringing down the 'costs' of production. Since these costs were not measured in money, but in human labour (which could otherwise be devoted to the cultivation of food crops or leisure), this meant that less energy was devoted to produce the same amount of tobacco of a lower quality. In this manner, the complaints of the merchants proved to be a self-fulfilling prophecy. It was written in 1874 that 'the peasants do not feel the obligation to go on cultivating with the same care and procedures, because they have the idea that the new prices will not compensate them for their efforts'.[18] And the *Eco del Pueblo* wrote in 1882: '. . . the problem is not that our cultivators do not know how to grow the leaf—they have proven the contrary in other times—; no, we have to search in a different direction to find the real motive of this neglect, which is, if you like, *conscious*'.[19] Other malpractices, of which the peasants were accused came about as a result of the same logic. It was weight which counted, not quality. Therefore, the grower tried to add weight to the tobacco in many different ways. A certain amount of moisture was added to the tobacco notwithstanding the danger of decay. Another method was putting stones, branches, etc. at the bottom of the *serones*, the tobacco bags. A way of saving labour and adding weight at the same time, was putting green, undried leaves in the *serones*, a practice which in the long run produced putrefaction as well. The merchants complained bitterly about the attitude of the peasants, but few people doubted that it was precisely their false scales, usurious interest (up to 10 per cent per month) and low prices which elicited these practices:

> Many people say that same growers augment the weight of the tobacco (...). There is some truth in this, we must acknowledge, but: who doubts that this conduct is an answer to the exaction of which they have been the victims? Who doubts this? Will he throw the first stone?[20]

The peasants also resisted interference in the production process, which made them more dependent on the cash-economy and required extra expenses. This became particularly clear in the case of the *Juntas*. This co-operative system of labour exchange was a way to deal with occasional labour shortages during the harvest, so that the tobacco could be harvested without financial expenses. In a community where money was so scarce this system offered considerable economic advantages. Moreover, it improved the internal cohesion of the peasant community. The merchants continuously tried to terminate this practice because they were convinced that the quality of the leaves was affected by the very fast way they were picked. However, until the 1950s the *Junta* remained a normal practice.

This reaction of the tobacco producers was typical for a cash-crop producing peasantry, which lived within a subsistence oriented economy and was not subject to regular extra-economic coercion. The peasants were inextricably linked to the world market and depended on a money income for a limited set of items, such as salt, guns and textiles, but they retained considerable freedom within their own sphere. Of course, the peasants did not have the means to influence the world market (nor had the merchants, for that matter), but they continued to organise their own production process. This became particularly clear after the 1929—world crisis, when the tobacco prices were lower than ever. The Cibao peasantry collectively stopped the tobacco cultivation and production figures fell from 20 million kilos in 1927 to 4.5 million kilos in 1932.[21] Many peasants migrated away into the mountains trying to maintain their independence. The Cibao peasant population in this period resembles, in this respect, Hyden's 'uncaptured peasantry' in East Africa. Although incorporated into the large world economy, their dependence on the system is marginal. 'They live', in the words of Hyden, 'in the boundary region of this system and there they have the unique prerogative of choosing to withdraw. They have a true exit option'.[22]

It was not only in economic matters that this exit option was resorted to. Onerous exactions of local leaders or military service were also instrumental in driving the peasants into the woods. It was above all the 'recruiting' of soldiers — consisting in 'detailing groups of soldiers with orders to seize any youths they found in passing',[23] which pushed many peasant families into isolated regions. Others flew from juridical persecution or unpayable debts and in the disorganised situation of the Republic in the nineteenth century few were caught. Many complaints are to be found in the municipal correspondence about the impossibility of catching fugitives and the rare lists of prisoners usually list more than half of them as *profugo*, (fugitive). The weakness of the state exposed the peasant population to all kinds of abuses and intimidation, but on the other side provided them with ample space for evading injustices and retaining some form of autonomy. For this reason, the peasant population of the northern provinces hardly ever resorted to open protest.

In the period with which we are concerned, it was only the construction of the railroad between Samana and Santiago (1881–1887), which elicited some violent resistance. The ruthless Dominican entrepreneur, Gregorio Rivas, who functioned as an intermediary on this project, started a large speculative scheme in which he tried to acquire as much land as possible around the projected trajectory of the railroad. His methods were far from scrupulous. He tried to sell his lands so expensively, that he even forced the Scottish entrepreneur of the railroad to look for another (and less favourable) harbour to start his enterprise. Along the way many peasants were thrown off their land, causing a deep and long-standing resentment. Until the very end of its construction works, it proved practically impossible to find Dominican labourers who were prepared to work for the company. The majority of the labour force therefore had to be brought in from the British West Indies.

Even after the railroad was finished, resentment did not fade. This was probably partly due to the decision of the entrepreneur not to extend the railroad to Santiago. This also alienated the urban élite and the merchants of the Cibao from the railroad project. Acts of protest were common: 'Lately a locomotive was held up...not far from La Vega, by a number of big pieces of wood, on which some men were standing...These kind of things happen almost daily'.[24]

The land question

These examples of autonomous behaviour and 'avoidance-protest' were only possible in a situation where the access to land was virtually free. Under the influence of the changing relations of production, however, the tendency to regulate the system of land ownership and to close land resources became slowly stronger.

The Dominican land-system was the result of a confusing Spanish heritage.[25] The peasant population lived in general on the so-called *terrenos comuneros*, remnants of subdivided colonial latifundias, the *hatos*. Although originally individually owned, they were in the course of time transformed into collective properties, in which several owners had a share or shares, called *pesos* or *acciones*. The property was never *physically* divided. This resulted in almost free access for the shareholders to the fruits of the entire property.

The municipalities had moreover their own municipal lands, called *ejidos*, with unclear boundaries. There was no such thing as a land register, often preventing local officials from actually disposing of these lands. 'Everybody just lives and benefits from them because no land registry (*Catastro*) exists of the lands which belong to the state'. The sensitivity of the land question was underlined by the fact that land-registration had to be done by armed men, because 'all inhabitants of these places believe themselves to be proprietor' and 'are capable of any kind of disorder'.[26] The situation became even more complicated by the law about the free transfer of State lands in 1876, according to which every Dominican or foreigner was allowed to take an uninhabited piece of land in order to cultivate it with crops, such as sugarcane, cocoa and tobacco.

To put an end to this situation, different land laws were proclaimed of which only the last in 1920 under the US government had the desired effect. The general aims of these laws were to reach an obligatory registration of land transactions and to destroy the system of collective landholding. Until 1920 the state did not dispose of the means to enforce these regulations and in the period 1880—1920 it was above all the activities of the capitalist sugar entrepreneurs which curtailed the use of land by the peasant population. Everywhere they bought large tracts of land for infinitesimal prices and, where needed, they drove the peasants away by forged land titles or force.

The southern sugar sector

The beginning of a large scale, mechanised and clearly capitalist sugar sector in the south-eastern part of the Dominican Republic is usually placed in the year 1874, when the first steam-mill was introduced. Within ten years, some thirty *ingenios*, steam-driven sugar plantations, were fostered, mainly with Cuban (and some Dominican and US) capital.[27] The world market crisis of 1884 with its dramatic fall in prices, eliminated the smaller and financially less sound enterprises and caused a concentration of property. In the last decade of the nineteenth century the sugar plantations started to accumulate large quantities of land.

The process of expansion and the monopolisation of land by the sugar industry accelerated rapidly in the first two decades of the twentieth century. Seven of the largest *ingenios* expanded their territory in the following manner:

1893	79,000 tarea	(16 tarea is 1 ha.)
1911/12	268,850 tarea	
1915	580,340 tarea	
1925	1,986,370 tarea[28]	

The sugar industry which emerged in the first two decades of this century, was all but completely financed by US capital and dominated by a handful of corporations, which had a trans-national character.

The initial peasant reactions to the opportunities of relatively well-paid wage labour which the new plantations offered, were far from averse. The Dominican peasants showed a remarkable willingness to adapt themselves to changing circumstances. According to Abad, small peasants flocked to the sugar plantations in great numbers, looking for a daily wage.[29] So great was the attraction of the sugar plantations, that state officials in other regions started to complain about the drain of people from their district.[30]

Soon this picture changed, however. The peasant-labourers did not object to selling their labour to the plantations, but they were only prepared to do that on their own conditions. Something of that attitude may be drawn from the disdainful remark of an anonymous correspondent: 'The labour force has been abundant at times and scarce at others, according to the position of the *fiesta*-barometer'.[31]

And they worked only as long as they perceived the work as

rewarding. When the sugar entrepreneurs in 1884 drastically lowered wages, the cane-cutters simply refused to work. The *Eco de la Opinion*, a journal in favour of the sugar interests, wrote in October 1884 on the eve of the next sugar harvest: 'Everyone worries about the stagnation of the *ingenios*. Some of them already want to start working, but they have no labourers. The *peones* refuse to accept the wages, which are offered to them'.[32] The situation did not improve and the Dominican labourers pulled out *en masse* in the subsequent years, leaving the sugar plantations with no other option than importing labour from the surrounding islands.[33]

Migration, many times almost indistinguishable from flight, can also be seen as an act of protest.[34] In this respect, a distinction must be made between migration *to* and migration *from* the centres of capitalist activity. The first can be considered as a positive, consenting reaction to new opportunities. The second was a clear sign of protest. This was even more the case where capitalist penetration entailed a considerable shortage of labour. In that case a clear confrontation sprang up between the state and capitalist entrepreneurs on the one side, devising *vagancia*-laws and work books, and a peasant population which stuck to its freedom.[35]

Slowly, it became clear that it was a fiction to think that the peasant economy could remain untouched and viable in the confrontation with a mode of production which adhered so completely to other values and introduced new economic means of domination. Leaving the sugar plantations, as the peasants had done after 1884, was not sufficient. The monopolistic plantations threatened the core of their existence as peasants.

The perplexed peasantry tried in vain to counter this increasing danger. Peacefully at first, by writing petitions to the state authorities, explaining the injustice done to them:

> until yesterday this community lived on these lands in the same way as in other parts of the Island, that is having a collective usufruct of its advantages and products, such as is determined by common law and custom.

> They (the owners) have been surprised by the seizure of almost the entire property by senor Seralles (a powerful Puerto Rican sugar entrepreneur), who has cut off all the land near the Jagua which was not occupied, in many cases violating rights of property. He acted so shamelessly, that he has even cut off the public road.

This behaviour is even more anomalous because the number of titles by far exceeds his.[36]

Petitions and defence leagues, however, could not arrest the penetration of capitalism. The large enterprises, which had many friends in high positions and disposed of ample rewards, constituted a superior force in a small and backward country. Unable to confront the plantations openly, the peasant population sometimes resorted to a kind of passive resistance. In cases when the plantations were in need of urgent help, the *peones* and the local peasants sometimes blandly refused to help. A correspondent in San Pedro de Macoris reported that in the case of a fire on the ingenio 'Puerto Rico' the 400 peasants and some labourers who were present at the ingenio at that time 'refused to help, such as was desired, and did not obey the overseer of the plantation'. When the same thing happened on the ingenio 'Santa Fe', 'it was not possible to find people to help, neither on the hacienda, nor in the nearby villages'.[37] Moreover, various reports appeared in the newspapers about fires in the cane fields, which had mysterious origins and were blamed on arson.

It was not only access to land, but also a way of life, grounded in a subsistence economy, which was threatened. In this same period, for instance, laws were proclaimed which limited the regions where loose cattle were allowed. Cattle holding was an essential part of the subsistence economy of the peasantry and these laws legitimised in another way violent means to undermine peasant existence. The rural guard had another pretext to harass the peasants. The large landowners had the cattle simply shot or used them for their own provisions.[38]

In the drier western parts of the country, the monopolisation of the water supply had similar consequences. The distribution of water had never been a problem but after the establishment of large scale agricultural enterprises, which used irrigation, a fierce struggle about the access to the water supply ensued. The clearest example of the monopolisation of water took place on the south-western coast. In 1917, the North American Barahona company devised here an extensive irrigation project with the water of the Yague del Sur.[39] The owners of this US enterprise orginally asked permission to take 40 cubic metres per second, but even the 21 metres which they were eventually allowed to take by the US military government, left almost nothing for the other farmers in the dry season.[40]

In this case the traditional landowning élite took the lead in the struggle. In 1921 a vigorous press-campaign started and the local newspaper, *El Cable*, published a long series of well-documented articles about 'The Seizure of the Southern Water'. At the same time the small proprietors organised themselves in 'Committees for the Defense of the Water' (*Comités de Defensa de Aguas*).[41] Although this movement could not put an end to the activities of this company, it prevented its most extreme abuser.

In the long run, violence seemed to be the only remaining option. Already before 1917 the south-east had been the scene of much warfare. The destruction of the local power structures, the destruction of the traditional agriculture, and the political anarchy led to a great deal of internecine struggle between different caudillo-led warbands.

After the US occupation these guerrilla-bands, known as *gavilleros*, took a revolutionary, nationalist flavour. In this 'volte-face' the ambiguities of the personalistic leadership became evident. On the one hand the US military government and the sugar enterprises used local strong men to maintain order. On the other, many local leaders took the lead in opposing the US occupation and the monopoly of the sugar companies.

The tenacious *gavillero* war, which raged through the south-eastern region of the Dominican Republic from 1917 to 1922 against the US occupation and the North American sugar plantations, was in the first place, a desperate attempt by a class of dispossessed peasants to change the future. The rank and file of the *gavillero* forces consisted of the expropriated peasantry, which had been pushed off their land by the sugar companies. Many of the men who fought with the caudillo-led bands were from the sugar *bateys*, the desolate villages in which the sugar cane cutters lived. After the mass surrender of guerrillas in 1922, military officials found a significant percentage to be men who had recently lost their land.[43]

The guerrillas were supported by the peasant population, which had maintained itself on the fringe of the sugar plantations, but were in constant danger of being eliminated themselves. These peasants provided the guerrillas with recruits, shelter and an extensive system of intelligence. Very quickly the movement began to take on revolutionary and nationalist overtones. Many guerrillas were aware of the importance of their struggle and displayed a sharp political insight. Some groups were in virtual control over definite areas and even constructed some kind of government structures. Opposing the label of 'bandits' which the marines had given them, they insisted on the ideological nature of their struggle.

Peasant culture and resistance

In the parts of the country which were situated further away from the centres of capitalist expansion, the picture was more complex.

Here the contradictions between the local peasant economy and the changing social and economic structures were more heterogeneous. Not so much a direct confrontation between different modes of production took place here, as much as a hardly documented struggle on the part of the peasants to retain their economic and cultural autonomy. This meant above all a refusal to make the peasant livelihood subservient to wage labour relations and a rejection of state interference.

On a few occasions we can obtain a glimpse of the cultural elements of the peasant struggle and the influence of a resilient peasant culture. A significant incident occurred at the canalisation project of the *Yague del Norte* in Monte Cristy. In April 1885 all work had to be stopped unexpectedly during an entire week, because the workers had gone home for the *Semana Santa* (the week before Easter, full of religious and social activities). The entrepreneurs who wanted to finish the project as quickly as possible could do nothing but acquiesce and wait.[44]

Dominican society as a whole was Catholic, but it was a popular Catholicism which prevailed in the countryside.[45] It was full of African and other non-Christian elements and allowed ample space for miracles and direct contact with the 'other side'. Moreover, religious practice was closely linked — interwoven one could say — with the subsistence economy. The religious holidays were times to accomplish with the *promesas* (vows) made during the year in order to provoke rains, bless the harvest or cure the sick. The dead were attended during *velorios*, wakes, which could last up to nine days and nights. The *pesáme*, a gift for the dead, took care of the immediate needs of those left behind. The 'innocent' children, who died shortly after birth, were sent to heaven in equally long lasting ceremonies (*baguinís*). The popular religion was an integral part of the peasant economy and as such played a significant part in the conflict between different modes of production. This became particularly clear in the attempts to put an end to certain elements of the popular culture, in order to bring them more in line with the new economic order. The official Catholic church started to dissuade 'extravagant' expressions of religious fervour, the press complained continuously about the disorders which accompanied religious ceremonies and the Guardia Nacional received explicit orders to prohibit popular religious practices.[46]

The consequences of all these activities on the lives of the peasant population are difficult to ascertain, but apparently it made little of these restrictive measures. It was only in the course of the twentieth century, that changing social and economic conditions slowly transformed what the legislators had been unable to eradicate.

The Olivorista movement

The only example of a more or less organised peasant movement with a clear religious, messianistic tendency, was the movement of the so-called Dios Olivorio in the San Juan region near the Haitian border. The frontier region, west of Azua, had shown a very specific development at the end of the nineteenth century. Because of the turbulent capitalist development in the eastern parts of the island, it had become a more or less marginalised region within the Dominican economy. Its sole economic base was the raising of cattle for the Haitian market, which was combined with small handicrafts and some agriculture.[47]

Within these general regional conditions, two processes had a profound effect on the livelihood of its population. First there was an increasing monopolisation of the land in the fertile San Juan valley by large landowners with large-scale agricultural enterprises. This pushed the small peasants uphill to the less accessible parts. Because the population was small, free land was still available, but traditional rights, of which the free movement of cattle was the most important, were severely limited.

The cattle economy was, in the second place, strongly affected by the government policy to limit cattle-holding in order to promote commercial agriculture. The determination of the so-called 'agricultural regions' in which loose cattle-holding was forbidden, meant the dislocation of the existing economic structure. The limitation of the frontier trade with Haiti by subsequent Dominican governments made the situation even worse and the archives of the Ministry of Agriculture in the first decades of this century, contain countless petitions of cattleholders to change the legislation and to improve their situation.[48]

It was against this background of social and economic dislocation that the rise of the Olivorista movement must be seen.[49] In 1908, Olivorio Mateo, who was a day-labourer and native of the San Juan region, disappeared during a hurricane. Having been given up for dead, he reappeared after nine days and constituted himself as messenger of God and proclaimed that everyone who believed in him would be saved. Within a short while, hundreds of people from all over the region flocked to his place of residence. Many poor people joined the brotherhood, which established itself in Olivorio's holy town, where everyone was equal and violence was not permitted.

The Olivorista movement was clearly a messianistic cult, which Adas took as an example of 'avoidance-protest'. It provided a place of refuge for a peasant population who wanted to withdraw from a changed society which was destroying their livelihood and autonomy. It was not meant as a direct confrontation with that society. Carlos E.Deive emphasises its initial peaceful character:

> As long as its moderate action did not encounter opposition of the system, Olivorionism took a peaceful and harmonious posture. Only when that changed, it resorted to an open confrontation with the opposing forces.[50]

And indeed, violent repression did not take long to materialise. First it was the Caceres-government (1906–1911) which, in its efforts to pacify the western part of the country where it had many enemies, all but extinguished the movement. Nevertheless, the government never succeeded in capturing Olivorio himself. After the assassination of Caceres and the subsequent civil strife, Olivorionism resurged stronger than before. The final repression came during the occupation of the Dominican Republic by North American marines who, in the same period, were trying to repress the strong Haitian *caco*-resistance on the other side of the border.[51] From 1917 onwards they took every effort to suppress the movement and to capture Olivorio. Diaries of the expeditions show how these activities at the same time functioned as a means to pacify the western part of the country. Many people were arrested on the accusation of illegal frontier trade, provisioning the guerrillas, or of simple vagrancy. Huts of 'bandits' were indiscriminately burned down. In 1919 Olivorio's camp was discovered and destroyed, 'eight deserted *bohíos* (huts), a large shed with benches fixed to the wall for sleeping and a dance hall or meeting place' and 'several foodplots (*conucos*) close by'.[52]

After the destruction of the camp, Olivorio and some loyal followers were driven to the mountains. The messiah was finally assassinated in 1922 and although Olivorionism as a movement dissolved, its ideas never disappeared. Until this day vestiges of Olivorista beliefs can be found in the San Juan region.[53] As a collective utopia, however, the avoidance of conflict had proved to be illusory. Centralisation and state-control had become the catchwords of a new political and economic élite, which was trying to regain its hold over Dominican society. In this context, organised autonomy was perceived as inherently subversive. As so often in history, the governing classes spotted 'subversion' way before the 'subversive' group itself; a factor which, of course, greatly facilitated its destruction.

Conclusion

The transformation of peasant society under the influence of the expanding world swept away in an irreversible process of proletarianisation. Concomitant with these theories was the suggestion that the role of the peasantry has been extremely passive and that it had undergone its destruction as a docile victim.

This viewpoint has neglected the active and sometimes decisive role of the peasant population in determining the outcome of these processes of change. Usually, the peasants were not at all averse to change and many times took an active part in it. As long as they could maintain a certain independence and their subsistence economy was not endangered, they did not feel particularly threatened by the new economic circumstances. They were accustomed to a tolerable amount of injustice and as long as they could maintain their subsistence base, they did not feel the need to resist these changes. Rather, they were eager to get some profit out of the new opportunities and were not averse to wage labour or cash-crop production.

It did not take long to become clear that in many cases the preservation of their subsistence economy was incompatible with new relations of production which were dominated by capital. De Janvry and Garramon point at the two essential processes which capitalist penetration in Latin American agriculture tries to enforce where labour is scarce: the alienation of labour from access to the land through its monopolisation and the imposition of social relations of production that prevent labour from capturing its own opportunity costs in the labour market.[54] Although these conditions were never completely met in this period, this remark underlines the fundamental conflict between capitalist logic and the autonomy of the peasants.

As long as avoidance of protest was possible, the peasants limited themselves to non-violent reactions to penetrating capitalism. In the more remote regions of the Republic land resources remained open until the 1940s and even longer. Many peasant families migrated to these regions. Others remained where they were and tried to hold their own against the growing pressure of merchants and the authorities. Less conspicuous forms of resistance can be found in the popular culture of the Dominican people. *Fandangos, fiestas* and popular Christian ceremonies, all served as a means of preserving some form of cultural autonomy. Looking over all the measures and laws to suppress these symbols of popular culture, there is no doubt that the Dominican élite very well understood that this retention of the 'old days' was an implicit rejection of a new economic and cultural system which was undermining peasant autonomy. Sometimes, the destruction of traditional social and economic structures led to religious fervour and open conflict, such as happened in the case of Olivorio Mateo. Generally it remained on a hardly documented, local level.

It is tempting to link the various forms of peasant protest to the different processes of capitalist transformation in the Dominican Republic. In the northern region, the processes of change were diverse and relatively smooth. Class antagonism was softened by *compradazgo*—relationships and inter-class alliances. The peasantry was able to pursue its agricultural and social activities without too much outside interference. The cultivation of cash-crops, which was an integrated part of the subsistence economy, linked them firmly to the market. Peasant resistance therefore focused on the terms of trade and credit and was meant, above all, to maintain its independence vis-à-vis the regional mercantile class.

In the southern provinces, the sugar industry had disastrous consequences for the peasant economy. The region seems to show the classic plantation-peasant antagonism, in which the peasantry is swept off its land by predominating capitalist-enterprises. Against this background, it is not surprising that it was especially in this region that collective and violent resistance surged. In the western frontier region, peasant behaviour reflected the disoriented and marginalised position of this region. Increasing state interference set bounds to the cattle-holding and the freedom of commerce with Haiti without offering any economic alternatives. This situation was a breeding ground for the messianistic movement of Olivorio Mateo which aimed at reorganising society and reordering social relations.[55]

The penetration of capitalism in the Third World has not been a uniform and linear process. Especially in a country, such as the Dominican Republic, with a weak state and a lack of a dominant central power, capitalist development was erratic and uneven. Sometimes it used existing economic and cultural institutions, sometimes it brutishly suppressed them. Research into the different forms of resistance to which the peasantry took refuge, may give us a better insight into the interplay between these different factors. This could modify the still widely held idea of an all-dominating capitalism in Third World agriculture. On the other hand, it could also provide a more prominent place in history to the peasantry as the subject of its own history.

Acknowledgements

This article was first presented at the 9th Annual Conference of the Society for Caribbean Studies (2—4 July, 1985).

I would like to thank Heather Sutherland and Willem van Schendel for their valuable comments on earlier versions of this paper.

Notes

1 Cf. H.A. Landsberger, (ed.) *Latin American Peasant Movements*, (Ithaca/London, 1969); J. Paige, *Agrarian Revolution*, (New York, 1975); B. Moore, *Social Origins of Dictatorship and Democracy*, (Harmondswoth, 1966).
2 Cf. J.C. Scott, *The Moral Economy of the Peasant. Rebellion and Subsistence in Southeast Asia*, (New Haven/London, 1976); J.A. Meyer, *The Cristero Rebellion. The Mexican People between Church and State. 1926—1929*, (Cambridge, 1976); B.J. Kerkvliet, *The Huk Rebellion*, (Berkeley, 1977).
3 Scott, *Moral Economy*, VII.
4 E.R. Wolf, *Peasant Wars of the Twentieth Century*, (New York etc., 1969), was the first who explicitly tried to write such an analysis, cf. pp. X-XIII. More recent examples are: G. Hyden, *Beyond Ujamaa in Tanzania: Underdevelopment and an Uncaptured Peasantry*, (London, 1980); F.E. Mallon, *The Defense of Community in Peru's Central Highlands: Peasant Struggles and Capitalist Transition, 1860—1940*, (Princeton, 1983).
5 J.C. Scott, B.J. Kerkvliet, 'How Traditional Rural Patrons Lose Legitimacy', *Cultures et dèveloppement*, Summer, 1975: pp. 501—540; 519—20. For the actual situation in Latin America: M.S. Grindle, *State and Countryside: Development Policy and Agrarian Politics in Latin America*, (Baltimore, 1986).
6 M. Adas, 'From Avoidance to Confrontation: Peasant Protest in Precolonial and Colonial Asia', *Comparative Studies in Society and History*, XXIII, 1981: pp. 217—247. J.C. Scott has taken up this point recently in *Weapons of the Weak: Everyday Forms of Peasant Resistance*, (New Haven/London, 1985).
7 Scott, *Moral Economy*, p. 173.
8 In this article I will use general concepts, such as 'peasantry' or 'peasant population'. This is not to deny that class differences already existed between different peasant producers. However, the purpose of this paper is only to describe some forms of peasant resistance in the absence of sources which would permit a class analysis of peasant protest. For a similar view, see: P.A. Marinez, *Resistencia Campesina, Imperialisms y Reforma Agraria en República Dominicana (1899—1978)*, (Santo Domingo, 1984).
9 Mallon, *Defense of Community*, p. 157.
10 This part is based on an unpublished manuscript: M. Baud, 'Agricultural Transformation in a Caribbean Region', (Amsterdam, 1982).

11   H. Hoetink, *The Dominican People, 1850—1900*, (Baltimore/London, 1983) (original in Spanish: 1972); p. 171.
12   Scott/Kerkvliet, 'Traditional Rural Patrons', p. 510. Also: R. Bartra, (et al.), *Caciguismo y poder político en el Mexico rural*, (Mexico, 1976).
13   Cf. Hoetink. *Dominican People*, Ch. 5.
14   E.R. Wolf, *Europe and the People Without History*, (Cambridge, 1982), pp. 310—13.
15   *Eco del Pueblo*, (Edp), III, 125; 24 August, 1884.
16   Baud, 'Agriculture Transformation', p. 28.
17   Good examples are given in: W. Roseberry, *Coffee and Capitalism in the Venezuelan Andes*, (Austin, 1983) and Mallon, *Defense of Community*. In respect to the tobacco production, the Colombian case is particularly instructive. Cf. J.P. Harrison, 'The evolution of the Colombian tobacco trade to 1875', *Hispanic American Historical Review*, XXXIII, 2, (1952) and *The Colombian Tobacco Industry from government monopoly to free trade, 1778—1876*, (Bogota, 1969).
18   *El Orden*, 1. 9, 4 October 1874.
19   *Edp*, 1, 33, 19 November 1882.
20   *Edp*, IV, 193, 24 January 1886.
21   P. Mutto, 'La economía de exportaciòn de la República Dominicana, 1900—1930', *Eme Eme, Estudios Dominicanos*, III, 15, (1974) 677—110, pp. 107—8.
22   Hyden, *Beyond Ujaama*, p. 32.
23   Hoetink, *Dominican People*, pp. 98—9.
24   *Eco de la Opinión*, 22 October 1887.
25   About the Dominican land-system: A. Albuquerque, *Títulos de terrenos comuneros de la República Dominicana*, (Ciudad Trujillo, 1961).
26   Letter of the Governor of Puerto Plata, March 21, 1872; *Archivo General de la Nación. Santo Domingo*, (AGN), Interior y Policia, legajo 15.
27   For this period: J.J. Sanchez, *La cana en Santo Domingo*, (Santo Domingo, 1893), reprint 1972.
28   F. Baez Evertsz, *Azúcar y dependencia en la República Dominicana*, (Santo Domingo, 1978), p. 47.
29   J.R. Abad, *La República Dominicana. Resena general geogràfico-estadistica*, (Santo Domingo, 1888), reprint 1973, p. 263.
30   M. Baud, 'Transformación capitalista y regionalización en la República Dominicana, 1870—1920', *Investigación y Cicucia*, I, 1, Enero-Abril 1986, pp. 17—45.
31   *El Mensajero*, VII, 9, 14 July 1887.
32   *Eco de la Opinión*, V, 274, 9 October 1884.
33   J. Del Castillo, 'La inmigración de braceros azucareros en la República Dominicana, 1900—1930', *Cuadernos del cendia*, CCLXII, 7, (1978).
34   Cf. A.I. Asiwaju, 'Migration as Revolt: The Example of the Ivory Coast and the Upper Volta Before 1945', *Journal of African History*, XVII, 4, (1976), 577—594. Also D. Nicholls, *Haiti in Caribbean Context: Ethnicity, Economy and Revolt*, (London, 1985), p. 16.
35   Contempt for the 'vagos' is of course a recurrent theme in Latin American historiography. A Dominican example may be found in the *Voz the Santiago*, (II, 98, 20˙February, 1882), under the heading 'La Vagancia': 'The influence of the *Vago* corrupts the society, because it is

generally easier to follow evil, than to imitate the hard-working man (. . .). It is impossible to sum up all the consequences of the *vagancia*. It influences everything. The vago lives in a pernicious atmosphere, always inventing lies in order to abuse the confusion which he consciously sows in the hearts of the people'. About the legislation in Puerto Rico: L.W. Bergad, *Coffee and the Growth of Agrarian Capitalism in Nineteenth-Century Puerto Rico*, (Princeton, 1983). See also: M. Baud, 'Ideología y campesinado: el pensqmicuto social de José Ramon Lopez', *Estudios Sociales*, XIX, 64, Abril-Junio 1986, pp. 63—87.

36 Petition to the Minister of Interior y Policia, July 10, 1891; *AGN* Interior y Policia, Legajo 133, exp. 8.

37 *Eco de la Opinión*, 673, 20 April 1892.

38 The peasants who lived near the ingenious 'La Duquesa' y 'Italia', complained to the Governor of the Province of Santo Domingo about the shooting of their cattle. His conclusion was clear: 'considering that these *ingenios* provide more profits for the country than the few cattle which can be held in their surroundings and taking into account that the owners of these *ingenios* are foreigners, which our sad experience learns us to handle with kid gloves, it is my opinion that this region is declared agricultural zone'. Letter Governor of Santo Domingo, 11 January, 1900; *AGN*, Interior y Policia, Legajo 171.

39 Cf. M.M. Knight, *The Americans in Santo Domingo*, (New York, 1970) original 1928, pp. 132/3.

40 Cf. letters to Lieut. C.C. Baughman from? (28 February, 1917) and Octavio A. Acevedo (10 March, 1917); *AGN*, Correspondence of Ministerio de Fomento y Obras Publicas, Legajo 26, 1917. Also *La Informatión*, 2173, 15 June, 1921 which wrote: 'They have given a concession for more water than the Yague contains in the dry season'.

41 V. Garrido, *En la ruta de mi vida, 1886—1966*, (Santo Domingo, 1970), pp. 111—13 and 120.

42 For this episode: B.J. Calder, 'Caudillos and Gavilleros versus the United States Marines: Guerilla Insurgency during the Dominican Intervention, 1916—1924', *Hispanic American Historical Review*, LVIII, 4, (1978), pp. 649—675; and: B.J. Calder, *The Impact of Intervention: The Dominican Republic during the US Occupation of 1916—1924*, (Austin, 1984), chapters 5—7.

43 Calder, *Caudillos and Gavilleros*, p. 658.

44 *Edp*, IV 158, 3 May 1885.

45 The reports of the *Inspectors de Instrucción Pública*, made in 1921—22 contain very interesting information about the popular culture in the different regions of the Dominican Republic. They are reproduced in: E. Rodriguez Demorizi, *Lengua y folklore de Santo Domingo*, (Santiago, 1975), pp. 91—277.

46 This is very eloquently illustrated in the 'Orden del Cuerpo' (1908) of the Guardia Republicana, in which all kinds of expressions of popular culture were summed up and then prohibited. Also: P. Bryan, 'La producción campesina en le Républica Dominicana a principios de siglo XX', *Eme Eme Estudios Dominicanos*, VII, 42, Mayo-Junio 1979, pp. 29—62.

47 This region begs for more detailed study. A good introduction is: E.C. Palmer, *Land Use and Landscape Change along the Dominican-Haitian Borderlands*, (Unpublished Ph. D, University of Florida, 1976).

48 Cf. for example the correspondence in 1918, when hundreds of people

asked for permission to hold cattle; *AGN*, Correspondencia del Ministerio de Agricultura e Inmigracion, legajo 12, 1918.

49   About this movement: C.E. Dieve, 'El mesianismo olivorista' in: *El Indio, el Negro y la Vida tradicional Dominicano*, (Santo Domingo, 1978), 177–205; E.O. Garrido Puello, *Olivorio: un ensayo histórico*, (Santo Domingo, 1963).

50   Deive, 'Mesianismo Olivorista', p. 205.

51   Cf. R. Gaillard, *Charlemagne Pèralte le caco*, (Port-au-Prince, 1982). For the Dominican-Haitian connection in the resistance movement, pp. 177–80.

52   'Report on Operations of a detachment of the 9th Company (26–12–1918 to 14–1–1919)', *AGN*, Correspondencia del Ministerio de Interior y Policia, legajo 379, 1919.

53   The Palmer Sola movement, which was destroyed by the Dominican airforce in 1963, was a direct sequel of the Olivorista messianism. Cf. L. Martinez, 'Palma Sola: Un caso de movimiento social campesino con caracteristicas mesianisticas' *Revista Estudios Dominicanos*, 11, 4, Abril 1985, pp. 9–20.

54   A. De Janvry, /C. Garramon, The Dynamics of Rural Poverty' *Journal of Peasant Studies*, IV, (1976/7), p. 207.

55   De Queiroz calls this a situation of 'anomie', or break-up of social cohesion: De Quieroz, MIP 'Messiahs in Brazil', *Past and Present*, 31, July 1965, pp. 62–86; p. 72/73.

CHAPTER 7 | Gender roles in Caribbean agricultural labour

Janet Henshall Momsen

Boserup[1] in her pathfinding study of *The Role of Women in Economic Development* identified the British Commonwealth Caribbean as an anomalous region in terms of gender roles in agriculture. She suggested that since Jamaica, as distinct from Cuba, the Dominican Republic and Puerto Rico, had a relatively high proportion of women farmers it was more like Africa than Latin America according to her continental-scale regional classification. Boserup explains this anomaly in ethnic terms relating it to the preservation of African farming traditions among a population mainly descended from African slaves.[2] This hypothesis appears to contradict her basic materialist thesis in which gender roles in agriculture are seen as being principally determined by the system of production, primarily through the workings of the labour market and the level of technology, with cultural perceptions of gender roles considered to be irrelevant. This essay examines the Boserup hypothesis using evidence from both historical sources and contemporary fieldwork.

The development of the sugar plantations in the Caribbean during the seventeenth century created a demand for labour which was met by the importation of slaves from West Africa. By 1663 it was said that 'the very being of the plantations depended on the supply of Negroes'.[3] More male slaves than female were imported and planters alleged that they preferred male workers. They blamed the low rate of reproduction among the slave population on this sex-specific migration which resulted in a shortage of women.[4] However, contemporary statistics belie this explanation as they show that by 1800 the sex ratio was in balance in most of the region and with the cessation of the slave trade women soon came to outnumber men. By 1817 there were 116 female slaves to every 100 male slaves in Barbados and Montserrat, 114 per 100 in Antigua, 108 and 104 in St Kitts and Nevis respectively while Jamaica and the Bahamas had a relatively balanced sex ratio.[5] This increasing predominance of women in the slave population, despite the plantation owners' declared preference for male slaves, occurred, according to Kiple[6] because women were physiologically better able to withstand the stress of the Middle Passage and slave life although they were often even less well nourished than the men. There was a higher rate of male than female fetal mortality and infant mortality in the slave population.[7] Reproduction remained low not because of the sex ratio but rather because malnutrition and overwork depressed the fertility rate of the female slaves while the mortality rate remained high.[8] In addition, even when slave owners improved conditions for female slaves in an effort to raise the birthrate, social factors still inhibited an increase in the fertility rate.[9] The numerical dominance of women in the slave labour force had a marked effect on the gender division of labour. Yet the planters generally refused to recognise the existence of a high female sex ratio and Bush[10] feels that this may have been done in order to conceal from the abolitionists the degree to which women slaves were exploited.

It is clear that under the forced labour of slavery the gender division of labour amongst Caribbean slaves was decided not by slave memories of African traditions but by the European slaveowners and their perceptions and traditions. Planters were aware that women worked in agriculture in Africa and used this knowledge as justification for their utilization of female slaves as field labourers in the West Indies. In fact, women had very specific roles in African agriculture and rarely undertook the heavy work of land preparation which was expected of them in the West Indies. The use of women as field labourers appeared natural to the planters because it was also the pattern of farm labour in England. There is strong evidence that between 1690 and 1750 in England there was little difference in male and female participation in agricultural work. During that period gender roles were undifferentiated by employers.[11] This metropolitan pattern, which in England continued for a relatively short period, was transferred to the Caribbean colonies and became associated with the slave labour system.

Gender in the 'formal' plantation economy

Under slavery men and women were seen merely as labour units. Not until the slave trade had been brought to a halt did women's reproductive role assume as much importance as her productive role. 'The woman was expected to work just as hard, she was as indecently exposed and was punished just as severely. In the eyes of the master she was equal to the man as long as her strength was the same as his'.[12] Women had a narrower range of occupations than men. Apart from the midwife, doctoress or traditional healer, the chief housekeeper (often a concubine of the master), and to a lesser extent, washerwomen, cooks and domestics, the slave élite consisted almost entirely of men. Reddock sees this as 'the introduction of the sexual division of labour that had been instituted in Europe into one sector of slave society while not extending it into areas in which it was not economically advantageous'.[13]

In agriculture the élite positions were held almost entirely by men. Consequently planters were increasingly forced to rely on women as field labourers. Craton[14] shows that as the overall proportion of women slaves on Worthy Park plantation 'rose from 46 to 60 per cent, their numbers in the fields increased almost proportionately: from around 58 per cent of the 'field' labour force in the 1790s, to over 65 per cent throughout the 1830s'. As early as 1756 on Roaring River Estate in Jamaica, of the ninety-two female slaves, seventy were fieldworkers, while of the eighty-four men only twenty-eight were labouring in the cane fields.[15] From the age of four years children were also expected to work in the fields and data from the Codrington estates in Barbados (Table 7.1) show that the gender divisions of labour of the parents were visited on the children. In 1781 73 per cent of the active slaves at Codrington were field labourers of which over half were women and young girls. Of the working child slaves 95 per cent of the girls but only 80 per cent of the boys were field hands.

Although fieldhands performed the hardest labour, their living conditions were far inferior to those of élite workers and, in con-

Table 7.1   Occupations of slaves at Codrington, Barbados, 1781

Occupation	Number of slaves				Percentage of slaves			
	Men	Women	Boys	Girls	Men	Women	Boys	Girls
Field workers	37	52	34	39	22.8	32.1	21.2	24.1
Artisans and watchmen	17	0	1	0	94.4	0	5.6	0
Stockkeepers	10	5	7	1	43.5	21.7	30.4	4.4
Personnel workers	3	15	0	1	15.8	78.9	0	5.3
Non-workers	4	4	19	27	7.4	7.4	35.2	50.0

Source: Adapted from Bennet, J.H. 1958. *Bondsmen and Bishops: Slavery and Apprenticeship on the Codrington Plantations of Barbados, 1710–1838*. Berkeley, University of California Press, p. 12.

sequence, they experienced a higher mortality rate and suffered more frequently from illness than the more privileged slaves, but, despite these hardships, women field labourers lived five years longer than men on average. Pregnancy did not guarantee a lighter workload nor a reduction in physical punishment until very late in the period of slavery. As Mathurin indicates 'Slavery, in many essentials made men and women roughly equal in the eyes of the master. Their jobs on the plantation were distributed not according to sex but according to age and health. In theory men were supposed to do the backbreaking tasks of the field and the factory; in fact as long as women were young and fit they were recruited into the same work force as men and shared more or less the same labour'.[16] The majority of women remained in the fields in harsh conditions and unlike the men, they had the dual burden of childcare and housework on top of their agricultural work. As Levy[17] points out in Barbados slave women in the fields 'toiled as strenuously as the men, carried baskets of manure weighing as much as seventy pounds, and when they returned to their cottages at night faced additional family duties'.

Gender in the 'informal' slave economy

The cost of feeding a large slave labour force persuaded the plant-ocracy to allow peasant-like activities to develop. Male and female slaves were granted plots of land on which to grow subsistence crops in their own time. Mintz has shown that as early as 1672 in Jamaica, slave women were involved in buying and selling the surplus produc-tion from their provision grounds on Sunday mornings in public markets.[18] This growth of marginal production and internal trade within the plantation slave economy with its concomitant gender division of labour occurred to varying degrees on other West Indian islands, including Montserrat, Tobago, St Vincent, Dominica, Grenada, Barbados and St Kitts, as well as in Jamaica.[19]

Such was the importance of the Sunday market to the entire population that the stringent laws restricting the mobility of slaves were relaxed where marketing activities were concerned. The con-sequent unusual mobility of market women enabled them to facilitate communication between plantations. Thus they came to play an important role in organised slave resistance and in the development of a creole society. By 1800 there were more women than men in the Jamaican Maroon communities. Women in these Maroon groups had special tasks during campaigns, such as helping to carry off spoils, but their main role was to grow food.

Post-emancipation gender divisions of labour

By the end of the eighteenth century in England regional variations in types of agriculture had produced different practices in the division of labour by gender.[20] In the new, capitalist agriculture of south-east England technological change had had the effect of squeezing women out of agriculture to a very large degree, with their role being reduced to work such as weeding and haymaking. Gradually women moved away from agriculture and rural areas into domestic service and later manufacturing in the urban areas. The increasing scale of production and commerce led to the separation of public and private spheres of work with the men in the public sphere and the women in the private sphere of the home. These developments have been identified with Victorian morality and new middle-class assumptions about the role of women. By the mid-nineteenth century such metropolitan attitudes had been transferred, with the usual time-lag, to the colonies and the planters found themselves torn between moral certitude and economic preference in their search for non-slave plantation labour.

With the ending of slave apprenticeship in the British West Indian colonies in 1838, many women ex-slaves sought the private sphere hitherto denied them and it was said that 'mothers of families have retired from the field, to the duties of the home'.[21] Even before 1838 many women came to dominate the movement to the towns but, as on the plantations, the range of jobs for women was much narrower than for men, with most women working as domestic servants or in retailing (Table 7.2). Inter-island migration, encouraged by regional differences in wage rates, was mainly undertaken by men, exacerbating the female sex ratio in the smaller islands and leaving many women as *de facto* heads of households. The mid-nineteenth century rapid rise in food prices forced many women back into the agricultural labour force in order to feed their children. Women's fluctuating participation rate in the agricultural work force during this period was reflected in the planters' ambivalent attitudes towards women workers, for 'while the planters criticized mothers for neglecting their offspring, they preferred to hire females, whom they considered more regular than males in their work habits'.[22]

Indentured labour from India was used to replace slaves in many Caribbean territories. Throughout the period of indenture the attitude to women immigrants from India varied with the problems of recruitment and with the perceptions of the role of women in both production and reproduction by the plantocracy and the Imperial power. As Reddock[23] indicates 'contradictions continued

Table 7.2 Occupations of slaves in Kingston, St Vincent, 1817

Occupation	Number of slaves		Percentage of slaves	
	Male	Female	Male	Female
Domestics	297	751	28.3	71.7
Skilled trades	249	32	88.6	11.4
Transport	187	0	100.0	0
Retailers	0	25	0	100.0
Other	179	98	64.6	35.4
None	178	227	44.0	56.0
Unknown	12	8	60.0	40.0
Totals	1102	1141	49.1	50.9

Source: Adapted from Higman, B.W. 1984, 'Urban Slavery in the British Caribbean.' In E. Thomas — Hope (ed.) *Perspectives on Caribbean Regional Identity*. Monograph No. 11, Centre for Latin American Studies, University of Liverpool, pp. 49–50.

between the planters' short-term preference for adult male migration and their long-term need for a self-reproducing, cheap and stable labour force. Among the male Indian workers, their desire for docile, secluded and controllable women as befitted their aspirations for higher caste status, conflicted with the planters' need for women as labourers and the non-availability of women of the "right kind" for migration to the colonies'. Both Reddock[24] and Emmer[25] have shown for Trinidad and Surinam respectively that the women who left India to work in the Caribbean were more independent than most Indian women. Indenture was an escape route for many Brahmin widows and child-widows offering both the opportunity for re-marriage and for economic improvement. Only about one-third of the women who arrived from India were accompanied by husbands. These women did not easily accept the prevailing male orthodoxy of the British view of women as 'housewives' or the Indian insistence on the seclusion of women of high caste. Indenture gave Indian women an escape from poverty and a chance for emancipation but Emmer[26] demonstrates that most women married and retreated to the private sphere. In Surinam, in principle, workers of both sexes were given equal pay but in Trinidad women indentured workers were paid less per task than men, as were all women workers. Emmer[27] indicates that the average number of days worked per year by women in Surinam was a quarter to a third less than men, while Reddock[28] asserts that in Trinidad, despite pay differentials, some women managed to earn as much as men by working harder.

In general, indentured labourers of both sexes were treated as severely as slaves had been since many estate managers wished to extract the maximum returns from their investment in labour during the period of the contract.[29] There was little gender division of labour and women were expected to perform a wide range of tasks on the plantation. Harry[30] quotes a newspaper report based on interviews with three women who had been indentured in Trinidad in the late nineteenth century. According to their story:

> In the cultivation you will find that the women dominated the group. They were out early in the fields performing hazardous duties like dropping lime and phosphate of ammonia, planting foods on the estates, that is vegetable crops and ground provisions, manuring, cutlassing, weeding, cutting canes, loading them on carts, and most of the time carrying the canes on their heads.[31]

In addition to this field work, women were responsible for childcare, housework and general family maintenance. Thus, under forced labour there was very little differentiation of agricultural activities based on either gender or ethnicity.

Gender roles under a free labour system

Since the ending of apprenticeship and indenture, gender roles in West Indian peasant agriculture have been largely determined by two factors: family structure, and, to a lesser extent, type of agriculture. Women have had to accept responsibility for the financial support of their children since emancipation because of both male migration and male economic marginality. In 1970 the Commonwealth Caribbean had 238,781 female-headed households constituting 35 per cent of all households in the region.[32] The proportion of female-household heads displays both cultural and spatial variation, ranging from one-half amongst the highly migratory Afro-Caribbean population of St Kitts-Nevis to one-quarter in Trinidad and Tobago where the rural population is largely East Indian. That this pattern is of long standing is clear from Brodber's[33] study of the Jamaican free women in which she showed that second generation free women even when married, chose and could choose economic independence and autonomy.

Female members of Caribbean farm households may play three economic roles related to agriculture. They may be the decision maker or they may assist on their own family farm, providing subsistence for their household, they may market the surplus production of their own and other farm enterprises or they may join the rural proletariat and work as agricultural labourers on other small agricultural holdings or on plantations. These roles are not mutually exclusive and any one individual may move between the informal and the formal economy at different times of year or at various stages in her life cycle.

Women as peasant farmers

Peasantries in the Caribbean have grown up in the crevices of their societies, interdependent but in conflict with, the capitalist plantation economy.[34] In this situation it was perhaps inevitable that women, in their reproductive role, should play a major part in the peasant sector.

Census data on gender divisions of labour on small farms is not widely available and is subject to the usual caveats concerning the effect of enumerator's and interviewees attitudes on under-reporting of women's economic activity rates in agriculture.[35] Although the data presented in Table 7.3 for the Eastern Caribbean comes from a wide range of sources and is somewhat spotty in its coverage it is adequate to identify certain trends related to type of agriculture, inter-island variation and changes over time.

Female farming is most common on subsistence holdings and less so on those farm enterprises oriented towards commercial cropping, as the figures for St Lucia, Montserrat and Grenada in Table 7.3 show. In the large island of Trinidad there are several distinctive types of farming, and Harry[36] in her survey found that one-quarter of the rice and dairy farmers, 22 per cent of the cocoa farmers, 18 per cent of the vegetable farmers, 14 per cent of the tobacco and 13 per cent of the cane farmers were women. These differences are related to income, land ownership and type of farm work. Cane farmers had the highest levels of living and women provided the smallest amount of labour on these farms. Most cocoa farms were on freehold land and the women farmers in this group had generally inherited their land from their spouse. Tobacco and vegetable farms were predominantly on rented land. Female labour inputs were relatively high in rice and dairy farming.

Examination of the structural characteristics of farms operated by women shows that these farms are generally smaller, have poorer

Table 7.3   Sex of decision makers on farms of less than 10 acres in selected Eastern Caribbean territories

Island	Year of survey	Sample size	Percentage farms with female decision makers
Barbados	1963	207	53.1
Barbados	1987	146	23.9
Barbuda	1971-73	234	28.2
Grenada	1969	256	20.7
Grenada*	1969	214	18.7
Martinique	1964	203	35.5
Martinique	1981	17,919	20.0
Montserrat	1972	527	44.2
Montserrat	1983	125	32.1
Montserrat*	1973	60	36.6
Montserrat*	1985	136	27.9
Nevis	1950	205	29.2
Nevis	1979	91	30.8
Nevis	1985	407	38.3
St Lucia	1964	187	42.8
St Lucia	1980/81	7,520	23.0
St Lucia*	1971	47	17.0
St Lucia*	1984	152	15.8
St Vincent	1972	6,862	46.2
Trinidad	1979	80	28.8

*Sample drawn from commercial farmers only.
Source: Field surveys for Barbados, Martinique (1964), Nevis (1979), Montserrat (1973) and St Lucia (1964 and 1971). Data for St Vincent and Montserrat (1972) comes from the 1972 Agricultural Census. Data for Grenada from John S. Brierley *Small Farming in Grenada W I*, Winnipeg, 1974; for Barbuda from Riva Berleant-Schiller, 'Production and division of labor in a West Indian Peasant community', *American Ethnologist*, 4, 1977, pp. 253–272; and for Trinidad from I.S. Harry, *Women in Agriculture in Trinidad*, unpublished MSc thesis, University of Calgary, 1980. St Lucia 1980/81 and 1984 data supplied by Department of Agriculture, Castries. Montserrat (1983). Census of Agriculture, 1985 data supplied by Department of Agriculture, Plymouth. Nevis 1950 and 1985, Farmers on Land Settlements, data supplied by Department of Agriculture, Charlestown. Martinique, 1981, Recensement General de L'Agriculture, 1980–81, Martinique, SCEES, SRSA-DOM DDA Martinique, 1983.

quality land, are less accessible to markets and are less likely to include rented land than those operated by men. The structure and economic level of the female-headed household, which is commonly associated with these farms, gives rise to labour problems and to a dependence on the land for subsistence rather than for commercial production. Women appear to view the farm as an extension of their domestic reponsibilities, concentrating on subsistence production of food crops and small stock rather than on the export crops and cattle preferred by men. Sometimes, where the land is jointly operated, women may see the land as a source of economic independence from the male partner and thus may specialise in the production of fruit, herbs and vegetables which they can sell on the local market. The overall picture of female-operated farms is that of marginality in terms of capital, land and labour resources, and largely reflects the economic insecurity of the matrifocal household. However, the dominant characteristics of these farms vary from island to island indicating intra-regional differences in the availability of human and physical resources.[37]

On the whole the proportion of small farms operated by women has declined over the last two decades as the economic base of most islands has widened and alternative opportunities in the labour market have become available (Table 7.3). Only in the small, impoverished island of Nevis, of those islands for which time-series data is accessible, has this defeminisation of agriculture not occurred. Indeed, in Nevis it is not merely the case that women are maintaining their operation of the family farm but that women are also actively taking up vacant lots on government land settlements in order to grow food with which to feed their families.

Women in the agricultural labour force

In addition to their role as peasant farmers, women have continued to play an important role in the agricultural labour force, as they did in the days of slavery (Table 7.4). The decade following emancipation was marked by a rapid decline in the agricultural labour force, as the women and children among the ex-slaves moved into domestic occupations and education respectively and, where land was available, the men became peasant farmers. The economic difficulties of the mid-nineteenth century resulted in a slight increase in the rural proletariat but then followed a century of relative stability in the absolute numbers of agricultural workers in most parts of the Caribbean. The food shortages of the Second World War brought the agricultural workforce to its highest level since slavery but this

Table 7.4   *Occupation of farm workers, Dennery Estate, St Lucia, 1985*

	Number of workers		Percentage of workers		
Occupation	Male	Female	Male	Female	Total
Labourers	109	111	49.5	50.5	100
Field supervisors	20	-	100.0	0	100
Tractor drivers	5	-	100.0	0	100
Totals	134	111	54.7	45.3	100

Source: Agricultural Statistical Unit, St Lucia, 1985.

peak was followed by a rapid decline as alternative occupations became available to the proletariat.[38] Within this overall trend the participation rate of women fluctuated as women came to see themselves as a reserve labour force responding both to seasonal and to longer term shortages in agriculture.

In the late nineteenth century, as men left the poorer territories in search of economic opportunities overseas, the unskilled agriculture workforce became once more predominantly female as it had been in the later stages of slavery. Brizan indicates a ratio of 132 female to 100 male agricultural workers in Grenada at this time.[39] Even in Guyana where labour shortages were less marked than on the smaller islands the proportion of women agricultural labourers rose from 31 per cent in 1881 to 39 per cent in 1891 and 41 per cent in 1911.[40] In Jamaica, on the other hand, women dominated migration to the towns and so their participation rate in the agricultural labour force fell from 49.2 per cent in 1891 to 19.9 per cent in 1943.[41]

The postwar decline in the agricultural labour force was accompanied by a relative increase in the proportion of female workers, especially in the unpaid family worker category. These postwar changes support Boserup's theory that agriculture comes to depend increasingly on unpaid female family labour as the number of paid agricultural workers decreases. However, as the tourism and manufacturing sectors of the Caribbean economy expanded under the stimulus of investment by trans-national companies, agriculture became less important as an employer and women, especially the younger, better-educated ones, moved into these new growing sectors. By 1970 only about one-third of the workers in agriculture were women and the decline was most marked in Antigua where agriculture was very depressed (Table 7.5).

Table 7.5   Percentage of women in the agricultural labour force of selected Caribbean territories, 1946 to 1980

Territory	1946	1961	1970	1980
Antigua	47.6	59.2	25.3	N/A
Barbados	48.8	52.5	38.3	36.0
Dominica	40.4	55.0	32.8	N/A
Grenada	48.9	48.9	40.4	38.0
St Kitts-Nevis	44.0	44.4	33.8	N/A
St Lucia	39.3	47.0	29.9	35.0
St Vincent	46.9	49.9	31.8	41.0

Sources: *West Indian Census, 1946, Vol. 1*, (Kingston, Jamaica, 1950); *Agricultural Census of the West Indies, 1961, Eastern Caribbean Territories*, (Bridgetown, Barbados, 1968); *1970 Population Census of the Commonwealth Caribbean Vol. 4, Part 16*, (Kingston, Jamaica, 1976). 1980/81 *Population Census of the Commonwealth Caribbean*; *Barbados*, Vol. 1. Statistical Service, Barbados. 1985 Le Franc, E.R. 1980. 'Grenada, St Vincent and St Lucia', in *Small Farming in the Less Developed Countries of the Commonwealth Caribbean*, Barbados. Caribbean Development Bank, 1–143.

The most striking development in the West Indian labour force since 1970 has been the increased economic activity rate of women, and the service sector, in which women predominate, has superseded agriculture as the major employer in the region. Yet agricultural labouring remains the main source of income for poor, rural women and in addition, there is anecdotal evidence that high inflation during the 1970s has forced many women back into dependence on subsistence agriculture. Agricultural surveys in the Windward Islands during this period indicate a continuing and in some cases increasing participation rate for women (Table 7.5).

Le Franc[42] found that women in Grenada made up 50 per cent of the unpaid family workers but had declined from 40 to 38 per cent of the paid workers whereas in St Vincent and St Lucia their role had increased with women constituting 47 per cent of the unpaid workers and 41 per cent of the paid in St Vincent and 34 per cent of the unpaid and 35 per cent of the paid workers in St Lucia. In Barbados, although agriculture's share of employment almost halved between 1970 and 1980, the proportion of women workers fell only from 38 to 36 per cent.[43] In Montserrat, on the other hand, the absolute number of male agricultural workers increased between 1970 and 1980, and the number of women workers decreased so that the female percentage of the agricultural labour force declined markedly from 33.4 to 22.6, in response to male return migration and increased female employment opportunities in tourism and the textile industry.[44] It is clear that West Indian women today, in general, consider agriculture as an occupation of last resort to be followed only when there is no alternative way of feeding their families.

Gender divisions of labour time

The local context, household structure and stage in the domestic cycle are all important in determining the gender division of labour time in any particular area. However, there is considerable evidence that, in general, women have shorter resting hours, greater intensity and fragmentation of work and more frequent recourse to multiple simultaneous occupations than men.

Throughout the Caribbean women members of farm families work long hours. Knudson and Yates[45] in their survey of small-farming on St Lucia, found that women worked five to six hours a day on the farm, three to four hours on housework, two to five hours on childcare depending on the age of the children, and occasionally spent time on marketing. It is scarcely surprising that 22 per cent of the women in this survey felt they had no leisure time at all. In terms of farm work, the relative time input of men and women varies with the economic status of the farmer, the type of farming, seasons, the importance of off-farm employment and the sex of the farm operator. Both Edwards[46] working in Jamaica and Macmillan[47] in Trinidad found that women's labour input on the farm differed according to the male partner's economic status: in poor families women performed all field tasks but as prosperity increased dependence on female and child family labour declined. Harry[48] in her Trinidad survey found very little difference in the mean hours worked on the farm by men and women, with men averaging 4.9 days per week and women 4.8. Both sexes worked seven hours a day in the busy season and three hours in the quiet season. However, women worked longer hours than men in rice and vegetable farming while men put in longer hours on cane and tobacco farms. Men who had off-farm jobs worked fewer hours on the farm than average and women who operated their own farms worked five to seven days per week on the farm. In the Leeward Island of Nevis, on the other hand, there were distinct gender-based differences in the average hours worked and in the seasonal pattern of employment. On average, women worked the same number of days per week as in Trinidad, 4.8, but men put in 5.5 days. At the busiest time of the agricultural year women averaged 25 hours and men 35 hours per week, while in the quiet season women worked 18 hours compared to 27 hours for men.[49] Thus the weekly hours worked by women fell from 72 per cent of male hours in the busy season to 66 per cent in the quiet season suggesting that women form, to some degree, a reserve supply of labour for the farm to be drawn on at periods of peak demand.

Gender divisions of agricultural tasks

The allocation of tasks by gender has become gradually more marked. Under slavery both men and women carried out the full range of farming tasks in the field and divisions of labour were based more on age than on gender. This situation was still evident in Grenada in the 1930s when, as Brizan[50] comments, 'rural womenfolk were engaged in all agricultural activities pursued by men, in addition to their domestic chores.' Today gender differences largely conform with the pattern found by Murdock and Provost[51] in their cross-cultural sample of 185 societies. In general, as shown by field surveys in Nevis, Trinidad,[52] St Vincent (Table 7.6), and St Lucia (Table 7.7), women perform the less strenuous tasks such as planting, weeding, fertilising, moulding up of soil around young plants and harvesting. Men undertake the preparation of the soil, the hoeing or ploughing, and the transporting of the crop from the field. Some of these tasks are gender-neutral or interchangeable, especially harvesting and fertilising. Pest control is least likely to be undertaken by women because they feel that the use of chemical sprays is dangerous to them, especially when they are pregnant or lactating. Women farmers without available assistance from male relatives will hire male agricultural labourers for this task alone. Weeding is the task most often seen as suitable for women only, especially on tobacco and vegetable farms, but weeding and pruning is considered a masculine task for crops such as cocoa and bananas.

The gender division of labour associated with livestock is often considered to relate to the size of the animal, with men caring for large animals and women for small stock.[53] In the West Indies these gender divisions appear to be more closely linked to specific tasks and to the level of commercialisation of the particular animal. Yates' work in St Vincent and St Lucia revealed that the construction of sheds and fencing for stock, and the slaughter of animals are jobs

Table 7.6 Gender divisions of labour on small farms in St Vincent

Type of job	Percentage distribution of labour			
	Male	Female	Joint	Not applicable
Preparation of soil	90	5	5	0
Planting	28	40	32	0
Hoeing	85	8	7	0
Weeding	8	50	35	7
Pest control	23	5	2	70
Fertilising	43	35	22	0
Harvesting	22	13	65	0
Storage	2	3	2	93
Marketing	25	45	27	3
Keeping records	5	3	0	92
Care of livestock	23	10	59	8

Source: Adapted from a sample survey of small farms in St Vincent undertaken by Barbara Yates in 1981, Women and Development Unit, Barbados.

done only by men. Women help with daily care of farm animals and with the milking and collection of eggs and are responsible for the marketing of these products. In Trinidad men care for the beef cattle and the equines while women do much of the work with the dairy cattle and look after all other animals.[54] In Nevis, where sheep and goats are of major economic importance, men are normally in charge of all the animals, except poultry, and do all the marketing of animal products.[55] It would appear that in both Trinidad and Nevis it is the level of commercialisation of stock raising which determines gender roles, rather than the type of animal.

Rural women in the West Indies fulfill their roles within the constraints of household structure, occupational multiplicity, time and space. The presence of older children reduces the demand for the mother's labour in the fields and possibly may determine how far the family is able to market its agricultural produce. Younger children keep the mother tied closely to her private sphere of the home but many women develop home-based income-earning opportunities such as baking, sewing or store-keeping. Women are responsible for the dooryard garden of vegetables and herbs and for the poultry and pigs which are kept close to the house and fed on household scraps. Women are least likely to work in the most

Table 7.7   Gender divisions of labour on small farms in St Lucia

Type of job	Percentage distribution of labour		
	Male	Female	Joint
Preparation of soil	83	3	14
Planting	76	4	20
Weeding	48	17	35
Pest control	75	15	10
Fertilising	56	22	22
Harvesting	54	8	38
Storage	52	25	21
Marketing	48	37	25
Care of livestock	55	23	22

Source: Adapted from Tables III-13 and III-15 in *The Economic Role of Women in Small Scale Agriculture in the Eastern Caribbean — St Lucia*, by Barbara Knudson and Barbara Yates, Women and Development Unit, Barbados, 1981.

distant fields which are usually kept in tree crops or crops unlikely to suffer from praedial larceny and requiring little attention. These fields may be left uncultivated on farms operated by women if adequate family labour is not available.[56]

Conclusion

Under slavery roles in agriculture were differentiated according to strength rather than sex. Only in the last 50 years have agricultural wage rates reflected gender differences. Today most rural people feel that women's roles are changing, according to Yates' surveys in St Vincent and St Lucia. In Trinidad, Harry noted that the 'female coolie syndrome', with women working up to sixteen hours a day in the fields and the home from the age of 10, was disappearing with the improved educational attainment of young women and the new opportunities for non-farm female employment. Yet the traditional pattern of male-dominated gender relations is not changing[57] and as women expand their horizons and become more confident they find themselves unable to alter their domestic work patterns.[58] It is essential if West Indian peasant agriculture, which depends so heavily on women's work, is to become more efficient that the conflicts between women's productive and reproductive roles at the household level are reduced.

This examination of gender roles in the rural Caribbean has provided evidence that productive activities organised through the relations of reproduction, of kinship and of community, have existed under a range of economic systems, though often in hidden and invisible form and varying in time and space. These activities adjust, counter-balance or disintegrate under the effects of the decline or continuing structural absence of capitalist relations. It is hoped that this study has shown the necessity for setting technological and economic developments in their local and historical contexts and has refuted Boserup's reliance on the preservation of African cultural traditions as an explanation of the role of women in Caribbean agriculture.

Acknowledgements

Thanks are due to the Social Sciences and Humanities Council of Canada for funding the field work in 1979 and to the Nuffield Foundation for supporting the 1985 field work.

Notes

1   For a critique of Boserup's theoretical approach see L. Beneria and G. Sen. 1981, 'Accumulation, Reproduction and Women's Roles in Economic Development: Boserup Revisited.' *Signs*, Vol. 7, pp. 279–99.
2   See Boserup, 1970. *op. cit.* p. 63.
3   Eric Williams, *From Columbus to Castro*, p. 136.
4   Bryan Edwards, 1801, *op. cit.* Vol. II. pp. 106, 118.
5   For details of the slave sex ratio in the British Caribbean see Higman, 1976, pp. 67–69.
6   For an analysis of gender differences in slave physiology see Kiple, *op. cit.* p. 149.
7   *Ibid.*
8   Kiple, *op. cit.* pp. 110, 114.
9   See Morrissey, *op. cit.*
10 Bush, *op. cit.* suggests this interpretation after considering female resistance to slavery.
11 See Snell, 1980, for a discussion of female agricultural labour in England.
12 Orlando Patterson, 1967, p. 67.
13 See Rhoda Reddock in *Latin American Perspectives*, Vol. 12 (1), p. 65.
14 See Craton, 1977, in *Searching for the Invisible Man*, p. 142.
15 See Sheridan, 1974, *Sugar and slavery*, pp. 257–8.
16 See Lucille Mathurin, 1975, *The Rebel Woman*, p. 5.
17 See C. Levy, 1980, *Emancipation, sugar and federalism*, p. 10.
18 This situation is described in Mintz, 1964. Currency problems in eighteenth century Jamaica.
19 M.R. Edwards, 1980, provides an overview of the growth of higglering in the region.

20   See R.E. Pahl, 1984, for a review of changing gender divisions of labour in England.

21   H. Morsen, 1841, provides a contemporary description of post-emancipation changes.

22   See Levy, *op. cit.* p. 113.

23   See R. Reddock, 1985 in *Economic and Political Weekly*, p. 81.

24   R. Reddock, *Ibid*.

25   See R.C. Emmer, 1986.

26   *Ibid*.

27   See Emmer, *op. cit.* p. 257.

28   See R. Reddock, 1985 in *Economic and Political Weekly*.

29   See Lowenthal, 1972, *West Indian Societies*.

30   See Indra S. Harry, 1980 for a discussion of women's role in Trinidadian agriculture.

31   See the *Battlefront*, 1978, Vol. 2, 19 May, p. 7.

32   This is reported in Buvinic and Youssef, 1978, *op. cit.*

33   See E. Brodber, 1980, *op. cit.*

34   See S.W. Mintz, 1985, *op. cit.* pp. 127–154.

35   Dixon-Mueller discusses these problems in *Women's work in Third World agriculture*.

36   See I.S. Harry, 1980.

37   A detailed description of female operated farms is given in Henshall, 1981, *op. cit.*

38   For a survey of agricultural labour in the Eastern Caribbean see Momsen, 1969.

39   See George Brizan, 1985.

40   Reported in W. Rodney, 1981, *History of the Guyanese Working People*.

41   See Roberts, 1957, *op. cit.*

42   See E.R. Le Franc, 1980, *op. cit.*

43   *1980–81 Population Census of the Commonwealth Caribbean, Barbados*, 1985.

44   *1980–81 Population Census of the Commonwealth Caribbean, Montserrat*, 1984.

45   In their 1981 sample survey of St Lucia, Knudson and Yates provide considerable detail on gender roles.

46   See David Edwards. 1961.

47   See A.A. Macmillan's, 1967 study of market gardening in Trinidad.

48   See Harry, 1980, *op. cit.*

49   See J.D. Henshall (Momsen), 1984.

50   This is mentioned in George Brizan, 1979.

51   See Murdoch and Prevost, 1973.

52   Henshall, 1984, compares gender roles in Nevis and Trinidad.

53   This is described in Murdoch and Prevost, 1973.

54   Harry, 1980 provides further details on women farmers in Trinidad.

55   See Henshall, 1984.

56   See Vasantha Chase's 1986 paper on farming systems.

57   Henry and Wilson, 1975, discuss female status in the Caribbean.

58   See John, Elwin, Charles and Clarendon's 1983 report on a project in Dominica.

Labour Control and
Political Power

CHAPTER 8

Labour 'scarcity' and immigration in the Dominican Republic c.1875–c.1930

Harmannus Hoetink

In the western hemisphere, sugar cane was first introduced in the island of Hispaniola, and it was there that sugar plantations making use of slave labour were first established. The Dominican Republic on that same island, however, was the last of all Caribbean societies concerned to witness the introduction of modern, large-scale sugar plantations, a process which started there around 1875. That was half a century after the abolition of slavery (1822). Thus, the Dominican Republic is the only country in the region which lacks an historical coincidence, or even continuity, between slavery and a modern sugar economy.

Just as in Cuba and Puerto Rico, economic prosperity following the *Conquista* did not last long in Santo Domingo. After the middle of the sixteenth century, with a sharply decreased population living off the land, the colony remained for over two centuries outside the main currents of the international economy. Whereas in Cuba since the middle of the eighteenth century, and in Puerto Rico since the early nineteenth century, sugar cultivation, based on slavery and other forms of unfree labour, changed these islands' economic and social configurations, the abolition of slavery in Santo Domingo hardly affected a society where for a long time and for the most part, slavery had existed *de jure* rather than *de facto*.[1] Apart from the traditional sugar area west of the capital, where indeed some slave revolts occurred at the end of the eighteenth century, slavery had been characterised by comparatively paternalistic relations both in the towns and on the cattle ranches where slaves, by virtue of their work, had to be accorded a considerable freedom of movement.

For those, then, who in writing the history of the Caribbean let themselves be guided by the twin key-words of 'sugar' and (harsh) 'slavery', the Dominican period from 1650–1875 must look like a negligible and peripheral epoch. And those who wish to see a logical connection between the release from slavery and that from colonial domination, denoting both as 'epiphenomena'[2] will have to find a special place in their scheme for the Dominican Republic. Although

the country's independence resulted from secession from neighbouring 'black' Haiti (1844), and its economy was not yet shaped by
sugar and no longer marked by slavery, the Dominican Republic
none the less served as a hotbed of anti-Spanish activities directed
from the 1860s, at Cuba and Puerto Rico.

The exceptionally long period between the early sixteenth century's boom and the introduction of modern large-scale agriculture
in the latter part of the nineteenth century was a significant factor in
the island's development. In addition, the manifold repercussions
which the Haitian Revolution and its aftermath had on the Spanish
part of the island (culminating, after an ephemeral independence in
1821, in a unification under Haitian flag, 1822–1844, to be followed
by a number of Haitian invasions and a reannexation by Spain,
1861–1865) gave the evolution of the agrarian structure in the
Dominican Republic some highly specific features. Let us, by way of
illustration, briefly sketch this structure *circa* 1870.

Background to the agrarian structure of the Dominican Republic

There was, first of all, an exceptionally low density of population.
Between 1789 and 1819 the number of inhabitants is estimated to
have declined from 125,000 to 69,000. In 1871 it was reported to be
150,000. From then on, it began to grow and by the end of the
century it was approaching half a million. Some ten years later,
Schoenrich observed that with a density of 39.6 per square mile, the
country, while less than half as large as Cuba, had only a quarter of
that island's population and even though five times as large as
Puerto Rico it had only half the number of inhabitants of that
island.[3]

Nor was the sparse rural population tied to a few large land-
holdings. On the contrary, for most rural dwellers land was still an
abundant resource, possession of which did not yet serve as an
important indicator of social or economic prestige. In large parts of
the country, a peasantry had evolved dedicated to the production of
fruits and root-crops, and to pig-hunting; in the fertile north-central
Cibao valley, sugar, rice and bananas were cultivated for local
consumption. On part of their land in this area peasant-farmers also
grew tobacco and cacao for the internal and foreign markets. But
even in this large valley, the most densely populated of the Republic,
nine-tenths of the land was still uncultivated and shifting agriculture
was common. An orderly partition of the land by surveying and

division was only just beginning. The city of Santiago was the centre of the Cibao economy and, until the 1890s, the largest city of the country. Puerto Plata on the north coast was at this time the main port.

With its cities, its many small and middle-sized landholdings with their mixed production and its export of tobacco, the Cibao valley clearly was, prior to the introduction of the modern sugar estates, the politically and economically dominant region of the country. At a later stage, and partly as a reaction to the foreign influences associated with the sugar-complex, many distinctive elements of the Cibao *campesino* culture were adopted as national cultural attributes. A similar phenomenon can be observed with regard to the Cuban *guajiro* and the Puerto Rican *jíbaro* culture; the difference being, however, that the Cibao area, particularly its economy and regional culture, *remained* of vital importance to the country although losing its dominating role.[4]

The owners of the traditional sugar *trapiches* west of the capital (especially around Azua) did not own large tracts of land either: a plantation of 600 acres was considered exceptional, especially if it was well kept. Their number was increasing, however, in these years. Some of the sugar was exported, but most of it was sold within the country; in 1862 one could still see the owners bringing it on muleback to the capital city.[5] The largest private lands were in the eastern part of the country and dedicated—as were some of the westernmost valleys—to cattle raising. In the eighteenth century when the slave economy of French Saint-Domingue demanded large imports of food, much cattle was exported from these areas. Many of these ranches—called *hatos*—had been subjected to a process of fragmentation during which the *hato* as such—often with undefined boundaries—may have remained intact, but an ever increasing number of persons had come into possession of *acciones* (shares), which entitled them to the use or possession of parts of its lands. Such *terrenos comuneros*, it should be said, were not unknown in other parts of the country and may perhaps be seen as the result of a process of regression and deconcentration of the quasi-feudal land-holdings established in the early colonial period.

Private estates owned by one person and of more than ten thousand acres were scarce around 1870, as in this period, between one third and one quarter of all land belonged to the state. The Church, after the confiscation of its land during the Haitian occupation, had succeeded again in accumulating considerable properties. Another type of corporate ownership was the municipal *ejidos*, lands endowed by the state to a town at the moment of its foundation and which in time came to be considered the common property of its inhabitants. Around 1870 such *ejidos* were still cultivated by individual families according to their needs, or were rented out for relatively small sums. Yet large parts of the country were still covered by woods. Trees were cut and transported by river to northern ports such as Monte Cristi or to Santo Domingo in the south from where some exporting took place.

We may therefore distinguish three main economic regions in the years preceding the introduction of the large sugar estates: an eastern region, based on extensive cattle raising, with a very sparse population partly employed by a number of large *hateros* and partly eking out a precarious existence on the *terrenos comuneros*, the proprietary claims on which were based more on custom than on legal registration; a southwestern area along the coast where amidst a 'traditional' peasantry there could be found a few hundred small and middle-sized sugar farms where trapiches were used similar to those of the early colonial phase; and the Cibao valley where the *campesino* in the course of the century had concentrated more and more—but by no means exclusively—on the cultivation of tobacco (and cacao) and where consequently the ties with the international markets were strongest. If we complete this picture by pointing to the country's defective infrastructure—both in terms of communication and of political control—it becomes clear that even during the relatively stable period of the Haitian domination, efforts such as President Boyer's *Code Rural* (1826), intended to increase the island's agricultural production by drastically limiting the freedom of agricultural workers and their families, hardly had any effect on the Spanish speaking part of the island.

The effects of the development of plantations after 1875

The introduction of modern plantations since about 1875, as well as of large scale cultivation of coffee, cacao, bananas and other fruits in the Dominican Republic, can of course be linked to several external changes, the most important of which was the rapid growth of the nearby US market. As for the main crop, sugar, the accidental effect of the Cuban Ten Years' War prompted a number of Cuban entrepreneurs to move their capital and know-how to the Dominican Republic. Further (but here cause and effect are not easily disentangled), by the late 1870s a long period of civil war and revolution had come to an end; the dictatorship of Ulises Heureaux ('*El Pacificador*') until 1899 gave the country a stability it had not known since Independence.

Sugar exports increased dramatically, from nearly 6 million kg in 1881 to more than 20 million kg in 1889 and from nearly 50 million kg in 1905 to over 120 million kg in 1916. By 1920 they had reached nearly 160 million kg.[6] Following Del Castillo, we may divide the period 1870—1930 in two phases:

> A first, competitive phase, characterized by the predomin-ance of Dominican and foreign capitalists, by individual forms of enterprise, by a largely Dominican labour force, by the growth of a class of owners-producers of sugar cane, by the dynamic function of the (sugar) industry in estab-lishing new industrial and commercial enterprises, etc. A second, monopolistic phase, characterized by the pre-dominance of foreign capital, by corporate property due, typically, to the fusion of banking and industrial capital, by the existence of predominantly foreign labor force, by the bankruptcy of the *colonato* and independent commerce in favor of the sugar corporations and banking institutions (. . .) (I)n other words, the configuration of an enclave economy, a slow process, but accelerated by the North American occupation of 1916 (−1924).[7]

The Cuban and Dominican initiators of the modern sugar economy established themselves at first in the same coastal areas—near Puerto Plata, and around and west of the capital city—where traditionally smaller scale sugar farms had existed. Soon, however, they moved to the region around San Pedro de Macoris, east of the capital, which grew into a typical boom town. The lands in this area formed part of the old cattle raising region as was also the case with the large properties around La Romana which would be converted to cane fields during the phase of corporate expansion.

The demand for labour

In the first decade after the establishment of the new sugar estates, efforts were made to meet labour demand by attracting native workers. As late as 1884, of an estimated total of 6000 workers in the cane fields, only 500 were thought to be foreigners.[8] But in the previous year it had already been observed that 'the natives will be sufficient to do the work on the existing plantations, but in case the number of the latter increases, it will be indispensable to start the introduction of foreign laborers'.[9]

The local labour was recruited from among unemployed 'idlers' in the Southern cities, from woodcutters who, partly due to agricultural expansion, were losing their jobs, from the rural population in the eastern provinces whose *terrenos comuneros* were gradually being bought or acquired by fraudulent means by the new estates, and from among the population in the traditional sugar areas. There, after a period of co-existence, the old *trapiches* had to give up competition, their owners and personnel being absorbed in part by the new enterprises as employees or *colonos*. Many of these local workers were seasonal migrants who hired themselves out during the *zafra*, the harvesting season, after which they returned to their *conuco* and their family for the remainder of the year.

Rather than a massive abandonment of their lands, it was probably this mobility and its attendant neglect of the peasants' crops, which led to increasing complaints by the urban population (itself growing quickly in these years) about rising prices and temporary scarcity of local foodstuffs. Contemporary observers, such as Hostos, when reviewing in the 1880s the adverse effects of the expanding sugar economy on traditional rural production, focused primarily on two regions: the cattle raising east and the traditional sugar area in the southwest:

> The *ranchos* have almost been wiped out by excessively avaricious mass exports; the sugar presses that dotted the fields of the South like ants have continued to disappear rapidly, and the worker in all these regions has been abandoning his small-scale production in order to become an agent of large-scale production. That is a bad thing.[10]

He and other social critics writing in these years showed a keen awareness of the ultimate economic and political consequences of large-scale, foreign-dominated agri-business, but they may have exaggerated the impact of the new plantations on the Dominican peasantry in general, certainly during these early years. While land was appropriated and labour absorbed by the new enterprises, it proved impossible to reduce a sufficient number of *campesinos* to the condition of sugar proletarians, entirely deprived of other means of production, and thus forced to sell their labour to the *ingenio*.[11] Moreover, in the eastern part of the country, where sugar production increasingly took place, population was exceedingly scarce. To conclude of this nearly empty region that 'poor, yet independent peasant farmers were pushed from their land to become a pauperized, marginalized rural proletariat'[12] easily suggests a phenomenon of such massive proportions that, had it occurred, it would have meant the successful formation of a large and pliable native work force. In fact, this never took place.

The native work force proved to be anything but pliable. A decidedly high wage level had attracted it to the cane fields in these early years. When, however, a long crisis in the world markets started in the 1883–4 season, leading to a drastic wage reduction and to protest strikes, their willingness to work on the estates decreased considerably. Indeed, Del Castillo writes of the crisis of the 1880s as 'a determining factor in the progressive withdrawal of the Dominican workers'.[13] This 'scarcity' of local labour became a permanent feature of the Dominican Republic's sugar economy although the factors which caused it varied over time.

The scarcity of local labour

Well into the present century low rural population density, combined with easy access to cultivable land, was undoubtedly one of the major causes of this scarcity. Only real wages in the sugar sector, as high as those in the earliest years, could have overcome this problem. The low wages that this sector was prepared to offer from the middle of the 1880s onwards proved insufficient to lure the thousands of labourers that the expanding sugar acreage needed during the *zafra*.

Complaints about the 'idleness' of the Dominican workers were often voiced by interested parties. Yet such complaints were nothing but a recognition — under the veil of a prejudiced accusation — that other options were available to the local population. As William Bass, a large plantation owner, observed in the early twentieth century: 'The natural fertility of this country, in combination with the sparsity of its population and the vast areas of virgin lands, not claimed by anyone, allow the lowest class to live without (having to) look for work in any of the principal modern enterprises',[14] and in 1910 the British Consul confirmed that 'the native Dominicans can rarely be induced to work in the plantations'.[15] William Bass further observed that the Dominican workers insisted on work contracts per job (*por ajuste*) which were always preceded by long and arduous discussions with the plantations' overseers. He saw this as 'a silent recognition that the worker is able to impose his conditions on the owner'.[16]

That Dominicans did not necessarily avoid hard work, however, is shown by the preference they had for cutting trees and clearing land in preparation for new cane fields. This work of *tumba, quema* and *habite* was, again, carried out *por ajuste*. The fact that it paid better than cane-cutting surely explains a good part of the natives' preference, but one should also keep in mind that such slashing and burning was part of the *campesinos*' traditional work. It could be organised along traditional lines and was much more an integral part of the independent *campesino's* or *montero's* work culture than the strictly regimented, factory-like, massive work during the *zafra*. As long as the rural worker in need of cash money could hire himself out *por dia* or *por ajuste* in areas with other crops — or in the harbours, or at the building of roads or railroads — where the type, rhythm and organisation of work had more affinity with what he was used to, such elements would enter into his calculations. At a later stage another largely non-economic consideration may have begun to play a part. Since foreign labourers came to form the large majority of the *ingenios*' personnel, the closer association of 'sugar' with 'non-nationals' in popular opinion would not have increased the Dominican workers' disposition to join the sugar proletariat as long as they could avoid it.

The 'scarcity' of local labour may also be attributed to political factors. Repeatedly, the Dominican government tried to increase the local work force by force or persuasion. In the 1890s, actions against vagrants were announced and in 1906 and 1911 anti-vagrancy laws were promulgated. In 1908 it was decreed that labour contracts should be registered and that anti-social elements should be obliged to join the work force. A few years later, a publicity campaign was launched to persuade rural workers from all over the country to work for the *ingenios*.[17] All these efforts were to no avail. The Government was too weak to enforce effectively the measures that it announced. A system such as the *régimen de la libreta* (workbook system), whereby each man in his productive years had to carry a booklet in which the name of his current employer was registered, was enforceable in a relatively well-policed and well-administered colony such as nineteenth century Puerto Rico. But measures of this type were not viable in a country with recurrent chaotic political conditions, with a defective infrastructure and considerable parts of the population virtually outside the reach of central government. Governmental weakness was of course shown also, and *a fortiori*, in relation to the sugar interests which proved reluctant to abandon the system of seasonal immigration of foreign labour, once it had been set in motion. As early as 1912 a law was passed designed to restrict (black) immigration, but provisions were included enabling the *ingenios* to circumvent its effects. Subsequent intermittent cries for 'dominicanisation' of the sugar work force — especially vocal during the crisis of the 'twenties when high unemployment seemed incompatible with a 'scarcity' of local labour — again had hardly any impact. Only in 1933, a law aiming at a 70 per cent 'dominicanisation' of all enterprises (reminiscent of similar legislation in Cuba at the time, and born out of the same crisis-induced nationalistic fervour) was taken more seriously. Even though it provided some loopholes for the *ingenios*, this law had 'a positive impact and many *ingenios* — where Dominican personnel had been zero — incorporated national workers in not unimportant numbers'.[18] By then, of course, the crisis was severe, the population pressure had increased, and the country was in the grip of a dictatorship able to impose its will on workers and employers alike. To put these matters in perspective it should be noted that today, with a large part of the sugar industry (previously bought by Trujillo) in the hands of the state, both state and private estates depend for the *zafra* on the recruitment of some 15,000 seasonal Haitian migrants.

In considering the 'scarcity' of local workers for the sugar industry, we should finally and for completeness' sake, consider the factor of political will. What I should like to argue here is that although the central government undeniably became ever more strongly influenced by the sugar interests, as these grew to become of supreme economic importance to the nation, it did not become beholden to them to the same extent as was the case in those Caribbean countries where the whole fabric of society, the whole economy and virtually all arable soil were dominated by it. By pointing here again at the large and densely populated Cibao valley, I do not wish to suggest that its tobacco, coffee and cacao could measure up in volume of exports, or in size of its labour force, to those of the sugar area in the south and east. But the Cibao remained important. It had a stable peasantry and farmer class, it had prosperous cities, it had a strong sense of regional pride, it had an active civic life, and it produced a large number of well-trained professionals. Its leading strata — at times in alliance with those of other non-sugar regions — were apt to see themselves as defenders of the 'true' national interests and culture, as opposed to those of the sugar area whose capitalists were predominantly foreign.

Since a disproportionate number of the country's presidents and major politicians came — and still come — from the Cibao area, it is perhaps not too bold to suggest that the small room for governmental manoeuvring was at times used to foster interests not in line with those of the sugar enclave. The negative answer given in 1916 (just prior to the US occupation) by a minister of the 'Northern' president Jimenez to the powerful sugar planter J.B. Vicini, who had asked for permission to contract one thousand foreign workers for one of his estates, should be seen in this light. Thus '. . . paying good wages (to local workers), it seems to me, would resolve the problem'.[19] One might also speculate whether, even if the government had been strong enough to enforce legislation to that effect, the Cibao interests would not have opposed or sabotaged the forced recruitment of labour in their area because it would have deprived its economy of whatever labour surplus it had. We would do well, then, not to blindly equate the state, weak as it may have been, with sugar, strong as it was.

To sum up: the durable 'scarcity' of local labour for the sugar sector may be attributed to a mixture, varying over time, of such factors as low population density in combination with easy access to land, wages during most of the period under discussion too low to ease the culturally and socially difficult transition from peasant to cane-cutter, the government's lack of political power and control during much of the period and, possibly, at times government's lack of political will. What the governments of the day lacked in effective force and control, the sugar companies in 'their' region had in abundance, and they showed it in the way they went about appropriating lands needed for their expansion and in the treatment of their workers.

The sparse rural population, basing its claims on the use and custom of the *terrenos comuneros*, was easily convinced to sell, and often fell prey to fraudulent lawyers and speculators, not to mention ruthless actions on the part of the *ingenios*. In 1921, two hamlets 'which stood in the path' of Central La Romana's expanding fields, were burned to the ground; one hundred and fifty families were left homeless. A few years earlier a similar case had occurred on lands bought up by the North American-owned Consuelo estate.[20] In this period of US occupation, guerilla bands in the area, known as *gavilleros* (whose existence pre-dated, to be sure, the occupation, going back to the soldierly traditions of the cattle ranch *monteros*), started fighting the US military presence and some displaced peasants may well have joined them.[21] It was also during the US occupation that, after several earlier efforts, a Land Registration Law was promulgated which effectively put an end to the *terrenos comuneros* (1920). On the estates, the system of *vales* (vouchers) for the *bodegas* (company stores) became a common way to put the workers in debt, thus binding them to the *ingenio*. The first notice (1893) in the press about this system dealt not with the sugar estates but with a large banana plantation in the Northeast of the country. In a letter to the editor, a certain Marius complained that

> the peons, sons of the country, are treated like animals... Instead of paying them weekly or fortnightly, the fruit of their labour is arbitrarily withheld from them for a month or more, and as these unfortunate weaklings necessarily need some advances in order to buy their food, the company gives them on account a kind of paper money...so that they find themselves obliged to buy in the store that the Company has established and where they are sacrificed in the most undescribable, cruelest fashion.[22]

Reports made during the US occupation about conditions in the estates' *bateyes* and *barracones*—overcrowded, unsanitary, with 70 per cent of the Haitian labourers suffering from yaws, dysentery, leprosy, malaria and elephantiasis,[23]—unfortunately would not need much editing to make them up-to-date.

Immigration as a solution to the scarcity of local labour

This brings us back to the ways in which, since the late eighties, the need for foreign labour was met. The planters, who were in need of a pliable, low-wage experienced work force, not easily absorbed into the Dominican mass of peasants and semi-proletarians, saw seasonal migration from the small impoverished Eastern Caribbean as a perfect solution. In the view of the planter William Bass, the migrants

> would have to come from the French, Danish and English possessions, where they are already used to respect the authorities, their neighbors and the property of these. ... They would not form discontented political elements, and they would not intrude in the work and aspirations of Dominican citizens. One cannot argue that a foreigner working in a sugar *hacienda* would prevent a son of the country who only wants to work in a *conuco*, from earning a living.

As Del Castillo observes, Bass was looking for an experienced, well-disciplined worker with a reduced negotiating capacity due to a lack of economic alternatives.[24]

Efforts to attract other migrants had been made but were not too successful. According to Bryan, in 1882 the British government had been approached to allow migration from British India, but the request was denied.[25] Canary Islanders and Puerto Ricans did come to the country but perhaps lacked the qualities Bass and his colleagues were looking for. In 1892 a party of the recently-arrived Puerto Ricans returned home 'because they were labourers accustomed to the easy work of harvesting coffee'.[26]

By the end of the first decade of the present century, the mostly British-workers from the Eastern Caribbean already constituted the main work force on the large Eastern sugar estates; the seasonal migration of some 3,000–4,000 of them had become a routine affair in which the government took no part. They arrived at the end of October and started to leave in May. Most of them were first brought to St Thomas where contracts were signed with individual estates, who were themselves represented by the ships' captains. Others, however, upon arrival in San Pedro de Macorís, were free to select the *ingenio* of their choice.[27] The majority of these migrants came from St Kitts, Nevis and Anguilla. On the latter island, during some years, close to ninety per cent of the male population moved back and forth to the Dominican Republic. On behalf of such labourers, a complaint was lodged as early as 1899: 'Your Majesty's black and coloured subjects in the West Indies...have to choose between death from hunger in their native islands, and the suffering and bad treatment in Santo Domingo, where many have sought work since their own islands are only Islands of Death'.[28]

In 1910 the British Consul in the country stated politely that the British workers were receiving wages 'somewhat lower than the level of wages earned by the few natives willing to do this type of work'.[29] By the early 1920s, somewhat late in the day, the British colonial government opened an office in St Kitts 'to keep track of British contract labourers and to boycott estates (in the Dominican Republic) which had records of abusing their workers'.[30] In 1919 the US military government issued several decrees dealing with the migrant workers. The sugar estates were ordered to repatriate their contract labourers within a month after the end of the *zafra*. From now on, those who wished to stay on had to apply for a special permit. Simultaneously, the migrants were forbidden to leave the country before the expiration of their contracts and shipping agencies and ship captains were prohibited from offering passage to those who, with a residence permit, had resided less than a year in the country.[31] A few months later, no work contracts were allowed to be offered, for a period of two years, to either Dominicans or foreign workers, if the place of work would be outside their country of residence or citizenship; this decree clearly was directed against Cuban efforts to hire migrant labour in the Dominican Republic at a time when the sugar industry in both countries was booming. With these and similar measures—which often referred explicitly to 'non-Caucasian' immigrants—the US military government, with its effective apparatus of administration and control, was the first to monitor adequately migration and to regulate it to some extent. Such efforts at regulation in this period were, however, never at variance with the interests of the large sugar estates, by now mostly US owned.

Virtually from the start, the massive seasonal waves of foreign migration had met with critical responses from at least three sides. First there was a feeling of uneasiness among the national political élite, which according to José del Castillo especially resented the weakening of their traditional clientelist base of political support in the sugar area. Second, there were frequent protests from the commercial sector which deplored not only the hold of the company-stores over the sugar workers, or the increasing successes of recently arrived 'Turkish' vendors but also, and perhaps especially, the circumstance that large amounts of money saved by the migrant workers left the country each year instead of being spent there. Finally, there were intermittent complaints from, or on behalf of, the Dominican working class whose power of negotiation was weakened by the presence of foreigners willing to work for low wages.

All these three sectors also expressed at one time or another their preoccupations and criticisms in xenophobic or frankly 'racist' terms, emphasising the impact the massive presence of foreigners was to have on national culture and 'racial' composition. In 1911 there were demonstrations against foreign workers on some of the largest estates, and in 1915 just-arrived workers from Anguilla were met with disturbances, instigated by a newly-formed association professing to defend the interests of the Dominican workers.[32] It was occurrences such as these which prompted the passing in 1912 of a law which was meant to limit 'non-Caucasian' immigration to cases of *utilidad general* (public interest) but of whose provisions the large estates were generally exempted. The average annual number of authorised seasonal immigrants during 1912–1920 was nearly 5,000, and during 1921–1928 it was close to 7,000.

There were, furthermore, many sugar workers among those foreigners (some 22,000 in 1919 alone) who opted for permanent residence, and there was a steady stream of illegal immigration. If we compare these figures with the total work force in the sugar sector, estimated at 15,000 in 1915, we may get a rough idea of the importance of foreign labour in these years.[33] During the second decade of the century, the composition of foreign labour started to change. Haitian immigration, although never absent, increased from 1916, when both Haiti (since 1915) and the Dominican Republic were occupied by the US marines. The precipitous fall of sugar prices in 1920, initiating a crisis which would virtually last until the Second World War, only accelerated the rhythm of Haitian immigration. British West Indians, though still arriving for each *zafra*—until legislation in the early 1930s prohibited this—came in smaller numbers, finding it hard to accept the ever lower wages, especially in view of the fact that better paying alternatives were opening up at the newly established refineries in Curaçao and Aruba.

Conclusion

Looking back at the period under discussion we may conclude that the early efforts to 'catch' the Dominican peasantry in sufficient numbers to satisfy the need of a rapidly expanding sugar industry proved unsuccessful. Neither the relatively high wage levels up to the crisis of the 1880s, nor the efforts at recruitment by force had the desired effects. Migrations to the new sugar area, both seasonal and permanent, did take place both from the eastern provinces and from the southwest, and had an adverse effect on the production of traditional food for the rapidly growing urban population, but such spontaneous migrations were not enough to satisfy the increasing demand for labour during the *zafra*. Once the crisis of the 1880s had made itself felt in a drastic lowering of wages, a process of 'withdrawal' of the native cane cutters began. Of course, such withdrawal was never absolute, but it was large enough to convince the sugar growers of the need for foreign labour. Dominicans remained interested, though, in the better-paid 'piece'-work of preparing lands for new sugar cultivation. Increasingly, middle-range jobs such as overseer or technician also came into Dominican hands. Owners of small traditional *trapiches* often became *colonos* first, only to lose their lands to the sugar corporations during one of the recurrent crises, especially that of the 1920s. The two major crises also marked the main changes in labour supply: that of the 1880s brought about the seasonal migration from the small eastern—mostly British—Caribbean, that of the 1920s fostered a preponderance of Haitian migrants.

The recruitment of cane cutters from nearby islands, and the negative reactions against this foreign presence, culminated in nationalist legislation and forced repatriation in the 1930s. These are but a few of the many parallel developments in twentieth century Cuba and the Dominican Republic. The two countries' competitive positions were not, however, identical. The presence of cheap and virtually empty land probably gave the emergent modern sugar industry in the Dominican Republic a competitive edge against such neighbours as Cuba and Puerto Rico as well as other, more distant sugar producers, and this consideration may well have influenced the pioneering capitalists of the 1870s. Soon, however, political interventions in the pricing and marketing mechanisms began to harm the country's position. After 1879, Hawaiian sugar had free access to the US market; for Puerto Rico sugar this was the case from 1901, and for sugar from the Philippines from 1909. From 1902 Cuba profited from a 20 per cent reduction in import duties for its unrefined sugar. The Dominican Republic, on the other hand, only started to participate significantly in the preferential sugar quota system of the United States in the early 1960s when, as part of the economic sanctions against Cuba, that island's quota was divided among several countries.[34] During this long period of comparative disadvantage the Dominican sugar growers' insistence on the necessity for the lowest possible wage level can only have increased. Nearby Haitian labour, the cheapest in the region, remains until today the mainstay of the Dominican sugar industry.

Notes

1   Juan Bosch, *Composición social Dominicana: historia e interpretación*, (Santo Domingo, 1970), p. 96.
2   Gordon K. Lewis, *Main Currents in Caribbean Thought: The Historical Evolution of Caribbean Society in its Ideological Aspects 1492–1900*, (Baltimore, 1983), p. 239.
3   Otto Schoenrich, *Santo Domingo, un país con futuro*, (Santo Domingo, 1979) transl. of *Santo Domingo, a Country with a Future*, (New York, 1918), cited in José del Castillo, *La inmigración de braceros azucareros en la República Dominicana 1900–1930*, Cuadernos del Centro de Investigaciones Antropológicas (CENDIA), Vol. CCLXII, No. 7 (Santo Domingo, no date), p. 29.
4   H. Hoetink, 'El Cibao 1844–1900: Su aportación a la formación social de la República,' *Eme Eme: Estudios Dominicanos*, 48 (mayo-junio 1980), p. 17.
5   See H. Hoetink, *The Dominican People 1850–1900: Notes for a Historical Sociology*, (Baltimore, 1982), p. 4 ff, and Del Castillo, *La Inmigración de Braceros*, p. 27.
6   Patrick E. Bryan, 'La cuestión obrera en la industria azucarera de la

República Dominicana a finales del siglo IXX y principios del siglo XX', *Eme Eme: Estudios Dominicanos*, 41 (marzo-abril 1979), p. 58.

7   Del Castillo, *La inmigración de braceros*, p. 7. All translations from the Spanish are mine.

8   E.M. de Hostos, 'Falsa alarma, crísis agrícola' in Emilio Rodríguez Demorizi (ed.), *Hostos en Santo Domingo*, (Ciudad Trujillo, 1939), p. 160.

9   Bryan, 'La cuestión obrera', p. 58.

10 Cited in Hoetink, *The Dominican People*, p. 12.

11 Del Castillo, *La inmigración de braceros*, p. 6.

12 Bruce J. Calder, 'The Dominican Turn Toward Sugar', *Caribbean Review*, X (Summer, 1981), p. 18.

13 Del Castillo, *La inmigración de braceros*, p. 31.

14 Del Castillo, *La inmigración de braceros*, p. 34.

15 Bryan, 'La cuestión obrera', p. 66.

16 Del Castillo, *La inmigración de braceros*, p. 36.

17 Bryan, 'La cuestión obrera', pp. 59−60.

18 José del Castillo, *Ensayos de sociología Dominicana*, (Santo Domingo, 1981), p. 128.

19 Del Castillo, *La inmigración de braceros*, p. 46.

20 Calder, 'The Dominican Turn Toward Sugar', p. 44.

21 Calder, 'The Dominican Turn Toward Sugar', p. 20.

22 Hoetink, *The Dominican People*, p. 15.

23 Calder, 'The Dominican Turn Toward Sugar', p. 20.

24 Del Castillo, *La inmigración de braceros*, p. 36.

25 Bryan, 'La cuestión obrera', p. 61.

26 Del Castillo, *La inmigración de braceros*, p. 33.

27 Del Castillo, *La inmigración de braceros*, p. 41.

28 Bryan, 'La cuestión obrera', p. 65.

29 Bryan, 'La cuestión obrera', p. 66.

30 Calder, 'The Dominican Turn Toward Sugar', p. 21.

31 Del Castillo, *La inmigración de braceros*, p. 47.

32 Bryan, 'La cuestión obrera', p. 69.

33 See Del Castillo, *La inmigración de braceros*.

34 Del Castillo, *Ensayos de sociología Dominicana*, p. 107.

CHAPTER 9

The Dominican working class: Labour control under Trujillo and after

Rosario Espinal

Modern authoritarianism has been linked to modernisation in various ways. Authoritarianism has been associated with the existence of a weak bourgeoisie or a 'weak bourgeois impulse' as Moore once said, and to the failure of the most modern sectors of society (those linked to industrialisation) to push forward industrialisation and modernisation from below without a strong alliance with the traditional agrarian classes.[1] The cases of Germany and Japan are quoted as examples of modernisation from above of a reactionary nature.[2] Authoritarianism has also been linked to revolutionary processes in 'backward' (i.e. pre-industrial) societies as in the cases of Russia and China.[3] Authoritarianism and modernisation have also been related in the case of societies that suddenly confront the challenge of modernisation 'from behind' without a revolutionary breakthrough of a socialist kind. This would be the case with many Latin American countries, including the Dominican Republic.[4]

Various studies have shown that the form and content of various 'authoritarianisms' differ, despite their similarities. In the first case mentioned above, fascism was the type of authoritarianism. In the second case, it was the dictatorship of the proletariat. And, in the third case, the variety of authoritarian experiences ranged from the old-type personalistic dictatorships such as Generalissimo Rafael Trujillo's, the Dominican dictator assassinated in 1961, to corporatist-populist or bureaucratic-authoritarian regimes.

For these 'authoritarianisms', society has meant different things whether the rulers have mobilised it, restrained it, or suppressed it. For instance, when one compares the most advanced economies of Latin America (primarily those of the South) with the less advanced (primarily those of the Caribbean and Central America), one finds that in the former case, the expansion and diversification of the market economy, which resulted from the expansion of import-substitution industrialisation in the first half of this century, led to more redistributive social arrangements and more competitive politics.[5] These are regimes of 'incorporation' of sectors of the dominant and subordinated classes linked to the urban-industrial economy,[6] which students of Latin American politics have labelled 'populism'.[7] On the other hand, dictatorships such as Trujillo's, which emerged in less advanced economies linked to the international market through a single crop (e.g. sugar, coffee, bananas) and highly controlled by foreign capital, were exclusionist in their political projects.

This chapter identifies two different strategies of labour control in the Dominican Republic, which have been instituted at different times or historical periods. The first one consists of 'exclusion through a corporatist subordination without incorporation or mobilisation', as in the case of the Trujillo regime. The second consists of 'exclusion through fragmentation', as has been the case during the post-Trujillo period.

Labour under Trujillo

The expansion and diversification of the Dominican economy throughout the first half of this century resulted in an expansion of wage-labour. Up until the 1930s, the working class was mostly made up of sugar workers. They constituted a mixture of industrial workers (those linked to the industrialisation of sugar cane) and agricultural or field workers (those involved in the cultivation of sugar cane). Given that most of the data available do not differentiate between these two groups of workers, the discussion will be pursued without making the necessary specifications about the heterogeneity of this labour force. It is important to keep in mind, however, that the unique condition of this labour force was tied both to industry and agriculture by the same product. This was different from other enclaves in the region where the main export product was an agricultural one (e.g. bananas). Sugar enclaves created from very early on both an agricultural and an industrial working class. These workers were either former peasants who had lost their land in the process of spoliation that took place at the turn of the century, which was accelerated during the US occupation of 1916, or immigrants from other Caribbean islands.

From the late 1930s, the number of wage-labourers increased in both the sugar and non-sugar industrial sector.[8] The post-Depression years, and primarily the Second World War, had brought about an increasing demand for basic export products, which in turn produced a surplus from international trade. This surplus was used to promote the expansion of import-substitution industrialisation, which brought about the diversification of the labour force. Thus, although the Dominican Republic had a working class since the turn of the century linked to the sugar economy, it was the new industrialisation for the internal market which accounted for the diversification of the labour force. It should be noted here that this process of economic transformation was highly manipulated and monopolised by Trujillo, including both the new import-substitution industrialisation and the traditional export economy which up to then had been largely controlled by foreign capital.[9]

Before 1930 there were some guilds, but a working class movement had not yet emerged. However, as wage-labour expanded, the government began enacting labour laws in the 1930s, continuing to do so into the 1940s and 1950s. In 1934, laws were passed concerning payment of agricultural workers. In 1940, the first minimum wage law was passed and the National Committee on Wages created. And in 1942, the Constitution was amended to allow for labour legislation to be enacted on work-hours, wages, vacations, and social security.[10] During the 1930s no major industrial action took place. These were years of terror and consolidation of the Trujillo dictatorship through the elimination of the opposition and the monopolisation of state power.

The 1940s were somewhat different for labour. The government continued enacting labour laws, but there was also an awakening of the working class. Union activism was expressed from the early 1940s in a series of strikes which were organised by sugar workers in the eastern part of the country, where production was heavily concentrated. The first major strike was organised in 1942 in La Romana, a province of the eastern region. Later, in 1945, sugar workers organised the first general strike in the region, which was repeated in January, 1946. The basic demands were an increase in wages, regulation of working-hours, and a reduction of the work-load. As a result of this unrest, wages were increased. Due to the rate of inflation of those years (1942–1947), the increase in real wages was much more moderate than the increase in the nominal wages. As indicated in Table 9.1, this was the case for sugar workers who were the majority of the labour force. Non-sugar workers did, however, increase their purchasing power. It is interesting to note for the purpose of political analysis that the opposition to Trujillo eventually emerged in the larger urban areas where the standard of living was higher than in the rest of the country.

At a time of an economic boom as a result of favourable international trade, the immediate reaction of the government was to make concessions to workers. Once the increase in wages, however,

Table 9.1   Mean annual salaries in the sugar and non-sugar industries

Year	Consumer price index (1953—100)	Salaries in the sugar sector		Salaries in the non-sugar sector (Dominican pesos)	
		Nominal	Real	Nominal	Real
1942	51	198[a]	388	202	396
1943	63	243	386	192	305
1944	73	272	373	191	262
1945	76	297	391	248	326
1946	85	359	422	331	389
1947	96	431	449	395	411
1948	97	455	469	490	505
1949	93	409	440	484	520
1950	93	344	370	518	557
1951	100	365	365	502	502
1952	101	442	438	555	550
1953	100	428	428	540	540
1954	98	397	405	533	544
1955	98	394	402	526	537
1956	99	365	369	633	639
1957	104	359	345	642	617
1958	102	372	365	619	607
1959	102	369	362	691	677
1960	98	324	331	720	735

a   The nominal annual salary was calculated based on the number of
    workers employed for each year and the total amount of salaries
    paid. Thus, the mean annual salary is per worker.

Sources: Consumer price index from the *Statistical Yearbook*, 1958
and 1961, United Nations.
Estadística Industrial, Oficina Nacional de Estadística, Santo Domingo.

was allowed, the subsequent reaction was to curtail union activity
through repression.[11] The main leaders were killed, jailed or exiled.
Also, the Dominican Labor Confederation (CTD) was reorganised
under official leadership at the very beginning of the labour struggles
in the early 1940s. The CTD had been created in 1929, but did not
play any major role during the first years of the regime. However,
in the early 1940s, the government granted official status to the

organisation, and the governor of each province was appointed
president ex-officio of the provincial labour federation.[12] Although
this official recognition would fit the criteria of 'state corporatism' as
defined by Schmitter,[13] in the sense that the CTD received state
recognition to represent the working class, it did not reflect a policy
of incorporation of a mass-based working class movement. It is
difficult to know precisely how many unions existed at the time in
order to substantiate this argument. The records available at the
Labour Ministry, beginning with 1956, show that there were very
few unions officially registered. Furthermore, soon after the fall of
Trujillo in 1961, the CTD disappeared and a much larger number of
unions were registered (Table 9.2). One can assume that without
strong roots in the working class, the CTD was not able to survive
the process of political change and labour activism sweeping the
country in the early 1960s. In 30 years of dictatorship, the labour
movement was only once able to organise a significant struggle for
better working conditions (1942−1946). Apart from that period,
rule was imposed from above. Besides repression, the government
continued introducing labour laws, culminating with the approval of
the Labour code in 1951.

Unlike other Latin American countries with experience of
working class mobilisation and incorporation, such as populist regimes
in South America, the Trujillo regime, despite the laws enacted and

Table 9.2 *Number of unions registered at the Labour Ministry
1956−1965*

Year	Number of unions
1956	2
1957	2
1958	7
1959	4
1960	14
1961	13
1962	145
1963	53
1964	18
1965	11

Source: Official records from the Labour Ministry (Unpublished).

the concessions made concerning wage increases in the mid-1940s, was far from having the working class as a 'support-class'. Despite the growth of the economy, and the surplus accumulated from foreign trade during the post-war years, the majority of workers concentrated in the sugar sector did not experience significant improvements in their living conditions.

There is no doubt that Trujillo ruled by force. There is plenty of personal testimony and academic information illustrating this.[14] Besides the use of coercion, however, the explanation for the limited working class mobilisation and/or incorporation may be related to two other factors. One was the limited development of capitalism when Trujillo came to power, which allowed him to consolidate his position without having to integrate specific social classes linked to the process of industrialisation, whether the bourgeoisie or the working class. The other was the social fragmentation of the sugar labour force, which made up the majority of the working class at the time. This was due to the different working conditions of field (agricultural) and factory (industrial) workers, and to the presence of immigrant workers from elsewhere in the Caribbean, who frequently did not speak the language of the natives. One may argue that the dispersal of sugar workers may have worked against the possibility of organising collective action, which is essential for class mobilisation and unification. In the case of migrant labour, one is faced with a widespread problem on this question: due to the more limited civil and political protection granted to migrant workers, political action (and therefore class action) becomes more difficult. When migrant workers speak a different language, this may exacerbate the position. Although a lengthy discussion on the question of race and ethnicity is not a central theme of this paper, it should be mentioned that in the Dominican Republic, there has been a history of social differentiation based on colour and its linkage to sugar production. One could put forward the argument that at the level of the dominant political culture, a differentiation is made between the black immigrant who traditionally has worked in the sugar field (who has 'cut the sugar cane' as it is said by Dominicans) and the rest of the population. Also, besides colour, language has been the other element used to differentiate between social strata. Those who are black, work in the sugar sector, and do not speak Spanish or do so in a 'funny' way belong to the lowest stratum in Dominican society, and are regarded as such by most of the population. Given this 'socially accepted' status of these immigrants, there has never been a strong movement seeking the incorporation and participation of this sector of society in the political process.

Labour after Trujillo: The incipient unionism

Unilke the 1920s and 1930s when Trujillo emerged as a ruler and consolidated his power, by the early 1960s the Dominican economy and social structures were more complex. Instead of *caudillos* as competing political figures, there were more clearly defined classes with varying strengths and weaknesses and various interests. Instead of only peasants and a tiny oligarchy of local and foreign entrepreneurs, there was an expanded urban population which increased from 16.6 per cent in 1920 to 30.5 per cent in 1960. The size of the working class had more than tripled from the 1930s to the 1960s, and the labour force was more diversified as a result of the initiation of import-substitution industrialisation. At the time when Trujillo was killed, however, (1961) there were very few civil and political organisations. Thus, an immediate reaction after the fall of the dictatorship was to promote the organisation of different civil and political groups such as political parties, unions and business associations.

Political parties were the first to emerge and, through them, trade unions began to be organised with links to specific political organisations. The first labour federation of the post-Trujillo period was the United Labor for Independent Unions (FOUPSA), formed in 1961. FOUPSA was backed by the major political parties opposed to Trujillo, both the National Civil Front (UCN) and the Dominican Revolutionary Party (PRD). FOUPSA played an important role in the organisation of trade unions, which was reflected in the registration and certification of a number of unions in 1962 (see Table 9.2). FOUPSA however, soon split, and a faction sided with the US union movement. Other labour confederations formed at the time were the Autonomous Confederation of Christian Unions (CASC), linked to the Christian Democratic Party (PRSC), and the Labor Confederation of Dominican Workers (CESITRADO) which had leftist leanings. There were not, however, any workers' parties, as neither of these confederations were labour organisations officially affiliated to a particular party or government. For instance, the PRD, traditionally strong in areas with large working class and low-income urban groups, has always claimed to be a 'multiclass' party.

All through the early 1960s, the working class, along with other sectors of society, were after 'social recognition', or in Bendix's words with an 'extension of citizenship'.[15] This process involved a struggle centred around a variety of issues such as political freedom, as expressed by the right to free elections and the right to organise, and corporate interests, such as salary increases and the right to bargain. This fusion between political struggle and corporate struggle was a feature of the incipient labour movement after 30 years of an exclusionary dictatorship. Two main conditions account for this fusion. First, unions were born in close connection with the expansion of political parties at the outset of the fall of Trujillo. Second, the labour movement began to grow and consolidate in the context of a general struggle for civil and political rights. These rights had been denied in the past not only to the working class, but to most of society. Thus, the incipient labour movement was involved not only in a struggle for better wages and working conditions, but also in a struggle against the remnants of the Trujillo regime and for the construction of alternative politics.

Besides the struggle for political rights, the question of wages was central to labour. Public employees and urban workers were particularly active in the struggle for better wages. Salaries went up in the early 1960s in real terms, but the government reacted quickly to curtail the activities of both public and private workers. In 1902, the Council of State enacted laws banning strikes in the public sector. It also added more conditions to the ones already in existence making strikes illegal if the strike had a political motive or if the reason for the strike was mere solidarity (Law No. 5915 of 1962). These regulations constraining union activity were a setback for the incipient labour movement. They helped to tie unions more closely to political parties, as they fought together against the various governments that ruled the country in the early 1960s.

In 1964 the government that followed the election of the Dominican Revolutionary Party which had been overthrown in a coup in 1963, passed two resolutions regulating the formation of unions, labour federations and confederations. Both resolutions (8/64 and 15/64) set higher standards of supervision on the part of the Labour Ministry over labour organisations. Resolution 8/64 set procedures to verify the validity of signatures endorsing the formation of a union and made it compulsory for all labour organisations to register monthly at the Labour Ministry any change in their structure and composition. Resolution 15/64 set the number of unions that were required to form a federation and the number of federations required to form a confederation. Up until then, the process of formation of unions, labour federations and confederations had been flexible, and the activism of the labour movement since 1961 had made supervision and control by the Labour Ministry very difficult. In 1964, the *de facto* government that followed the coup of 1963 began promoting rival unions. The most relevant case at the time was the division of the Dock Workers' Union of Santo Domingo (POASI). This policy was pursued by Joaquín Balaguer after he gained power in 1966.

In summary, it can be said that the incipient labour movement was closely tied to various political parties, most of which were small and weak, and to international organisations with different ideologies. While in 1961 the organisation of workers was promoted by FOUPSA, by 1963 there were already five different so-called 'labour confederations' claiming to represent the working class. By 1965, the number had come down to three as some amalgamated or were dismantled: FOUPSA-CESITRADO amalgamated and were linked to the centre-left of the political spectrum (the PRD and some Marxist organisations); CONATRAL (the National Trade Union Confederation of Free Workers) was linked to the US labour movement; and the CASC was linked to the Christian Democrats. Thereafter, labour confederations have been dismantled, amalgamated, reconstructed, and created anew. These changes have been related to the political upheavals of the last decades, and the various parties and political ideologies that have flourished.

The institutionalisation of labour fragmentation

Once the government headed by Joaquín Balaguer was installed in 1966, the main objectives of labour policy were to demobilise the incipient labour movement and to minimise overt class conflict[16] in order to guarantee higher levels of accumulation to investors. To facilitate the analysis of labour policy, the basic mechanisms utilised to achieve those goals are classified in two categories: institutional and coercive mechanisms of labour control. The former refer to those measures based on legal provisions or facilitated by these provisions. The latter refer to those measures that derive from the repressive capacity of the state as the institution in society with a legitimate monopoly of the means of coercion. In order to illustrate how these mechanisms were utilised, the following discussion is based on case studies. In so doing one has to be aware of the fact that precise and definite information cannot be provided, since there are no systematic records on these issues. For instance, there is no quantitative information available to determine how widespread was the implementation of these mechanisms. Thus, we have to rely on newspaper information in order to reconstruct what happened to organised labour.[17]

a) Wage policies were central in the regulation of labour-capital relations during the Balaguer regime, and they helped to neutralise the bargaining capacity of labour on legal grounds. The Austerity Law (Law No. 1) of July 1966 froze all wages in the public and private sectors and set the minimum wage at 60 pesos a month. The only nationwide increase of the minimum wage during the Balaguer regime (1966–1978) took place in 1974, when the minimum wage was increased by about 50 per cent. Earlier modifications of the Austerity Law consisted of allowing collective negotiation to take place in the case of businesses that declared a profit and whose 'nature' permitted wage increases. The law (Law No. 478 of 1969) did not specify, however, what was meant by the 'nature' of the business. Furthermore, the Labour Ministry had to agree in each individual case on the viability of wage negotiations. Thus, the law made collective negotiation possible only when employers and the government decided to do so. This shows that the austerity laws set not only restrictions concerning wage levels, but also restrictions upon the conditions under which collective negotiations were possible.

Wage control policies had both economic and political implications. On the economic side they guaranteed low and stable salaries to investors. However, they resulted in the deterioration of the purchasing power of the working class (Tables 9.3 and 9.4). It is important to note here that the decline in real salaries during the 1970s took place at a time of high rates of growth of the Gross

Table 9.3   *Minimum wages in the city of Santo Domingo*

Year	Nominal wage	Price index 1969–100	Real wage (Monthly salaries in pesos)
1966	60	98	61
1967	60	100	60
1968	60	102	59
1969	60	100	60
1970	60	105	57
1971	60	108	56
1972	60	117	51
1973	60	134	45
1974	60	152	39
1975	95	174	55
1976	95	189	51
1977	95	212	49
1978	95	219	43

Source: Calculations based on basic information from the nominal wage set by the austerity laws and the price-index from *República Dominicana en Cifras,* National Bureau of Statistics, 1980.

Table 9.4 *Average annual salaries in the industrial sector*[a]

Year	Price Index[b] 1969–100	Real salaries (In pesos)
1964	101	1,005
1965	100	968
1966	98	927
1967	100	746
1968	102	813
1969	100	954
1970	105	880
1971	108	874
1972	117	870
1973	134	747
1974	152	751
1975	174	906
1976	189	1,028
1977	212	857

a   It includes not only manual workers but all employees as well.
b   Calculations of the price index are based on the city of Santo Domingo.
Source: Calculations based on industrial statistics, *Estadística Industrial*, National Bureau of Statistics

Domestic Product (GDP), particularly in the manufacturing and construction sectors.[18] On the political side, they reduced the possibilities of labour conflicts over wages since the austerity law declared illegal all labour actions concerning struggles for better wages. In other words, the austerity law minimised overt class conflict on legal grounds.

b)   The formation of rivals was also a mechanism utilised to weaken the most active and powerful unions, especially those difficult to transform from within. In these efforts, the regulations of the labour code concerning the formation of unions facilitated these anti-labour moves. The code established that 20 workers, who either work at the same plant or share the same occupation, had to agree to form a union so both the government and the private sector were able to promote the fragmentation of the labour movement on legal grounds. An important example of this action was the case of the Unified Trade Union of Central Romana (the union of a large sugar company owned—at the time—by Gulf and Western). During the early 1960s, the union had become the largest and best organised in the country, and was linked politically to the PRD and the Marxist left. In 1965, prior to the Civil War, the union had organised a major National Labour Congress, aimed at uniting against the anti-labour policies. The union continued to be active in the following years and by 1967, the tensions between the union and the company had worsened. Early in that year, the union threatened the company with a major strike if abuses against workers and itself did not stop.[19] Soon after the threat was made a rival union by the name of Free Union of Central Romana appeared publicly. In a press communiqué,[20] the newly created union stated its objectives as:

> The Free Union has been formed out of the conviction that the activities of the Unified Trade Union are aimed at destablising the company. A handful of professional agitators linked to international communism have taken advantage of the good faith of many workers who have innocently risked their jobs by following their advice.

With the formation of this rival union and the repressive actions against the activists, the Unified Trade Union was severely weakened. Moreover, in 1973 the Labour Ministry cancelled its certification. This action was illegal since it could only be taken against a certified union in Court.

One of the effects of the formation of rival unions was that it diminished the chances of success of labour struggles, since the rival union was more willing to accept the conditions rejected by others. Although, due to the lack of adequate data, one cannot establish how many rival unions were formed during the Balaguer regime, one could assume that if the largest and best organised union in the country was dismantled, the formation of rival unions must have played a role as part of the anti-labour policies. One could refer here to a 'demonstration effect', in the sense that if a strong union was the victim of such action then a message was sent to the rest of organised labour.

c) The replacement of a union board was another mechanism utilised to foster docile unions. The process consisted of firing labour activists who opposed the company's and/or the government's plans and policies, and appointing a new more amenable board. Since the labour code did not grant job security to any worker (including labour activists), this was not difficult to carry out. One of the best known cases where this action was taken was at the National Cement Factory (partially owned by the state). Labour problems started there soon after Balaguer took power in 1966. Initially, workers protested against the austerity law and the government's plans to fire the manager, who had been in charge of the factory from before the inauguration of the Balaguer government.[21] By late 1966, the conflicts had worsened and the union protested very actively against repressive actions such as the direct intervention of the police within the factory, violation of the collective labour contract, the dimissal of workers, and the threat to union leaders.[22] In January, 1967, workers went on strike and in February, a new union board came out publicly denouncing statements made by former union leaders against the company. The new board was certified by the Labour Ministry, and once it was installed, it announced the withdrawal of the union from FOUPSA-CESITRADO (the labour confederation linked to the political left).[23] Similar events took place in the state-owned flour factory. In this case, the conflict started in September 1966, when the union protested against violations of the collective contract and the hiring of new workers without considering seniority rights.[24] By March 1967, a new board had replaced the old leadership with the support of the Labour Ministry. The new board then proclaimed its allegiance to 'free unionism' and against what they called 'ideological unionism' of communist inspiration. This was the first union to proclaim its allegiance to this movement, followed by the Free Union of La Romana in April of the same year.

d)   The use of repressive measures was quite widespread during the Balaguer regime, primarily during the first half of his twelve-year long presidency.[25] The most typical examples of repressive actions were assassination, incarceration, the seizure of union headquarters, and the occupation of plants by the police. Among the existing labour confederations, FOUPSA-CESITRADO was the most heavily attacked by the government, and the unions affiliated to this confederation (e.g. the Unified Trade Union of Central Romana, the union of the Cement Factory) were the target of anti-labour policies. FOUPSA-CESITRADO went underground and disappeared by the end of the 1960s. The Autonomous Confederation of Christian Union (CASC) initially opposed the Balaguer regime but was later partially integrated to participate as labour representative in state-run institutions such as the Dominican Institute for Social Security (IDSS).

The two labour confederations linked to the Balaguer regime were the National Confederation of Free Workers (CONATRAL) and the Trade Union Confederation of Organised Workers (COSTO). They had very limited impact upon the government as representatives of the working class. For instance, in 1967, Balaguer created a national commission to revise the labour code but neither of these organisations was in the commission representing labour, nor did the commission achieve any results in terms of modifying the code. Furthermore, they never gained support among the working class. Both CONATRAL and COSTO were dismantled by their own promoters soon after Balaguer lost power in 1978. The weakness of these two labour confederations can be taken here as an indication of the lack of a corporatist strategy of incorporation by the Balaguer regime. Instead, the anti-labour policies of fragmentation and exclusion prevailed.

Besides these mechanisms of labour control the government added in 1974 a regulation to the labour code which increased the role of the state in the internal affairs of unions. Resolution 13/74 established that all meetings to form a union, labour federation, or confederation, to elect the governing board, to change the by-laws, and to affiliate a union to a federation or confederation had to be attended and approved by a Labour Ministry supervisor. Then, based on this certification, the Secretary of Labour would decide upon the validity of the event and grant final approval. Two problems, with political connotations, stem from this regulation. First, the regulation allows the state to interfere in a private activity of an organisation, consequently violating the freedom of association. Second, the resolution opens up the possibility of an arbitrary decision on legal grounds by the Labour Ministry, either by their own supervisor or by the Secretary of Labour. The latter had already been a problem before the approval of resolution 13/74, when the government cancelled, arbitrarily, the certification of the Unified Trade Union of Central Romana in 1973, and when it denied certification to the newly formed General Trade Union Confederation (CGT) in 1972.

Resolution 13/74 represented a corporatist attempt in the sense of imposing state controls upon union activity, but not in the sense of granting any official representation to a limited number of unions within the state. Although the resolution could have been implemented to move towards a unified system of representation of the working class under state control, this was not the case. For instance, the Labour Ministry granted certification to the CGT in 1974, a labour confederation openly opposed to the regime, and with the potential to grow and confront the government. It can be argued, then, that Resolution 13/74 had, primarily, the purpose of establishing legal regulations so that the state could have more 'legal' control of union activity. A reason for making this claim is that when Resolution 13/74 was approved, the labour movement had already been weakened; none the less, there were already signs of a resurgence of the movement. As evidence of this resurgence one can point at two main events: first, the formation of the CGT in 1972 (certified in 1974), which brought together former members of the dismantled FOUPSA-CESITRADO and a dissident faction from the Christian Democrat CASC (these two groups represented the most militant factions in the labour movement). Second was the increasing number of unions certified by the Labour Ministry beginning in 1972. To illustrate this, while the annual mean number of unions certified by the Labour Ministry between 1966 and 1971 was 11.8, the mean for the period 1972–1977 was 38.6. Despite this increase, it is important to keep in mind that as a whole, the 12 years of Balaguer's rule represented a reversal for the labour movement in terms of the number of certified unions. This is evident when one compares the annual mean of certified unions in three different political periods during the post-Trujillo period (Table 9.5).

Overall, during the Balaguer regime, the labour movement was repressed and fragmented. The working class saw its standard of living decline as salaries and services deteriorated. The government invested very little in the reproduction of the labour force, both in the form of social services and in facilitating the conditions for labour negotiation to take place. For example, the Central Government, in violation of the law, never made a fiscal contribution to the social security system.[26] Also, the share of the National Budget assigned to the Labour Ministry, decreased over time from 0.25 per cent in 1967 to 0.01 per cent in 1977.[27]

With the victory of the Dominican Revolutionary Party (PRD) in the 1978 elections, there was a resurgence of labour. The inauguration of the PRD government meant the loosening up of the more

Table 9.5   Unions certified by the Labour Ministry during the post-Trujillo period

Periods	Annual mean
1962–1965	45.4
1966–1977	25.2
1966–1971	11.8
1972–1977	38.6
1978–1981	87.5

Source: Calculations based on list of unions certified by the Labour Ministry (Unpublished).

repressive traits of the state since the PRD represented a democratic alternative in Dominican politics. The first indicator of the resurgence of labour was the increasing number of unions that were registered at the Labour Ministry during the months following the inauguration of the PRD government.[28] Along with this increasing organisation of unions at the grass-root level, there was also underway a process of reorganisation of labour confederations. By late 1978, the labour movement was clustered among five different labour confederations with different political and ideological orientations. The Autonomous Confederation of Christian Trade Unions (CASC) — now the Autonomous Confederation of Clasist Trade Unions — was the only one still in existence from the early 1960s; it continued to be linked to the Christian Democrats. The General Trade Union Confederation (CGT) was linked to the Marxist left, except for the Communist Party. The Workers' Movement for Labour Unity (MOSUO) — named later the Unified Labour Confederation (CUT) — was linked to the Communist Party. The Central Trade Union Confederation of Dominican Workers (UGTD) was formed by the PRD soon after taking power. And the National Confederation of Dominican Workers (CNTD) had links with the US labour movement.

The attempts made to unify the labour movement have failed. The most important one was that of 1980, when all the labour confederations (except for the UGTD which had been excluded for being linked to the ruling party) formed the National Council for Trade Union Unity (CNUS). In spite of all the critical self-evaluation that was proclaimed by the various organisations, the CNUS failed. The CASC withdrew from the CNUS about two months after joining it, claiming to do so because the CGT had tried to divide its unions. Although the CNUS continued to function for a few months after the withdrawal of the CASC, it lacked a strong base of support within organised labour for neither the CASC nor the UGTD — the two largest and most important labour confederations besides the CGT — were participating. Furthermore, after 1982, during the second PRD government, the existing labour confederations have divided even further as a result of internal conflicts and rivalry having to do, primarily, with conflicts among the political parties backing a particular labour confederation, or tensions among factions within a political party. The CGT was divided in two. One group is linked to the Dominican Liberation Party (Juan Bosch's party), and the other to several Marxist organisations. The UGTD has not been officially divided, but the conflicts among the various factions within the PRD affect the organisation. The CUT was also recently divided as a result of divisions within the Communist Party.

Conclusion

The problems and dilemmas of the Dominican labour movement are complex. Although this chapter has not discussed the role of important economic factors that work against the possibilities of unionisation, one should be aware of this issue. The most important one is the high rate of unemployment and underemployment, which generates a reserve of labour that facilitates replacing workers. To this, one should add the lack of labour laws granting job security to workers. Having acknowledged this, one can conclude by saying that labour control in the Dominican Republic has been imposed from without and within the labour movement. As explained in this paper, the government's labour policies have not fostered the strength and power of workers, but on the contrary, their weakness through exclusion, either by means of 'corporatist control without mobilisation or incorporation', or by means of 'organisational fragmentation'. Employers, in turn, have favoured, benefited and followed the course set by the state. And, under these circumstances, employers have done little in terms of negotiation with the working class.[29]

Political parties (of all orientations) have also damaged the labour movement by dealing with labour organisations in an instrumental way. With a small grass-root movement — although there are not good data on the degree of unionisation, labour leaders estimate that it is about 18 per cent — labour organisations respond more to the strategies of the political parties to which they are related than to the working class who they claim to represent. This problem has become more evident with the decline of authoritarian rule after the PRD took power in 1978. Despite the reduction in the use of coercion as a method of social control since 1978, the labour movement has not been able to expand its bases of support among the working class. Neither have the various labour confederations been able to unify those already organised. The Dominican labour movement is, thus, a product of an unfavourable economic structure and political history, and of the incapability of both workers and labour leaders to transform these negative conditions by struggle and change.

Notes

1   See Barrington Moore, *The Social Origins of Dictatorship and Democracy*, (Boston, Beacon Press, 1966), pp. xv–xvi.
2   *Ibid*.
3   *Ibid*.

4 See among relevant works, Samuel Huntington, *Political Order in Changing Societies*, (New Haven, Yale University Press, 1968).

5 Guillermo O'Donnell, *Modernisation and Bureaucratic Authoritarianism: Studies in South American politics*, (Berkeley, Institute of International Studies, University of California, 1973).

6 David Collier, 'Overview of the Bureaucratic-Authoritarian Model'. In David Collier, (ed.) *The New Authoritarianism in Latin America*, (Princeton, Princeton University Press, 1979), pp. 19–24.

7 See O'Donnell, *op. cit.* and Collier, *ibid.*

8 While in 1936 the size of the industrial labour force was 20,000 workers (90 per cent in the sugar sector and 10 in the non-sugar sector), by 1960, it was 90,000 (72 per cent in the sugar sector and 28 in the non-sugar sector).

9 By 1955 Trujillo had acquired two-thirds of the sugar mills. He owned also abour 60 per cent of the industrial assets in the non-sugar industrial sector.

10 Jesús de Galindez, *The Era of Trujillo*, (Tucson, University of Arizona Press, 1973).

11 Roberto Cassá, *Historia económica y social de la Républica Dominicana*, (Santo Domingo, Editora Alfa y Omega, 1980).

12 Jesús de Galíndez, *op. cit.*

13 Philippe C. Schmitter, 'Still a Century of Corporatism', in Gerhard Lehmbruch and Philippe Schmitter, (eds.) *Trends Toward Corporatist Intermediation*, (Beverly Hill-London, Sage Publications, 1979), p. 20.

14 See Robert D. Crassweller, *Life and Times of a Caribbean Dictator*, (New York, MacMillan, 1966). Also, Jesús de Galíndez, *op. cit.*

15 Reinhard Bendix, *Force, Fate, and Freedom: On Historical Sociology*, (Los Angeles, University of California Press, 1984), p. 102.

16 See for a similar argument in the case of Brazil, Kenneth Mericle, 'Corporatist Control of the Working Class: Authoritarian Brazil Since 1964'. In James Mally, (ed.) *Authoritarianism and Corporatism in Latin America*, (Pittsburgh, University of Pittsburgh Press, 1977), pp. 303–338.

17 A problem with this source is that the most prominent cases tend to be covered the most. Thus, one has to be aware of the limitations of providing convincing proofs based on case-studies. One could suggest, none the less, that if the most important unions were weakened as a result of anti-labour policies, those policies were likely to have an impact on the labour movement as a whole. Therefore, showing what happened to the largest and/or most active unions has some relevance as an indicator of what may have happened to the labour movement as a whole.

18 From 1970 to 1973, the annual rate of growth of the GDP in both manufacturing and construction was over 10 per cent. After 1973, it has been about 50 per cent lower.

19 *Listín Diario* (A daily newspaper), 6 and 7 March 1967.

20 *Listín Diario*, 29 April 1967.

21 *Listín Diario*, 11 July 1966.

22 *Listín Diario*, 16 September 1966.

23 *Listín Diario*, 19 January 1967.

24 *Listín Diario*, 16 September 1966.

25 See for an account of repression during the first few years of the Balaguer regime, José Moreno, 'Class Domination, Repression and

Economic Penetration in the Dominican Republic'. (Buffalo, Council of International Studies, University of New York at Buffalo, 1976).

26   Oficina Nacional del Presupuesto, Ejecución Nacional del Presupuesto, Santo Domingo, various years.

27   *Ibid*.

28   According to press reports in *El Sol*, 14 October 1978, a new union was registered every two days at the Labour Ministry during the first two months of the first PRD administration.

29   A lengthier analysis of these issues can be found in Rosario Espinal 'Classes, Power, and Political Change in the Dominican Republic'. (Ph.D. dissertation, Washington University, St Louis, 1985).

CHAPTER 10

British officials and the West Indian peasantry, 1842–1938

Richard A. Lobdell

In the view of West Indian planters and British officials, the most pressing socio-economic problem of the immediate post-emancipation period was the apparent inability of estates to command adequate numbers of wage labourers with which to produce sugar at competitive prices. Above all else it was this consideration which determined the attitude of officials towards the emerging West Indian peasantry during the first six decades following emancipation. The peasantry was then seen as antagonistic to and subversive of the plantation sector. Hence, it was generally supposed, the prosperity—indeed the very civilization—of the West Indies was endangered. At the end of the nineteenth century, however, a different attitude began to emerge among British officials who increasingly regarded the peasantry as a legitimate and vital element of the West Indian economic and social system.

This chapter attempts to understand this remarkable change in the attitude of British officials towards the West Indian peasantry. The first section traces the evolution of official thinking on this issue during the century following emancipation. The second explores three possible explanations of the change in attitude which became evident during the 1890s.[1]

Post emancipation changes in the British official attitudes to the peasantry

At the time of emancipation, it was generally held that 'the freed slaves would naturally and necessarily continue to earn their livelihood in employment on estates'.[2] That this did not occur uniformly throughout the West Indies was something of a puzzle to many officials who, on the basis of British experience, had come to believe that 'the dependent position of the agricultural and industrial working class' on wage labour was a universal rule of economic behaviour.[3] Reacting to heated representations from West Indian planters and British mercantile interests, a parliamentary Select Committee was appointed in 1842 to enquire into economic conditions throughout the West Indies.

After gathering evidence presented in London by witnesses, the majority of whom 'were interested as Proprietors or Managers of Estates', the Committee reported in July, 1842.[4] Notwithstanding 'the great advantages which have resulted from Emancipation' in so far as 'the character and condition of the Negro Population' was concerned, the Committee was troubled by the 'great diminution of the staple production . . . to such an extent as to have caused serious, and, in some cases, ruinous injury to the proprietors'. In the Committee's judgement this was the result of the inability of planters to secure sufficient labour at wages consistent with profitable sugar production. This in turn was 'principally to be attributed to the easy terms upon which the use of land has been obtained by Negroes'.

The Committee suggested three courses of remedial action. First, 'much might be effected by judicious arrangements on the part of Planters themselves, for their own general advantage'; that is, planters should exercise greater control over the alienation of estate lands. Second, the Committee urged immigration 'of a fresh labouring population, to such an extent as to create competition for employment', thereby containing or possibly even reducing wage rates. Third, in order to ensure 'the just rights and interests of the West Indian Proprietors, and the ultimate welfare of the Negroes themselves', the Committee recommended 'early and careful revision' of 'the relations between employers and labourers'; in particular, steps should be taken to control vagrancy and eliminate squatting by freedmen on abandoned estates or crown lands.

Thus the Select Committee of 1842 generally adopted, without hesitation or qualification, the planters' view of the immediate post-emancipation crisis. In particular, the Committee accepted the argument that in many West Indian colonies the prosperity of estate agriculture had been and would be threatened by a general shortage of wage labour, the root cause of which was the growth of small settler and peasant cultivation. In the Committee's view, the appropriate remedy lay within the authority of colonial administrations which were urged to enact measures designed to reduce the viability of peasant cultivation.[5]

But the West Indian plantation sector also faced a serious external threat to its prosperity after 1840, as political debate in Britain increasingly favoured the adoption of unfettered free trade. Thus quite apart from the perceived problem of a chronic labour shortage, West Indian planters were confronted with a new crisis:

the proposed abolition of protective duties favouring colonial sugar. The effects of the Sugar Duties Act of 1846 were so controversial that another Select Committee was established, under the chairmanship of Lord George Bentinck,[6] to enquire into sugar and coffee planting in Mauritius and the West Indies. During the spring of 1848 this Committee heard and published several thousand pages of evidence given in the main by residents of Britain who had direct interests in the production of tropical staples.

In its final Report[7] the Committee concluded that the 'great distress' in the West Indies sugar industry was largely the result of misguided policy which had encouraged, if not actually caused, a chronic insufficiency of low wage estate labour. The Committee apparently accepted the planter argument that modernisation of the industry had been hindered by the unjustifiably low compensation payments made to slave owners at the time of emancipation. Because modernisation had not been possible, it was argued, sugar estates had become dependent upon the whim and caprice of wage labourers; thus, emancipation had been 'carried into effect without sufficient provision having been made for providing many of the Colonies with an adequate command of free labour'. The result was that West Indian sugar had become uncompetitive with the slave grown sugar of Cuba and Brazil.

In his draft report, Lord George Bentinck had gone even further in attacking past policy. Since emancipation, he wrote, 'an unchangeable spirit and hereditary evil genius' had 'perverted the judgement of the Colonial Office' with respect to 'the unfortunate planter' who had been 'relentlessly persecuted as though he were still an enemy of humanity and the African race'. He was not alone in this view. The Under-Secretary of State for the Colonies, Benjamin Haes allowed: 'I quite admit that the past policy of (Britain) has been prejudicial to the cultivation of estates in the West Indies; I think it has narrowed the supply of labour...In so far as (the allegation that) the policy of the country may have injured those who were engaged in sugar cultivation and weakened their general power to cultivate and to improve, I am disposed to admit it'.[8] The staff of the Colonial Office were distressed by such claims, believing themselves to have acted in accordance with parliamentary instructions.[9]

Defects of past policy notwithstanding, the Committee of 1848 clearly believed the most pressing problem facing the West Indies was the insufficiency of estate labour. Small settler villages continued to prosper and expand in Jamaica. In both Trinidad and Demerara freedmen were said to be acquiring small holdings on crown land or on abandoned estates. Even in Antigua a 'native peasantry' was reported to be emerging. And everywhere, the Committee concluded, vagrancy and squatting had greatly reduced the supply of estate wage labour. The Committee thus urged that 'Laws be enacted against Vagrancy and Squatting', but accepted that planters were probably 'unable at present to bear any portion of the expense of enforcing' such laws. Consequently, the Committee's major recommendations were that indentured immigration be encouraged and that colonial sugar be granted a six year preferential duty in British markets.

Thus, by the middle of the nineteenth century, most British officials appear to have shared the view of Lord Grey, Secretary of State in 1847: '...the highest interests of the Negroes require that the cultivation of sugar should not be abandoned, and that the proprietors of European race should be enabled to maintain their present place in the society...which can only be done by giving them a greater command of labour'. The governor of Trinidad, Lord Harris, predicted 'A state of comparative barbarism' in the event of the 'ruin of the larger proprietors'. And yet, he did not believe it either practical or wise to 'place the labouring population in circumstances in which a greater amount of labour than at present shall be required to supply their wants'. Although an outspoken defender of planter interests over those of freedmen, Lord Harris felt obliged to urge the removal of restrictions on the sale of crown land to small settlers in order to ensure a measure of harmony and goodwill in Trinidad.[10] But the doubts of Lord Harris and a few others were surely exceptions at mid-century.

Indeed throughout the period 1850–1883, most British officials continued to accept the planters' view that West Indian social and economic progress was endangered by the growth of independent peasantries.[11] To be sure, both declining sugar prices and outmoded production techniques were acknowledged to have contributed significantly to planters' distress.[12] None the less, the prevailing official view continued to be that West Indian prosperity might be rejuvenated if planters were afforded more effective control over wage labour.

During the early 1880s, the continuing economic depression in the West Indies took on a new urgency. European subsidised beet sugar had depressed world market prices to such an extent that colonial governments, as well as individual planters, were faced with financial ruin. Tax revenues had precipitously declined, public expenditures had proved difficult to reduce, and colonial debt had become chronic. It appeared the West Indies might become a significant drain on imperial funds. Thus in 1883 a Royal Commission, under the chairmanship of William Crossman, was dispatched to enquire into the finances of the most affected West Indian colonies. The Commissioners took a very broad view of their mandate; their report, published in 1884, addressed many aspects of the economic and social conditions which they observed during their visit to the Caribbean.[13]

Perhaps not surprisingly, the Commissioners reported that one of the principal difficulties they had encountered was the inability of 'capitalists', by which they meant planters, 'to obtain at all times a reliable supply of labour'. This they attributed 'in a great extent to the natural indolence of the negro' and the multiplicity of economic alternatives, including peasant cultivation, open to the labouring classes. But the Commissioners did not consider the peasantry an unmitigated evil: 'we found that to a very welcome degree, and in a steadily increasing proportion, negroes are becoming prosperous peasant proprietors, and already in many Islands, and especially in Jamaica and Grenada, (are) appreciably increasing the exports'. This was of special significance to British officials whose theory of finance held that public revenues were intimately tied to duties on imports, the volume of which depended on income derived from exports. For the first time in any official report, the West Indian peasantry was 'altogether to be commended' even though its success adversely affected 'the supply of labourers willing to work for wages (on estates)'. Since 'the industry of sugar planting requires at times continuous trained labour, a kind of work experience has shown to be distasteful to the majority of negroes', the Commission felt obliged to recommend that indentured immigration should be encouraged. Thus the Commission could not quite break away from the traditional view that peasant cultivation and estate agriculture were incompatible.

In late 1896 the economic position of the West Indies had become so precarious as a result of the virtual collapse of world sugar prices that another Royal Commission, under the chairmanship of Sir Henry Norman, was appointed to enquire and make practical recommendations. The Commission's Report, submitted in late 1897, was certainly the most significant and imaginative official investigation into the state of the West Indies during the nineteenth century.[14]

The Norman Commission of 1897 and its successors

The principal innovation of the 1897 Commission was the recognition of 'peasant proprietorships' as a key element in the West Indian social and economic system. In the opinion of the Commissioners, there was no possibility that acreage then under cane cultivation could be maintained in the face of present or reasonably anticipated world sugar prices. It was therefore essential 'that no time should be lost in making a beginning of substituting other industries for the cultivation of sugar-cane'. Since there did not appear to be any prospect for the establishment of a manufacturing industry, the Commissioners were driven to their most famous recommendation: '(N)o reform affords so good a prospect for the permanent welfare in future of the West Indies as the settlement of the labouring population on the land as small peasant proprietors'.

While such a policy was more feasible in some places than in others, the Commissioners none the less argued that every colony had crown lands which should be made available to small cultivators, who were expected to produce food for themselves and for local markets as well as exports which would inevitably increase public revenues. The Commissioners went even further: circumstances in some colonies, notably in Carriacou and St Vincent, were sufficiently dire to justify expropriation of private estates for resale to small settlers. In a remarkable break with the past, the Commissioners declared: 'A monopoly of the most accessible and fertile lands by a few persons who are unable any longer to make a beneficial use of them cannot, in the general interest of the island, be tolerated, and is a source of public danger'.

In the Commissioners' view, it was not enough merely to provide land for the peasantry. It was essential that roads and bridges be built to facilitate peasant access to local markets and that shipping services be improved to encourage inter-colonial trade. Moreover, measures were needed to improve the techniqures of peasant cultivation. In this regard, the Commissioners recommended the creation of the Imperial College of Agriculture in Trinidad and the establishment of extension services modelled on the Jamaica Agricultural Society. Both colonial and imperial governments were encouraged to promote the export of peasant grown minor staples to North American markets.

At the same time the Commissioners emphasised the dangers inherent in the production of agricultural products for export. Not only were markets for tropical produce unstable and untrustworthy by their very nature, over-specialisation would 'result in a preponderating influence in one direction tending to restrict development in other ways'. Policy had been in the past, and might be in the future, dominated by the needs of the sugar industry which had not always been beneficial to colonial economic and social progress.

Indeed, the Commissioners believed that the estate cultivation of sugar 'unfits the people, or at any rate gives them no training, for the management or cultivation of the soil for other purposes'. Hence any serious decline in the sugar industry, which the Commissioners had documented for the recent past and fully expected to continue into the foreseable future, would leave the population 'without either the knowledge, skill, or habits requisite for making a good use of the land'. So long as the West Indies 'remain dependent upon sugar their position can never be sound or secure'. This represented a complete abandonment of the established doctrine that social stability and economic progress in the West Indies depended on the production of sugar by plantations.

It is interesting to note that the Commissioners of 1897 considered, in the final section of their Report, the 'Obligations of the Mother Country'. Because of its past colonial policy, Britain was under a powerful moral obligation to act as trustees of West Indian welfare: 'We have placed the labouring population where it is, and created for it the conditions, moral and material, under which it exists, and we cannot divest ourselves of responsibility for its future'. However patronising this may now sound, it stands in sharp contrast with Britain's obligatons as seen by Lord Harris in 1847: 'How shall the vast capital already expended on the estates in the first place be saved? And then, how shall it be rendered profitable to the possessors? For there is this difficulty — Great Britain encouraged the outlay of this capital; she even enforced certain terms upon capitalists, and then was the first to fly from them'.[15] Thus during the half century 1847–1897, the concern of British officials appears to have shifted away from the interests of 'capitalists' towards those of 'the labouring population'.

The Report of the 1929–30 West Indian Sugar Commission[16] chaired by Lord Olivier, and the Report of the West India Royal Commission of 1938–39[17] chaired by Lord Moyne, may be seen as extensions into the twentieth century of the views expressed by the Norman Commission in 1897. As had the Norman Commission, both the Olivier and Moyne Commissions expressed genuine admiration of the social, economic, and political strengths inherent in peasant proprietorships. All three Commissions urged the creation or expansion of agricultural extension services in order to improve the productivity of peasant cultivation; denounced over-specialisation in agricultural exports, whether produced by peasants or by plantations; stressed the obligation of the imperial government to intervene directly and forcefully to ensure West Indian social and economic development. Finally, all three Commissions held that peasant cultivation and estate production were complementary rather than antagonistic forms of agricultural organisation.

In summary, there are significant differences in the expressed attitude of British officials towards the West Indian peasantry before and after 1897. To be sure, the later commissions shared certain misconceptions with the earlier enquiries. Assertions of labourers' 'natural indolence', specious arguments favouring indentured immigration, general disparagement of industrial development—these and other misjudgements were commonly shared by officials before and after 1897. But, in contrast with early views, official opinion after 1897 generally argued that the economic crises experienced within the West Indies had not been caused by the peasantry. On the contrary, if such crises were ever to be overcome, the peasantry would have to be encouraged and strengthened.

Reasons for the British change in attitude to the peasantry

There are at least three possible explanations for this remarkable change in the attitude of British officials during the last decade of the nineteenth century. What might be termed the orthodox interpretation focuses attention on the profound economic crisis which descended upon the West Indies after 1880.[18] At the international level, the crisis resulted from a severe and apparently permanent depression of sugar prices caused by chronic over-supply as European beet sugar production expanded rapidly. As the tenuous profitability of West Indian sugar production came under relentless attack in world markets, estates and small cane farmers reduced output and faced ruin. Both relatively rapid population growth and the apparent absence of alternatives to cane cultivation added to the sense of despair as wage employment and other income earning opportunities narrowed. Vocal discontent and open restlessness became common among landless labourers and those elements of the peasantry closely tied to the declining sugar industry.[19] As economic conditions worsened throughout the 1890s, British officials were forced to consider alternative means by which economic and social stability might be assured in the West Indies. According to this interpretation, the pro-peasantry attitude which finally emerged was the result of 'discontent and restlessness among peasants and labourers combined with prolonged depression in the sugar industry'.[20]

A second interpretation would emphasise the role of the 'Colonial Office mind' in altering expressed attitudes towards the West Indian peasantry.[21] While acknowledging the importance of economic circumstances within the West Indies, such an interpretation would focus consideration on the general atmosphere of political unrest, economic stagnation, and philosophical radicalism which characterised Britain after 1880. During these years the Colonial Office was increasingly staffed with recent university graduates. Influenced by the reform agitation of the times, many of these new recruits were disillusioned with traditional methods of colonial administration and established doctrines of socio-economic development within the empire. The concept of an imperial trusteeship took root within the Colonial Office which slowly came to see its role as that of protecting the interests of labourers and peasants against those of merchants and planters. This view was especially evident in the West India department which, according to Hyam, was convinced that the planter oligarchies of the Caribbean were 'ignorant, narrow-minded, shifty, improvident, selfish, and provocative'.[22] Such an interpretation would argue that the 'Colonial Office mind', altered by the critical environment of the age, came to prefer 'native' forms of economic organisation to the more vulgar forms of colonial capitalism which had hitherto prevailed. This general attitude was in turn reflected in the views and recommendations of the later commissions of enquiry.

A third interpretation would be that specific individuals played a crucial role in altering official attitudes towards the West Indian peasantry. The views expressed in the Select Committee reports of 1842 and 1848 were inevitably dominated by the political inclinations and personal interests of committee members.[23] Members of the later commissions, however, were direct appointees of the Colonial Office which, as suggested above, had begun to view the West Indies from a different perspective. Moreover, certain members of the later commissions held strong views concerning the relationship between estate agriculture, peasant proprietorships, and overall colonial economic development. Most notable among these were Sir Henry Norman and Sydney (later, Lord) Olivier.

Prior to his appointment as governor of Jamaica in 1883, Sir Henry Norman had been a distinguished administrator and military commander in India for some thiry-eight years.[24] During his years in Jamaica, Norman introduced a controversial new constitution and pursued various policies designed to facilitate peasant cultivation.[25] Norman is said to have believed himself a Radical and, as chairman of the 1897 Royal Commission, he was in general sympathy with arguments favouring the development of a peasantry, the merits of which he had come to appreciate in India.[26] The Report of the

Commission was clearly influenced by Norman's predisposition towards the peasantry.[27]

The secretary of the Norman Commission and the person most directly responsible for the contents of its report was Sydney Olivier. An influential member of the Colonial Office staff, Olivier was a leader of those who were critical of West Indian plantocracies and sympathetic towards small settlers and peasants. More eccentrically, Olivier had declared himself a socialist and for many years was an active member of the Fabian Society's committee. He frequently participated in public debates on doctrinal and practical issues connected with the establishment of socialism in Britain. During the 1880s and 1890s Olivier regularly contributed articles to the radical press in England, most notably arguing the case for the nationalisation of both land and capital.[28] Olivier's views were strengthened by first hand experience in British Honduras and in the Leeward Islands during the 1890s. During his service in Jamaica as colonial secretary (1900–1904) and as governor (1907–1973), he attempted to apply his ideas by initiating policies designed to expand peasant cultivation and to reduce Jamaica's economic dependency on plantation produced exports.[29] Based on his enquiries for the 1929–1930 West Indian Sugar Commission, Olivier was persuaded that the 1897 Royal Commission's positive recommendations with respect to the peasantry were still valid. Giving evidence before the Moyne Commission in 1938, Olivier resolutely defended his earlier views on the value of the peasantry in the West Indies.[30]

Conclusion

By way of summary, the change in attitude of British officials towards the West Indian peasantry during the late nineteenth century may be explained in a variety of ways. One explanation argues that profound change in the international markets for sugar caused such economic and social instability within the West Indies that imperial authorities were forced to seek alternatives to the traditional plantation system. Thus it has been argued, positive official attitudes towards the peasantry evolved as a desperate attempt to counter chronic economic depression in the West Indies. A second explanation argues that during the late nineteenth century the overall outlook of the Colonial Office changed significantly. According to this explanation, the new 'Colonial Office mind' was the product of changes in the social, political, and ideological environment of Britain during that period. The result, it is argued, was a tendency on the part of the Colonial Office as an institution to favour peasant as opposed to plantation forms of production. A third explanation argues that knowledgeable and influential individuals played a significant role in reforming official attitudes towards the peasantry. According to this explanation, key members of the later commissions of enquiry were strongly predisposed to favour the peasantry. By virtue of their experience and position, these individuals were particularly influential in altering the overall attitude of British officials towards the peasantry.

It is tempting to try to locate these separate explanations along a spectrum ranging from least to most important. The prevailing scholarly view does so unambiguously: economic conditions in the West Indies were overwhelmingly important. In so far as they are considered at all, the role of particular individuals and the general outlook of the Colonial Office are viewed as quite incidental. But this overlooks the complicated mechanism by which economic conditions effectively alter attitudes. Economic events in and of themselves cannot alter attitudes directly; it is the interpretation and assessment of such events that matters. In the case at hand, West Indian economic conditions were imbued with significance by the interpretations of experienced and imaginative individuals such as Henry Norman, Sydney Olivier, and others. These interpretations were inevitably conditioned by the individual's experience and personal inclinations. Not least of all, these individuals were influenced by and in turn influenced the general environment within which Hyam's 'Colonial Office mind' evolved. Thus economic conditions in the West Indies, the general outlook of the Colonial Office as an institution, and persuasive individuals all seem to have played significant roles in changing the attitude of British officials towards the peasantry. Far from being separate or contending explanations, these must be seen as complementary and dynamic elements in any comprehensive understanding of that remarkable change in attitude.

Acknowledgements

The author thanks Stanley Engerman, Gad Heuman, and Howard Johnson for helpful comments on previous drafts of this chapter.

Notes

1 A number of significant and controversial issues connected with the growth of the West Indian peasantry during the nineteenth century are beyond the scope of this paper. Among these are conceptual and analytical problems of what constitutes a 'peasantry', the internal economy and social organisation of the peasantry during this period, and the views of colonial government and local plantocracies concerning

both the attitudes of British officials and the policies they recommended. The extensive literature on such topics owes much to the pioneering studies of Sidney Mintz. See, for example, his *Caribbean Transformations*, (Chicago, Aldine Publishing Co., 1974), especially pp. 131–250. A very useful survey of the literature on Caribbean peasantries may be found in Peter Fraser, 'The Fictive Peasantry: Caribbean Rural Groups in the Nineteenth Century' in Susan Craig (ed.), *Contemporary Caribbean*, Vol. 1, (Port of Spain, Susan Craig, 1981), pp. 319–347.

2   Sydney (Lord) Olivier, *Jamaica: the Blessed Island*, (London, Faber and Faber, Ltd., 1936), p. 108. Olivier quotes at length the views of Joseph Sturge and other leaders of the emancipation movement on this point.

3   *Ibid.* p. 108. James Stephen was one official who thought otherwise: 'I am convinced', he wrote in 1840, 'that the inevitable tendency of things (in Jamaica) is toward the substitution of small holdings and Peasantry living on detached Plots of Land, for the old system of large Plantations'. Quoted in W.A. Green, *British Slave Emancipation*, (Oxford, Clarendon Press, 1976), p. 85. Recent research has uncovered much ill-ease among Colonial Office staff on this point. See, Stanley L. Engerman, 'Economic Change and Contract Labour in the British Caribbean: The End of Slavery and the Adjustment to Emancipation', *Explorations in Economic History*, Vol. 21 (1984), pp. 133–150.

4   All quotations with respect to the findings of this Committee are from the *Report of the Select Committee on the West India Colonies*, 25 July 1842. (Parliamentary Papers, 1842, Vol. XIII).

5   See, for example, Eric Williams, *The Negro in the Caribbean*, (Westport, Connecticut, Negro Universities Press, 1971. Reprint of the 1942 edition), Chapter 5; W.K. Marshall, 'Notes on Peasant Development in the West Indies Since 1938', *Social and Economic Studies*, Vol. 17, No. 3 (1968), pp. 252–263.

6   An eccentric of the first rank. See, Benjamin Disraeli, *Lord George Bentinck: A Political Biography*, (London, Archibald Constable and Company, 1905), especially chapter XXVI.

7   Unless otherwise noted, all quotations with respect to the findings of this Committee are from the *Eighth Report of the Select Committee on Sugar and Coffee Planting*, 29 May 1848. (Parliamentay Papers, 1848, Vol. XXIII).

8   *Seventh Report of the Select Committee on Sugar and Coffee Planting*, 6 April 1848. (Parliamentary Papers, 1848, Vol. XXIII).

9   'Memorandum on the Charges Brought Against the Home Govt. by Witnesses before the Recent Committee on Sugar Duties, &c., 1848', C.O. 318/179.

10   These quotations are from correspondence between Lord Harris and Lord Grey which was published in the 1848 Committee's *Eighth Report*, cited above.

11   Olivier, *op. cit.* chapter X: Green, *op. cit.* chapter 5 and 6; Williams, *op. cit.* chapter V; S.J. and E.F. Hurwitz, *Jamaica: A Historical Portrait*, (London, Pall Mall Press, 1971), pp. 127–147.

12   R.W. Beachey, *The British West Indian Sugar Industry in the Late Nineteenth Century*, (London, Oxford University Press, 1957); Richard A. Lobdell, 'Patterns of Investment and Sources of Credit in the British West Indian Sugar Industry, 1838–97', *Journal of Caribbean History*, Vol. 4 (1972), pp. 31–53.

13   All quotations with respect to the Crossman Commission are from the *Report of the Royal Commission to Enquire...C.* 3840, Feb. 1884. (Parliamentary Papers, 1884, Vol. XLVI).

14   All quotations with respect to the Norman Commission are from the *Report of the West India Royal Commission*, C. 8655 (Parliamentary Papers, 1898, Vol. L).

15   Quotations in the *Eighth Report* of the 1848 Select Committee, cited above.

16   *Report of the West Indian Sugar Commission*, Cmd. 3517 (Parliamentary Papers, 1929–30, Vol. VIII).

17   *Report of the West India Royal Commission of 1938–39*, Cmd. 6607 (London, H.M.S.O., 1945).

18   See, for example, Gordon K. Lewis, *The Growth of the Modern West Indies*, (London, MacGibbon & Kee, 1968), chapter 3 and 4; W.K. Marshall, *op. cit.* Eric Williams, *op. cit.*

19   For a useful summary of these outbreaks, see 'Notes on West Indian Riots, 1881–1905', Colonial Office Confidential Print, West Indian No. 147, March 1905, C.O. 884/9.

20   W.K. Marshall, *op. cit.* p. 262.

21   Ronald Hyam, 'The Colonial Office Mind, 1900–1914', *Journal of Imperial and Commonwealth History*, Vol. 8, No. 1 (1979), pp. 30–55. See also, Howard Johnson, 'The West Indies and the Conversion of the British Official Classes to the Development Idea', *Journal of Commonwealth and Comparative Politics*, Vol. XV, (1977), pp. 55–83.

22   Hyam, *op. cit.* p. 40.

23   Not surprisingly, members of these Committees tended to represent landed and mercantile interests in Britain or the West Indies. Brief biographical sketches of Committee members may be found in *The Parliamentary Companion*, (London, Whittaker & Co., 1847 and 1850 editions).

24   See the entry for Norman in *The Dictionary of National Biography, 1901–1911*, (London, Oxford University Press, 1920), pp. 21–24.

25   H.A. Will, *Constitutional Change in the British West Indies, 1880–1903*, (Oxford, Clarendon Press, 1970), especially chapter 1.

26   Olivier, *op. cit.* pp. 247–248.

27   *Ibid.* pp. 255–265.

28   Margaret Olivier (ed.), *Sydney Olivier: Letters and Selected Writings*, (London, George Allen and Unwin, 1948).

29   J.J. Carroll, 'The Government of Jamaica, 1900–1913, with Special Reference to the Role of Sir Sydney Olivier'. Unpublished Ph.D. thesis, University of London, 1972.

30   See Olivier's file in the Moyne Commission's archive, C.O. 950/28.

CHAPTER 11

Sydney Olivier, Jamaica and the debate on British colonial policy in the West Indies

Paul Rich

The West Indies have been ill-served in recent British imperial historiography. The importance of the Caribbean possessions in the evolution of empire has generally been seen to decline markedly in the wake of emancipation in the 1830s and attention has usually turned towards the dynamics of free trade imperialism in the middle years of the nineteenth century followed by the scramble for African colonies in the 1880s. For the last decade of the century most historical writing has dwelt on the significance of capitalist imperialism in Southern Africa culminating in the outbreak of the Anglo-Boer War of 1899–1902. Reflecting the general attitude of the British official mind of the time, historians have generally chosen to view the West Indian colonies as mere provincial backwaters with no significant importance for wider trends in imperial policy.[1]

If the West Indian possessions had, however, only a marginal economic significance with the decline in the sugar industry through competition with European bountied beet sugar by the close of the Victorian age, the same cannot be said for their symbolic and ideological importance. The British imperial system had always been a loose one, with weak structures of control emanating from the Colonial Office apparatus in London and a high degree of administrative autonomy located in the colonial governor and 'The man on the spot'. What ultimately held the empire together was the common loyalty of administrators towards general standards of trusteeship rather than an automatic obeisance to a centralised administration.[2] Given the high degree of importance attached to standards and criteria of imperial governance, the West Indies in fact acted as a forum of some significance in an increasingly sophisticated debate on the nature and functions of imperial government and its ultimate political objectives. In this debate, the model of colonial administration in Jamaica proved to be an important one by the early years of the twentieth century, especially under its Fabian governor from 1907–1913, Sydney Olivier. It will thus be the purpose of this chapter to discuss Olivier's significance in the British debate on empire, especially in terms of the Jamaican pattern of race relations which was upheld as an important alternative for colonial administration when compared with the emergent segregationist system in South Africa in the aftermath of the Anglo-Boer War.

The evolution of the debate

Olivier's entry into the society and politics of the West Indies occurred in the wake of a protracted period of debate in British intellectual and policy-making circles, for his thought, like that of most British imperial observers, was conditioned by a tradition of social and travel observation which had developed strong roots in colonial political discourse. As Gordon Lewis has recently argued, the Caribbean in many respects was the most completely colonised region in the western hemisphere exhibiting features not only of a mercantile-based capitalism but also of a racial society amounting to a two-dimensional process of exploitation.[3] Most external observers, in such a setting, generally interpreted Caribbean social processes in terms familiar to a European audience, so imposing a Eurocentric set of criteria through which to judge its dominant features.

In the wake of emancipation, the West Indian possessions raised the question of the role and function of colonial government in a new and acute form. Carlyle's imprint on the debate from the time of *The Nigger Question* in 1849 had helped shape a strong affirmation of Christian duty to impose force on the newly emancipated black slaves in the face of threatened anarchy.[4] Though this was mistakenly likened by some to an early doctrine of state fascism, Carlyle's justification for strong colonial government found a number of champions, despite a growing Victorian distaste for justifying government policy mainly in terms of Christian faith.[5] It was in particular Carlyle's Calvinist application of the doctrine of work to the black West Indian peasantry which found such a ready audience, enunciating a principle of 'teleological racism' and the justification of colonial rule in terms of forcing the work-shy Quashee into the labour market.[6] It was this principle which was to help shape the thinking of later liberal observers too, such as Anthony Trollope in *The West Indies and the Spanish Main* in 1859. For Trollope, British colonial rule in the Caribbean was essential in the absence of any perceived sense of 'country', 'pride of race' or 'religion' by the Jamaican blacks. Furthermore, it was necessary to protect the Jamaican black given that he was 'the very idlest brother with which a hardworking workman was ever curst, intent on getting his mess of pottage without giving anything in return'.[7] The Carlylean doctrine of 'ascendancy' was thus necessary, argued Trollope, for the country, given the incompatability of two races to live together on terms of complete equality. This foreshadowed the later Darwinian doctrine of racial struggle which was to make such an impact on imperial thought by the last two decades of the century:

> Ascendancy is a disagreeable word to apply to any two different races whose fate it may be to live together in the same land. It has been felt to be so in Ireland, when used either with relevance to the Saxon Protestants or Celtic Roman Catholic; and it is so with relevance to those of various shades of colour in Jamaica. But none the less it is the true word. When two rivers come together, the waters of which do not mix, the one stream will be the stronger— will over-power the other—will become ascendant. And so it is with people and nations. It may not be pretty spoken to talk about ascendancy; but sometimes pretty speaking will not answer a man's purpose.[8]

Trollope's apologetic tone regarding racial 'ascendancy' was fortified, though, by 'scientific' doctrines of climactic fitness which had a widespread popularity in Victorian thought. While black races were seen as fitted for labour in tropical climates, the 'white European creole' was not, and biological inter-breeding of the two races, Trollope believed, would produce a new hybrid race 'fitted by nature for the burning sun, in whose blood shall be mixed some portion of northern energy, and which shall owe its physical powers to African progenition—a race that shall be no more ashamed of the name of negro than we are of the name Saxon?'[9]

The climactic theory would come to be increasingly interlinked with Darwinian notions of racial fitness in the latter half of the century, especially after the Morant Bay insurrection and the resulting Governor Eyre controversy hardened mid-Victorian racial attitudes. Despite a degree of economic advancement by the brown middle class in Jamaica in the years following emancipation, there was still a high degree of racial exclusiveness amongst the white planter and governing class and Trollope's hopes for an active policy of biological social engineering in order to produce a new mixed race met with a generally cool response. In Britain, Thomas Huxley, the biologist and follower of Charles Darwin, reflected the approach of the liberal 'scientific' school on race when he saw emancipation as providing the opportunity for a generally *laissez faire* policy. 'The highest places in the hierarchy of civilisation will assuredly not be within the reach of our dusky cousins', he wrote in 'Emancipation-Black and White' in 1865, 'though it is by no means necessary that they should be restricted to the lowest'. The point was that 'whatever the position of stable equilibrium into which the laws of social gravitation will bring the negro, all responsibility for the result will henceforth lie between Nature and him. The white man may wash his hands of it, and the Caucasian conscience be void of reproach for evermore. And this, if we look to the bottom of the matter, is the real justification for the abolition policy'.[10]

This attitude reflected the general political climate in Britain in the aftermath of Governor Eyre which sought a return to the Carlylean doctrines of the 1840s, though with a greater regard for the disciplines of political economy, the 'dismal science' which Carlyle had held in generally low esteem. Lord Grey, for instance, in speaking in the Lords on the Jamaica Government Bill in 1866 regretted that a land resettlement scheme for Jamaican blacks had not been initiated at the time of emancipation and urged the establishment of a crown colony administration which 'should have a full acquaintance with all those great questions of social organisation which have of late years attracted so much attention, in addition to a knowledge of the principles of political economy'.[11] Jamaica, therefore, in the late 1860s was beginning to raise the questions of the principles of good colonial administration in a new and acute form. The Governor Eyre episode had touched a sensitive nervous chord in the Victorian imagination, attuned as it was to the possible breakdown of civil law and bourgeois civilisation before the forces of demagogy and mob rule. It was a nightmare which had been made respectable through the writings of Macaulay and Carlyle and perpetuated the frightening images of the guillotine and the French Revolution.[12] To many of the followers of Eyre only strong government could prevent such an eventuality re-emerging in the case of Jamaica and the other Caribbean colonies and the frightful imagery invoked embedded horrors which would resemble later images invoked by the East African settlers some ninety years later at the time of Mau Mau. Thus the barrister W.F. Finlason urged that the Morant Bay disturbance did not necessarily produce the 'danger...not of open insurrection in the sense of large assemblies of armed men seeking encounters with the troops, but rather of sudden surprise and massacre of the whites by the blacks, who everywhere surround them...The danger was not to the troops, nor of encounter with troops, but of universal massacre in districts distant from the troops'.[13] Morant Bay thus in some degree shifted attention away from classic revolutionary models on the French pattern to more modern images of terrorism then prevalent in Irish Fenianism.

The theme of 'black peril' indeed became increasingly prevalent amongst sections of informed opinion in Britain by the later 1860s as the liberal impulse attenuated in some degree in the wake of the 1867 reform of the electoral franchise.[14] Fears of black insurrection were also popularised through the vehicle of the novel and Grant Allen, a prolific journalist and popular writer on biology who had also taught as a school master in Trinidad, wrote a novel in this vein, *In All Shades* in 1886.[15] This story in some respects acted as a forerunner for the theme of black revolt against white rule in the African context by such writers as Rider Haggard, John Buchan, Bertram Mitford and George Heaton Nicholls. The novel is shot through with colour consciousness linked both to the ideal of social gentility and racial caste which is continually threatened by black mob insurrection. In England, it is observed, the dark complexion of the supposed white aristocrat Harry Noel might pass unnoticed, while in Trinidad it becomes a matter of social comment. Both whites and blacks in the novel are concerned with purity of race, which tends to be associated with geographical areas. Louis Delgado, who tries to lead a black revolt against white rule, considers that 'England is de white man's Africa' while the land of Trinidad he considers to be 'black' for 'when de black man his burst him heart like ribber burst him bank in de rainy season, white man's house snap off before his like bamboo hut when de flood catch it'.[16] Faced with this prospect of black revolution, white rule is affirmed at the end of the novel in a somewhat mystical manner. Harry Noel succeeds in winning over the mob that Delgado has raised by overawing them 'with the strange power of a superior race over the inferior in such critical moments of intense passion'.[17] Ultimately the Carlylean doctrine of racial ascendancy succeeds over a black population and the plea to the mob to disperse which would be 'comparatively powerless upon an English mob at home in England' succeeds 'like magic on the fierce and half naked throng of ignorant and superstitious plantation negroes'.[18] With the leader, Delgado, removed at the end through death by cardiac arrest, Harry Noel seeks to reaffirm the justice of white colonial rule by travelling to London to place before the Colonial Office the blacks' grievances.

The novel reflected the uncertain direction in colonial policy in the West Indies in the two decades following the Morant Bay rebellion. After 1884 the sugar market collapsed as competition from European beet drove down the price per hundred weight from 13s 3d in 1884 to 10s by 1897. A period of mounting panic led some sections of British opinion to doubt the possibility of British rule, though the example of Haiti led many to place a continuing faith in the doctrines of strong colonial government. Spencer St John's account of the black republic in 1884, *Hayti or the Black Republic* did much to reinforce the Victorian conception of the general unfitness of black races for self government. St John boosted this notion with lurid descriptions of voodoo practices in Haiti and the general governmental instability in the country as, he claimed, the mixed race or coloured element declined in political influence and 'constant intermarriage' caused 'the race to breed back to the more numerous type', such that 'in a few years the mulatto section will have made disastrous approaches to the negro'.[19] This racial propaganda added strength to the plea by James Anthony Froude in 1888 *The English in the West Indies*, for a reassertion of British rule on the model of the imperial government in India. Under such a regime, Froude asserted, the West Indian colonies 'would be peopled in a generation or two with dusky citizens, as proud as the rest of us of the flag under which they will have thrived, and as willing to defend it against any invading enemy as they are now unquestionably indifferent'.[20]

Froude's account was essentially an apologia for the plantation interests and represented more the end of a traditionalist assertion of white racial superiority in the region rather than the affirmation of a more modern set of doctrines in keeping with the changing climate of thought in the last quarter of the twentieth century. The rise of Darwinism in the context of a renewed outburst of imperial expansion in Africa in the 1880s led Victorian racial ideology to assume an increasingly dynamic and protean form, absorbing in many cases some of the arguments of its liberal opponents and resting its case on the capacities of a superior civilisation to transform and develop underdeveloped tropical colonial economies. In this context the rather static Carlylean appeal to the inherent beneficence of strong government and to imperial rule on the lines of the Raj appeared somewhat out-dated. A new set of propositions regarding West Indian colonial economy began to come into play by the 1890s, rooted in the requirement to stimulate and develop peasant agriculture and cope with the economic transition from sugar production to the growing and marketing of other tropical products.[21]

Since the 1860s a group of radical economists had begun to doubt the applicability of the classical theories of political economy to such peasant societies as India and Ireland where the monopoly of land by a parasitical landlord class hampered the possibilities of a flourishing peasantry. By 1870 John Stuart Mill had begun to widen this issue to England itself, linking it to general problems of the poor at a time of a rising tide of interest in social reform. Whilst not being necessarily opposed to market principles *per se*, Mill's critique of the classical tradition began to abstract land from the market and undermine the tradition of *laissez faire* theory by urging state intervention to restructure social relationships on the land in order to ensure the operation of a fair market system.[22]

This attack on the sacred tenets of nineteenth century classical political economy drove the Manchester economic liberals into alliance with the landed interests to defend property rights. However, the new radical cause came to be epitomised by the mid 1880s with Joseph Chamberlain's programme for three acres, a cow and the establishment of state-created small-holdings. While initially confined to Britain, the ideas of the former mayor of Birmingham were to have more widespread ramifications in the colonial setting by the middle of the next decade as they seeped through into Colonial Office thinking in the crisis years before the Anglo-Boer War. In 1894 the Glen Grey Act, introduced by Cecil Rhodes in the Cape Colony, pinpointed the new interest in colonial circles in fostering peasant economies, though in the South African case this proved a somewhat half-hearted attempt to resist the forces of proletarianisation stimulated through the growth of the mining industry and its rapacious demands for cheap migrant labour.[23] By the mid 1890s, a general consensus began to be established in colonial policy in a number of quarters of the empire rooted in the notion that peasantries were the best means of stabilising British control and influence.

The last years of the century, in fact, were marked by a growing nervousness regarding the long-term possibilities of white settlement and colonial rule in the band of tropical territories stretching north and south of the equator around the globe. The former history lecturer at Trinity College, Cambridge and minister of education in the colony of Victoria in Australia, Charles Pearson, reflected some of this anxiety in 1893 in his book *National Life and Character*. He prophesied an advancing band of tropical territories under the control of black and yellow races threatening the imperial hegemony of white Anglo Saxon races from the temperate areas.[24] A less pessimistic view was expressed by Dudley Kidd, author of the popular *Social Evolution* (1894) in a series of articles in *The Times* in 1898 and later published as a book *The Control of the Tropics*. Kidd argued that the temperate areas under the rule of white nations were still the motive forces of world history, but that at the end of the nineteenth century 'another epoch of instinctive rivalry' was taking place between these nations for control of tropical areas and their raw materials. This control could no longer be based on the old plantation model which was linked with slavery while Kidd believed — in the face of growing scientific evidence to the contrary — that white races were ill-suited for settlement in tropical areas. In essence, the tropics represented a challenge for the white races to uplift them to the level of nationhood according to the ideals of the imperial government of India. Kidd thus up-dated the old Carlylean conception of white racial ascendancy to one of trusteeship which no longer depended upon the assumption of white genetic superiority but on a superiority of social inheritance. It was the duty of the colonising race to bequeath this inheritance to its less developed wards.[25]

While Kidd's doctrine by no means found universal favour in late Victorian England, his social liberalism and search for scientific methods endeared him to a section of the progressive intelligentsia both in Britain and the United States, which was becoming increasingly involved in the Caribbean following the war against Spain in 1898 and the conquest of Cuba and Puerto Rico.[26] In Jamaica the writer W.P. Livingstone was considerably influenced by Kidd's arguments in his book *Black Jamaica: A Study in Evolution* in 1899 for the shift of focus on race reinforced the view that the negro could adapt to the 'civilisation' of the white race whether in Africa, the United States or the West Indies. Contact with the white race, though, was essential, Livingstone argued, for the white race's presence 'is to him (the negro) what the invigorating climate of the temperate regions is to the white — a necessary condition of progress'.[27] This progress meant in particular the encouragement of a class of black yeomanry on the land while politically there needed to be a 'strong and unprejudiced government of English gentlemen'.[28] This would by no means eliminate racial division for 'broadly speaking, the position of all...classes is governed by the caste of colour'. However, 'based on sentiment, colour-caste is by no means so rigid in its application as the religious castes of the world, and society is established on a system of mutual tolerance, which, however, has its well understood limitations'.[29]

By the turn of the century, therefore, a new impetus had occurred in the debate on race and politics in the West Indies which, in the light of a government Commission appointed in 1897 to investigate the sugar industry, promised to extend to the level of formal policy-making too. After decades of benign neglect, it appeared that the Colonial Office, under the reforming aegis of Joseph Chamberlain, was going to take a renewed interest in its underdeveloped colonial estates and integrate them more fully into the British imperial system. These hopes, however, were to be somewhat prematurely dashed by the outbreak of the Anglo-Boer War and the concentration of imperial attention after 1899 on South

Africa. But the longer term influences of the debate in the late 1890s were to have an important impact on the thought of Sydney Olivier when he became governor of Jamaica after the return of the Liberal government in 1906.

Olivier and the comparative study of race

Olivier's entry into West Indian affairs occurred at the highpoint of the debate of the 1890s. Coming from a relatively provincial background as a clergyman's son (with Huguenot ancestry) born in 1859, Olivier had had no immediate colonial connections, though at Corpus Christi College, Oxford he had become involved in the debate on evolution between Charles Darwin and Samuel Butler and had imbibed the positivism of Auguste Comte and Herbert Spencer. Like a number of his generation, Olivier became attracted to the rationalism of Fabian socialism and in 1885 he joined, along with Sidney Webb, the Fabian Society, three years after he had entered the Colonial service. In the Fabian discussion circles, Olivier soon got involved in discussion on land and rent and in 1888 propagated a neo-Ricardian critique of the land nationalisation campaign in England accusing it of failing to see that capital could exploit as much as land. With the Irish example especially prominent, he pointed out that when tenants on farms tried to improve their properties the landlords appropriated the resulting capital created by raising rents on the expiry of the lease. It was absurd therefore to discriminate between capital and land values of estates and it was necessary to recognise the socialist principle that 'labour has contributed to capital, and that labour gives some claim to ownership'.[30]

Olivier was soon able to start testing these ideas as he developed his career in the Colonial Office. In 1890–91 he was Colonial Secretary in British Honduras and between 1891–95 worked in the South African department. This was followed by a transfer to the West India Department at a time when the Jameson Raid in December 1895 indicated a rising political temperature in South Africa and the prospect of British imperial intrusion. Olivier's growing dislike and distrust of jingoism and the philosophy of imperial annexation was probably a major reason for this transfer, though the effect was to stimulate an interest in West Indian economic development which remained a major concern for the rest of his life. He later recollected that Dudley Kidd's *Social Evolution* and later *The Control of the Tropics* had been a major influence on his thought at this time for they formulated the trusteeship conception in a new and intelligible form in keeping with the evolutionary and social Darwinian atmosphere of the 1890s.[31]

As Secretary of the Norman Commission in 1897 Olivier began to gain some public attention, especially from the West India Committee who praised his work as 'excellent and able'.[32] The Commission, though, championed 'a class of small proprietors among the population' which it thought would be 'a source of both economic and political strength',[33] and it was by no means clear that the Commission would be willing to back the planters' demands for countervailing duties in order to protect the West Indian sugar estates from European competition. In a memorandum on the Commission's report, Olivier considered its recommendations on peasant proprietorship essentially 'just and right' for outside Jamaica the sugar plantations in colonies such as Guiana and Trinidad were considered an 'exotic and artificial business conducted by absentee capital with imported labour' or else, as in Barbados, Antigua, St Kitts and St Vincent 'by a strict land monopoly and an entire subjection of the negro which is equivalent to the system of slavery'. It was thus necessary to recognise, in areas where the sugar industry had broken down that the negro 'granting all his imperfections and slovenliness' was 'distinctly more prosperous, self respecting and progressive than where the land monopoly has been maintained'. It was in any case possible to develop village communities of black peasants 'with due regard to the maintenance of the sugar industry, and in such a manner as not to withdraw from the estates those who are under contract to work upon them'.[34]

This view reflected a more general predilection in the Colonial Office at this time for a middle course between the demands of the plantation interests and those of the peasantry who, in selected evidence to the 1897 Commission, had pointed out the problem of marketing peasant produce in the mountainous interior areas as well as the perennial question of theft and 'praedial larceny'.[35] As Olivier's colleague C.P. Lucas pointed out it would be 'impolitic' to seek a direct confrontation with the plantation owners for they were 'an influential class, and if not attended to would, feeling a strong sense of injustice, in no way co-operate with the government in efforts to regenerate these colonies'.[36] The Colonial Office thus began one of its early ventures into colonial development which presaged later effects in the inter-war years after the 1929 Colonial Development Act and, in the wake of the 1936—37 riots, the 1940 Colonial Development and Welfare Act. The measures in the late 1890s were, though, on a small scale and mainly designed to encourage more scientific experimentation in tropical agriculture: in August

1898 an Imperial Department of Agriculture was established with £17,000 per annum funds, though the House of Commons agreed to support it for ten years up to a budget of £250,000. The research, located at Kew, was designed in part to improve the quality of cane sugar by increasing its saccharine content in order to meet the beet competition. Combined with this was a campaign to establish schools of horticulture in the West Indian colonies in order to stimulate an interest in agricultural efficiency on lines similar to the Tuskegee Training Institute developed by Booker Washington in Alabama or the Lovedale Mission in the Eastern Cape. 'I trust to see the day', declared Dr D. Morris, the Imperial Comissioner for Agriculture in the West Indies in November 1898, 'when the young men of the West Indies will not be rushing into the overcrowded professions of law and medicine, but that they will devote themselves to improve the agricultural interests of these adopted lands'.[37] This was a view that found some support from sections of the educated black and brown population and a memorial to Joseph Chamberlain in March 1898 by H.M. Joseph, President, and Henry Sylvester Williams, Secretary, of the *African Association* attacked the sugar industry which it saw as having 'contributed very largely towards the abortion of free and progressive institutions'. It was necessary to establish central factories, the memorial continued, so that 'the care and responsibility could be distributed beneficially among small peasant farmers as well as large planters as one of the staples, even if it does not remain the great staple'.[38]

This general consensus amongst Colonial Office, philanthropic and black and brown educated opinion on the desirability of peasantisation reflected the fact that both the area of cultivation and the number of holdings in Jamaica had significantly increased. Between 1880 and 1911, for example, the cultivated area of the island rose from 108,000 acres to 273,000 acres and the number of holdings between 5 and 50 acres doubled between 1880 and 1902. In the banana parishes of Portland and St Mary the cultivated area rose from 10,000 acres in 1880 to 68,000 acres in 1911 and small farming was in some respects starting to come into its own. It also appeared to a number of observers like A. Norman that, even if the European sugar bounties were removed, the West Indian sugar planters would not be significantly affected for they would still be dependent, given the cost of transportation, on American rather than European markets. It would thus be necessary, Norman wrote to Chamberlain, to recognise that 'for many years to come' the West Indian colonies would 'need very careful and efficient administration by able and sympathetic governors and close attention by the Colonial Secretary'.[39]

Such attention, however, was no longer forthcoming once war broke out in South Africa in 1899 and marked for a number of liberals a turning point in their perceptions of empire and imperialism. For Olivier, the decision to go to war against the Boer republics represented not merely an unjust attack upon a pastoral 'seventeenth century people' but the capitulation of the British government to landlordism and labour exploitation. Writing to his fellow Fabian George Bernard Shaw in 1899, Olivier expressed his opposition to the 'imperialist microbe' and his lack of belief in 'the White Man's Burden theory'. It was clear that the 'imperialist militarist movement' did not seek the welfare of 'native races' still less 'the regulation of capitalism in the interests of wage earners'. The advent of popular imperialism was not the result of conscious exertion but of commercial and militarist pressures which had taken up the same morality of their Boer opponents, namely 'might for might' which Olivier saw as a departure from the central ethos of British imperial rule. Hearkening back to the period of mid-Victorian free trade imperialism, Olivier considered it would have been better for Britain to have let the Boers shape their own mode of South African 'industrial democracy' free of British or American influences.[40]

These arguments reflected a renewed search for a liberal ethos in British imperial policy amongst sections of liberal and radical opinion, though Olivier found himself at odds with the Fabian Society as a whole which for the most part supported the war, especially after the publication of Shaw's *Fabianism and Empire* in 1900. But Olivier in essence began to look back to the era of mid-Victorian liberalism as a moral base on which to reformulate principles of colonial government and as a challenge to the alternative strand of Victorian thought on colonial government represented by Carlyle and Froude which had ended up in the militarism on the South African veld. He also began parting company with the expansionist social Darwinism of Dudley Kidd which had led to the justification of military conquest, and to look on the mode of colonial government in the West Indian colonies as markedly different to that in South Africa. Though some liberals in Britain after 1900 saw in South Africa a new opportunity after the war for a new impetus to 'Christian Imperialism' based on an expansion of education for the African peasantry,[41] Olivier and a number of other colonial critics began to see a new threat to imperial policy in the emergence of the ideology of racial segregation.

Unlike its equivalent in the Jim Crow South of the United States, the South African racial segregationism that emerged in the years of reconstruction after the Anglo-Boer War was of a markedly territorial or 'possessory' kind. In contrast to Southern segregation which forbade racial intermarriage and the denial of the franchise and civil rights to blacks, South African segregation represented an extension of previous colonial practice separating white and black land areas. This became the official doctrine of South African 'native policy' in the years after the Report of the South African Native Affairs Commission of 1903–5 and eventually became ensconced in the first major Act separating white and black land areas in the new South African Union, the 1913 Native Land Act.[42]

South African segregation was thus a markedly more radical and sociologically penetrating doctrine than its American equivalent, though the common term 'segregation' appeared to a number of contemporary observers, including Olivier, as marking a more general resurgence of landlord interests allied to those of the state and military conquest. Here seemed to be a rebirth of the slavery and plantation interests which Victorian liberals had imagined to be a spent force after the emancipation of the 1830s. In the early years of the twentieth century some liberals began to note the comparisons between West Indian and segregationist modes of administration and in 1905 B. Pullen Burry wrote in *Ethiopia in Exile* that 'under British rule we have evolved the fact that with a minimum of education but with a maximum of the white man's guidance, in contrast to the segregation policy of the Americans, a great deal has been done in converting a backward race into helpful members of a civilised community'.[43] Furthermore, he noted that, despite the 'depressed state of the island at the time of the 1897 Royal Commission there was a recognition that 'through the cultivation of the land this island will some day win her way to a permanent substantial prosperity'.[44] A further favourable comparison was made by the Harvard philosopher Josiah Royce in 1906 who was impressed by the administration of the Jamaican colony in which blacks were trained to man some of the lower echelons of the police and civil service. Contrasting this with the repressiveness of the Southern system, Royce considered that the success of the Jamaican system lay in its relatively high degree of tolerance which allowed the ventilation of black grievances and so worked 'in the direction of making the negro a conscious helper toward good social order'.[45]

Olivier accepted a considerable part of this liberal critique of authoritarian colonial government and in a book *White Capital and Coloured Labour* in 1906 pointed out what appeared to be the strong features of Jamaican colonial administration compared to Southern and South African models of segregation. His work at the Colonial Office had allowed him to read fairly extensively on colonial policy and he had been especially impressed by the writings of Mary Kingsley, the traveller and amateur ethnologist, whose writings in the late 1890s did much to awaken interest in British colonial circles in West African cultures and stimulated an early version of the indirect rule doctrine whereby colonial government to some degree worked in collaboration and alliance with traditional African chiefly and social structures. For Olivier, Mary Kingsley had been an eye-opener, as for a number of his generation, into recognising the importance of African cultures and values and acknowledging that, as people, Africans were to be considered 'as rational human beings to be weighed in the same scales as the white races'.[46] There was the continuing existence of racial prejudice which had to be recognised 'as a fact of social importance in regard to colonial societies' for the relations of white and black races were 'obscured by a mass of prejudice and ignorance and blindness'.[47] But this was no major reason for considering that, in the Jamaican context, these relations were worsening and Olivier attacked Grant Allen's novel *In All Shades* as a 'grotesque extravagance' which might have been imagined by a writer who had never been to the island (though Allen's novel was in fact set in Trinidad). Olivier considered the picture Allen had painted more typical of a society like the American South than of contemporary Jamaica and made a strong plea for recognising the reality of inter-racial marriage which could no longer be condemned in terms of the old theory of degeneracy of the mixed race offspring.[48] The white race was by no means 'the furthest advanced in effective human development' and it was important to recognise that the coloured population was 'a valuable and indispensable part of any West Indian community and...a colony of blacks, coloureds, and whites has far more organic efficiency and far more promise in it than a colony of blacks and whites alone'.[49]

In his case for 'organic efficiency', Olivier was to some extent trying to capitalise upon the contemporary reactions against the Anglo-Boer War and the campaign for improvement in national efficiency in Edwardian Britain in the wake of the military disasters in South Africa.[50] The concept, though, represented in part the ideal of evolutionary social liberalism imbibed from Dudley Kidd ten years earlier and applied to the West Indian context in order to offset it from the rival segregationist systems. The point about the 'balance of feeling' that had been achieved in Jamaica was that it was very much 'healthier' than anything in South Africa or the South and demonstrated that 'industrial harmony between white and black races may be established more effectively by human understandings and sympathies than by what the sociologists call "economic motive"".[51] Olivier was thus in some degree able to extend the debate in Britain between Cobdenite *laissez-faire* liberalism and the more socially inclined liberalism of L.T. Hobhouse and J.A. Hobson which argued for a measure of state intervention into market processes. By arguing in effect for a healthy racial 'balance' in the West Indian context, Olivier sought to justify a policy of benevolent colonial adminstration as opposed to a market-orientated one which he saw as leading to racial segregation and the polarisation of white and black economic classes. Like a number of his fellow liberals, Olivier considered black races the world over to be especially prone to economic exploitation by white settler and capitalist interests. As a peasantry, blacks had not been disciplined into the rhythms of proletarian wage earning, and he considered that it would be quite possible that a wage system applied to blacks would break down:

> The European wage proletariat and its standards of industrial virtue were only created by long evolution arising out of private landlordism and the pressure of climate and poverty. So long as the African has access to the land, and is saved from poverty by the simplicity of his needs and the care of meeting them, so long the capitalist employer is sure to find his labour unmanageable under the 'free' wage system.[52]

Thus so long as land was not monopolised 'no oppressive industrial system' could be established and Olivier considered that the African peasants could successfully resist exploitation and proletarianisation by industrial landlords.[53] Racial prejudice, though, 'intensifies the tendency to oppression in exploitation' and it needed to be recognised that 'the contacts of human races seeking subsistence have always for the most part begun with war, and that if we are hostile to any European nation today it is chiefly from economic jealousy'.[54] The relationships of white and black were for the most part no different to those of European classes and nations and the problem colonial policy-makers faced was trying to avoid the same class polarisation which had defined nineteenth century English history:

> ...white and black are, or will be, most distinctly confronted in the class division of employer and employee, and in such countries in the comparative absence of (a) hybrid 'middle class' this confrontation appears likely to persist most stubbornly. The biological race distinctions which are the basis of so much race antagonism, will be the less subject to modification, and any bridging of the gulf must be effected the most exclusively by intellectual influences.[55]

Olivier hoped that policy in the West Indies and elsewhere in the empire would evolve through a growth in moral humanitarianism and an increasingly attuned British intelligentsia. He did not speak of a growth in black or coloured political pressure and his description of the racial balance in Jamaican society had a somewhat static quality. For some black critics Olivier's argument seemed faulty at a number of points. Theophilus Scholes, for example, pointed out that, while Olivier was clearly not pandering to popular racial prejudice, there was the feeling that 'if Mr Olivier had given a reason for the existing disproportion between the progress of the mulatto and the progress of the Negro in the West Indies, it would have been the presence of the white blood in the one and the absence in the other'.[56] Racial determinants may have operated in Olivier's argument at one remove and he had by no means made any radical break with Victorian racial thought, but only a humanitarian elaboration upon it.

Indeed, the mid-Victorian axis to Olivier's argument prevented him from seeing a more fundamental feature to the segregationist ideology he castigated. In South Africa territorial segregationism did not reflect a simple *laissez-faire* dependency on market forces but a high degree of state involvement in both economy and society which was epitomised by the domination of Lord Milner and his kindergarten in the working of the post-war Transvaal administration.[57] Olivier tended to underestimate, certainly at this point in his career, the general resilience of segregationist ideology and its capacity to absorb modernising ideas of state-initiated social engineering. For the moment, though, Olivier was not able to follow up his book for a year later, in 1907, he was appointed governor of Jamaica where he got involved in the more detailed aspects of colonial administration which he had hitherto tended to criticise from a distance.

The Governor of Jamaica

In 1900 as a Colonial Office clerk, Olivier had considered, on a visit to the West Indies, that the 'political tone' there was one of 'continuous ill will and suspicion' and 'very disagreeable to deal with'.[58] Despite this apparent reluctance to get involved in West Indian politics, Olivier saw in his appointment as governor a good opportunity to try and apply some of his ideas on the administrative rationalisation of colonial government.

His elevation to the governorship occurred in the wake of the resignation by Sir James Swettenham due to his ordering off the island a company of US marines which had landed to assist in reconstruction after an earthquake had shattered Kingston.[59] Olivier had been a strong critic of Swettenham's *laissez-faire* approach which he argued amounted to nothing more than a 'starvation policy' which would fail to regenerate Kingston and its environs unless the colonial government stepped in to assist the commercial class.[60] His appointment therefore occurred as a result of his concern for the predominantly brown trading and commercial middle class which he considered so important a stabilising factor in Jamaican society. The government had been petitioned early in the year by the Kingston Restoration Committee for the rebuilding of Kingston in order to secure sea defences, wider streets and better housing for the expanding working class population which, the Committee, argued, would be raised in 'tone' by gaining greater selfrespect. These appeals met a sympathetic reception from the Liberal Minister Lord Elgin and Olivier found himself in a political climate favourable to cautious social and economic reform.[61] One civil servant, though, minuted against 'splendour' in the economic reconstruction of the city, which Olivier hoped would act as a stimulus for creating a commercial middle class and, in response to calls for strengthening the police force, Olivier suggested its budget be increased by £2280.[62]

By the time Olivier became governor, the Brussels convention securing European sugar bounties had been revoked and it was the hope of some planters, that with the growth of sugar factories and modern production processes on the larger estates, work could be found for most of the Jamaican population. Since 1904 there had been a continuous emigration of Jamaicans to work on the Panama Canal where contracts lasted for 500 days at 10 cents a day.[63] Though the conditions were harsh with segregationist practices imported from the South (many of the white overseers were Southern), there was a continuous temptation on British colonial governments to encourage this trend which brought back cash wages into the local economy as well as appearing to instil labour disciplines into a population which was seen as generally lacking them. Olivier was generally favourable to this emigration for he saw it as a means of providing the 'surplus' Jamaican population with employment and cash wages while initiating reforms in agriculture to boost the production of peasant small holders.[64] On some occasions, though, the peasant ownership of small plots of land appeared to inhibit the possibility of commercial development, as in the case of a proposal by the Sisal Fibre Company Ltd in the Bahamas to recruit labour in Jamaica. While noting that there were no restrictions on this, Olivier pointed out to Elgin that 'it is true also of Jamaica as of the Bahamas that the labourers are very generally the owners of lots of land which they are unwilling to leave for any length of time.'[65]

Combined with this willingness to see black labour exported to Panama and other West Indian colonies, Olivier placed a considerable faith in the continued importation of Indian indentured labour. Since 1904 this had been at the annual rate of approximately 600 labourers a year, though there had been no special inducements and the granting of free plots of land to the immigrants on the termination of the indentures had ceased in 1906. It is generally true that the English philanthropic spirit failed to take much interest in the indentured system in the wake of the abolition of slavery and the advent of free trade and the Sugar Act in 1846.[66] The limited scale of the system in Jamaica, however, probably encouraged Olivier to think well of it, especially as it seemed from reports of the colony's Surveyor General that there were still thousands of acres of land in the hills which could be opened up by an Indian peasantry once it was freed of its indentures. But there still remained continuing doubts on the fitness of the Indian immigrants who came predominantly from lowland areas of Bengal, for life in the hills and the lack of roads there indicated that there would be marketing problems for any produce grown.[67]

Olivier, however, had no particularly strong faith in the existing black peasantry on the island, whose culture had developed in a tradition of resistance both to slavery and rule by the plantation owners.[68] There was only limited pressure during his governorship for the abolition of the indentured labour system, which some critics compared unfavourably to the segregationist system in South Africa.[69] In general the Colonial Office rejected proposals that the work which the indentured immigrants were currently doing would be taken up by the Jamaican blacks considering the Indian coolies were better suited for the labour disciplines of the sugar plantations. These views reflected the strong local pressures from some of the sugar planters in Jamaica for the continuation of indentures for, as Charles Pringle of Annotto Bay wrote in 1908, 'as may be suspected the proletariat is no paragon of industry and strongly objects to hoeing the light grass, which is well suited to the inferior physical capabilities of the East Indian, and I may add essential to the cultivation of bananas'. On the other hand, though, he pointed out that 'the natives willingly labour at the heavier and more important work'.[70]

By 1910 to 1911, however, it became increasingly difficult to obtain the same annual number of Indian indentured labourers as the number leaving India dropped and there was growing competition for those who did go from other colonies such as Fiji, Trinidad and Mauritius.[71] A proposal to import coolies from Madras introduced problems of language, while those of high caste were considered unsuitable for agricultural labour.[72] It began to look as though indentured labour would eventually dry up in the future and Olivier began to look towards the extension of West Indian commercial interests in the Caribbean as the long run solution to the colony's economic problems. Following a visit to Panama and Costa Rica in 1911 he wrote of the longer term importance of the emigration of Jamaican labour to work on the Panama Canal which could initiate a pattern of colonisation extending to the coastal areas of Central America. He pointed out the growing American threat to British imperial hegemony and called for the British consular presence in Central America to be stopped for:

> A very big process is taking place, and if the British govern-
> ment is at all interested in this part of the world, it is
> desirable that it should as fully as possible understand it, as
> it will have a considerable bearing on relations between the
> U.S.A. and Great Britain in the course of the next ten or
> twenty years...If we do not follow our people into these
> territories we shall have in the alternative to hand over
> Jamaica to the United States.[73]

Such a plea for an aggressive programme of commercial imperialism in the Caribbean met with no positive response from London at a time when the earlier enthusiasm for imperial consolidation of the Chamberlain era had waned and the British government was increasingly preoccupied with domestic issues and Ireland. One civil servant at the Colonial Office considered that the United States was only gaining high returns in Central America as a result of the exploitation of virgin soils and as these became exhausted would eventually find itself in the same position as the British colonial possessions in the region, so bringing down wage levels.[74] The proposal was quietly shelved and Olivier eventually ended his gover-norship in 1913 having failed to shift British colonial policy in any substantial manner, though imprinting some of his ideas on later colonial thinking.

The longer term implications

As Olivier returned from the Jamaican govenorship, his policy appeared to have won a considerable degree of support from amongst the emergent creole political élite in the colony. At a paper delivered to the 1911 Universal Races Congress in London while still governor, he had considered it impossible to arrive at any 'generalisation' regarding the government of 'native races', though hastened to point out that it was 'probably in South Africa that there have been developed the greatest conflicts of opinion, as between the efficient class of colonists in those lands and the mother country in regard to the principle on which the native races should be dealt with'.[75] In the case of the West Indian colonies, however, British policy appeared in effect to be a triumph of Whig statecraft for here government was based on 'no distinction of persons before the Civil Law' and the 'transplanted proletariat' of blacks and Indians was 'regarded as being in semi-tutelage and as not fully qualified for the exercise of responsible self-government in democratic institutions'. With government remaining the responsibility of the colonial power, government remained in the hands of whites 'or of those who have imbued themselves with the civilisation and ideals of the sovereign nation'.[76]

For some of the Jamaican brown élite such as the editor of the *Daily Gleaner,* Herbert De Lisser, Olivier's championing of Whig progress in Jamaica acted as a powerful reinforcement for viewing the creole middle class as the nucleus of a unified Jamaican social order. Furthermore, there seemed almost to be a racialising influence stemming from this conception of social progress for 'no experienced observer', De Lisser wrote in 1913, could fail to be 'struck in these days by the difference between the features of presumably pure-blooded Jamican peasants and the features of African Negroes. The prognatheous face is gradually disappearing in this West Indian colony, the features are being relined. This, of course, is not merely the effect of race mixture. To some extent it is also the consequence of civilisation, and possibly of climactic influence'.[77] For some more radical critics, though, such as Egbert T. Morris Gordon, writing in the Pan Africanist *African Times and Orient Review*, there still remained the question of providing agricultural land for the Jamaican peasantry and the development of docks, transport and hotels to stimulate commercial trade in the island. Blaming Olivier for setting the price of land at £5 an acre too high, Gordon complained that Jamaicans were being forced to work on the Panama Canal for lack of any adequate alternatives.[78]

Such criticisms of colonial policy were to grow in the years ahead as the heyday of the peasant small proprietor came to an end. Though co-operative loan banks had been started in 1905 (growing to some 119 branches by 1949), the peasantry in Jamaica faced a mounting economic crisis by the end of the First World War which the promised 'agricultural revolution' of the early years of the century failed to alleviate.[79] From 1911 onwards the urban parishes started to increase by at least a thousand persons per year through internal migration as a steady exodus from the land began. Kingston started to grow rapidly by the 1920s and 1930s, spawning a nascent labour movement which was eventually to lead to strike action, political parties and the riots of 1936—37[80] Thus the class harmony which De Lisser tried to portray in his novel *Susan Proudleigh* in 1915 in which the 'white and the higher classes of fine coloured folk belonged to one world' while those of blacks 'belonged to another' but 'envy and hatred did not embitter the relations of one class with another' was rapidly becoming an article of mere middle class folk memory.[81] Something of Olivier's earlier portrayal of social harmony in Jamaica lived on, though, into the inter-war years and filtered into British colonial propaganda in its fight against Garveyism. The Colonial Under-Secretary, W. Ormsby-Gore, for example, wrote in 1922 of the 'growth of strong local patriotism in which each and all sections of the community can co-operate, without distinction of race or colour' as the main means of meeting the Garveyite challenge.[82] By the 1920s furthermore Olivier, now a peer, had a reputation as an authoritative figure on colonial policy in the circles of Westminster and Whitehall.

Despite an awareness of what he termed the 'scandal' of West Indian labour conditions, Olivier remained an ardent exponent of the peasant model of economic development. Some analysts such as the South African observer W.M. Macmillan in *Warning from the West Indies* (1936) argued for a plan of collective farming planned by the state,[83] though Olivier still forcefully maintained in evidence to the Moyne Commission in 1938 for peasant settlement combined with a programme of 'liberal education' by which 'people can write and talk in a manner which appeals to the intelligence of educated men all over the world'.[84] An increasingly bitter critic of the Colonial Office, which he felt had sold out to financial interests and had betrayed the Victorian ideal of a *mission civilisatrice* in the British colonies, Olivier's voice remained one of radical protest until his death in 1943. In many respects he helped found a tradition of liberal debate and analysis in the British West Indies which, while removed from a wider school of historical understanding of West Indian social processes in the tradition of José Martí, later contributed to the growth of plural society theory in the 1950s and 1960s. While the exact development of this intellectual tradition must await further analysis, it is clear for example that M.G. Smith's early work laid a similar emphasis on the 'creole complex' as a basis for a new multiracial West Indian culture.[85] Furthermore, with the strong hand of colonial government removed at independence, the more amorphous concept of 'differential incorporation' was seen as binding the segments of the Jamaican plural society together in a manner substantially similar to that envisioned by Olivier in 1906. Thus, in both political debate and social analysis, Olivier should be considered a figure of considerable importance in both the Jamaican and West Indian intellectual and political tradition.

Notes

1   D.K. Fieldhouse, for example, does not refer to the West Indies at all in *The Economics of Empire, 1830–1914*, (London and Basingstoke, The Macmillan Press, 1973).
2   J.M. Lee *Colonial Development and Good Government*, (Oxford, Clarendon Press, 1967), p. 141.
3   Gordon K. Lewis, *Main Currents in Caribbean Thought*, (Baltimore and London, Johns Hopkins University Press, 1983), pp. 2–8.
4   Ian Campbell, 'Carlyle and the Negro Question Again', *Criticism*, XIII, 3 (Summer 1971), pp. 279–290.
5   Eric Williams, *Capitalism and Slavery*, (London, Andre Deutsch, 1964) pp. 195–6.
6   Philip Curtin, 'Scientific' racism and the British theory of Empire', *Journal of the Historical Society of Nigeria*, 11, (1969), p. 44. See also Paul B. Rich, *Race and Empire in British Politics*, (Cambridge, C.U.P., 1986) pp. 12–13.
7   Anthony Trollope, *The West Indies and the Spanish Main*, (London, Frank Cass, 1968; I ed. 1859), pp. 55–56.
8   *ibid*. p. 74.
9   *ibid*. p. 64. For Trollope's attitude to the colonies see J.H. Davidson, 'Anthony Trollope and the Colonies', *Victorian Studies*, 12 (1968–9), pp. 305–330.
10 T.H. Huxley, 'Emancipation-Black and White'.
11 *Parliamentary Debates*, House of Commons, 182, 1866, col. 132.
12 J.W. Burrow, 'A Liberal Descent', *Victorian Historians and the English Past*, (Cambridge, C.U.P. 1981), p. 84.
13 W.F. Finlason, *A History of the Jamaica Case*, (London, Chapman and Hall, 1868). pp. 661–662.
14 John Roach, 'Liberalism and the Victorian Intelligentsia', *The Cambridge Historical Journal*, XIII, I (1957), pp. 58–81; Christopher Harvie, 'Ideology and Home Rule: James Bryce, A.V. Dicey, and Ireland, 1880–1887', *The English Historical Review*, XCI (April 1976), pp. 298–314.
15 For Allen's novel see Lewis, *Main Currents*, pp. 233–34.
16 Grant Allen, *In All Shades*, Vol. 1, (London, Chatto and Windus, 1886), pp. 122–23.
17 *ibid*. Vol. 2. p. 155.
18 *ibid*. p. 166.

19   Sir Spencer St John, *Hayti or the Black Republic*, (London, Frank Cass, 1971; I ed 1884), p. ix.

20   James Anthony Froude, *The English in the West Indies,* (London, Longman, 1888), p. 79.

21   Lewis, *Main Currents*, p. 311.

22   Clive J. Dewey, 'The Rehabilitation of the peasant proprietor in nineteenth century economic thought', *History of Political Economy*, 6, I (1974) pp. 17–47.

23   Colin Bundy, *The Rise and Fall of the South African Peasantry*, (London, Heinemann, 1979), pp. 134–40.

24   Charles Pearson, *National Life and Character*, (London, 1893); see also Oscar J. Falnes, 'European Progress and "Superior" Races: as viewed by a *fin de siècle* liberal, Charles H. Pearson', *Journal of the History of Ideas*, XV, 2 (April 1954), pp. 312–321.

25   Benjamin Kidd, *The Control of the Tropics*, (London, Macmillan, 1898), pp. 2–3.

26   D.P. Crook, *Benjamin Kidd: Portrait of a Social Darwinist*, (Cambridge, C.U.P. 1984), pp. 117–141.

27   W.P. Livingstone, *Black Jamaica A Study in Evolution*, (London, 1899), p. 15.

28   *ibid.* p. 150.

29   *ibid.* pp. 165–166.

30   Sydney Olivier, *Capital and Land,* Fabian Tract No. 7, (London, 1888).

31   *C.W. Greenidge Papers*, Rhodes House Library, Oxford, MSS Brit. Emp. S285 31/2 Lord Olivier, 'The Dual Ethic in Empire', (Unpub. ms., n.d.), pp. 3, 8.

32   CO 318/289 West India Committee, Circular No. 738, 25 January 1897.

33   *Report of the West India Royal Commission*, 1897, Cmnd 8655, London, 1897, p. 17, para 115.

34   CO 884/5 S. Olivier, memorandum dated 28 September 1897.

35   *West Indian Royal Commission, Report*, minutes of evidence Messrs C. Gordon and Gosset, pp. 292–4; Hon. J.T. Palache, p. 300.

36   CO 884/5 C.P. Lucas, memorandum October 1897.

37   CO 318/293 *Address delivered before the Agricultural Society of Trinidad by Dr D. Morris, Imperial Commissioner of Agriculture for the West Indies*, 8 November 1898, p. 7.

38   CO 318/293 *The Memorial of the African Association on the Distress in the West Indies*, 30 March 1898.

39   CO 318/290/2 A. Norman to Under Sec of State, C.O., 7 December 1897.

40   *George Bernard Shaw Papers*, British Museum Add 50543 S. Olivier to G.B.S. 1899.

41   'The Settlement of South Africa', *The Quarterly Review*, CXCIV, 385 (1901), p. 583.

42   See John Cell, *The Highest Stage of White Supremacy: the origin of Segregation in South Africa and the American South*, (Cambridge, C.U.P. 1982).

43   B. Pullen-Bury, *Ethiopia in Exile: Jamaica Revisited*, (London, 1905), pp. 67–8. The book owed much to Charles Pearson's *National Life and Character*.

44   *ibid.* p. 79.

45 Josiah Royce, 'Race Questions and Prejudices' in *Race Question, Provincialism and other American Problems*, (New York, 1908), p. 24.
46 Sydney Olivier, *White Capital and Coloured Labour*, (London, I.L.P., 1906), p. 18. For Mary Kingsley's influence see *Race and Empire in British Politics*, pp. 29–49.
47 *White Capital and Coloured Labour*, p. 20.
48 *ibid*. pp. 36–7.
49 *ibid*. pp. 37–8.
50 G.R. Searle, *The Quest for National Efficiency*, (Oxford, O.U.P., 1971.)
51 *White Capital and Coloured Labour*, p. 42.
52 *ibid*. p. 84.
53 *ibid*. p. 118. Olivier's argument rested upon the static portrayal of African tribal life in Dudley Kidd's *The Essential Kaffir*.
54 *ibid*. p. 131.
55 *ibid*. p. 142.
56 Theophilus E. Samuel Scholes, *Glimpses of the ages: or the 'superior' and 'Inferior' races, so called, discussed in the light of science and history*, (London, 1905), p. 159.
57 Eric Stokes, 'Milnerism', *Historical Journal*, V, I (1962), pp. 47–60; Shula Marks and Stanley Trapido, 'Lord Milner and the South African State', *History Workshop*, 8, (Autumn 1979), pp. 50–80.
58 *G.B.S. Pap.* Add 50543 S. Olivier to G.B.S. 11 April 1900.
59 An account of this episode is given in Ronald Hyam, *Elgin and Churchill at the Colonial Office*, (London, Macmillan, 1968), p. 479–481.
60 CO 137/656 S. Olivier to C.P. Lucas 7 April 1907.
61 CO 137/658 S. Olivier to Lord Elgin 6 June 1907; CO 137/656 S. Olivier to C.P. Lucas; Lucas, minute., n.d.; CO 137/662 S. Olivier to Lord Elgin 14 February 1907.
62 CO 137/663/68 S. Olivier to Lord Elgin 25 February 1908; minute by HQC 13 March 1908; CO 137/656 Deputation of the Kingston Restoration Committee 1 March 1907.
63 Lancelot Sebastian Lewis, 'The West Indian in Panama (Black Labor in Panama) 1850–1914', Ph.D Thesis, (Tulane University, 1975), pp. 33–4.
64 For Olivier's commitment to reform in Jamaica see Richard A. Lobdell, 'Socialism, Imperialism and Sydney Olivier', (unpub. ms. University of Manitoba, 1984).
65 CO 137/659 S. Olivier to Lord Elgin 28 August 1907.
66 Hugh Tinker, *A New System of Slavery*, (London, O.U.P.), 1974, p. 237; Philip Curtin, 'The British Sugar Duties and West Indian Prosperity', *Journal of Economic History*, XIV, 2 (Spring 1954), pp. 157–164. See also William A Green, 'The West Indies and Indentured Labour Migration-the Jamaican Experience', in Kay Saunders (ed.) *British Labour in the British Empire, 1834–1920*, (London and Canberra, Croom Helm, 1984) pp. 31–2.
67 CO 137/685/217 P.C. Cork to L. Harcourt 2 June 1911.
68 Sydney W. Mintz. 'The Origins of Reconstituted Peasantries', *Caribbean Transformations*, (Baltimore and London, Johns Hopkins University Press, 1984) pp. 146–56: 'Torn from societies that had not yet entered into the capitalist world and thrust into settings that were profoundly capitalistic in character on the one hand, yet rooted in the need for

unfree labour on the other, the slaves saw liquid capital not only as a means to secure freedom, but also as a means to attach their paternity—and hence, their identity as persons—to something even the masters would have to respect. In these terms the creation of peasantries was simultaneously an act of westernisation and an act of resistance' (p. 155).

69   CO 137/662 C. Ton Evans (National Negro Baptist Convention) To W. Churchill, 27 July 1907; HQC minute 31 July 1907.

70   CO 137/666/561 Charles Pringle to Protector of Immigrants September 1908: George D. Murray to C.W. Doorly 26 September 1908; Charles W. Doorly, 'Note on the Alleged Competition between Coolies and Creole labour in Jamaica'.

71   CO 137/871 S. Olivier to Sec. of State, 12 March 1909; CO 137/679/352 S. Olivier to Lord Crewe 27 August 1910; CO 137/684/134 S. Olivier to L. Harcourt 21 April 1911.

72   CO 137/685/217 P.C. Cork to L. Harcourt 2 June 1911.

73   CO 137/690 S. Olivier to Anderson 29 November 1911 and to L. Harcourt 20 January 1912; See also John Joseph Carroll, 'The Government of Jamaica, 1910–1913, with special reference to the role of Sir Sydney Olivier', Ph.D Thesis, (University of London, 1976), p. 270.

74   CO 137/690 minute by G.G., February 1912.

75   Sir Sydney Olivier 'The Government of Colonies and Dependencies', in *Papers on Inter-Racial Problems communicated to the First Universal Races Congress held at the University of London, July 26–29, 1911, edited, for the Congress by G. Spiller, Hon. Organiser of the Congress*, (London, P.S. King and Boston, The World's Peace Foundation, 1911), p. 295. For the historical significance of the Congress see Michael D. Biddiss, 'The Universal Races Congress of 1911', *Race*, XIII, 1 (1971), pp. 37–46; Paul Rich, 'The Baptism of a new era: the 1911 Universal Races Congress and the liberal ideology of race', *Ethnic and Racial Studies*, 7, 4 (October 1984), pp. 534–50.

76   'The Government of Colonies and Dependencies', pp. 295–6.

77   H.G. De Lisser, *Twentieth Century Jamaica*, (Kingston, The Jamaica Times, 1913), p. 148.

78   Egbert T. Morris, 'Jamaicans and the Panama Canal', *African Times and Orient Review*, 7 April 1914.

79   Woodville K. Marshall, 'Notes on Peasant Development in the West Indies Since 1838', *Social and Economic Studies*, 17–18, (1968–69), p. 261.

80   G.E. Cumper, 'Population Movements in Jamaica, 1830–1950', *Social and Economic Studies*, 5, 3 (1956), pp. 272–3.

81   H. De Lisser, *Susan Proudleigh*, (London, Methuen, 1916) p. 70.

82   W. Ormsby-Gore, 'British West Indies', *United Empire*, XIII, 7 (July 1922), p. 463.

83   W.M. Macmillan, *Warning from the West Indies*, (Harmondsworth, Penguin Books, 1936); Mona Macmillan, 'The Making of *Warning from the West Indies*: Extract from a projected memoir of W.M. Macmillan', *Journal of Commonwealth and Comparative Politics*, XVIII, 2 (July 1980), pp. 207–19. See also Sydney Olivier, 'The Scandal of West Indian Labour Conditions', *The Contemporary Review*, CLLII, (March 1938), pp. 282–89; *Race and Empire in British Politics*, pp. 79–82.

84   Royal commission to the West Indies: verbatim report of the 1st Session of the Commission, 20 September, 1938, ed. Lord Olivier, pp. 28−9 in *Arthur Creech Jones Papers*, (Rhodes House, Oxford), ACJ 25/1 (4).

85   M.G. Smith, *The Plural Society in the British West Indies*, (Berkeley and Los Angeles, University of California Press, 1965); see also R.S. Bryce-Laporte, 'M. G. Smith's version of Pluralism - the Questions it raises', *Comp. Stud. in Soc. and Hist.* X (1967−68) pp. 114−70; Malcolm Cross, 'Cultural Pluralism and Sociological Theory - A Critique and Re-evaluation', *Social and Economic Studies*, 17, (1968), pp. 381−97.

CHAPTER 12 | The imperatives and complexities of the Cuban labour movement

Alistair Hennessy

For size and complexity the Cuban labour movement dwarfs that of any other Caribbean country. This essay can only skim the surface of its tortuous history but by stressing some distinctive features may contribute towards a realistic assessment of the relevance which the Cuban experience might have for the rest of the Caribbean. Because organised labour played an unheroic role in the struggle against Batista its historical importance can easily be underestimated. It is arguable that it was the complexity and contradictions within the movement which enabled a small group of determined revolutionaries to fulfil the role which in more orthodox revolutionary theory should have been played by the organised working class.

The Cuban labour movement developed under constraints which were very different from those operating in other Caribbean countries so that labour radicalism took a distinctive form but quite apart from these constraints the context within which the labour movement operated as well as the imperatives of Cuban history need to be spelt out in order to make comparisons more effective.

Cuba has had a much longer relationship with the United States than any other island, stretching back to the late eighteenth century, to such an extent that it has been part of the North American economic and cultural universe rather than that of the Caribbean or Spanish America.[1] Annexation to the United States, for example, has been a persistent sentiment among members of the Cuban élite since the mid-nineteenth century and the degree of Americanisation of the élite is symbolised by the American citizenship of Estrada Palma, the first president of independent Cuba. It was not until the revolution of 1959 that Cuba was wholly reincorporated into the orbit of Latin America.

In common with other Spanish speaking islands, Puerto Rico and the Dominican Republic, but to a greater extent, Cuba was a settlement as well as a plantation colony with its population almost equally divided between those of African and European descent until the racial balance began to swing in favour of whites after the last importation of slaves in the 1850s. This created a much more complex racial and class structure as well as a multi-layered culture, affecting the process of slavery abolition which was longer and more protracted than elsewhere in the Caribbean.

The process of abolition was further complicated by the war of independence against Spain which lasted from 1868–78 and 1895–98, the longest and bloodiest war experienced by any Caribbean nation. The intervention of the United States at the end of that war and subsequent occupations between 1898 and 1902 and 1906 and 1909 strengthened an already powerful nationalist tradition and fuelled the myth of a continuous but frustrated revolution.

Under Spain, Cuba was not simply dependent on a European power but on one which was itself dependent economically on other European powers, notably Britain. By inhibiting industrialisation this compelled the middle class to seek employment in the bureaucracy in Spain or in the colonies at the same time as an economically backward industry, unable to face competition in Europe, became increasingly dependent on a protected colonial market. This had the effect of binding Spaniards and Cubans together in a much tighter web of relationships than those existing between any other Caribbean colony and its metropolis.

With the impact of the sugar revolution in the early nineteenth century Cuba was modernising more rapidly than Spain and in contrast to declining and stagnant economies in the rest of the Caribbean the first and second sugar revolutions created a dynamic industrial system which provided the basis for an industrial working class for eclipsing in size that of any other island.[2]

One consequence of the immense wealth generated by a monocultural economy was that Cubans became bemused by 'King Sugar' and the sugar mirage. This created a fatalism and a boom-slump psychosis which deeply influenced the national self-image. As the smallest fluctuation in sugar exports sent a ripple effect throughout the economy no class or group remained unaffected.

Excessive wealth also produced a leisure class. Exclusion from politics under Spanish rule led to a boredom which could only be assuaged by conspicuous consumption and a hedonist ethic, bequeathing a legacy to Havana which was not easily thrown off. But another by-product of leisure was the emergence of a nationalist intelligentsia, the student sector of which was to arrogate to itself from the 1920s a national regenerationist role, in which they saw themselves as redeemers of an exploited working class, and the vanguard of the anti-imperialist struggle against the United States.

Although corruption was not unique to Cuba its extent and

depth were.[3] This was a consequence of the spoils system and a by-product of the neo-colonial relationship with the United States as well as being a legacy of Spanish rule. All sectors of Cuban society, especially in Havana, were affected by corruption from which union leaders were not immune. Although one purpose of the American occupation after the war was to establish an uncorrupt administration, Americans themselves soon found opportunities for self-enrichment — as the mafia were to discover in the 1920s. This was merely one aspect of the way in which Cuban society after independence was to be distorted by the neo-colonial relationship expressed in the Platt Amendment which permitted Americans to intervene should life or property be threatened or in the event of civil disturbances which might encourage intervention by a third power. The implications both for the political system and for labour relations were profound.

Havana dominated Cuba after the achievement of independence as effectively as it had during the colonial period and only after 1959 was an attempt made to downgrade the capital in the interests of the rural areas. Part of the explanation for Havana's dominance stems from the settlement pattern created by the expanding sugar frontier. As this moved into empty land it created plantations rather than viable rural communities. This influenced the structure of the rural population round which a vigorous debate has developed as to what proportion should be classified as peasants and what proportion as rural proletarians. Sugar plantations created rural proletarians 'culturally and behaviourly distinct from the peasantry', a class more concerned with job security, a living wage and access to social services than with access to land.[4] There is no Cuban equivalent of peasant movements wedded to the reconstruction of an idealised communal past such as may be found in *zapatismo*. The sugar *colono* class of cane growers, the heroes of Guerra y Sánchez's seminal book, was highly differentiated between large landowners, medium size farmers and mere small tenant farmers. Other crops such as tobacco produced recognisable peasant farmers such as those who constituted the ANAP (*Asociación Nacional de Agricultores Pequeños*) after 1959, or the *guajiros*, descendants of squatters or the marginalised squatters of Oriente who were to be the first recruits of the guerrillas in the revolt against Batista but there was very little sense of peasant class consciousness.

As a nominally Catholic country, Cuba had no sect tradition before the twentieth century and so was deprived of the stimulus of Protestant educational, entrepreneurial, charitable or cultural values.[5] After independence the secularisation of the state, combined with a weak Catholic church, provides one explanation for the intensity and variety of ideologies which extended to the labour movement, and for the prevalence of a Marxist and *marxisant* political culture.

Finally, and for the purposes of this chapter, the most distinctive feature of Cuban society in the twentieth century was the unusual fact that Cuba continued to be a net importer of immigrants at a time when the rest of the Caribbean was exporting labour.[6] Labour history has to be interpreted in terms of a dialectical interaction between enforced black immigration from Africa, indentured Chinese labour and white immigration from Europe (and the Canary Islands) in the colonial period, and between free Spanish immigration and free black seasonal immigration in the republican period.

With these factors in mind the rest of this chapter will be concerned with the emergence of an organised labour movement in the nineteenth century, represented by the tobacco industry; the major trends in twentieth century labour; the significance of the colour question and the sugar industry; the influence of immigration; intellectuals and the labour movement, and the revolutionary crisis of 1933 and its aftermath in the first period of Batista's rule between 1934 and 1944.

The emergence of organised labour in the nineteenth century

Cuba's labour system began to diversify earlier than in the rest of the Caribbean and many decades before the end of slavery as the sugar revolutions gathered momentum based on technological innovation and steam power. Squatters, displaced peasants, Canary Islanders (*isleños*), indentured Chinese and manumitted slaves coexisted during the apogee of the slave-dominated sugar revolution, at the same time as the tobacco industry produced an industrial proletariat and the genesis of a factory system.

From the 1850s tobacco workers were the cutting edge of Cuban labour and were to remain so up to 1959.[7] But even in this most advanced sector of the labour force as many as a third of cigar makers were slaves working beside free labourers of whom 15 per cent were coloured. Although the tobacco industry has never accounted for more than a small proportion of the national production, it has nevertheless played a crucial role in the labour movement and was the scene of early conflict 'whose ideological ramification spanned annexationism, abolitionism, nationalism, anarchism, anarcho-syndicalism, socialism and communism'.

A tradition of resistance can be traced back to the *vegueros* of the early eighteenth century when tobacco farmers resisted the imposition of a royal tobacco monopoly but it was the growth of the cigar industry in the nineteenth century which made tobacco comparable with the contemporary textile industry in England. Some factories employed as many as 300 in the 1860s, and some a thousand or more by the end of the century. Mutual aid societies were formed in the 1850s not much later than in Spain itself; craft guilds, white, male and urban were founded in the 1860s, and *Aurora* the first workers' weekly appeared in 1866. The practice of reading in rolling rooms, a secularised version of homiletic readings in monasteries and still practised, was an indication of the stress laid by tobacco workers on the written word and was rightly suspected by employers for its potentially subversive implications. Censorship was enforced, provoking the first recorded strike in the industry, and eventually the practice was forbidden. Cigarmakers, with the highest literacy rate after typographers, were described as 'intellectuals of the proletariat', and from their ranks were recruited some of the most prominent working class leaders such as the anarcho-syndicalist Enrique Roig in the 1880s, the socialist Carlos Baliño in the 1900s, and the communist Lazaro Peña who built up Cuba's first strong industrial union the *Federación Tabacalera Nacional* in 1936 as well as the first National Workers' Federation (CTC) in 1939 and who, as a black, reflected the breakdown of the earlier white exclusivity of unionised tobacco workers.

Although anarcho-syndicalists spearheaded the strikes of the late 1880s for higher and standardised wage rates, anarchism was not incompatible with 'respectable associationism', possibly because employers were less intransigent than their Catalan counterparts whose inflexibility contributed to the solidarity of Catalan anarchism. The tobacco industry was particularly prone to strike waves over a wide spectrum of issues, ranging from differential wage rates, apprenticeship issues, technological innovation, political repression, mechanisation and the challenge from United States manufacturers. Even in the early period, labour organisation was related to political issues such as abolition and independence, foreshadowing the politicisation of the labour movement in the twentieth century.

Many tobacco workers had started to leave for Florida as early as the 1860s, tempted by higher wages or fleeing for political reasons and it was among the Cuban communities in Key West, Tampa, Ibor City and elsewhere that José Martí was to find some of his most dedicated supporters for the PRC (*Partido Revolucionario Cubano*). When many of these workers returned to Cuba at the end of the war after 1898 they brought with them anarchist ideas, socialism, Martían populism, and American unionism. Views among these exiles were more eclectic than among immigrants coming straight from Spain for whom an addiction to forms of anarchism seemed almost to provide a form of bonding in the new environment. The Florida Cubans in contrast were steeped in Cuban and American traditions.

Martí's views have been subjected to a variety of interpretations as every sector of Cuban political opinion has tried to legitimate their own actions by reference to them but, however varied these interpretations, the fundamental fact was that Martí's ideas and activities—and the two were inseparable—were conditioned by the independence struggle against Spain and by an acute awareness of the need to build an alliance between hardened *caudillos*, sophisticated lawyers, literate artisans, skilled workers and semi-literate ex-slaves.[8] His views were not only conditioned by immediate tactical needs but by strategic necessity as he saw, with a clarity unmatched by any of his contemporaries, the nature of the threat to a future independent Cuba from the United States. His programme for *Cuba Libre* was one of political democracy, social justice, racial equality and land reform to break the economic tyranny of the plantation system. His views, heavily influenced by Henry George, envisaged a society of independent peasant farmers, producing a variety of crops so as to break the monocultural dependence on sugar. Martí's populist nationalism stressed class harmony as he believed that class conflict, by undermining national consensus, would expose Cuba to the expansionist ambitions of the United States. Killed at the beginning of the war in 1895, he was not able to put his ideas into practice but his vision became integral to the Cuban revolutionary tradition.

His associates in exile, faced with practical problems on their return to Cuba modified his ideas.[9] Notable among them was Diego Tejera who founded the *Partido Socialista Cubano* in February 1899. Although it collapsed within four months the socialist tradition was taken up on his death by another associate of Martí, Carlos Balino who founded the *Partido Obrero* in 1904. His marxism brought him into contact with Julio Antonio Mella the student leader and founder member of the communist party first constituted in 1925, thus establishing the party's reputable nationalist ancestry.[10]

Labour trends in the twentieth century

Three main strands within Cuban labour organisation in the twentieth century illustrate the diverse source of influences feeding into it.[11]

First in time were anarchism and anarcho-syndicalism introduced by Spanish immigrants—mainly from Catalonia, the stronghold of anarcho-syndicalist sentiment. In 1924 anarchists founded and dominated CNOC (*Confederación Nacional Obrera de Cuba*) the first labour confederation. But this leadership was shortlived. Terrorised by Machado who became president in the same year, and with their leader assassinated, control passed to the communists. Anarchism proved unable to compete with rival labour ideologies partly because of a refusal to accept centralised leadership and because, with the decline of Spanish immigration in the late 1920s, recruits with an anarchist background from Spain dried up. Although Machado outlawed CNOC in 1928 when it protested against his continuing in office the communists were able to turn labour into one of the major opposition groups.

The second trend was socialism but because of the corrupt nature of Cuban parliamentary life socialists were unable to organise themselves into a social-democrat party and leaders such as Baliño were attracted to the newly formed communist party, the core of which included foreign immigrants of whom the Pole, Yunger Semjovich of the Comintern, was the most prominent representative and who as Fabio Gobart, is the oldest veteran of the Cuban labour movement alive today. The communist party attracted intellectuals such as Julio Antonio Mella, the founder of the students' federation, the FEU, and the poet Rubín Martínez Villena. Their early deaths, one by assassination in Mexico in 1929, the other by tuberculosis in Russia in 1934 deprived the party of able intellectual leadership and left it as a sectarian group who were able to increase their influence in the Havana and Manzanillo unions and to turn labour into one of the major opposition groups against Machado contributing, through their organisation of strikes, in overthrowing him in the revolution of 1933. But a rigid adherence to the party line of non-cooperation with bourgeois 'social fascists' diminished their influence and contributed to the collapse of the Revolution with Batista's army coup in January 1934. Sectarianism had reduced them to impotence, and discredited them among labour unions.

The third period was ushered in by Batista who dominated Cuban politics until 1944. After breaking a general strike in 1935— called by the non-communist unions—he began a period of reconstructing the labour movement with the co-operation of the communists who since 1936 had changed the party line to popular front tactics of co-operation with progressive forces. This period was marked by government patronage of labour unions, legalisation and preferential treatment of the communists, and protective legislation enshrined in a workers' charter incorporated in the 1940 Constitution. After Batista stood down in the 1944 elections the strong hold of the communists on the unions which they owed to Batista's patronage was challenged in a period marked by terror and bribery, which by dividing and demoralising the labour movement prevented it from playing a leading role in the opposition to Batista in his second and dictatorial period after his coup of 1952. After the success of Castro's revolution in 1959 collaborationist unions were purged and the communist dominated unions came into their own, building on the foundations laid during the first *Batistato*.

In addition to the international links of the communist party through affiliation with the international communist federation unions, reformist unions in the 1920s had links with American unions. Samuel Gompers and the AFL had been active supporters of Martí and the independence struggle through the tobacco workers in Florida and these contacts were carried over into the republican period. Links were institutionalised through the Pan American Federation of Labour (PAFL) of which Gompers and the Puerto Rican Santiago Iglesias were founder members. Carlos Loveira, who began life as a railwayman in Camaguey and finished as Cuba's leading novelist of the 1920s was a close friend of Gompers and a member of the executive committee of the PAFL.[12] He returned to Cuba in 1915 from Mexico where he had been involved in the revolution but attempts to repeat in Cuba the successes which the PAFL had had in Mexico failed in the face of divisions between Cuban anarchists, syndicalists and socialists as well as of nationalist resentment at the way in which the PAFL appeared to be controlled by the State Department.

The sugar industry and the colour question

In chapter four Rebecca Scott has highlighted some of the issues involved in the transition from slavery to free labour during the last years of colonial rule but the transitional period overran into the first decades of independence when the new republic had to face serious problems of social and economic readjustment. A crippled economy and the post-war legacies of an uprooted rural population in a devastated countryside posed problems for the sugar industry which were exacerbated when the sugar frontier started expanding into Camaguey and Oriente after 1904 and when the Great War created a spiralling demand for sugar.

Ex-slaves could either squat on unoccupied land (as many did in isolated parts of Oriente) and run the risk of eviction by the newly established rural guard or they could move to the cities in search of work.[13] The puzzling fact of the absence of legal coercion compelling ex-slaves to work on the plantations has already been mentioned. With the majority of plantations in ruins after the war there was no shortage of rural labour nor was there a shortage of labour in the towns as Spanish immigrants once again became available, and once on the plantation payment by *fiches* instead of money (a recurrent motive behind strike action) effectively tied down the labour force. There was therefore little alternative to work on the plantations and even a free spirit such as Esteban Montejo drifted back to the cane fields, and for thousands like him independence did not alter the facts of pre-war life.

The sugar industry was by far the largest employer of labour but even so it proved difficult to organise a united front. A distinction must be made between the industrial sector of the sugar industry in the centrals, for the most part white and skilled, and the rural sector, mostly black and unskilled. Both suffered from the arbitrariness of seasonal labour but this shared disability was not sufficient to draw the two very diverse components together. Whereas it was comparatively easy to organise those in the industrial sector, those in the agricultural sector were disadvantaged for reasons connected with colour—a dimension of the history of twentieth century Cuba which has only recently received attention from historians—and through the immigration of seasonal labour from the rest of the Caribbean.

The colour question

Racial tensions between abolition in 1886 and the outbreak of war in 1895 had been heightened as increasing geographical mobility brought freed slaves into contact with whites in cities and with colour conscious Spanish immigrants competing for scarce jobs. This hostility was partly offset by the Spanish government's attempt to head off black discontent by social and educational reforms but these did not extend to land distribution which would have undermined the basis of the plantation system. Black *gremios*, nascent black workers' organisations and the emergence of a small black professional group with their own paper was cut short by the outbreak of war again in 1895.[14] Although the war put an end to this it opened new avenues of social mobility in the Liberating Army where blacks served as officers, including Antonio Maceo a leading general whose death in 1896 deprived the blacks of a leader if not a legend.

Although racial friction and discrimination existed before independence there was sharpening antagonism during and after the American occupation which led to increasing discrimination.[15] The origins of the black crisis which was to explode in the Race War of 1912 stemmed from disappointed expectations raised by black involvement in the war. The promise of black advancement seemed less after independence than in the late 1880s and 1890s.

The Platt Amendment and the retention of the naval base at Guantánamo were seen by both Americans and the Cuban élite as an insurance against social revolution and rebellion by blacks. Spanish immigrants were welcomed as part of a 'whitening' policy and some 200,000 entered between 1920 and 1910. Black immigration, in contrast, was forbidden by decree in 1902. Racial discrimination was not only practised by Americans but by incoming Spaniards.

So far from links with Spain becoming weaker as happened when the mainland colonies broke away, they became stronger so that blacks could well wonder who had won the war. As Spanish immigration had militated against Cubans in the colonial period so now it militated against blacks who through lack of educational qualifications were excluded from all but the most menial occupations. Nor did they receive any help from unions in which, as Carlos Baliño commented, they were conspicuous by their absence.

Settling blacks on the land, as Martí had proposed, was never a possibility as this would have spelt the end of the plantation economy on which Cuba's revival was posited. As Scott has shown, only 4.5 per cent of *colonos* were coloured. It was the disillusioning experience of independence for the vast majority of blacks which prompted Evaristo Estenoz to found the PIC (*Partido Independiente de Color*) in 1906 with a programme demanding access to land, to education and the spoils system, as well as labour reforms, the eight-hour day, child labour laws and preferential treatment for blacks over immigrants.[16]

Faced with the threat of politics polarising along colour lines a law was passed in 1910 named after Morúa Delgado, the black president of the Senate, forbidding the formation of parties based on colour. This was to be a major factor goading the PIC into revolt. The subsequent race war of 1912 cost at least 3000 lives and prompted the intervention of US marines. Crippled by this experience blacks tended to withdraw into their own subculture in the shanty towns of Havana and other cities until the growth of Afro-Cubanism as part of the nationalist *prise de conscience* of the 1920s drew attention to the central role which Africanisms had made to Cuban culture. The growth of Afro-Cuban cults was the most distinctive feature of this sub-culture. It has been argued that they rather than Christianity have been the traditional opium of the people and that unlike the black churches of the United States they failed to provide a counter-institutional structure or to generate a national black leadership.[17] However, they did serve as a defence mechanism which in the case of port-workers in Havana was used to protect jobs ensuring, through the *nañigos*, access to unskilled and casual labour, a process which lasted until the 1950s.[18]

Any hope that blacks would benefit from new demands for labour as the sugar economy expanded in the years before and during the First World War were to be dashed by the introduction of immigrants from the rest of the Caribbean.

Black immigration

Elsewhere in the Caribbean, slavery abolition exacerbated the problem of labour supply. Cuba was unusual by starting to import indentured labour in 1848, forty years before the abolition of slavery. There was, however, no need to import workers from as far afield as Asia when lack of opportunities in neighbouring Haiti and Jamaica provided a more convenient pool of cheap labour.[19] In contrast to shrinking sugar economies elsewhere, Cuba had new land to open up and in the decade before the First World War the sugar frontier pushed into Camagüey and Oriente creating a demand for some 105,000 additional cane cutters. In 1914 the American Nipe Bay Company petitioned the Cuban president to rescind the prohibition of 1902 and to allow the importation of seasonal migrants from Haiti and Jamaica. Attitudes to this new black immigration were hostile except for those planters who were beneficiaries. In the 1920s the labour press loudly denounced immigrants who were depressing wages and being used as strikebreakers while the bourgeois press ran articles raising visions of Cuba being swamped by Africans and scare stories of imported disease, witchcraft and child murder much in the style of the 'Africanisation of Cuba' scare of the 1850s. It would seem, however, that the 'yellow invasion', although minimal (one per cent of all immigrants between 1900 and 1931 were Chinese) was perceived as an even greater threat because of the more immediate challenge they posed to the Spanish domination of shopkeeping.

There were wide differences between Haitian and Jamaican

immigrants. Although both were concentrated in the new areas of sugar production in the Eastern provinces, Jamaicans were more socially and geographically mobile and were inclined to move to cities and to Havana where it was the proud boast that their carpenters and masons had made a major contribution towards the construction of the pretentious Congress building.[20] Their literacy rate was over 90 per cent compared with 20 per cent for Haitians. They were proud of their British nationality and expected (although not always receiving) the protection of British consuls, who, in spite of Jamaicans' generally exemplary behaviour, complained of their being a disruptive element.[21] Haitians though, were exploited financially by Haitian and Cuban migration officials alike. There was a striking disparity in sex ratios with women regularly comprising each year 45 per cent of Jamaican immigrants. They were highly prized as cooks and domestics by American employers as well as for their knowledge of English. Jamaican men, however, were not as popular as Haitians because of their higher cultural level and desire to better themselves by moving away from the plantations. Employers nevertheless welcomed an un-unionised and culturally disadvantaged workforce. It was cheaper to import labour from outside than to recruit from other parts of the island. The new immigration had all the advantages of slavery with none of the disadvantages. Because of the isolation of the immigrants living in barracks, patrolled by plantation guards, they had little contact with Cubans and although intermarriage did occur it seems to have been rare.

To what extent this immigration depressed wages is difficult to estimate although *prima facie* it would seem to have done so as the labour press argued. What is clear is that the presence of two culturally diverse groups made the task of political proselitisation and union organisation among field workers more difficult. One of the consequences of the 1933 revolution was to implement anti-migrant legislation for which labour unions had been clamouring since the early 1920s. The communists opposed this legislation in the interests of international solidarity but in doing so they misjudged the sentiments of most Cuban workers. They also argued, following the current American communist party line, for a separate negro state in Oriente, the 'black belt' where blacks numbered 77 per cent of the population in comparison with 23 per cent in the nation as a whole—a view which was abandoned in 1934.

Back in Jamaica and Haiti this migration acted as a useful safety valve and it is not accidental that once this valve was closed after 1933, disturbances broke out in both Haiti and Jamaica.[22] In Haiti demographic pressures on the Dominican frontier led to the massacres by Trujillo of 1938 and in Jamaica it was a contributory factor in the outburst of labour militancy there. Whether any political influence can be traced still remains to be researched although Bustamante's period in Cuba may have had some influence on his populist style of politics. Within Cuba itself, immigrant workers seem to have avoided militancy for fear of being deported but also because in the case of Jamaicans, Garveyism was an important influence as in all the West Indian enclaves throughout the Hispanic circum-Caribbean. Garveyism gave a sense of dignity, self-respect and pride in conditions of squalor rather than encouraged workers to become militant. Garvey, himself, who visited plantations in 1921 was still, at that time, a believer in American style self-help.[23]

If black immigration provides one key to an understanding of the slow emergence of unionism among agricultural sugar workers, the pattern of Spanish immigration is a key to explaining some of the peculiarities of the development of urban labour and of unionism among industrial sugar workers.

Spanish immigration

Continued large scale white immigration after independence differentiated Cuba from the rest of the Caribbean and, by constantly renewing the inflow of Spaniards, perpetuated Spanish attitudes towards labour organisation. In spite of the importance of this migration process it has gone virtually unstudied.[24] Unlike other Latin American countries—Argentina, Uruguay, Brazil—which received a wide variety of European immigrants, those in Cuba were predominantly from Spain or from the Canary Islands (*isleños*) and thus immigrant stock was not diluted by non-Spaniards. This gave a peculiar Spanish intensity to the Cuban population and in spite of one of the bloodiest colonial wars of the nineteenth century, bonds between Spain and Cuba grew closer with independence. Whereas in the colonial period government and administration had been monopolised by Spaniards, with independence this became the preserve of Cubans, and Spaniards were forced into commerce and finance so that internal trade became virtually a Spanish monopoly. In rural areas this meant that Spanish shopkeepers fulfilled an informal banking role as providers of credit. The perpetuation of clannish regional associations together with *compadrazgo* and family ties made it difficult for Cubans to break into Spanish preserves (except by intermarriage) whereas for blacks it was impossible to do so.

As in Brazil after emancipation, blacks were forced to compete on unequal terms with aggressive and highly motivated immigrants. White Cubans, for their part, were compelled to look to government for a livelihood as many white collar and technical posts in the expanding sugar industry were staffed by Americans or foreigners. Fierce competition for positions in the bureaucracy provided a rationale for the spoils system of government and accounts for the baleful phenomenon of *continuismo*. Corruption permeated the political system — as it did that of Spain (although there it took the form of rural *caciquismo*) but without an appreciation of the extent to which the Cuban political and social system was permeated by corruption it is difficult to understand the appeal of austere, moralistic anarchism for Spanish immigrant workers and to account for the domination of early labour organisations by the anarcho-syndicalists with their rejection of parliamentary politics, belief in direct action and the use of the strike as a political weapon. In the 1920s a new dimension was added to this corruption in the wake of the post-war sugar speculation — the 'dance of the millions' as well as by the repercussions of Prohibition in the United States when Havana became a refuge for gangsters and a paradise for whoremongers and gamblers — when it became in Carlos Loverai's words the 'trashcan of the Caribbean'. It was not by chance that anarcho-syndicalism found some of its strongest support among the union of waiters and cooks of Havana's restaurants, bars and hotels.

Intellectuals and workers

The moral degradation of the early years of the republic contributed to the rediscovery of the idealism of José Martí by students and intellectuals and to the forging of links between them and workers. This became a distinctive feature of Cuban revolutionary politics marking it off from the rest of the Caribbean. In 1923 Julio Antonio Mella founded the *Federación de Estudiantes Universitarios* and established the *Universidad Popular José Martí* in which students gave night classes to some 500 workers. This symbiotic relationship reflects the influence of the University Reform Movement and of the Peruvian Apra party although Mella's critical views of the latter attracted him to marxism and to becoming a founding member of the Cuban communist party in 1925.[25] It also echoes the belief which tobacco workers had expressed half a century earlier that educational enlightenment was a prerequisite for healthy unionism, a point not lost on Machado who closed down the José Martí

University in 1927. Mella himself was forced into Mexican exile where he was gunned down in 1929.[26]

Mella tried to overcome workers' suspicion towards intellectuals by showing the common interest of intellectuals and workers in resisting the growing US influence caused by Machado's 'Business nationalism' and collaboration with US corporations. Idealistic students and intellectuals excluded either by temperament, ideological conviction or frustrated ambition from the spin offs of the American connection, spearheaded the political revolt against Machado after he decided to stand for office for another period in 1928.

The success of Machado's policy had depended on dampening down militant unionism.[27] US investment was equated with national welfare and had, therefore, to be attracted by favourable conditions. The foundation of CNOC in 1925 posed a threat to this stability and so Machado attacked unions, terrorising and exiling their leaders. Political anger at Machado's *continuismo* combined with the devastating effects of the Great Depression to bring together middle-class nationalist groups and labour in an opposition movement which finally overthrew Machado in the Revolution of 1933.[28]

The 1933 revolution and its aftermath

The revolution which overthrew Machado in August 1933 was not only the most extreme expression of radicalism anywhere in the Caribbean in the inter-war years but was also a turning point in the history of the Cuban labour movement. It not only signified the inability of labour to capitalise on the key role it had played in the events leading up to Machado's overthrow but left a legacy of distrust towards the communists in what many considered to be their sectarian and opportunist behaviour.[29]

The withdrawal of communist support for the general strike which brought the crisis to a head, and their subsequent opposition to the revolutionary nationalist government of Grau San Martín was condemned for its adhesion to the comintern line of non-cooperation with bourgeois parties but their decision was based on a realistic assessment of the weakness of political preparation in the labour movement and on a justified fear that any attempt to impose extremist policies would lead to American intervention.[30] The chances of this happening were real as the repercussions of the Havana strike throughout the island were indicative of the success which the communists had had in organising sugar workers.[31] Thirty six centrals, representing 30 per cent of national production, were occupied and in some cases soviets were established.

Reluctance to push the revolution further was also rooted in an attitude of 'geographic fatalism' which argued that revolution in the United States was a necessary prerequisite for successful revolution in Cuba. 1933 illustrated very clearly the constraints on any revolutionary government operating in an international context where no outside support would be forthcoming. Objectively correct though communist tactics may have been, it cost them the support of many workers. By the late 1930s, however, the change to a popular front line and Batista's support had enabled them to recover their hold on the unions to such an extent that the foundations were laid on which the party's power after 1959 could be based.[32]

Although Batista's coup of January 1934 destroyed political democracy, the legislative achievements of the five month's revolutionary government were nevertheless to be implemented in the course of Batista's ten year domination of Cuban politics until 1944. Apart from decrees affecting a wide range of political, social and economic issues (which included abrogation of the Platt Amendment) there were gains for organised labour. The decree illegalising the importation of Haitian and Jamaican workers removed a long-standing grievance among agricultural labour. For urban workers, the Cubanisation law, which made it obligatory for at least 50 per cent of employees in industry and commerce to be Cuban nationals, widened possibilities for employment in the cities, and the 8-hour day for which unions had agitated since the late nineteenth century was at last recognised. The most important decree for the future development of the labour movement was the establishment of the Department of Labour which from 1933 became a government instrument regulating relations between employers and workers, giving preferential treatment to those unions accepting government patronage and encouraging unions to approach the Department directly in cases of conflict with their employers.[33]

The immediate effect of Batista's coup of January 1934 had been a severe repression of the unions which goaded them into the general strike of March 1935. As in 1933, this spread throughout the island, involving an estimated 200,000 workers. Havana was paralysed; the sugar industry brought to a halt. In contrast to 1933, though, a united and loyal army was available to suppress the strike. After its failure, and with his opponents divided and intimidated, Batista began to widen the basis of his support, using an expanded, bureaucratised army as the spearhead of a comprehensive Three Year Plan in which the social gains of 1933 were consolidated in a wide ranging programme.[34] This included state control of the sugar and tobacco industries, insurance and health schemes for workers, an expansion of rural education, and a law giving security of tenure to the *colonos*, a potentially discontented group in a period of declining sugar production.

The nationalists of the failed revolution of 1933 remained Batista's implacable foes and the unions remained suspicious. When therefore the communists, now pursuing a popular front line, made approaches to him he saw the opportunity to win union support. The party was legalised, allowed to publish its own daily, open a radio station and to organise the unions. The CTC (*Confederación de Trabajadores Cubanos*) was established in 1939 with Lazaro Peña, the veteran communist tobacco leader as its president. When Batista drew up the 1940 Constitution to legitimise his position, communist influence was partly responsible for the inclusion of far-reaching labour provisions.

Labour had never been stronger than during the period of Batista's constitutional rule between 1940 and 1944 which coincided with the war boom and of friendship with both the United States and the USSR as allies in the war against the Axis. When Batista was replaced in the 1944 election by the Auténticos under Grau San Martín, his old adversary from 1933, the situation for both the labour movement generally and the communists in particular deteriorated. An early honeymoon period between Grau and the communists collapsed under the strain of the Cold War in 1947. The communist hold on the unions was broken by the Auténtico unions by a mixture of patronage, suborning and violence. Even their control of the sugar workers was ended.

The gangsterism and corruption which permeated Cuban political life in the later forties involved the unions as it did the students' union of Havana University where Fidel Castro was serving his political apprenticeship. When Batista staged his coup in 1952 there was to be no general strike as he had already assured Eusebio Mujal, the president of the CTC, of his support. The onus of opposition would be borne by the middle class student revolutionaries of the 26 July movement, heirs of their 1933 predecessors, and not by organised labour.

Conclusion

Today the labour movement in Cuba constitutes one of the main pillars of the Revolution with unions fulfilling a post-revolutionary function of acceding to the dictates of the party. This apparent unity contrasts with the pre-revolutionary history of labour since the late nineteenth century which has been distinguished by fierce rivalry between anarchist, communist, reformist and collaborationist unions. This can be explained by the varied influences feeding into the labour movement, from the United States, Spain, the Cuban populist tradition, and from international communism.

These diverse influences have had to be adapted to the specific conditions of a sugar economy. The seasonal nature of employment, the divisions between a skilled industrial work force and unskilled transitory and geographically dispersed agricultural workers, internally divided by language and culture, isolated from the major centres of labour activity in Havana and subjected to military forms of social control, have compounded the difficulties of organisation. Of all groups, the communists have perhaps been the most successful in overcoming these difficulties by accepting the challenge of the colour issue and by recognising the strategic importance of the sugar in- dustry and its agricultural work force, but their organisational ability and the dedication of their leaders was often nullified by mistaken tactics dictated by external considerations.

The attitude and behaviour of both employers and employed were conditioned by the relationship with the United States and the fear that strike action, as often as not directed against American interests, would provoke intervention. Similar constraints operated in the British West Indies where colonial authorities intervened in labour disputes but in many ways the neo-colonial relationship under the Platt Amendment made matters worse, as illustrated by the remark of a railway manager in 1919 who commented that 'the fact that these strikes are carried out peacefully only makes them more dangerous because it is difficult for the Government to find grounds in which to employ the public forces'.[35] The military continued to be responsive to appeals twenty three years later when an American vice-consul could report that 'the military continues to be most solicitous of the needs of the consulate and any help or co-operation they can give is always extended graciously and efficiently'.[36] Cuban workers lived in a culture of violence which could not be tempered by appeals to either parliamentary opinion where worker interests were scarcely represented or to metropolitan opinion, and even appeals made to the AFL for assistance tended to be ineffectual. The violent suppression of strikes with accompanying loss of life was accepted as a matter of course. It was this persistence of violence which made politics seem irrelevant.

Urban workers were divided over whether to participate in politics or not. The major difficulty was that the spoils system on which politics was based militated against a party system with which unions could co-operate or affiliate. The personalist pattern of politics contributed to recurrent instability. Furthermore, at the centre of the anarchist tradition was a distrust of any form of bourgeois parliamentarianism. Hence the addiction to the strike as a political weapon and a repudiation of mediation or bargaining as mere palliatives. Another difficulty was that the particular ambience which gave a rationale to anarcho-syndicalism in Catalonia could not be replicated in the Cuban environment, and when to this is added a natural reluctance to accept centralised control the eventual demise of anarchism, which spearheaded the early labour movement, is easy to understand. As losers, anarchists have not had a good press. Praised for their militancy in the pre-1917 period, once there was the model of a vanguard Marxist Leninist party to be emulated, any refusal to do so was condemned as backsliding or worse. Mutual recrimination over issues of corruption and suborning gave an edge of bitterness to fierce ideological conflicts.

Communist emphasis on ideology raises the question of the role which ideologies play in labour movements and their relationship to particular forms of labour activity. For the industrial worker in an urban environment there is no past to idealise and so ideology can become the equivalent of the collective memory of the rural folk. An obsession with ideological questions led the communists into adopting sectarian attitudes which lost them support, but workers did not necessarily vote for union leaders because of their ideological convictions. 'You understand', a barber explained to José Yglesias, 'that Jesús Menéndez being loved does not mean that the sugar cane workers were communist. Look at us barbers, we were Liberals, Auténticos, of all political opinions, but our union leaders were communist and when it came to union matters, we were as one in supporting them'. Batista, the racially mixed self-made son of a poor cane-cutter benefited from this admiration for personal leadership qualities and when there were tangible benefits to be derived from his populist policies he became a hero figure to many workers.

The phenomenon of a labour movement heavily dependent on government patronage, in which organised workers share some of the features of a labour aristocracy can be found elsewhere in Latin America although less so in the Caribbean. This type of movement reflects the sharp distinction between unionised workers enjoying the benefits of social security and the unemployed and underemployed who do not. They are the *damnés de la terre*, the marginalised groups among whom the predominantly middle-class revolutionaries of the 26 July movement were to find their initial support. It was not until after Batista's overthrow in 1959 that labour unions, under communist control, would regain that prestige and influence they had once enjoyed under an earlier and very different period of Batista's rule.[37]

The Cuban labour movement shares many of the characteristics of labour in peripheral developing societies but the deeper penetration of foreign, and in particular American, capital in the economy has given to its struggles a complexity and bitterness which is not easily matched in other Caribbean countries. For those interested in discovering any relevance of the Cuban revolution to their own societies, it is as well to understand the distinctive form which labour struggles have taken. However attractive the revolution may seem as an example or however compelling as an inspiration, as a model its relevance is more questionable.

Notes

1 The relationship began with the American Revolution when Cuba replaced the British West Indies as North America's major trading partner. Annexationism was a planter-led movement supported by New Orleans filibusters anxious to add a new slave state to the South. Cuban links with Latin America were attenuated until the 1959 revolution, hence the importance of José Martí to the revolution's ideology as Martí was as much a Latin American, in his life, writings and outlook as a Cuban. The success of the Cuban community in the United States may be related to their long presence there.

2 The first sugar revolution from the mid eighteenth century to the 1870s was based on slave labour, Spanish and Cuban capital, and steam power with creole planters both growing and grinding cane in the *ingenio*. The second sugar revolution from the end of the Ten Years' War separated the milling and growing processes with, on one side, the *centrales*, who were under the control of impersonal, foreign, mostly US corporations. On the other, the growing of cane was in the hands of Cubans—*colonos*, economically dependent on the *centrales* as the plantation owners had previously been dependent on Spanish capital.

3 Although dated, C.E. Chapman, *A History of the Cuban Republic*, (New York 1927 & 1969), illustrates the corruption theme well.

4 The Plattist relationship has been studied in L.A. Pérez, *Intervention, Revolution and Politics in Cuba, 1913–21*, (Pittsburgh, 1978).

5 See S. Mintz, introduction to R. Guerra y Sánchez, *Sugar and Society in the Caribbean*, (New Haven, 1964). This was the classic attack in the sugar plantation, idealising the middle class farmer—the *colono*. They were, in fact, prisoners of the *centrales* and in order to survive in the sugar depression from the late 1920s were forced to squeeze their labour force. This accounts for the radicalisation of sugar workers in the pre-1933 period. For a view that the landless rural proletariat had not been so landless after all see, B. Pollitt, University of Glasgow, Institute of Latin American Studies, Occasional papers, 27 and 30.

6 This was particularly noticeable in the case of blacks who had scarcely

any access to schooling in contrast to the Church schools in the British West Indies. Cuba was comparable in this as in many other aspects to Brazil.

7　Those Cubans who did emigrate did so for political rather than demographic reasons. The political emigration reaches a peak after 1959.

8　J. Stubbs, *Tobacco on the periphery: a case study in Cuban labour, 1860–1958*, (Cambridge, 1985), is a minor classic in labour history, full of insights and not only on tobacco workers. Estimates of blacks are on p. 69. Women were prominent among stemmers.

9　There is a huge bibliography on Martí. Two of the best books in English are C. Abel and N. Torrents (eds.) *José Martí, revolutionary democrat*, (London, 1986) and P. Turton, *José Martí: architect of Cuba's freedom*, (London, 1986).

10　J. Ibarra in Abel and Torrents *op. cit.* discusses the relationship between Martí and socialism.

11　Whereas Martí was used by every political faction to legitimate their views, Mella has always been a hero to the communists and the student movement. The beginnings of the labour movement in the independence period are discussed in J. Rivero Muñiz, *El movimiento obrero durante la primera intervención*, (Universidad Central de las Villas, 1961).

12　The standard official history of the labour movement is the two volume *Historia del movimiento obrero cubano*, Vol. I, 1865–1935 and Vol. II, 1935–1958, published by the Instituto de Historia del movimiento comunista y de la Revolución Socialista de Cuba, Havana, 1985. It is a fundamental source book and important for both facts and interpretation. See also the book length chapter by Aleida Plasencia Moro, in P. González Casanova, *Historia del movimiento obrero en América Latina*, (Mexico, 1984). The official party paper *Granma* is a key source, publishing many historical articles on little known facets of labour history.

13　Carlos Loveira's most famous novel *Generales y Doctores* was published in 1920. He had been a union organiser on the railways and labour journalist until forced out of Cuba in 1913. In Mexico he became involved in labour activity and during a period in the United States came to know Samuel Gompers.

14　The Rural Guard was formed in 1901 with the purpose of acting as a buffer between the occupation army and the Cuban population, and of safeguarding rural property. Only 28 out of their 288 posts were owned by the state. Recruitment was selective and blacks were excluded although many had been officers in the Liberating Army. Banditry had been a serious problem in the aftermath of the Ten Years War and the abolition of slavery. There were fears of its recurrence after 1898. For the Rural Guards' pacification and social control functions see L.A. Pérez, 'The pursuit of pacification: banditry and the United States occupation of Cuba, 1899–1902', *Journal of Latin American Studies*, 18:2, November 1986. R. Schwarz in 'Bandits and rebels in Cuban Independence: predators, patriots and pariahs' *Biblioteca Americana* does not subscribe to the social bandit model but sees banditry as a response of lower class entrepreneurial agricultural workers, artisans and shopowners to opportunities in a market oriented agricultural system. There seem to have been fewer black than white bandits.

15 One of the most important, Juan Gualberto Gómez, an associate of Martí has been studied in E. Roig de Leuchsenring, *Cuba libre, Juan Gualberto Gómez*, (Havana, 1954).

16 A large proportion of the US occupying army were southerners at a time when racial friction was reaching a climax. Cartoons in the American press depicted Cubans as wayward black urchins needing the firm hand of Uncle Sam.

17 The race war has not been as fully studied as its importance warrants. A useful introduction is R. Fermoselle Lopez, *Black politics in Cuba: the Race War of 1912*. Ph.D. the American University, 1972, University Microfilms, Ann Arbor. Estenoz had been an official in a building union. There was no support from a divided labour movement. A useful overview of blacks is in H. Thomas, *Cuba or the pursuit of freedom*, pp. 514–24, 1117–1126.

18 D. Booth, 'Cuba, Color and Revolution', *Science and Society*, xl, 2, (Summer 1976).

19 Stevedores are a key labour group throughout the Caribbean and deserve a separate study. A major demand in Cuba of dockers was the right to select their own labour rota and to control the allocation of casual labour. Dockers have an additional importance when the important role played by seamen as propagators of Garveyism is recalled.

20 A useful analysis of black immigration is J. Pérez de la Riva, 'Cuba y la migración antillana, 1900–1932' in *Anuario de Estudios Cubanos*, (Havana, 1979), pp. 1–76. For, Haitian labour see Mats Lundahl, 'A note on Haitian migration to Cuba, 1890–1934, *Cuban Studies*, 12–2, (July 1982). The opening up of Oriente both to a sugar and mining frontier is discussed in R.B. Hoernel, 'Sugar and social change in Oriente, Cuba, 1898–1946', *Journal of Latin American Studies*, 8.2. 1976.

21 From conversations with Jamaicans in Havana in 1961. These had come to Cuba in the early 1920s and most had set up small businesses and wished to be repatriated after the Revolution.

22 F. Knight's chapter 'Jamaican migrants and the Cuban sugar industry' in M. Moreno Fraginals, F. Moya Pons and S.L. Engerman, *Between Slavery and Free Labor*, (Johns Hopkins University Press, Baltimore, 1985) is a long overdue analysis with some oral testimony.

23 Jacques Roumain's novel *Masters of the Dew*, (London), echoes the Cuban experiences of returned migrants back in Haiti. For Jamaica see K. Post, *Arise ye Starvelings: the Jamaican labour rebellion of 1938 and its aftermath*, (The Hague, 1978).

24 See the speech by Garvey on his visit to Cuba in 1921 in *The Marcus Garvey and Universal Negro Improvement Association Papers*, (U. California, Berkeley, 1984), Vol. III, pp. 532–4. While there, he had interviews with the president Menocal and the president elect Zayas, both of whom were 'in hearty sympathy with the work of the organisation'. Menocal had been the manager of the Chaparra central the largest belonging to the Cuba American Sugar Company. It is not known how many West Indians were involved in strikes. One of the largest strikes in 1933 was at the Preston central which Garvey had visited in 1921. The flow of Jamaicans began to dry up with the sugar recession from the late 1920s and it is not known how many stayed in

Cuba. Those who did probably kept a low profile for fear of being deported.

25   There is a useful introduction by M. Kenny 'Twentieth century Spanish expatriates in Cuba: a sub-culture?' *Anthropological Quarterly*, 34, 2. (1961).

26   Mella's recognition of the importance of culture and education for workers and the role of intellectuals echoes Gramscian ideas. He may have derived these views from the Peruvian Mariátegui and the Peruvian Apra. For a good analysis of the conflicts of ideologies in the late twenties see A. Anderle, *Algunos problemas de la evolución del pensamiento anti-imperialista en Cuba entre las dos guerras mundiales: Comunistas y apristas*, (Szeged, 1975).

27   It was widely believed he was killed by Machado's henchmen although there is a view that he was a casualty of inter-communist factionalism. Anarchists accused Mella of being suborned by employers. No holds were barred in the disputes of the twenties.

28   An excellent analysis of the pre-1933 period is J.R. Benjamin, *The United States and Cuba: hegemony and dependent development 1880– 1934*, (Pittsburgh, 1977).

29   The most accessible account of 1933 is L. Aguilar, *Cuba 1933: Prologue to Revolution*, (New York, 1972).

30   Grau was a professor at Havana university. His radical Minister of Labour, Antonio Guiteras was a student. The communists have always had an ambivalent attitude towards him. He was killed in the repression of 1935 and his followers in Joven Cuba scattered. Many fought in the Spanish Civil War and those who returned formed the ARG, one of the many terrorist groups active in the late 1940s.

31   The communists have admitted their tactical mistake attributing the lack of political preparation in the labour movement to residual anarchist attitudes.

32   The first national sugar workers union the SNOIA (*Sindicato Nacional Obrero de la Industria Azucarera*) was founded in 1932 in the wake of strikes during the sugar harvest. Jesús Menéndez, a black sugar workers' leader, became one of the towering figures of the labour movement and was assassinated in the conflicts with the Auténtico unions in 1947.

33   The 1930s is the least researched decade in modern Cuban history. A useful interpretation is S. Farber, *Revolution and Reaction in Cuba, 1933–60*, (Middletown, 1976). For a hypothesis explaining Batista's understanding with the communists in terms of the Spanish Civil War acting as a catalyst see A. Hennessy, chapter on Cuba in M. Falcoff and F. Pike (eds.) *The Spanish Civil War, 1936–9: American hemispheric perspectives*, (University of Nebraska, Lincoln, 1982). The communists were effusive about his 'conversion' to democracy. A concise overview of the relationship is H. Sims, 'Cuban labor and the communist party, 1937–58: an interpretation', *Cuban Studies*.

34   The most accessible and in some ways the best accounts of labour practices and legislation are *Problems of the New Cuba*, Report of the Commission on Cuban Affairs, Foreign Policy Association, (New York, 1935), and the *Report on Cuba*, by the International Bank for Reconstruction and Development, (Washington, DC, 1951).

35 The ideology of 'septembrismo' (after Batista's sergeants' coup of September 1933) is L.A. Pérez, *Army politics in Cuba, 1898–1958*, (Pittsburgh, 1976). Army sergeants were used as rural schoolteachers, Batista anticipated many of the nasserist ideas of the Latin American militarys' 'civic action' programmes of the 1960s.

36 Quoted in Pérez *op. cit.* p. 61.

37 Quoted in Pérez *op. cit.* p. 102.

38 A major lacuna in Cuban historiography is a good study of Batista. He was an admirer—as many Cubans are—of the American self-help ethic. Son of a racially mixed cane cutting father his career was a rags to riches story via the army. Never accepted socially by the white élite he patronised Afro-Cuban cults and had a rapport with labour leaders. There is a marked difference between the Batista of the 1930s and 1940s and that of the 1950s when he had come under the influence of the 'Trujillo miracle' in the Dominican Republic.

Postscript: A remarkable piece of oral testimony indicative of the interesting oral history work now being done in Cuba is 'Angel Santana Suarez: Cuban sugar worker' by Ana Nuñez Machin, in W.H. Beezley and J. Ewell (eds.) *The Human Tradition in Latin America* (Scholarly Resources Inc. Wilmington 1987). pp. 75–88.

CHAPTER 13 | The labour movement and the genesis of modern politics in Belize

O. Nigel Bolland

Labourers in Belize,[1] as elsewhere in the Caribbean, have persistently struggled against the various systems of control that have been imposed upon them. The revolts and desertions that punctuated the era of slavery gave way after 1838 to spontaneous strikes and absenteeism in an economy that was largely stagnant after about 1850.[2] Disturbances occurred periodically, such as the riots of 1894 and 1919, but the turning point, in Belize as elsewhere, came in the 1930s. As Arthur Lewis noted in 1939, it was not until then that there was 'anything that could be called a movement'[3] among the working people of the West Indies. A number of common factors, including wage cuts, unemployment, and increased taxation, a drift of the unemployed to the towns, and a rising political consciousness, provoked the emergence of trade unions and political organisations throughout the British West Indies in that decade of depression. Accounts of this developing labour movement, which formed the basis of nationalist movements and modern politics in the 1940s and 1950s, have ignored the similar developments that occurred in Belize, though the demonstrations, strikes, and riots began in Belize a year before those in St Kitts that are generally held to have started the widespread disturbances.[4]

The Great Depression, and a devastating hurricane that destroyed Belize Town on 10 September 1931, shattered the economy of Belize and made still worse the chronically poor living conditions of the majority of the people.[5] Governors and employers, who had resisted progressive labour legislation, were forced to give way before the increasing determination and organisation of the working class. Beginning with the Labourers and Unemployed Association of 1934– 36, and continuing with the British Honduras Workers and Tradesmen Union of 1939–43, in both of which Antonio Soberanis Gomez played a key role, the labouring poor of Belize organised and pressed for improvement in their working and living conditions. In so doing they became increasingly conscious and active politically. Their labour organisations, culminating in the General Workers

Union (registered under the new trade unions law in 1943), and radical nationalist agitation during World War II, presaged and prepared for the nationalist movement of the 1950s. While most of the respectable middle-class members of the Legislative Council seemed eager to behave like British parliamentarians, crucial support for the young and more radical members of the Belize City Council in the devaluation crisis of 1950 came from the members and leaders of the General Workers Union (GWU).

The importance of the labour protests and organisations of the 1930s and 1940s in the emergence of modern Belizean politics has not been adequately recognised or documented.[6] The fact that the People's United Party (PUP) sprang from the devaluation crisis, and that the PUP had close links with the GWU, has been generally recognised, but it is often held that it was the devaluation of the dollar and not the labour movement that gave rise to modern politics in Belize. Grant, for example, asserts, 'The political calm remained generally unruffled throughout the first fifty years of the twentieth century and in particular during the 1930s when the West Indian colonies were engulfed in disturbances and riots'.[7] He relegates the 1930s protests to insignificance and concludes that it was only with 'the British government's decision to devalue the Belizean dollar that Belize was rudely awakened from its apparent slumber'.[8] Shoman and Ashdown have begun to revise this view, but the former has not documented the 1930s events[9] and the latter, who describes them in detail, characterises them as 'stillborn' and fails to examine their connections with the later nationalist movement.[10]

This paper aims to give the labour protests and organisations before 1950 their due. Belize, far from slumbering through the 1930s and 1940s, was actually one of the first of the West Indian colonies to participate in the widespread labour unrest that, when organised, provided the mass political base for a generation of middle-class leaders. I will describe the early labour protests and organisations of Belize and will show that there were important links between them and the PUP in the early 1950s. First, however, it is necessary to provide the economic and political context of these events.

The economic background to the labour movement

The economy of Belize, since the origins of the British settlement in the seventeenth century, consisted of the extraction of a limited natural resource, namely timber. Logwood and mahogany provided successively the staple exports of Belize and its economic *raison d'être*. This monocrop economy suffered, not only from the usual susceptibility to fluctuations in demand and prices, but also from the fact that heightened demand led to a more rapid depletion of limited accessible resources and hence to increasing costs. The techniques and technology of timber extraction, which depended upon human and animal power to cut and haul the huge trees to river banks whence they could be floated to a boom near the coast, remained essentially unchanged until the 1920s when the introduction of cater-pillar tractors and log wagons permitted logging operations in more remote areas. But it was not until the 1930s that the construction of roads and the use of great trucking camions signalled the end of dependence on animal haulage and water transport, while the use of mechanical saws replaced axes and two-handled saws. Since no attempt was made to conserve or replace forest resources, it appeared that the colony's timber would soon be exhausted.

At the same time, the mechanisation of felling and hauling meant that more timber could be extracted with a smaller labour force. By the time legislation was introduced in the 1940s to protect labourers from exploitation and to enforce some measures of forest management, the mahogany trade was in its final decline. The export of other forest products, including particularly cedar and chicle (extracted from the sapodilla tree to make chewing gum), declined at the same time.

Forest products in the 1920s accounted for about 85 per cent of exports by value (they continued to predominate until about 1958) and most labourers sought employment in that sector. The forestry and mercantile interests had long dominated the colony and had used their dominance to suppress agriculture and hold back expen-diture on the development of communications and social services. Under a variety of constitutional forms the 'forestocracy' continued to exercise power, and control the colony's land and labour. One company in particular, the Belize Estate and Produce Company, which owned over a million acres or about a fifth of the entire colony, was for a century the biggest landowner and employer.[11] The structure of this economy, and the political processes associated with it, left Belize and its working people especially vulnerable to the effects of the Great Depression.

The *Colonial Report for 1932* stated that the total volume of exports was less than half those of 1931, which were themselves half those of 1930. 'Mahogany cutting was entirely stopped' and there was 'no market for the Colony's staple products, mahogany and chicle, and unemployment was more severe than in 1931'.[12] The export of products, such as coconuts, also declined. By June, 1931, the colonial administration was organising relief work, but for only about 150 of the unemployed. Despite these grave problems the Governor complacently reported labour conditions as 'generally satisfactory' in July 1931.[13] This blind official optimism was shattered by the great hurricane that killed over a thousand of the 16,000 inhabitants and demolished at least three quarters of the buildings of Belize Town.

The economic and social conditions of the depression, aggravated by the disastrous hurricane, were responsible for severe hardship among the working people of Belize. As the economy continued to decline after the hurricane, conditions worsened and people became increasingly desperate. Whether conditions are evaluated by the purchasing power of wages, by levels of unemployment, by housing standards, or health, the effects of the depression and hurricane simply made a chronically bad situation even worse. Labour conditions and living standards in the 1930s were similar to what they had been in the nineteenth century.[14] Forest workers were paid pitiful wages, supplemented by inferior rations from truck shops; they lacked medical attention and lived in insanitary accommodation in the camps. Bad as the living and working conditions were in the camps, however, the brunt of the poverty was often borne by women, children and old people who, separated from the working men by six-month logging seasons, had little security of income. They suffered in Belize Town from poor diet and, particularly after the hurricane, from overcrowded housing.

Yet such conditions in themselves seem to lead as often to fatalism as to activity, so what can account for the politicization of the people in Belize in the 1930s? Judging by the nature of their demands and protests, they seemed to hold the colonial administration increasingly responsible for their situation. On two previous occasions, remembered by many people in the 1930s, there were serious popular protests in Belize Town in which people openly criticised the colonial system of government.

Political unrest and Soberanis' leadership

The first of these occurred in December 1894 when forest workers rioted over a currency devaluation that effectively reduced their wages. The second was a more serious outburst, starting on 22 July 1919, among demobilised soldiers of the British West Indian regiment who objected to racist treatment and the injustices of British colonial domination. Both disturbances suggest that something more than persistent poverty provoked people into protesting against the colonial government.

The same was true in the 1930s when the government began to take some responsibility for relief for the unemployed and hungry and for reconstruction of hurricane damage. There was considerable dissatisfaction with the way the government responded to the crisis after the hurricane. Faced with the huge task of feeding and housing thousands of people while starting to clear up the mess, avoid epidemics, and begin reconstruction, the government opened soup kitchens, established a temporary camp at the airport and kept open public buildings to shelter the homeless each night. People made their own shacks from the wreckage, called 'dog-sit-downs' while government constructed a series of barracks of single rooms, for which a weekly rent of 75 cents was charged. It probably seemed insensitive, if not exorbitant, to charge about a day's pay to the needy in such a situation.

Three months after the hurricane, the Acting Governor was still trying to raise a reconstruction loan in England.[15] The British government would guarantee such a loan only if reserve powers were restored to the Governor. The unofficial members of the Legislative Council passed a resolution to the effect that they agreed to the constitutional change only to secure the needed financial aid and that they realised it was against the people's wishes. What seemed to the British government to be an opportunity to impose Treasury control on its colony, probably seemed to Belizeans uncomfortably like kicking a man when he was down. There can be no doubt that the callous attachment of this condition to the Hurricane Loan, and the inordinate delay in obtaining the loan, fostered resentment against the British officials. This resentment smouldered through the 1930s and 1940s and exploded when the Governor used his reserve powers to impose devaluation in 1949.

When a group calling itself the 'Unemployed Brigade' marched through Belize Town on 14 February 1934 it started a broad movement that had a lasting effect on Belizean politics. In the depths of the depression and two and a half years after the hurricane had destroyed the town, unemployment and poverty remained widespread and housing was deplorable. Though the people were desperate, the demonstration was orderly. In answer to their appeal, Governor Kittermaster promised immediate outdoor relief for the hungry, told the unemployed to register at the Belize Town Board offices, and said that the Hurricane Loan Board would not foreclose on debtors.[16] The Governor's relief measures, redolent of the nineteenth century, proved woefully inadequate and provoked further resentment. A daily ration of a pound of badly cooked rice and three ounces of local sugar issued at the prison gate was started on 21 February and people were allowed to break rocks in the Public Works Department yard for five cents each day to 'keep them from starving'.[17] The usually pro-Government *Clarion* called the proferred relief 'degrading and humiliating'.[18]

The complete inadequacy of the Governor's response can be gauged by the fact that 1,100 men and 300 women registered as unemployed as soon as the list was opened and this was recognised by the Governor to be a 'large proportion' in a town of 16,000 people.[19] 'By this time', according to the Police Superintendent's report, 'the masses of the unemployed had become restless'[20] and were dissatisfied with the leaders of the Unemployed Brigade. At a meeting held in the Battlefield, an open square in front of the Court House, on 16 March 1934, a new leader emerged. Antonio Soberanis Gomez (1897−1975), a barber who had travelled in Central America and the USA,[21] denounced the Unemployed Brigade's leaders and took over the movement.

Soberanis held meetings in the Battlefield, two or three times a week, with between six and eight hundred people attending. Soberanis was joined by a group of colleagues that included Benjamin Reneau, John Lahoodie and James Barnett. Though the Governor first referred to Soberanis as a 'man of no importance', the organisation that Soberanis created and led, called the Labourers and Unemployed Association, (LUA) soon became a major political force in Belize. It was reported that Soberanis 'always said he was forming a labour union',[22] but unions could not be legally registered at the time. His association, though not quite a union, was nevertheless far more political than the numerous Friendly Societies that existed to provide mutual aid and support for their members. Though the LUA organised food and medical care from time to time, its chief orientation from its inception was political in so far as it used such techniques as petitions, demonstrations, pickets, strikes, and boycotts to pressure the employers, merchants, and colonial officials into making concessions in favour of working people. Increasingly, Soberanis' attacks on the Governor and various colonial officials, which were said 'to please the people immensely',[23] became an attack on colonial government itself. According to the Police Superintendent, 'the more violent the language used from the rostrum the more the crowd enjoyed it. Soberanis was called the Moses of British Honduras who had been sent by God to lead the people to better things'.[24]

In April Soberanis was convicted of threatening the Police Superintendent and cautioned. Undeterred, he organised a petition signed by several hundred people, demanding that the Government find work for the unemployed at a minimum wage of $1.50 per day. He led a procession of about 500 people around the town and the crowd waited outside the Court House while their leader presented the petition to the Governor. Soberanis called for 'British Honduras for British Honduraneans. . . We are a new People, . . . we are only asking for our rights. Justice to all men. . . British Honduras has been sleeping for over a century, not dead, only sleeping. . . Today British Honduras is walking around'.[25] While the specific demands were for relief work and a minimum wage, these demands were couched in broad moral and political terms that began to define and develop a new nationalistic and democratic political culture.

Kittermaster replied that wages were governed by the world market price. A minimum wage of $1.50 a day, he said, would force enterprises to close for lack of profit, so 'It is better to get work steadily at 50 or 75 cents a day all the year'. This was an astonishing recommendation in a situation where hundreds of Belizeans could obtain no work at all and where most labourers had never had contracts that lasted all year. The Governor said he could do no more about the unemployed: 'It is only by asking for charity from England that there will be enough money this year to pay for services such as schools and hospitals. England herself has 4,000,000 unemployed and yet she is generously helping us here in our difficulties'.[26] Soberanis rejected this argument and pointed out that many officials drew large salaries while 50 cents per day is considered 'sufficient for the poor man and his family'. He also rejected English charity: 'What we are receiving from England is only what belongs to us. . . We will not throw up the sponge, but continue to agitate for our rights'.[27] Soberanis and the LUA continued to agitate and developed new and successful tactics in the next few months.

Kittermaster obtained only $2,000 to provide relief work building the Northern Highway. Eighteen men were sent up every week on a rotation basis, each given ten days work; for each eight hour day they received 60 cents, mostly in the form of credit for provisions at local stores. Since about 1,500 men were registered for work this was a woefully inadequate response. In August, it was reported that 'unemployment will get worse shortly. The Belize Estate and Produce Company are practically closing down', and the Chairman of the Belize Town Board observed that there was 'considerable want and even distress', especially hungry children, among the unemployed.[28] Soberanis and the LUA responded to this urgent need by pressuring local merchants and tradesmen to donate to the poor. When some merchants refused (among the largest were: Harley, Brodie, and Melhado), the LUA organised a boycott. During the 10 September celebrations, with the town full of unemployed, Soberanis led a march of about 3,000 people that culminated in a huge picnic for the poor. The Police Superintendent commented, 'This procession and feed added greatly to the prestige of Soberanis and he was referred to as a "Moses" more than ever'.[29]

Encouraged by his success and widespread support, Soberanis broadened his attack and became increasingly militant. He demanded that Denbigh Phillips, a notoriously severe magistrate, should be removed from the bench, and that C.S. Brown, the manager of the Belize Estate and Produce Company and a member of the Legislative Council, should not be allowed to live in Government House. Soberanis frequently held meetings in Stann Creek, which was then the second largest town with a population of about 3,000. On 27 September he organised a strike there among the stevedores who loaded grapefruit, and achieved another encouraging victory when their pay was raised from eight cents to 25 cents per hour.

On 29 September, Soberanis, back in Belize Town, reiterated his demands concerning Phillips and Brown and announced that on Monday, 1 October, the LUA would picket the big stores and organise a strike at the Belize Estate and Produce Company sawmill. The police arrived at the sawmill before Soberanis and 200 of his followers, so the mill started as usual at 7.00 a.m. When all seemed quiet the police dispersed, but by 8.45 a.m. some 500 people, 'armed with sticks', succeeded in closing the mill. When the police returned this crowd split and went to different parts of the town. One group broke down the gates of the Public Works Department and told the director he should pay his labourers more; another group closed the office of Mr Esquivel, a coconut exporter; another stopped the dredger working at Fort George; and another closed Harley's lumber yard. In the Police Superintendent's words, 'It was not a case of workmen striking for more pay but a case of unemployed men forcing employed men to strike for more pay'.[30]

About 300 men and women, armed with sticks, went to the Belize Town Board. When Matthews tried to arrest a man for threatening the Deputy Chairman of the Board, a struggle ensued. Eight men and one woman were arrested and, when the crowd increased to about 1,500, the police, in two ranks, pushed it back down Queen Street. Several constables were assaulted, shots were heard and one of the crowd was wounded.[31] At 10.50 a.m., with the situation threatening to get out of control, the Acting Governor ordered the police to halt and return to their station while he talked with the crowd's leaders. It is not clear who these leaders were. None of the LUA leaders were named, nor were any of them among those arrested during the riot. At noon Soberanis arrived at the police station in a 'very truculent' mood, and demanded bail for all those arrested. At 5.00 p.m. he bailed out 16 of the 17 persons who had been jailed, but he was promptly arrested himself and charged with threatening Mr Phillips on 29 September. As this news spread, the crowd at the station increased to 2,000. Several efforts to release Soberanis on bail were refused, and he remained in custody. Heavy rain dispersed the crowd, a planned meeting at the Battlefield was abandoned, and the night passed peacefully.

On 2 October, Soberanis was charged in court and refused bail. About 500 people abused the magistrates and 1,000 gathered in Market Square. Some, it was said, 'were inclined to be disorderly... it was women who were the most virulent', but no one was armed.[32] At 8.00 a.m. on 3 October, about 150 men who were assigned jobs refused to work for 60 cents per day and, demanding $1.00, they dispersed. On the following day a 'large gang of men' failed to stop others from working for 60 cents per day.[33] The crisis was over, and the British cruiser that the Acting Governor had inquired about was not needed. The sawmill remained closed until 18 October and the people obtained a promise of $3,000 for immediate outdoor relief. Meanwhile, 26 of the 32 persons who were prosecuted for participating in the riot were sentenced, receiving between three days and one year of hard labour. The jurors having failed to agree, Soberanis was released on bail on 6 November and his freedom was celebrated by a big rally. In January 1935, Soberanis was acquitted of the charge of threatening Phillips, who it transpired, had threatened to horse-whip him. Soberanis continued to lead the LUA but the movement was weakened when Lahoodie and Reneau split away and formed the British Honduras Unemployed Association.

Shortly after the peak of the disturbances in October 1934, a new Governor, Alan Burns, arrived. While he viewed Soberanis as a professional agitator who should be locked up, Burns was shocked by the people's condition and he made a major effort during his six years in Belize to bring relief. In March 1935, the Senior Medical Officer reported that the people, especially the children, were dangerously undernourished and hence susceptible to disease. Burns commented that the unemployment situation was still acute, that those who were employed were receiving lower wages and that when their contracts ended in June these wages could not tide them over the season. He considered 'the situation is most serious and that it will shortly become desperate...The people have behaved, in the circumstances, with admirable restraint, but their temper is rising and matters must come to a head within a few months unless something is done'.[34] Since Soberanis continued to hold mass meetings and his speeches became increasingly 'offensive and inflammatory',[35] Burns prepared legislation to help control the situation, namely a law to prohibit processions without police permission, one to give the Governor emergency powers to maintain order, and a seditious conspiracy bill.

In May 1935 Soberanis helped organise a strike among railway workers in Stann Creek, whose wage of 65 cents per day was below the rate for Government workers elsewhere, which ranged between 75 cents and $1.00. Soberanis had made several visits to the Stann Creek and Toledo Districts, 'holding meetings and preaching discontent', in the words of Superintendent Matthews.[36] On 20 May, following a meeting in Stann Creek Town, a crowd of about 300 unemployed stopped the railway workers at Havana Bridge and told them to strike for $1.00 per day. The workers went home and made no attempt to go to work the next morning. That afternoon four railway employees who tried to pass the bridge were beaten by pickets and the police could not make arrests because of 'the very threatening attitude' of a crowd of about 400 people. Later the crowd dispersed peacefully and the District Commissioner spoke with the local leaders, Abraham Dolmo and Zacharias Flores, Soberanis having left by boat. That night police reinforcements arrived from Belize Town 'to crush the disorders without bloodshed'. One woman and five men were convicted of impeding passage and disorderly conduct and were fined. None of the strikers was re-employed and those workers who were hired received the usual 65 cents per day. Burns felt that 'in consequence Soberanis has suffered in repute as a leader'.[37] Burns claimed that Soberanis' support and influence in general was waning as a result of the colonial development grants that employed people in road work and thus changed people's attitude to the government, but he still kept the police 'constantly on the alert in case of a possible sudden outbreak'.[38] By July, Soberanis himself acknowledged that the LUA was declining. He blamed Lahoodie and Reneau for splitting the organisation, and suggested 'that they must have been paid to do so'.[39]

When Burns refused to allow Soberanis or any member of the LUA to Government House on the anniversary of emancipation, Soberanis responded in a rather quieter manner than usual. The LUA, he states, was 'organised to agitate for a living wage and justice for the workers of British Honduras', and he insisted that they had the right to try to better their situation. He claimed that, by organising a band of 22 nurses, they helped and cheered up the workers and unemployed and that the LUA's community work had benefited hundreds of people.[40]

For months the government had been planning to change the law so that 'Soberanis could be successfully prosecuted for sedition'.[41] Shortly after the seditious conspiracy ordinance was passed on 24 October 1935, Soberanis was charged for using 'abusive and seditious language' at a public meeting in Corozal, though this meeting was held on 1 October, the first anniversary of the riot, *before* the amendment was passed.[42] Burns was determined to put Soberanis behind bars, but without provoking further disturbances. He instructed E.A. Grant, the magistrate of Orange Walk, to try Soberanis at Corozal because the Corozal magistrate was 'suffering from cold feet'. He added that 'One of my reasons for sending Grant to try "Tony" was that he was a black man. I did not want the trial to be a black v white affair'.[43] He wanted Soberanis 'put away for a good long sentence'. The trial was, as anticipated, a tense affair. People in Corozal and nearby Indian villages contributed over $200 to Soberanis' assistance and, because of 'a state of civil commotion which threatens the public safety', meetings were prohibited in the District. Soberanis was fined $85 (or four and a half months hard labour), plus $30 costs, for using insulting words concerning various people. In January 1936, Soberanis was acquitted by the Supreme Court on the charge of attempting to 'bring His Majesty into hatred, ridicule or contempt', but the Corozal conviction, along with the split in his organisation, the muzzling effects of the new laws, the Governor's efforts to expand relief work,[44] and an improvement in the economy in 1935 and 1936, combined to spell the decline of his influence and of the LUA. The LUA continued to hold meetings and processions in 1936, but much of Soberanis' effort consisted of attacking Lahoodie's BHUA.

The influence of the LUA as a political force

After the persistent agitation and tension of 1934–35, during which Soberanis and his LUA made a mark on Belizean history, there was a distinct lull in the labour movement, but Soberanis and his associates did not disappear and, with another slump in the economy in 1938 and 1939, labour militancy reappeared. Before examining these later events, however, let us first assess the important of the LUA. Ashdown has correctly stated that Soberanis' movement was of 'greater historical importance than the earlier disturbances' because 'Soberanis had a definite political purpose'.[45] Soberanis linked the concerns of his followers, which were chiefly with wages, prices, employment, food, health and housing, with an attack on the colonial administration and the merchant élite, whom he characterised as incompetent and overpaid, ruthless and callous in their relations with workers and the poor, and as the cause of much of the poverty and injustice experienced by most Belizeans. Soberanis, who organised the working people who were unrepresented in the Legislative Council, developed a variety of techniques to help the voiceless be heard, namely petitions, processions, boycotts, strikes, mass meetings, as well as mutual aid efforts. Though the core of these activities was in Belize Town, where a third of the colony's population was concentrated, Soberanis was active in the districts from north to south, among the Maya Indians around Corozal and the Garifuna in Stann Creek. He initiated a national movement, in which labour issues and interests were in the forefront of a critique of colonial government, and a developing national working-class consciousness, thereby presaging the labour and national movements elsewhere in the British West Indies. When Ashdown says that Soberanis' 'mantle was not to be taken up again until the coming of the People's Committee and the revitalisation of the General Workers' Union in 1950',[46] he ignores many connections and continuities in these political developments during the late 1930s and 1940s.

The constitution that was pressed in April 1935 readmitted the elective principle for the first time since 1871, though with the high property and income qualifications demanded by the unofficial majority. In 1922 the Hon. E.F.L. Wood, M.P., had recommended a reduction of the official majority and the inclusion of elected members in the Council,[47] but it was not until the Governor was granted reserve powers in 1932 that the elective element was readmitted in Belize. From 1936 to 1954 the Council consisted of the Governor and five (later three) other officials, two (later four) nominated unofficial members, and five (later six) elected members. Voters had to be 21 years old (30 years for women, until 1950) and receive an income of $300 per annum, or own real property worth $500 or be a householder paying rent of $97 per annum. Candidates were required to have real property valued at $500 or an annual income of $1,000. In 1945 (after Jamaica had achieved universal adult suffrage) the entire registered electorate of Belize numbered 822. The working people could not vote, but could support opposition to the 'establishment' candidates. Some of the Creole and *mestizo* élite resented the control of land, commerce and government by a

coterie of expatriates and developed a liberal 'Natives First' orientation. With support from working people, who had neither votes nor
candidates of their own, these early 'nationalists', like Arthur
Balderamos, a black lawyer, Robert S. Turton, a chicle millionaire,
and L.P. Ayuso, a local businessman, were elected to the Legislative
Council, defeating two Englishmen and a lawyer from Guiana.

Never having been allowed to represent itself, the working class
of Belize was used to looking to members of the élite to represent it.
The 1936 constitution encouraged this, with the result that much of
the political activity of the working people and the LUA in 1936 was
focused on supporting the 'people's men' in the elections. Endorsed
by the LUA and a middle-class Citizens' Political Party, these men
became the chief 'parliamentary opposition' after 1936. As working-
class agitation continued, all six seats on the Belize Town Board,
which was elected with a broader franchise, went to middle-class
Creoles who appeared sympathetic to labour in 1939.

The reappearance of labour militancy and the growth of union membership

Though the LUA disappeared, Soberanis and several of his associates
continued to agitate and organise in the late 1930s. At a Battlefield
meeting attended by about 500 people on 20 June 1938, Soberanis,
along with James Barnett alias Bangula (who had helped in the
Stann Creek strike in 1935), John Neal, and Thomas Sabal (a
Garifuna from Stann Creek), complained about wages and rations
and demanded that Governor Burns must go. Soberanis, speaking
in Spanish and English, said he had collected $40 from people in
Stann Creek to register a union but when he asked for donations
people began to leave. He chastised them and said they needed
more loyalty, like the Jamaicans who had demanded Bustamante's
release, if they were to get what they wanted.[48]

Later that year, Burns reported that unemployment was much
worse and that he needed to provide work for more men so as to
prevent disorder. On 19 November over 600 men gathered to apply
for work at the Public Works Department where only 200 could be
hired. One man was arrested for assaulting the Clerk, but danger of
serious trouble was 'averted by a promise to the men that more
would be taken on in a few days'.[49] Burns organised a series of road
works, reclamation and drainage projects, as relief schemes for the
unemployed. Under the *quincena* system gangs of labourers were
hired for two week periods so that, by rotation, all the unemployed

were given a chance of intermittent work. At any one time there were about 600 men so employed, but Burns, concerned that about 1,000 fewer men would be hired in the mahogany industry in 1939, proposed opening a quarry at Gracy Rock to provide work for 300 men and stone for the Belize-Cayo road. The development of better communications in Belize through road construction was clearly of secondary importance to Burns, whose primary concern was to avoid trouble in the streets. 'This year there appears to be very little money and crowds of unemployed men are in the streets. The local agitators have not missed the opportunity to stir up trouble'.[50] While it seems that the Governor's strategy was largely successful, as further widespread disorders were avoided, it was not because Soberanis and his colleagues had retired. In fact, their continued agitation was clearly a factor in pushing Burns and the Colonial Office to expand the relief schemes.

The economy deteriorated in 1939 and Burns had to lay off half of the men working on the Northern Highway, leaving 847 men in Belize Town seeking work.[51] In March, the following telegram was sent from a public meeting to the Secretary of State for the Colonies:

> Suffering and uneasiness acute Belize. Due to unemployment. Developing into dangerous situation. Cannot continue without disastrous results. Government approached and admits situation grave but unable to help. Wholesale laying off by Government on public workers not understood by the masses. Population pray for immediate intervention.[52]

Burns attempted to belittle this by saying that the chairman of the meeting, L.D. Kemp, was 'trying to make capital out of the situation'.[53] Kemp, an associate of Soberanis and cousin of Lahoodie, was a journalist who, under the *nom de plume* of 'Prince Dee', had for years attacked the colonial administration and supported Soberanis in the *Belize Independent*.[54] He continued to be politically active and influential in the 1940s.

Shortly after this meeting a crowd became disorderly, when only 75 men were engaged for road work out of 591 applicants, and was ejected from the Public Works Department by the police.[55] The number of unemployed men registered in Belize Town alone rose from 1,200 in April to 1,953 in August.[56] Once again, public anxiety and the prospect of unrest were relieved by announcements of continuing relief work, though everyone knew this was only a palliative in a sick economy.

Early in 1939, Soberanis and R.T. Meighan, a former member of the Belize Town Board, founded the British Honduras Workers and Tradesmen Union (BHWTU),[57] the first organisation to be called a union in Belize, though it could not be legally registered as such at that time. In July 1939 the BHWTU supported a strike of about 170 Garifuna road workers near Stann Creek. While Meighan had the title of President of the BHWTU in 1939, Soberanis held that office from 6 March 1941, when he was reported as saying that 'Trade Unionism is...the only medium by which the working class can get a square deal'.[58] The BHWTU was said to have branches in Stann Creek, Corozal and San Ignacio el Cayo, that is, in the south, north and west of Belize. Later that year Soberanis petitioned the Commissioner of Cayo District to do something about the awful living and working conditions of Maya labourers at Baking Pot,[59] but in 1942, discouraged by trying to organise people under wartime conditions when they 'could not give vent to their feelings',[60] he went to Panama where he stayed for six years.

In a confidential report written after the visit of the Moyne Commission in 1938, Burns attributed most agitation and discontent to 'colour feeling...fomented by a small group, of whom the principal is R.S. Turton'.[61] He named four 'professional agitators' (Soberanis, Adderley, Kemp, and Balderamos) but devoted three quarters of his report to Turton, whom he accused of financing the agitators 'in order to discredit and embarrass the administration and its officers. The agitation appears to be on behalf of the working class: actually it is in the interests of the worst type of capitalist'.[62] Whatever may be the truth of Burns' assertion, it cannot apply to Soberanis who was always desperately poor and whose efforts over eighty years to create a union were independent of Turton and were certainly inspired by working class interests. Perhaps the organisations formed by Lahoodie and Reneau (British Honduras Unemployed Association) and by Kemp (British Honduras Federation of Workers Protection Association), neither of which functioned as unions, were supported by Turton. Kemp was said to live rent-free in one of Turton's houses.[63] A radical nationalist group, first called the British Honduras Independent Labour Party, then the People's Republican Party, and finally the People's Nationalist Committee, was formed in 1940, and may have been supported by Turton. The radical nationalists' pro-American and anti-British stance (which became confused when the US joined Britain in the war) reflected the interests of Turton, who sold chicle to Wrigley's of Chicago.

Among the leaders of this group were John Lahoodie and Gabriel Adderley, alias Nehi, who had formerly been with Soberanis in the LUA, but the chief figure was Joseph Campbell, known as the 'Lion of Judah'. Born in 1901, of a Jamaican father and Belizean mother, Campbell had worked for many years for United Fruit in Honduras. He daily attacked the British and predicted their coming defeat as just punishment for all the 'dirt the English had done'.[64] At their meetings the nationalists demanded the expulsion of all white men, the creation of a local republic in union with the USA, and the substitution of the national flag of 'Belize Honduras' for the Union Jack. They were often attacked at these meetings by loyalists, who called themselves the 'Unconquerables'. Campbell was repeatedly imprisoned and the Governor tried to deport him in July 1941. On 5 September, with Campbell already in jail, Lahoodie and Adderley were held in a special detention camp in Corozal. The Governor indicated that he was avoiding a trial and holding the prisoners far from Belize Town in order to keep trouble from spreading.[65] While Kemp protested his cousin's detention, the 72 year-old Lahoodie refused to appeal, saying 'He has asserted his desire to be rid of the British administration of this colony and would have no truck with it'.[66] By 14 February 1942 the Governor felt confident enough to release Lahoodie and Adderley, subject to certain restrictions. Lahoodie and Adderley went to live in Guatemala but Campbell was active again in 1948.

In the meantime, mass meetings were held in various parts of the colony in 1941 to demand adult suffrage and the right to elect the government. A broad spectrum of Belizean politicians took part in these meetings, including elected middle-class members of the Legislative Council and the Belize Town Board, like Arthur Balderamos and E.S. Usher, as well as radicals and trade unionists, such as L.D. Kemp and R.T. Meighan.[67] Though the Governor himself felt that the Council was 'undemocratic if not oligarchic',[68] the Colonial Office decided that Belize, unlike Jamaica, was too backward and so made only minor constitutional changes in 1945. These constitutional issues did not go away, however, and became a primary part of the PUP platform in the early 1950s.

Another link between many of these labour and political activities in the 1930s and 1940s was provided by Garveyism. The 'official' flag and colours of the LUA were the red and green of Garvey's Universal Negro Improvement Association (UNIA) and several leading figures in Soberanis' organisation were members of the Belize branch of UNIA that was founded in 1920. Kemp was a Garveyite, as was Calvert Staine, who was a vice-president of the Belize UNIA and later chairman of the Belize Town Board and a member of the Legislative Council. When the parent UNIA split in 1929 over the disposal of the estate of Isiah Morter, a wealthy Belizean benefactor, there was a split in the local branch that was not healed by Garvey's visit to Belize in February of that year.[69] Cain, Kemp, and Staine remained loyal to Garvey but in February 1941, Lionel Francis, the Trinidadian President of the rival UNIA Inc., came to administer the Morter estate and decided to settle in Belize. In 1942 he won a seat on the Belize Town Board as leader of the 'People's Group', displacing Staine in the process. Francis and his group controlled the Belize City Council (as it became in 1943) until 1947. An Edinburgh-educated physician, he was seen as a 'respectable' spokesman of Creole Belizeans and, as president of the British Honduras Trades and Labour Union, he attended the Caribbean Labour Congress in Jamaica in August 1947.

Staine, who was nominated to the Legislative Council by Governor Hunter in 1942, joined with R.T. Meighan (they were both members of a Creole middle-class group called the Progressive Party) to support the Employers and Workers Bill in 1943. Though trade unions were legalised in 1941, it was only when the Employers and Workers Bill was passed on 27 April, 1943, that breach of labour contract was removed from the criminal code and the infant trade unions of Belize could pursue the struggle for improving labour conditions. The bill had previously been defeated by the employers among the unofficial members in August 1941, so it was the efforts of men like Staine and Meighan that made the crucial difference in 1943.

After the passage of the Employers and Workers Bill the first trade union, the BHTWU, was registered in May 1943, its name soon to be changed to the General Workers Union.[70] Though strikes in the mahogany industry were forbidden by a war-time essential services law that was not amended until 1953, and the Belize Estate and Produce Company refused to allow union officials to visit the lumber camps, the GWU quickly expanded into a nationwide organisation. Beginning with about 350 members in the forest industry and on the waterfront, this union engaged in a militant struggle to improve labour conditions and wages. For just a few years in the middle of the war the unemployment problem in Belize was in remission, partly because of a revived demand for mahogany but largely because about 900 men were recruited into a Forestry Unit to work in Scotland[71] and even more went to work in Panama. In early 1944 over 400 of the men who had gone to Scotland and about 1,000 of the labourers from Panama returned to Belize. Although by June some of these were recruited to work in the US, the problem of re-absorbing all these workers remained acute. In this context, a successful unionised strike of stevedores in July 1944 and the election of a radical, Clifford E. Betson, to the presidency of the

GWU were responsible for the rapid growth of that union.

By the late 1940s the GWU claimed a membership of over 3,000. Based in Belize City, with branches in the districts and in remote chicle and mahogany camps, this organisation, more than any other, helped to raise the political consciousness of the working people of Belize in the 1940s. The wretched conditions in which these people lived and worked were translated, through protracted struggles with the Belize Estate and Produce Company and the colonial government, into a protest against colonialism itself. The part played by the BHTWU-GWU, in the eleven years of their existence prior to 1950, in establishing a basis in both consciousness and organisation for the nationalist movement and the PUP, can hardly be exaggerated.

An example of the GWU's growing power and influence in this period is the strike against the Belize Estate and Produce Company at the sawmill in Belize City in 1947. The sawmill hands had been negotiating for a raise since 3 January when Betson, the GWU President, urged them to unite: 'The inertia of B.H. workmen in respect of their rights must disappear and there must be an end to the exploitation of workers'.[72] By early February some 300 men were on strike and Betson told them, 'we are dealing with a company who are in a position to pay what we ask of them...It is only right that we should share some of the profits of our land'. This nationalist note was echoed by the GWU treasurer, who said, 'a meeting of this kind stretches into the life and economy of British Honduras. You men are here to decide whether you shall live as slaves or as freemen in your homeland'.[73] For twenty days the employer ignored GWU's demand for a raise from \$1.25 to \$2.00, and when he eventually offered a 10 per cent increase the men refused it. Farmers from Santana, Salt Creek and other villages on the northern highway, many of whom were unemployed persons from Belize Town who were settled there in the mid-1930s, offered free food for the strikers. In early March an arbitration board awarded the sawmill men \$1.90 a day, which was a major victory for the workers and their union.[74]

The success of this strike in early 1947 led to others at the Corozal sugar factory and on the Belize waterfront where 45 long-shoremen walked off the job in a wildcat strike. It was in the context of this labour agitation that George C. Price and some other middle-class alumni of St John's College, members of a Jesuit Christian Social Action Group, got their feet on the bottom of the political ladder. Price, who was R.S. Turton's secretary, had failed to get elected to the Belize City Council in 1943 but in November 1947 he succeeded. Price, along with John Smith, Herbert Fuller and Karl

Wade (and the editors of the *Belize Billboard*, Philip Goldson and Leigh Richardson) belonged to the 'Natives First' Independent Group. These middle-class Catholic nationalists succeeded in ending the domination of the Belize City Council by Lionel Francis' People's Group, by linking Belize's social and economic troubles to the wider colonial context. However, when Betson, in his New Year message to the GWU in 1948, called for a 'united labour front, the election of representatives of labour', and the introduction of socialism to Belize, the *Belize Billboard* editors, though they published Betson's message, dissociated themselves from its 'dangerous tendency'.[75]

Soberanis returned to Belize in 1948 and joined 'Kid' Broaster and L.D. Kemp in the Open Forum[76] in a further public challenge to British colonialism. Their meetings were characterised by pro-Americanism, complete with renditions of the 'Stars and Stripes' and 'God Bless America', and a rather equivocal attitude towards the Guatemalan territorial claim. While their goal was political independence, they argued that 'The Guatemalan stand opens the gateway for natives to have legal rights to self-determination'.[77] The Open Forum group sharply distinguished itself from the Legislative Councillors who expressed loyalty to the British Crown and who, like the lawyer Harrison Courtenay, favoured the proposed West Indian Federation. Soberanis and Kemp saw advantages for Belize, especially in labour opportunities, in a closer association with the Central American republics.

Belize in the 1940s, far from slumbering, was in a political ferment. Among the chief issues that agitated Belizeans, including universal suffrage and constitutional reform, West Indian Federation, import controls and immigration, and the Guatemalan claim, was the widespread economic distress and unemployment that followed the return of almost two thousand labourers from abroad and the renewed depression in the chicle and mahogany industries.[78] Of the many groups and organisations involved in politics after the war, including the People's Group, the 'Natives First' Independent Group, the Christian Social Action Group, and the Open Forum, the only mass organisation involved in political issues was the GWU, that sprang from the LUA and BHWTU. The intense labour and political activity of the union prepared the ground for the middle-class politicians who seized the opportunity provided by devaluation at the end of 1949. The independence movement in general, and the PUP in particular, grew out of the labour movement that had been developing for sixteen years before devaluation.

The People's Committee, formed in response to the devaluation of the dollar on 31 December 1949, included people of diverse social backgrounds and political opinions who united over the issue of devaluation because it dramatically brought together economic and labour problems with concerns about colonial control and constitutional reform. Devaluation produced an immediate fall in the people's purchasing power and standard of living whilst protecting the interests of the Belize Estate and Produce Company and others who traded in the sterling area. Serious as the economic effects of devaluation were, the event was politically explosive because it came after repeated assurances by the British Government (which had devalued the pound in September) that the BH dollar would remain at parity with the US dollar, and it was enforced against the majority of the Legislative Council who could at least claim to be the elected representatives of Belize. The Governor passed devaluation on the instructions of the Colonial Office, by the use of the reserve powers that were incorporated in the constitution in 1932. There could hardly have been a more perfect issue for the incipient nationalist movement to exploit.

On the night that the dollar was devalued, the Open Forum held a protest meeting at the Battlefield and John Smith and George Price were among the guest speakers.[79] When the People's Committee (PC) was formed, with Smith as Chairman and Price as Secretary, one of the members was Clifford Betson. Within a month the PC and the GWU were holding joint meetings, discussing issues ranging from devaluation to labour legislation and from federation to constitutional reform. Many of the labour and political pioneers of the 1930s and 1940s were active in the months following devaluation, often at meetings organised by the PC and GWU. In early February, the Open Forum and the PC were said to have 'amalgamated and started a vigorous campaign by means of public meetings, processions through Belize, and petitions'[80] but soon the 'old hands of the Open Forum', namely Broaster and Soberanis, split from the PC.[81] In November Soberanis and Meighan contested the Belize City Council elections as Independents. They lost and the PUP lost five of the nine seats.[82] Soberanis wrote later that he and Kemp decided to hand everything over to Price in 1950, 'to carry on the same fight for Independence'.[83] In 1951, Joseph Campbell was reported to have said at a meeting at the Battlefield that 'the PUP have some educated young men to lead them, and he is very glad that at least some young fellows have come along to form this movement'.[84] While Soberanis, Meighan, and Campbell no longer had the influence or following they once had, it is important to note these continuities between the early political agitation in Belize and the PC and PUP in 1950 and 1951.

Above all, the links between the GWU and the PC were important in the rapid rise of the nationalist movement after 1950. Without the support of the GWU, the only extant mass organisation of the working people with branches nationwide, the early success of the PUP would have been unthinkable. The President and General Secretary of the GWU were national figures before 1950. Henry A. Middleton, the Secretary, had been an organiser since 1939 when he was the representative of forest workers on the BHFWPA.[85] Despite the PC's dependence on the experience and organisation of the GWU's leaders, the middle-class members of the PC, all of whom were St John's College alumni and members of the Christian Social Action Group, took over the leadership of the union at its Annual Meeting on 28 April 1950. Nicholas Pollard, President of the weak Mercantile Clerks Union, became President of the GWU, John Smith Vice-President, and George Price and Philip Goldson members of the Executive Council. Betson fought the takeover in vain. After seven years as a militant and pioneering union chief, he was given the dubious honorific title of 'Patriarch of the Union'. Middleton remained as General Secretary, and in April, 1951, he apparently objected to the further consolidation of PUP control over the union, when Price was made Vice-President, Goldson became Assistant Secretary, and Richardson joined the Executive Committee. Shortly after, Middleton was dismissed by the PUP officials, and when Kemp claimed in the *Daily Clarion* that this was a conspiracy to get rid of black officials who were not Catholic, he, too, was expelled from the GWU by the new committees. Betson, who had been made a life-member of the Executive Council in 1950, attended no Council meetings after June 1951.[86]

The PUP and GWU had become essentially identical and were entirely dominated by former members of the Christian Social Action Group. It is hard not to conclude that this group deliberately set about to take over the union for its own political purposes. The labour movement declined in the 1950s as it became increasingly dependent upon the politicians. The middle-class leadership of the PUP was successful in achieving constitutional decolonisation, but at the expense of an authentic and autonomous working-class voice in the nationalist movement.

Conclusion

The labour movement in the British West Indies in the 1930s produced modern trade unions and nationalist movements that have led, in most cases, to universal adult suffrage and independence. Belize was no exception to this pattern; indeed, the movement may even be said to have started in Belize in 1934. As in the rest of the West Indies, the working people of Belize, beginning to act as a class for the first time in the 1930s and 1940s, unwittingly served as the vehicle for the relatively weak but intensely manipulative middle classes in their rise to political power.[87] When, in 1954, twenty years after the beginning of the labour movement in Belize, universal adult suffrage was attained, it was the middle-class leaders of the PUP who reaped the benefits of the labour struggle and the GWU's organisaton.

The explanation of these events in Belize is broadly parallel to that of the similar events elsewhere in the British West Indies, with some variations. Conditions of the working people everywhere were terrible — low wages, intermittent employment and spreading unemployment, atrocious housing, hunger and bad health, poor education or none at all, and an absence of the civil rights of suffrage and union organisation. Immediate concerns about jobs, food, and housing quickly grew into demands for rights and social justice, and hence into nationalist demands for self-government and independence. The reaction of the colonial administration in Belize was similar to that of such administrations elsewhere, in part because they all followed broadly defined Colonial Office policy, but also because similar structurally defined conditions limited their options. One of the chief functions of the colonial state was to maintain the property of capitalists (whose leading members were invariably nominated to the Legislative Council in Belize), and, as part of that function, to ensure the supply of a cheap labour force. When this could no longer be provided by the immigration and coercion of slaves, the colonial judicial and police system enforced labour laws that made breaches of labour contract by the workers a criminal offence. It was this system that, in the 1930s crisis, was challenged by the working people.

The colonial administration responded to this challenge essentially in three ways. First, by police action, with surveillance, intimidation, force and legal action. When the laws were seen to be inadequate, new ones were quickly passed in order to detain, punish, and isolate the more radical elements and to divide the movement. Second, by making concessions, largely in the form of providing (or sometimes just promising) relief to assuage a proportion of the working people. This began early in Belize and was developed as a deliberate response to the labour movement by Governor Burns in 1935. This strategy, like that of repression, was later used in response to labour rebellions throughout the British West Indies,[88] and became part of the Colonial

Development and Welfare programme (which was always more welfare than development).[89] This policy was still prevalent in 1949 when the Governor wrote, 'Very early launching of relief schemes is necessary owing to the serious position in the Belize and Cayo districts particularly, where I am advised riots might break out if quick action is not taken'.[90] Third, the formation of a Labour Department in 1939, ostensibly 'to assist and guide the labouring classes in the formation of trade unions along the right lines',[91] retarded the development of autonomous trade unions by usurping union functions. 'The Labour Department was the institutionalisation of the colonial approach to trade unionism',[92] namely, to paternalistically organise labour and encourage 'responsible' labour leaders in order to control the labour movement. The British Trades Union Congress, especially under Sir Walter Citrine who was a member of the Moyne Commission, worked closely with the labour advisors of the Colonial Office and the various Labour Departments in the colonies to propagate 'responsible' trade unionism by stressing 'the separation between industrial disputes and militant political action'.[93]

Even when the Colonial Office and its local representatives identified their immediate task as restoring order and quashing rebellion, they retained their role of maintaining a suitable supply of cheap labour for local capitalism. But it was in this regard that the colonial administration became entangled in contradictions. When, for example, Garifuna road workers demanded a raise in July 1939, it was acknowledged by the Acting Governor that 'Any increase in the rate of wages paid by Government would of course create difficulties for other employers of labour in the locality'.[94] Yet, at the same time, the administration was forced by the workers, who 'bitterly resented'[95] the miserable wages paid by the Government, to concede wage increases from time to time. Moreover, as relief work began, with the collapse of the mahogany and chicle industries, to be reconceived less as a temporary palliative and more as a permanent necessity, Government itself became the largest single employer of labour in the colony.[96] That was surely the central contradiction: the colonial state was forced, by the bankruptcy of the very capitalist economy it was there to serve, to substitute a long-term relief work economy. Such welfare became a permanent means of social control because of the inadequacies of the economy, but this only served to raise working people's demands on the government whose economic role was increasingly transparent.

A casual labour market, in which seasonal low paid work and frequent unemployment were the norm, was always a structural condition of the Belizean economy, with resultant insecurity and persistent poverty for the working people. When this economy collapsed in the 1930s the colonial government itself became the chief employer of labour, not simply the means of ensuring its supply to local capitalists. The expanding economic role of the government, and its inability to meet the people's demands in this context, sowed the seeds of nationalism within the labour movement in the 1930s and 1940s and thereby fuelled the anti-colonial and independence movement that followed.

Notes

BA-Belize Archives, Belmopan
CO-Colonial Office records, Public Records Office, London.

1 Belize was known as British Honduras from the mid-nineteenth century until 1973 and, before that, as the Belize Settlement or the Settlement in the Bay of Honduras. The chief town and, until 1970, the capital, was Belize Town, redefined as Belize City in 1943. To avoid confusion, Belize is used throughout this article to refer to the territory that has been an independent nation since 1981.

2 O. Nigel Bolland, 'Systems of domination after slavery: the control of land and labor in the British West Indies after 1838', *Comparative Studies in Society and History*, 23, 4, (1981), pp. 591–619; O. Nigel Bolland, *The Formation of a Colonial Society: Belize, from conquest to Crown Colony*, (Baltimore, 1977).

3 Arthur Lewis, *Labour in the West Indies: the Birth of a Workers' Movement*, (London, 1939; new edition, London, 1977) p. 18.

4 See Richard Hart, *Origin and Development of the Working Class in the English-speaking Caribbean Area—1897 to 1937*, (London, n.d. (1984); W.M. Macmillan, *Warning from the West Indies*, (London,1935) refers to the St Kitts riots of January 1935, but does not mention Belize.

5 O. Nigel Bolland, 'Labour conditions in Belize: The century after 1838', *BELCAST Journal of Belizean Affairs*, 1,1, (1984), pp. 48–54.

6 Narda Dobson, *A History of Belize*, (London, 1973) makes no mention of labour protests and organisations prior to the GWU in her discussion of the development of trade unions and her discussion of politics in the two decades prior to 1950 is almost entirely limited to the Legislative Council and constitutional changes.

7 C.H. Grant, *The Making of Modern Belize: Politics, Society and British Colonialism in Central America*, (Cambridge, 1976) p. 61.

8 *Ibid*. 61. Grant gets the name of Soberanis' first organisation wrong and is incorrect when he says that the agitation 'never spread beyond Belize City', p. 67.

9 Assad Shoman, 'The Birth of the Nationalist Movement in Belize, 1950–1954', *Journal of Belizean Affairs*, 2, (1973), pp. 3–40.

10 Peter Ashdown, 'Antonio Soberanis and the disturbances in Belize 1934–1937', *Caribbean Quarterly*, 24, 1/2, (1978), pp. 61–74.

11 O. Nigel Bolland and Assad Shoman, *Land in Belize, 1765–1871: The Origins of Land Tenure, Use and Distribution in a Dependent Economy*, (Kingston, 1977), *passim*.

12 Colonial Report for 1932, No. 1 1647 (London, 1933), pp. 12, 31.
13 Gov. Sir John Burdon to Secretary of State (S.S.), 23 July 1931, BA 158.
14 Bolland (1984), pp. 49—50.
15 Act. Gov. H.G. Pilling to S.S., 12 Nov. 1931 and 3 Dec 1931, BA 158.
16 *Clarion*, 22 Feb. 1934, p. 165.
17 Police Superintendent P.E. Matthews Report to the Governor, 27 Nov. 1934, CO 123/346/35524 and BA, SP 25.
18 *Clarion*, 15 March 1934, p. 232.
19 Gov. Sir Harold Kittermaster, to S.S., 7 March 1934, CO 123/346/35524.
20 Matthews, *op. cit.*
21 See the autobiographical letter, A. Soberanis to Vernon Leslie, 10 July 1973, BA, SP 27. Soberanis' father, Canuto Soberanis, came to Belize from Yucatan in 1894 and lived in San Antonio, Orange Walk. His mother, Dominga Gomez was born in Corozal. Antonio, the eldest of seven children, was born on 17 January 1897. He attended R.C. Primary School in Belize Town until 1912, went to Honduras and all the other Central American countries and the U.S.A. Soberanis was a member of the Volunteers Guard in World War I and served in the Cayo expedition in 1914. See also 'Oral History: The L. and U.A.', *National Studies*, 2, 3, (1974), pp. 3—10.
22 Matthews, *op. cit.*
23 *Ibid.*
24 *Ibid.*
25 'Memorial in regard to conditions in the Colony', Soberanis to Kittermaster, 17 May 1934, BA, MP 700—34.
26 Kittermaster to Soberanis, 18 May 1934, BA, MP 700—34.
27 Soberanis to Kittermaster, 21 May 1934, BA, MP 700—34.
28 See reports enclosed in Acting Gov. Hunter to S.S., 14 Aug. 1934, CO 123/346/35524.
29 Matthews, *op. cit.*
30 *Ibid.*
31 Absolom Pollard recovered from his wound and it was never discovered who shot him. The police contended that it was a member of the crowd but it was widely believed that Corporal Building was responsible.
32 Matthews, *op. cit.*
33 *Ibid.*
34 Gov. A.C. Burns to S.S., 31 March 1935, CO 123/352/66554.
35 Burns to S.S., 26 July 1935, CO 123/353/66571.
36 Matthews report, 12 June 1935, included in Burns to S.S., 13 June 1935, CO 123/253/66568.
37 Burns to S.S., 13 June 1935, CO 123/253/66568.
38 Burns to S.S., 23 May 1935, CO 123/353/66571.
39 Serg. A.B. Clarke's report, 20 July 1935, CO 123/353/66571.
40 Soberanis to Burns, 23 Sept. 1935, CO 123/353/66571.
41 Att. Gen. S.A. McKinistry to Burns, 22 July 1935, CO 123/353/66571.
42 Burns to S.S., 30 Oct. 1935, CO 123/353/66571.
43 Burns to Beckett, 15 Nov. 1935, CO 123/354/66648. A Colonial Office official approved of Burns' action: 'The Governor took the right line in putting Mr. Grant on to try Tony, so as to avoid any suspicion of colour clash', Rootham's minute, 13 Dec. 1935, CO 123/354/66648.

44 The amount spent on outdoor relief, distributed largely in Belize Town, had increased rapidly from $2,600 in 1931 to about $10,000 in 1935 and 1936; see R.L. Cheverton and H.P. Smart, *Report of the Committee on Nutrition in the Colony of British Honduras*, (Belize, 1937), p. 47.

45 Ashdown, *op. cit.* p. 67.

46 *Ibid.* p. 68.

47 E.F.L. Wood, *West Indies and British Guiana*, (London, 1922).

48 Corpl. Cornelius A. Building to Supt. of Police, 21 June 1938, CO 123/367/66648.

49 Burns to S.S., 22 Nov. 1938, CO 123/366/66553.

50 *Ibid.*

51 Burns to S.S., 5 Jan. 1939, CO 123/373/66553.

52 Burns to S.S., 13 March 1939, CO 123/373/66553.

53 *Ibid.*

54 This paper was owned by a black radical, Herbert Hill Cain. Kemp's column, called 'The Garvey Eye' was viewed with suspicion by the colonial administration.

55 Burns to S.S., 24 March 1939, CO 123/373/66553.

56 Act. Gov. Johnston to S.S., Aug. 1939, CO 123/373/66553.

57 This was not related to the British Honduras Federation of Workers Protection Association, which Kemp formed earlier in 1939, and which was still functioning in 1941, though not really as a union. The newly created Labour Department reported that the BHFWPA 'could not qualify as a trade union' and that it often proved of considerable assistance to the Department in relief work and other matters', (Labour Department Report, 1940).

58 *Belize Independent*, 26 March 1941.

59 Soberanis to S.J. Hudson, 3 June 1940, BA, SP 25.

60 Soberanis to Leslie, 10 July 1973, BA, SP 27.

61 Burns to S.S., 28 Dec. 1938, CO 123/376/66824.

62 *Ibid.*

63 *Ibid.*

64 Gov. J.A. Hunter to Lord Moyne, 24 Oct. 1941, BA 174.

65 Hunter to Viscount Cranbourne, 5 March 1942, BA 174.

66 *Ibid.*

67 *Belize Independent*, 27 Aug. 1941.

68 Hunter to Stanley, 8 Feb. 1943, CO 123/380.

69 Garvey had previously visited Belize in 1910 and 1921. This account of Garvey and the UNIA in Belize is indebted to Peter Ashdown, 'Marcus Garvey, the UNIA and the black cause in British Honduras, 1914–1949', *Journal of Caribbean History*, 15, (1981), pp. 41–55.

70 Annual Report of the Labour Department, 1943.

71 See Amos A. Ford, *Telling the Truth: The Life and Times of the British Honduran Forestry Unit in Scotland, 1941–44*, (London, 1985).

72 *Belize Billboard*, 12 Jan. 1947.

73 *Belize Billboard*, 2 Feb. 1947.

74 *Belize Billboard*, 9 March 1947.

75 *Belize Billboard*, 3 Jan. 1948.

76 Joseph Campbell was probably one of this group. It was later reported that he had 'preached anti-British propaganda' in 1948 (Gov. R.H.

Garvey to S.S., 5 Sept. 1951, CO 537/7375.

77   A. Soberanis, G. and L.D. Kemp, *The Third Side of the Anglo-Guatemala Dispute*, (Belize City, 1945) p. 10.

78   1,166 people were registered as unemployed in Belize City in October 1949 and the situation was expected to get worse; Bradley's report, 31 Oct. 1949, CO 123/401/66985. By March 1950 there were 2,415 unemployed; Garvey's report, 30 Sept. 1950, CO 123/406/66985.

79   Since much of the story of the development of nationalist politics between 1950 and 1954 has already been told it will not be repeated here; see Shoman, *op. cit.* Grant, *op. cit.* Chap. 4.

80   Garvey, to S.S., 26 Feb. 1950, CO 537/6132.

81   Garvey to S.S., 29 March 1950, CO 537/6132.

82   Garvey to S.S., 25 Nov. 1950, CO 123/403/66152/2.

83   Soberanis to Leslie, 10 July 1973, BA, SP 27.

84   C.M. Flores police report, 14 Aug. 1951, CO 123/403/66512/6.

85   *Daily Clarion*, 25 May 1939. He was a delegate at meetings of the Caribbean Labour Congress and the Free World Labour Conference in London in 1949; Garvey to S.S., 20 Jan, 1950, CO 537/6132.

86   GWU newsletter, 25 April 1952, CO 1031/784.

87   For a monumental study of the Jamaican case, in which this argument is made, see Ken Post, *Arise Ye Starvelings: The Jamaican Labour Rebellion of 1938 and its Aftermath*, (The Hague, 1978) and *Strike the Iron: A Colony at War — Jamaica, 1939–1945*, 2 vols. (The Hague, 1981).

88   A Colonial Office official advocated the use of relief work in Jamaica in December 1938 as an 'insurance against disorder', quoted in Post, *Arise Ye Starvelings, op. cit.* p. 438.

89   The general case about welfare as a means of social control appears in Frances Fox Piven and Richard A. Cloward, *Regulating the Poor: The Functions of Public Welfare*, (New York, 1971).

90   Garvey to S.S., 26 Aug. 1949, CO 123/394/66620/5.

91   Labour Department Report, 1939. The Governor recognised that the sole Labour Officer was 'not qualified to assist and guide the labouring class in the formation of Trade Unions, or to speak with any authority on questions of labour legislation', Hunter to S.S., 5 Aug. 1940, CO 123/379/66807.

92   Don Hamill, 'Colonialism and the emergence of trade unions in Belize', *Journal of Belizean Affairs*, 8, (1978) p. 12; see also Peter Ashdown, 'Control or Coercion: The Motive for Government's Nurture of Organised Labour', *Journal of Belizean Affairs*, 9 (1979), pp. 36–43.

93   Susan Craig, 'The Germs of an Idea', in Arthur Lewis, *op. cit.* (1977) p. 79.

94   Act. Gov. Johnston to S.S., 22 Aug. 1939, CO 123/377/66853.

95   Burns to S.S., 3 Jan. 1939, CO 123/373/66553.

96   'The Public Works Department employs the largest labour force in the Colony...(exclusive of relief work)', namely 1,284 workers compared to 1,091 employed by the Belize Estate and Produce Company; Garvey's report on Economic Development and Employment, 30 Sept. 1950, CO 123/406/66985.

CHAPTER 14

The political representation of organised labour in Trinidad and Guyana: A comparative puzzle

Malcolm Cross

In an outstanding recent book, the philosopher and sociologist, W.C. Runciman, advises the social scientist and historian to search out and explore the 'suggestive contrast'.[1] Trinidad and Guyana from 1930 to the mid 1950s provide an excellent example of what he means. At first sight there is an extraordinary puzzle. In Trinidad, class-based unity in the 1930s appears to have been strong enough to bridge the racial divide between Afro-Trinidadians and Indo-Trinidadians and to have permitted the rise of industrial trade unions. These appear to have had a marginal effect, however, on political organisation in the post-war period. If there is one dominant feature of the Peoples National Movement (PNM), which governed the island from 1956 to 1986, it is that of a populist organisation eschewing any connections with organised labour. In Guyana, by contrast, inter-racial unity did not survive attempts to achieve class based politics in the form of the first Peoples Progressive Party (PPP) administration which '...had brought together for the first time politically (the) two main racial groups...'.[2] Organised labour, however, has always played a more important political role in Guyana, with each major post-war party being connected with a trade union. From this we might formulate the puzzling proposition that organised labour has a more powerful effect on nationalist politics where class unity is less evident.

There are four questions that appear to flow from these opening remarks, two in relation to Trinidad and two concerning the Guyanese position. First, is it really true that Trinidad had a class-based labour movement by the late 1930s? If so, then *why* did it appear to have so little impact on post-war politics? In Guyana, the opposite questions need to be addressed. Was it true that inter-racial and inter-ethnic divisions were such that it was not until the early 1950s that inter-ethnic unity became part of the political agenda? We know already that this political aspiration was realised for less than two years, but then why have trade unions appeared to figure so prominently in Guyana's contemporary history? To explore these issues, we need to look in turn at each country, starting with the 1930s which was throughout the anglophone Caribbean a decade of unprecedented working class struggle and resistance.

Trinidad after 1930

As early as July 1934, retrenchment of labour and tasks made harder by abnormally dry weather conditions had prompted labour unrest amongst the mainly East Indian workers on the Caroni, Esperanza and Brechin Castle estates. On 20 July 400 labourers marched in protest to Port of Spain and three days later the field manager and overseer at Esperanza were attacked and badly beaten.[3] Even the Acting Governor was moved to write to the Sugar Manufacturers Association later that year that:

> ...sufficient consideration for the condition of the labourers was not shown by the management, and...had there been a more adequate regard for their needs the disturbances which occurred in the latter part of July would almost certainly have been avoided.[4]

Certainly the wage bill for the three estates in question bore out the thesis that the management had acted in disregard of labour interests for it fell by 64 per cent for the eight weeks up to 21 July 1934 when compared with the same period the preceding year.[5] Yet these facts were merely triggering mechanisms; the underlying problem in Trinidad, as elsewhere, was that so little had been done to liberate labour from the 'new system of slavery' that had followed with the demise of the old. Nowhere is this more apparent than in the wages paid to agricultural labourers for a 'task' or job that was estimated to take a day's labour, but which could take from as little as six hours to a day and a half or longer. Under the old Indenture Ordinances, which governed the treatment of East Indian labourers from 1845 to 1917, a task for an unskilled labourer was paid 25 cents. In 1920 this was raised to 30 cents, and another five cents were added after the island-wide disturbances of 1937. The official Annual Report of 1932, entitled with unintentional irony the 'Annual Report on the Social and Economic Progress of the People of the Colony of Trinidad and Tobago', recorded that:

> The average wage for agricultural labourers varies from 5s to 12/6 per week of six days for men and from 4s 2d to 8s 9d per week of six days for women. The average hours of

work are 9 hours a day, i.e. from 7 a.m. to 5 p.m. with an
hour for lunch. Labourers who reside on plantations are
provided with free quarters but those who do not, have to
provide accommodation at their own expense. Skilled agricultural labourers may earn as much as 2s 11d a day.[6]

The latter figure was still the top of the range for skilled field
workers five years later so that even the élite of labourers could
expect the equivalent of about 97p for a 54 hour week. At wages
like these no agricultural labourer could afford to work all week but
had to rely on cultivating subsistence provisions on whatever land he
could find. As a result most labourers worked three or four days
only on the estates for an annual income of between £20.00 and
£30.00. A memorandum submitted by the Sugar Manufacturers
Association to the Moyne Commission in 1939 showed that in the
1936/37 season ten forkers 'randomly' selected from the roll at
Orange Grove Estate had earned between them £113.00 for 1,218
man-days or an average of nine pence per day. The two who had
worked longest received an *annual* income of £21.68 ($104.05) and
£18.62 ($89.40) for 237 and 202 days respectively.[7] Meanwhile another
memorandum to the Moyne Commissioners from an association of
labour organisations had estimated the minimum needs of a family
of two adults and three children living in a rural area at £3.04
($14.60) per week in 1938 or £158.00 per annum.[8] In these circum-
stances, it is no small wonder that anger and frustration kept boiling
through the deceptive calm of the colonial order.

Although we lack an adequate appraisal of the experience of
the 1930s throughout the anglophone West Indies, we know enough
to realise that the same pressures were being experienced elsewhere.
Most people worked on the land and workers on the land were
particularly subject to economic privations that were unusual during
this period even by the oppressive standards of plantation history.
But Trinidad had two special features in the 1930s that added a
particular vibrancy and significance to the period that it might
otherwise have lacked. These were, first, the presence of an oil
industry whose advanced structure and profitability brought into
high relief the contradictions between capital and labour and, second,
the combination of a highly sophisticated labour leadership with an
economic and administrative élite weakened by internal divisions.

The *peculiar* vibrancy of Trinidad's experience in the 1930s can
be accounted for by the class contradictions arising from relative
economic prosperity which gave opportunities for effective political
leadership seldom found elsewhere in the Caribbean. Moreover, the

historical accident that brought a liberal rather than conservative governor to Trinidad in 1936 revealed chinks in the colonial armour that served to excite rather than quell opposition. As a result the golden opportunity for dividing the working class against itself, typically afforded by an ethnically split work force, failed on this occasion — and perhaps on this occasion only — to stop movements of inter-ethnic unity from articulating Trinidad's share of the region's more general troubles. We can examine these two issues in turn.

The class factor

It is hardly possible to exaggerate the importance of the oil industry in the recent history of Trinidad. By 1932 petroleum products accounted for 57 per cent of export revenue, compared with 21 per cent from sugar and 14 per cent from the rapidly declining cocoa industry. The largest oil company in terms of mining was Apex Oilfields operating at Fyzabad and Siparia, but it sold most of its produce to the second largest mining firm, and largest employer of labour, Trinidad Lease-holds, which refined the crude oil at Point-a-Pierre and marketed it in the UK under the trade name 'Regent'. These two firms dominated the oil industry; both were public companies wholly owned by British interests, as were the fourteen other firms which by 1936 employed over 8,000 workers. With rising profitability there was a sudden scramble for oil leases on Crown Lands which increased in area by 79 per cent between 1936 and 1937 to occupy two-fifths of Trinidad's total land area.[9] Royalty payments were, however, a tiny proportion of the value of petroleum products comprising, for example, only 3.6 per cent in 1935 and 3.9 per cent in 1936.[10] Moreover, considering that oil was now contributing almost two-thirds of export revenue, the industry was contributing only minute amounts to public funds through royalties, as Table 15.1 shows.[11] In terms of profitability the picture was clear. From a position of good profits at the beginning of the decade the situation changed to one of very high return, followed by an almost explosive rise which lasted through the war years. For example, the dividends in Table 15.2 were obtained by Trinidad Leaseholds[12] between 1930 and 1936.

The following year profits rose again. The Chairman's annual report for Apex in 1937 records a total dividend for the year of 45 per cent (52.25 per cent gross) and this was after £2m had been written off in depreciation and amortisation.[13] Indeed most companies wrote off the *whole* cost of wells every year, which meant that profits were actually much higher, since wells often went on producing crude oil

Table 15.1   Proportion of public revenue obtained from royalties on oil in Trinidad, 1929–1938 (per cent)

1929	4.3
1930	4.6
1931	5.6
1932	6.3
1933	5.9
1934	5.7
1935	6.5
1936	7.0
1937	6.6
1938	7.5

Table 15.2   Dividends paid by Trinidad Leaseholds, 1930–36 (per cent)

1930	7.5
1931	5.0
1932	12.5
1933	15.0
1934	12.5
1935	17.5
1936	25.0

for decades. As the Chairman of Apex announced at the Company's AGM in London on 12 January, 1938:

> I have no doubt you will agree that there is good reason to be satisfied with the position disclosed in our balance sheet.[14]

Labour, on the other hand, was far from persuaded that they had been treated in a '. . . just and reasonable' fashion, as the Annual Report also suggested, and news of these figures was quickly circulated in the oilfields through popular papers such as the *People*. Prices had risen by at least 11 per cent between 1935 and 1938 (the governor was later to put the figure at 17 per cent) while wages remained very low, estimated by the employers at approximately $1.20 (25p) a day. Discounting price inflation, wages were never restored to pre-Depression levels.[15] The result was widespread unrest and disquiet which greatly increased both racial and class consciousness and culminated in the riots of Saturday 19 June, 1937. It is also true that Mussolini's adventures in Abyssinia had aroused anti-white feeling, as had the employment of South African managers on the oilfields, but the racial (anti-white) element was of much less significance than the economic. What was clearly perceived by labour as an exploitative situation created an awareness of class identity that was rare and compelling.[16]

The political dimension

The strike itself, which was called to force a wage increase of six cents an hour and the abandonment of the 'red book' by which management recorded information of black troublesome labour, was shortlived. It started at the Forest Reserve Field at midnight on 18 June and by 5 July 90 per cent of workers had returned to work. It gained a particular significance when the police tried to clear strikers from the Apex and Leaseholds oil fields. A mass meeting was called where 'Buzz' Butler, by now a familiar figure and already bound over to keep the peace by earlier brushes with the law, was addressing a crowd of 400–500 workers. Four policemen tried to arrest Butler and, after the warrant was read, another Detective Constable Carl 'Charlie' King tried to pull him away. King was beaten by the crowd, forced into a shop doorway and eventually thrown from the back window where, while he lay injured, someone threw a paraffin lamp on top of him with the result that he was burnt to death. Police reinforcements arrived that evening at which time more shooting and rioting broke out and Inspector Bradburn was killed.[17] Butler meanwhile had fled and did not reappear until he gave himself up to the authorities on 27 September.

What is critical here, apart from the emergent class consciousness, is the response of the authorities. Although in the vast majority of similar cases, the colonial authorities sided with capital in a dispute with labour, this was not always the case. The colonial service contained a minority of officials of liberal rather than conservative persuasion and this was most certainly true in Trinidad with the arrival of the new governor, Sir Murchison Fletcher in September, 1936. From the first, Fletcher, who was regarded by a senior official in London as '...the ablest man that the Colonial Service has had within my memory', had been sympathetic to demands for greater justice in wages and, in particular, he had taken a stand on the widespread malnutrition amongst the East Indian population.[18] As a result the *People* had referred to him as 'friend Fletcher' as early as January, 1937, while an *ad hoc* working class group dubbed him 'the Greatest Administrator that it is Trinidad's lot and luck to get'.[19]

The statements of the Governor and the Acting Colonial Secretary, Howard Nankivell, at the time of the 1937 riots provide ample reason for these unusual sentiments. At the first signs of unrest, Fletcher had cabled London with the statement that 'I am satisfied that the oilfield workers have legitimate grievances' and that 'the wages of unskilled labour throughout the Colony are admittedly too low'.[20] This was followed a week later by further telegrams giving in more detail the governor's specific complaints about the intransigence of the new South African General Manager of Leaseholds, H.C.W. Johnson, who would not consider meeting labour 'half way' even when 'there is ample evidence of legitimate grievances which must be remedied'.[21]

Two other actions by Fletcher brought the crisis to a head. First on 26 June, he obtained approval for an immediate 20 per cent rise for unskilled manual workers in public employment, and on 9 July he made his famous speech to the Legislative Council which, when taken with that of the acting Colonial Secretary on the same day, aroused a chorus of approval from labour and violent protests from vested interests.[22] The flurry of lobbying that eventually ensued culminated in Fletcher's dismissal and Nankivell's banishment.

The speeches make essentially the same points as the telegrams and despatches, although criticisms of the sugar industry were also included. Fletcher, noting the greatly enhanced profits in sugar, implored the industry to 'spare something more for labour than they now pay' and went on to suggest that 'they might either declare no dividend until labour conditions are better or declare a minimum dividend and apply the balance to the improvement of those conditions'.[23] Nankivell went even further saying that:

> ...thousands of labourers have to be kept employed and the only means that we can find at present for keeping them employed is the sugar industry and that is why the sugar industry has been subsidised; and not only must we keep them employed but we must keep them employed in decent conditions and not in conditions of economic slavery.[24]

Commenting on the oil industry, he suggested that 'it is far more in the interests of this Colony that the profits of oil should be expended on our own people than on the shareholders in other countries' while a few days later, after the governor had seen representatives of the oil workers, he wrote to the Employers Association that:

> ...the men have legitimate grounds for complaint and the Governor appeals to the managements to give to the re-

presentations their earnest and sympathetic consideration, and to act with the utmost expedition.[25]

As the Manchester Guardian noted at the time 'vested interests had never before been spoken to in that strain by an official speaking publicly in the Legislature' and a later Leader in the same paper praised the speeches for displaying '. . . an awareness of the deep rooted social and economic evils of the island that is wholly rare in the utterances of high colonial officials'.[26] Captain A.A. Cipriani, who had played such an important role in early movements to establish labour organisations in the previous decade but whose influence with the workers had been in decline for three years, and who subsequently approved of Fletcher's removal, lamented that he had '. . . been villified for years and called a red agitator for making remarks not half so strong as those made by the Government'.[27]

The official response to the outbursts makes a fascinating case study on the influence of pressure groups who are defined as legitimate by those in power. The immediate reaction of vested interests was to make representations to the Secretary of State for assurance that the speech by Nankivell in particular did '. . . not represent the considered policy of His Majesty's Government' but later a more considered policy was adopted.[28] In London the representatives of oil and sugar interests met under the auspices of the West India Committee on 6 August to prepare their evidence to the five-man commission of inquiry into the disturbances under the chairmanship of John Forster, a British Deputy Umpire for unemployment insurances.[29] Sir Alexander Rogers, managing director of Leaseholds' parent company, was particularly active. He made sure that he travelled out to Trinidad with the three British members of the Forster Commission, who left London on the *Colombia* on the 21 August. Later in the same year he was back in London dining with the Secretary of State himself, who was later to minute that after the meeting 'I am clearer than ever that Sir M. Fletcher must *go*'.[30] It was almost inevitable that the Forster Commission's report would be highly critical of the colonial administration and even before the report was published the Secretary of State had cabled Sir Mark Young (the Governor of Barbados and Acting Governor of Trinidad after Fletcher's recall in November, 1937) that 'I find it somewhat difficult to envisage Fletcher's return to the Colony'[31] although this did not appear to deter him from complaining in the subsequent House of Commons debate on the report itself that 'I resent the suggestion that Sir Murchison Fletcher was dismissed'.[32] The House was informed that Fletcher had resigned due to a 'nervous disorder'. A similar malady might have been said to have struck Howard Nankivell. He committed suicide in France in January, 1939.

The crucial point is that this manoeuvring by capital and the view from London were well known in Trinidad at the time. The speeches had encouraged labour organisations and made it easier for men like Adrien Cola Rienzi to apply his ample talents to forming both the Oil Workers' Trade Union (registered 15 September, 1937) and the All Trinidad Sugar Estates and Factory Workers' Trade Union (registered 24 November, 1937). Before Fletcher's resignation became known the new oil union had sent a memorandum to London describing him as an '. . .able, impartial and fair minded administrator' and declaring that:

> The Unions are aware that reactionary vested interests have for some time been disappointed and annoyed at Sir Murchison's impartial attitude towards the solution of the economic problems which have lately been confronting the Colony.[33]

After it was announced that Fletcher would not be returning, a large mass meeting on 16 January 1938, estimated to have contained 8,000 oil workers, 5,000 sugar workers and 2,000 cane farmers, and principally called to demonstrate support for Adrien Cola Rienzi's campaign for election to the legislature, passed a resolution which read as follows:

> That this public assembly of workers record strong protest if causes other than illness have produced this great loss to the Colony and is of the opinion that unless another Sir Murchison Fletcher be sent as Governor of Trinidad, the Colony will relapse into its past position of retrogression from which it began to recover with the advent of Governor Fletcher.[34]

It is not, therefore, fanciful to suppose that Rienzi's important and overwhelming victory in the constituency of Victoria, especially when taken with Cipriani's failure the previous autumn to regain his position as mayor of Port of Spain, was stimulated by the anger and resentment consequent upon the dismissal of the governor at the behest of financial interests.[35] In this sense the rift within the ruling élite of Trinidad galvanised support for class-based movements.

Trinidad: The post-war period

The war years in Trinidad and Tobago saw an unprecedented boom. The growth in the oil industry continued apace despite the imposition of an excess profits tax based on returns over the highest rates achieved in 1937–39. For example, oil profits rose by 68 per cent in June 1940 over the previous year.[36] In agriculture, too, these were years of increasing demand and rising prices.

Wage rates were more responsive than in the past to this increased demand and profitability. Partly as a result of fears that the events of 1937 would be repeated, but more because of a major labour shortage, real incomes tended to rise ahead of inflation. The single most important reason for this was the signing in March 1941 of the leasing agreement between Britain and the US of land for military bases. Twelve square miles were included in the 99 year leases at Chaguaramus, eighteen square miles at Wallerfield and a further two on the Toco road in the north-east of the island.[37] No charge was made for these leases but the building work at Chaguaramus at one time employed 28,000 men. As the industrial advisor wrote in 1942:

> In 1941 the Colony had the unique experience of an unfulfilled demand for almost all classes of labour. Towards the end of the year approximately 20,000 manual workers were employed in the construction of the US Defense Bases alone, and the importation of additional workers from neighbouring colonies was, at that time, receiving the close consideration of the Government and the US authorities.[38]

Although 2,000 workers were recruited in Barbados and illegal migrants from Grenada continued to arrive, this did not undermine the favourable position that labour enjoyed. The result was a dramatic decline in trade union support and organised activity. While it was true that Afro-Trinidadian labourers worked side by side with East Indians brought in daily from the sugar areas, the wages the latter received and, in particular, their lack of opportunities for overtime and promotion, undermined any attempts to harness their energies for pressing home political advantage on a united class front.

The result was that serious, popular leaders like Rienzi, who had based their appeal on working class unity, saw their support evaporate as attention become focused on the increasingly bizarre antics of men like Buzz Butler. In fact the unity of 1937–1939 fractured into four. First there was the emotional Afro-Trinidadian following surrounding Butler. Released from detention on 6 May 1939, he had urged his followers to work tirelessly to '...rid the Colony, the Empire and the World of fascism, Imperialism, Capitalism and Sin'.[39] Having been expelled from the OWTU for 'activities subversive to the discipline of the union', the vehicle for his struggle was to be the Butler Party (British Empire Workers and Citizens Home Rule Party). However, the Party and the workers' newspaper, *The People*, spent more time projecting Butler and soliciting funds for his sojourn in the UK than in promoting de-colonisation or labour interests. He eventually left in September 1948 to return nearly two years later in time for the elections of 1950.

The second focus for support was again projected through the personality of one man, Albert Gomes. Gomes, a Trinidadian of Portuguese extraction, had emerged in the late 1930s as a journalist. By 1944 he was Deputy Mayor of Port of Spain and, after Cipriani's death in 1945, he became one of nine elected members returned under the 1940 constitution. In the elections under the new constitution of 1950, Gomes became Minister of Labour, Industry and Commerce. Despite being a radical by nature, Gomes was staunchly anti-communist and eventually turned against organised labour, largely because he felt that the Trinidad economy needed foreign capital for industrial development. As he describes in his autobiography, he originally 'joined battle on labour's behalf' only to live long enough to realise 'that the irresponsibility of labour is today the outstanding threat to that rational ordering of the economic and social forces without which development is impossible'.[40]

Another fraction of labour was represented by the rural sugar workers. During the period after the war their undoubted political concerns were channelled into an ethnic revival that was to lead eventually to the founding of the Democratic Labour Party and nearly two decades of rather inept opposition to the PNM. In the mid 1940s, it was men like Ranjit Kumar who were able to stir Indian passions by referring to events on the sub-continent. Kumar also rose to prominence through organised labour but rather than struggle to retain the inter-racial unity of the pre-war days, he found it easier to revive the symbols and emotions of Indian communalism. The inter-weaving of anti-colonialism and ethnic separatism is well illustrated in Kumar's approach to the 1948 constitutional issue. As a member of the Reform Committee under Sir Lennox O'Reilly, which reported on 17 February, Kumar joined with Patrick Solomon in refusing to support the conservative Majority Report which retained the power of the Governor and colonial officials. Rather than promote Solomon's Minority Report, however, Kumar stuck out for his own amendment, claiming it to be more radical than anyone else's and in line with agreed resolutions from the 1947 meeting of the Caribbean Labour Congress. This earned him a sharp rebuke from CLC Secretary Richard Hart for not rallying around the main opposition to the official resolution.[41] There seems little doubt that Kumar's position was heavily influenced by the growing Indian ethnic revival. Two months earlier, it had been reported that Kumar had organised a meeting in San Fernando in which he proposed separate seats for Indians in the Legislative Council or, failing that, a voting system that only permitted Hindus to vote for Hindus and Moslems for Moslems.[42]

The final fraction was represented by the urban-based socialists with some support and certainly leadership from the middle classes. The two most important groups were the West Indian Nationalist Party and the Caribbean Socialist Party. The two leading lights in the former were the San Fernando lawyer, Jack Kelshall, and Clifford Sealy, while the latter was led by Solomon and Simbunath Capildeo. Despite the fact that both attempted to combine with major union figures, such as Ralph Mentor and John Rojas from the OWTU and Quintin O'Connor from the FWTU, nothing was to become of these attempts. In the elections of 1950, Mentor and O'Connor failed to win a seat and Solomon lost his, only to reappear in 1956 as Minister of Education and Culture in the first PNM administration.

Thus by the early 1950s the voice of organised labour had become much less strong. The usual explanation for this is to blame individuals, but this is a limited approach. Trinidad had ready made alternative symbols to those of class whose appeal grew as the urgency of change receded with the post-war boom. The oil workers, for example, came to see that the best way of retaining their leadership in the wages league was to throw in their lot with the urban Creoles, who in turn were perfectly happy to sustain a conservative nationalist government acting in the interest of a newly enlarged, home grown middle class. The threat of Indian domination was always enough to disarm organised labour mobilised on a class interest.

The events of the 1930s in Guyana

The first point to note is that this was a decade of ferment here too. As early in the decade as February 1930 there were demonstrations in Georgetown, which led the Colonial Office to inquire whether warships were available should they be needed.[43] By 1933 a major strike was called by the British Guiana Labour Union under Hubert Critchlow which called for a national 'down tools' day on 14 August. The union demanded an eight hour working day, a forty-four hour week, workers' compensation legislation, old age pensions, un-employment assurance, the abolition of 'catting', universal suffrage and a reduction in rents and taxes. This wholesale agenda, led from Georgetown by Guiana's earliest union (established in 1922) was enough to lead to the official suppression of all meetings, rallies or protests in Georgetown.[44] There were also disturbances at Estate Diamond in 1933 and others on West Coast Demerara in September 1934, following very heavy rainfall and consequent flooding.

In fact strikes had broken out in September 1933, 1934 and 1935 at the beginning of the grinding season. Each year they grew in intensity so that by 1935 they occurred throughout the sugar areas. On 30 August 1935 a so called 'boy' gang of field labourers on the West Coast, Demerara went on strike demanding more wages. The strike soon spread to the East Coast and East Bank of the Demerara River and eventually to the West Bank, Demerara. As the Governor wrote:

> The general complaints have been that wages are too low and that prices for work should be fixed before the task is commenced and these complaints have usually been coupled with demands that some over-managers or overseers should be dismissed.[45]

What is interesting and important here is that in addition to an emerging class consciousness there was a racial division which was clearly anti-white. This was seen officially as having been stimulated not only by racist attitudes locally but by the Italian invasion of Abyssinia in October 1935. The official report on the disturbances in September and October 1935 lends credence to this argument by noting the very significant role that African labour on the estates played in these uprisings and describes the events at Enmore and Lusignan when a British overseer called Hares was attacked by a cane-cutter called Daniel Pollard. Hares was made to march to hospital carrying a flag at the head of 400 strikers who are reported to have been shouting:

> Bad Abyssinia—all you white bitches got no business here—our country—you go back where you came from.[46]

Strikes and disturbances continued throughout the period. For example, between January-October 1938 there were thirty-six strikes, all on sugar estates and by this time a much more central role was being played by East Indian field labour. For example at Non Pareil 975 workers out of 1568 adults on the estate, struck from 31 August to 13 October. Although the strike failed to attain any of its objectives (increase in rates of pay, dismissal of one headman and withdrawal of sacking notices), it is significant that it was a united stand which included eighty African cane cutters.

On 14 February 1939 a major uprising occurred at Plantation Leonora after a shovel gang downed tools because of inadequate wages. The strike spread and involved African factory hands as well. On 16 February, the unrest was put down by the police who fired indiscriminately into the crowd, killing four workers and injuring six.[47] The picture that emerges from working class action itself is of continuous ferment against continued exploitation. This appears to have taken precedence over inter-community differences. In fact there are no reported instances of hostility between African and East Indian workers.

The causes

There are three major reasons why the strikes and uprisings occurred when they did. First, there are the obvious contradictions between capital and labour. After the depression of 1929 and 1930, prices fell dramatically for sugar but the weight of the depression was felt by labour and not capital, seventy per cent of which was externally owned. From time to time even the Governor would lament the effects of the imperial process. Writing in 1931 Governor Denham records:

> It is unfortunate for this Colony that so much of the money that has been made in sugar has been taken out of the Colony.[48]

At this time the finances of the colony were in a parlous state. The sea defences alone were accounting for more than a third of gross debt and it was proving impossible to obtain money from plantation owners. Between 1933–37 two per cent of government expenditure went on debt charges and administration and seventy cents out of every dollar were coming from taxes on tobacco, flour and oil. Thus taxes on the poor were being used to finance the plantations. In 1932, against bitter opposition, income tax was levied at low rates on 3000 wealthy individuals instead of 1000 as before, but by 1937 only 1,625 separate returns (including companies) were recorded. Evidence on the strategies used to avoid the appearance of profitability and repatriate profits is revealed from time to time. For example, an 'insider' view comes from John Dodds, an elected member of the Court of Policy 1924—26 and a former Curtis Campbell manager on the Essequibo coast. He records how profits were re-invested and how directors' fees, agency charges and buying and selling commissions for work carried out by the owners were used to export capital.

> Plantation Diamond, the largest sugar producer, belonging to an English company with a dividend record that would enthuse even a Wall Street financier in the boom days.

> This company started in a small way in the City of George-town as traders and agents for the plantations. From the money earned in BG, plantations were acquired from time to time, as gradually did the removal occur of those con-cerned to the happier clime of England there to enjoy all that money could procure. Education of the best for their children, society and club life for their elders, all from an industry that never makes a profit—on paper.

He calculated that while food prices had risen by 138 per cent during the Great War, wages had risen by only 50—60 per cent.

The inadequacy of wages was noted by every inquiry, even when these were set up by the colonial administration and excluded representatives of labour. By 1935 annual average wages in the sugar industry were recorded as $97 to Indians and $112 to all labour (including Africans), thus indicating the degree to which African cane cutters and factory workers, who were a small minority of all sugar workers, were better rewarded. It is important to notice that these differences are recorded by ethnic group and not by occupational category.

Secondly, there was the constitutional issue. Under the old Dutch system, even as modified after 1922, there was an equality between elected and non-elected representatives. In 1928, this was suspended, ostensibly on the grounds that the finances of the colony were going to require grant in aid from London and that therefore this must entail greater control. As a result Crown Colony government was introduced. What is more, the suffrage was undermined by the recession as more and more previous electors fell below the $300 minimum property qualification. There was a real sense, therefore, that politically things had got worse as power moved through the indirect system to London.

Finally, there was the crucial issue of anti-black racism amongst

the planter class and officials. This was very often present in statements from the planter class and a fine example is contained in the
memorandum from the Sugar Producers Association to the Moyne
Commission. This document is a model of special pleading which,
inter alia, argues that since wages are lower in the rice industry than
in sugar:

> ...this raises the question whether the recent disturbances
> on the sugar estates have not been instigated mainly, if not
> entirely, for the purpose of exploiting the sugar industry.[49]

More particularly, the memorandum quotes from an article appearing
in the *West Indian Review* of 1938 in which the Jamaican peasant is
described as 'lazy, feckless and oversexed' and claims that this is
'substantially true' for BG. This brought an instant reaction and the
labour union held a mass meeting in Georgetown on 12 February
1939 to protest at these widely reported remarks. In turn a bitter
row ensued between Frederick Seaford, President of the SPA and
Walter Citrine, head of the British TUC and a member of the
Moyne Commission, in which the latter attacked the planters for
their exploitation of labour and for profiteering. Seaford responded
by saying that his remarks were directed only at Afro-Guianese and
not at the Indians and he makes an interesting comment on the
necessity of racial stability for preserving the existing relationship
between capital and labour:

> I would point out that in a cosmopolitan community such
> as this, where public confidence can be maintained only by
> a common harmony among the different races making up
> the population, Sir Walter Citrine's apparent setting up of
> labour against capital cannot but be most disturbing to the
> well being of the colony.[50]

What we have, therefore, are all the ingredients for a powerful class
reaction against entrenched, external capital apparently bent on
continued and relentless exploitation. But is this what occurs? To
answer this we need to look at the response of the mass organisations.

The response of the mass organisations

At one level the events of the 1930s led, as elsewhere, to the
founding of unions and the growth of working class consciousness.
For example, up until 1931, the only union to register under the
Ordinance of 1921 was the Labour Union (1922). In 1931, this was
joined by the Workers' League, but between November 1937 and

the end of 1938, seven more unions had been formed, including the Man-Power Citizens' Association (MPCA) which was to play an important role on the estates. A reading of the documents, however, produced by these and other voluntary associations during the decade shows that in most cases, they come to represent one or other of the two major races. At one level this was obvious by the titles of the organisations themselves. Thus the African population was represented by organisations like the Afro-American Association and League of Coloured Races, the United Aid for People of African Descent and, in particular, the Negro Progress Convention, founded in 1922 by E.F. Fredericks, Theo Nichols, E.P. Bruyning and Hubert Critchlow. On the other side, there were the usual religious groups representing major Muslim and Hindu orders, but also the East Indian Association and groups such as the East Indian Intelligentsia. The important point is that the men behind these organisations were also the leading trade unionists. Thus Critchlow, for example, was president of the Labour Union and, somewhat later, C.R. Jacobs and Ayube Edun led the MPCA. It was Jacobs who wrote leading articles in the *Guiana Review* in the late 1930s calling for Indian communal representation.

But why was this the case? Three reasons stand out. First of all, there is no doubt that divisive policies and views had permeated down from the top. Not only were Afro-Guyanese abused by whites, they also had to contend with racially specific attempts to promote the Indians over them. For example, there were the settlement schemes at Bush Lot and Anna Regina, which were specifically for East Indians. These officially sanctioned divisions seem to have become adopted on both sides; the Indian organisations coming to assume they were representing the natural agriculturalists, and the African ones seeking to counting racist slurs with an attempt to revive black pride.

Secondly, there is no doubt that Indian organisations sensed that the size of the Indian population and its rate of growth would eventually permit a powerful, perhaps commanding, voice to be theirs eventually. Finally, there seems little doubt that bodies representing the Africans did resent what they saw as a progressive take over of established positions by the Indian population. This was true in the estates, in the villages and also in the civil service and other posts in Georgetown and elsewhere. The Workers' League, for example, spoke of being supplanted by the 'very much cheaper but less efficient East Indians' on the estates and others wrote in a similar vein.[51] The point was that, unlike Trinidad, there was little or no alternative to agriculture.

Organized labour and party politics after 1953

It is attractive to argue that racial divisions in Guyana were born of the 1953 debacle, when the newly won pre-independence constitution was suspended by the British government, and raised by CIA interventions in the years after. Certainly these are events of importance, since the British and Americans worked assiduously to split the Peoples Progressive Party (PPP) down racial lines in order to outflank the Soviet marxism of Dr Cheddi Jagan, but it is only fair to note that for at least fifty years before there had been frequent occasions when inter-ethnic rivalry had surfaced.[52] What emerged at the Moyne Commission, for example, was not evidence of organised labour bridging the racial divide but rather unions or voluntary associations pressing for sectarian interests. Thus, the British Guiana Workers' League in evidence presented by its president, A.A. Thorne, complained of the supplanting of Africans by the 'less efficient' East Indians and of exclusive land settlement schemes at Anna Regina and Bush Lot that were designed to persuade Indians not to return to the sub-continent.[53] On the Indian side the Man-Power Citizens Association, formed on 5 November, 1937 under its president, Ayube Edun, represented sugar estate workers. Edun regarded communal representation as '. . . the only equitable solution to the British Guiana problem'.[54] There is evidence, of course, that these divisions were fomented by the plantations themselves. Certainly the Sugar Producers' Association went out of its way to support racist generalisations against Afro-Guyanese to the point where the Moyne Commissioners themselves found it difficult to conduct their business because of the anger this produced in Citrine and the intervention of the public against the utterances of F.J. Seaford, president of the SPA.[55]

It has to be said however, that a striking feature of the evidence to the Moyne Commission, when compared with Trinidad, was the prevalence of organisations representing one or other major ethnic group. In addition to the East Indian Association and the major religious groupings, evidence was presented by the 'East Indian Intelligentsia', calling for the importation of five million Indian immigrants, while on the other side the commissioners heard from the Afro-American Association and League of Coloured Races, the Negro Progress Convention and the United Aid for Peoples of African Descent.

The war years did nothing to heal this divide. In fact, growing

Indian nationalism in the years before partition stirred similar sentiments in Guyana. Meanwhile organisations on the other side, like
the League of Coloured Peoples led by Claude Denbow, struggled
to promote parallel ethnic consciousness amongst the Africans. As
the recently returned young lawyer, Forbes Burnham, wrote to
Richard Hart in 1949 'I've been having a hell of a time being
friendly with Denbow and other Negro leaders while not adopting
their anti-Indian philosophy'.[56]

The key point is that labour disturbances in 1935 and again at
Plantation Enmore in 1948 were largely East Indian affairs, unmatched by any similar protest amongst the urban working class.
What this evoked was a fear of domination to the point where some
labour leaders with stronger support from urban areas, like A.A.
Thorne, took an anti-progressive stance, opposing universal suffrage
and constitutional change. Hart, writing in 1948, noted this 'virus of
racism' which was being used to '...advance one of the principal
racial groups, Negro or Indian, at the expense of the other'.[57] Thus
well before the split in the PPP following the suspension of the
constitution in 1953, labour organisations were widely seen as reflecting a racial interest.

On the basis of the foregoing, we should not be surprised to see
an important role for organised labour after the formation of the
PNC in 1956, as party politics came also to express a sectarian
interest. This is to miss, however, another very important theme.
From the very beginning of the PPP there was a commitment,
guided for the most part by ideological persuasion, to underpin
party political development with organised labour. It was initially
the conservatism of the MPCA and its leadership by a Muslim,
Edun, that led to the founding of the Guyana Industrial Workers'
Union, first registered on 5 April 1948. It was this union that was
used as the first labour base for the PPP and one of the main
struggles in 1953 was for its recognition. Indeed the passage of the
Labour Relations Bill through the House in September 1953 was the
pretext for the suspension of the Constitution.

This close affinity between party politics and organised labour
can be seen at every major turning point in Guyana's post-war
history. For example, in the Budget crisis of 1962, when the PPP
was in office under the 1961 Constitution, the opposition formed by
the unholy alliance of the conservative United Force with the PNC
was sustained by the Trade Union Congress. Indeed the strike
called by Richard Ismael of the TUC on 13 February 1962, which
was *supported* by the Chambers of Commerce, was the immediate
precursor to the famous disturbances of the following Friday which

were to further entrench the racial divisions and lead to the tragic years of 1963–64.[58] In other words organised labour became diverted to narrow political and sectarian ends.

Conclusion

The answer to the comparative puzzle should now be clearer. In both countries, of course, the threat of inter-ethnic hostility was ever present. In both, the so called East Indians were introduced in the years after slavery *specifically* to compete with the manumitted blacks. In both they came to supplant African labour in the sugar fields. The greater wealth and prosperity of Trinidad had, however, two contradictory effects. In the first place it led to a greater opposition between capital and labour, which was so intense that it managed to suppress the inherent tension between the two wings of the working class. Out of this was born a decade of extraordinary unity boosted by a rare, although not unique, strand of liberal colonial administration. Secondly, however, the Trinidad case points to the effects of relative affluence in defusing class conflict. The Afro-Trinidadian working class monopolised the labour in the burgeoning oil industry that was also able to benefit enormously from the growth of Port of Spain as a major regional capital and, perhaps more than anything else, they were never seriously threatened politically by a numerical Indian majority. The Indians meanwhile retreated from their class support in the 1930s to concentrate upon cultural retention and survival, apparently content with their supremacy in the rural areas and some small involvement in the new, urban labour market.

The result was thirty years of conservative Creole control in which ethnic symbolism was frequently used to maintain the status quo but which was always successful enough economically to minimise the possibility of inter-ethnic violence. Trade unions in this setting came to represent one or other ethnic group but always with a limited, industrial function. The hallmark of Trinidad politics in the post-war period, at least up until the mid-1970s, was that organised labour occupied a completely separate arena to that in which political debate took place.

The broad pattern of the 1930s is not dissimilar in Guyana. Here too the decade represented a watershed in which labour sought to reformulate the colonial order. The crucial difference was that labour organisations never overcame, but in fact reflected, the racial and ethnic divisions that have scarred Guyana's history in the twentieth century. What radicalism there was started from the assumption of ethnic separation. Guyana always lacked in this period the affluence that in Trinidad both sharpened class divisions and ameliorated ethnic competition. This mobilisation of ethnic interest continued after the war, except for the brief period of rapprochement in the first PPP administration, and for perhaps two years after the suspension of the constitution in 1953. Organised labour became a vehicle for ethnic interest.

There are two conclusions that emerge from this comparison. The first is, of course, that labour organisations can reflect an interest held in common with others in the same class position. These will be driven to the fore in times of extreme contradiction between capital and labour. On the evidence here, they dissipate relatively easily when short run advantage is achieved or when ameliorative measures are promulgated. Class unity may emerge only to become dissipated by the very affluence that brought it into being. Second, labour organisations can easily express other interests which relate to the position of one industry relative to another or one political ideology over another. When this happens, labour organisations come to represent those people who work in that industry or who support that ideology. But they are not the only organisations to fulfil this broader representational purpose. Political parties are another. The PNM in Trinidad filled the vacuum created by the decline in organised labour by entrenching a coalition of the urban middle and working classes. In that sense the PNM eschewed labour organisation because *it* organised labour. Trinidadian politics became class based, but in the interests of an urban *middle* class. In Guyana the PPP and PNC in their early years were not strong enough to stand alone. But the support they received pushed them inexorably away from home grown class politics. In the former case, the anti-colonialist but also anti-regionalist attractions of Soviet socialism fitted the bill, while for the latter the more familiar appeal of racial domination proved irresistible. In other words one went for foreign class politics, the other for domestic race politics. In this case, therefore, ethnic separatism did not succumb easily to socialist rhetoric because deeply entrenched interests were involved and labour organisations came to reflect these interests as readily as those of social class. Thus in neither country did organised labour come to fulfill a progressive class function.

Notes

1 'It is...likely to be more rewarding to look for hypotheses of which history has happened to furnish a chance of quasi experimental test

than for hypotheses which, however significant their theoretical implications, history has not furnished the means of testing even with the help of the most ingenious statistical or other techniques'. W.C. Runciman, *A Treatise on Social Theory*, Vol 1, (Cambridge, C.U.P. 1983), p. 169.

2 Ashton Chase, *133 Days Towards Freedom in Guiana*, (Georgetown, the author, n.d. (1953) p. 3.

3 *Report of the Labour Disturbances Commission*, Legislative Council Paper 109, 1934.

4 CO 295/585. Grier to the Secretary of the Sugar Manufacturers Association, 15 October, 1934. Enclosure.

5 *Report of the Labour Disturbances Commission, op. cit.* This report identified most of the immediate reasons for the disturbances but located the blame squarely on the labourers themselves, particularly the younger generation, who were said to reveal a 'lack of restraint and absence of a sense of responsibility' when dealing with the estate management. It is significant that among the ten members of the commission which was heavily biased in favour of established interests, was Captain A.A. Cipriani whose support for its findings must have contributed to his waning popularity. Even the governor makes reference to the commission's biases when he informed Whitehall that:

> . . . there can be little doubt that it was the definite wish of the Commission to avoid expressing their views in terms which might be regarded as justifying in some measure the conduct of the labourers

CO 295/585 Hollis to Cunliffe-Lister, 16 October, 1934.

6 *Annual Report on the Social and Economic Progress of the People of the Colony of Trinidad and Tobago*, Legislative Council Paper 78 933, p. 27.

7 CO 959/816 *Memorandum of the Sugar Producers Association to the Moyne Commission 1939*. These figures are transformed into sterling equivalents at the old exchange rate of £1 = \$4.80.

8 CO 950/814 *Memorandum from the Committee of Industrial Organization to the Moyne Commission*, 24 January, 1939.

9 In 1936 these sixteen companies held 264,665 acres of Crown Land under long term leases which specified that the lessee, directors and at least 85 per cent of the local staff had to be British subjects. The following year 473,855 acres of Crown land or alienated land were held under these leases. *Administrative Report of the Land and Surveys Department for 1937*, Legislative Council Paper 49, 1938.

10 *Times*, 19 April, 1937.

11 CO 950/832 *Memorandum from the Colonial Treasurer to the Moyne Commission*, 1939.

12 *Ibid.*

13 *Financial News*, 13 January, 1938.

14 *Ibid.*

15 *Legislative Council Debates*, (1371), 12 March, 1954.

16 In fact the racial element was often cited by officials and managers as a prime reason for the strike. See CO 295/599/70297, Tweed to Ormsby-Gore 13 July, 1937. Enclosure.

17 Five rioters were killed at Fyzabad and another four at Rio Claro.

18   CO 950/16, Stubbs to Moyne, 25 September, 1938.
19   *People*, 2 January, 1937; CO 950/796, *Memorandum by the People's Royal Commission Evidence Committee to the Moyne Commission*, 15 August, 1938.
20   CO 295/599/70297, Fletcher to Ormsby-Gore, 28 June, 1937.
21   CO 295/599/70297, Fletcher to Ormsby-Gore, 6 July, 1937.
22   The wage rises to manual workers were from 50 to 60 cents a day in the rural areas and 56 to 72 cents per day in town. It is worth recording that this did little more than restore earlier cuts in wages after the depression of 1929/30.
23   *Legislative Council Debates*, 9 July, 1937.
24   *Ibid.*
25   CO 295/599/70297, Acting Colonial Secretary to the Secretary of the Petroleum Association of Trinidad, 14 July, 1937.
26   *Manchester Guardian*, 10 August, 1937 and 2 February, 1938.
27   CO 295/599/70297, Quoted in General Manager, United British Petroleum (I. Farquharson) to Secretary of State, 20 July, 1937.
28   *Ibid.*
29   In addition to Forster the Commission consisted of the General Secretary of the Iron and Steel Trades Confederation (Pugh), a former Postmaster General in Kenya, Uganda and Tanganyika (Fitzgerald) and two Trinidadians—Brown (3rd Puisne Judge) and A. Jones (Commissioner of Agriculture ICTA). Their report, entitled *Report of Commission on Trinidad and Tobago Disturbances, 1937*, (Cmd 564) was published simultaneously in London and Trinidad on 1 February, 1938.
30   West India Committee, *Executive Minutes*, 6 August, 1937; CO 295/600/70307, Minute by 'W.O.G.' dated 17 December, 1937 (Emphasis in original).
31   CO 295/600/70307, Ormsby/Gore to Young, 7 December, 1937.
32   *Manchester Guardian*, 1 March, 1938. The paper was not, however, persuaded by this argument and recorded the hope that '...the Home Government will take less heed of what British capitalists tell it and more of the interests of its West Indian fellow subjects'. The best British comment on the Forster report came from Lord (Sydney) Oliver who wrote that:

> The Commission's report reeks, as the London oil people took care that it should do, of crude petroleum (Letter, *Manchester Guardian*, 16 March, 1938).

33   CO 295/600/70307, *Memorandum from the OWTU (Signed E.R. Blades) to the Secretary of State*, n.d. Enclosure. An annotation by J. Emmens, an Assistant Principal in London, sums up the impact of the speeches and couples it with an acutely racist remark:

> I cannot help feeling that the speeches made in the Legislative Council by the Governor and Mr Nankivell after the riots broke out in the summer are to some extent responsible for the attitude shown by the labourers. The speeches may have been warranted but it was not the kind of food on which to feed excitable negroes (*Ibid.* Emmens, 19 October 1937).

34   *People*, 22 January, 1938.

35   The election took place on 22 January, 1938. Rienzi beat his opponent, H. Piper, by 2,003 votes to 546.

36   *Financial News*, 24 March, 1941.

37   Legislative Council Paper No 22, 1941.

38   *Industrial Advisors Report for 1941*, Legislative Council Paper No 48, 1942, p. 3.

39   *People*, 27 May, 1934.

40   Albert Gomes, *Through a Maze of Colour*.

41   Hart to Kumar, 22 June, 1948. (Hart Papers).

42   *Clarion*, 17 April, 1948.

43   Darnley to Denham, 8 May, 1930.

44   Denham to Parkinson, 25 Sept. 1933 (CO 111/15140,).

45   Northcote to Thomas, 7 December 1935.

46   Report of the Commissioner on the Labour Disputes in Demerara and Belize, Legislative Council Paper No. 15, 1936.

47   Report of the Leonora Enquiry Commission, Paper No. 10, 23 March, 1938.

48   CO 111/696/85104/1971.

49   CO 950/649 Memorandum from the BG Sugar Producers Association to the Moyne Commission, 11 October, 1938.

50   Moyne, oral evidence.

51   CO 950/651.

52   Malcolm Cross, 'Indentured Immigration and Afro-Indian Conflict in Trinidad and British Guiana'. Unpublished ms.

53   CO 950/651, Memorandum from British Guiana Workers' League to the Moyne Commission, 14 November 1938.

54   *Guiana Review*, 4 December 1938.

55   CO 950/649.

56   Burnham to Hart, 14 April 1949.

57   Caribbean Labour Congress, *Monthly Bulletin*, August 1948, p. 3.

58   *Report of a Commission of Inquiry into Disturbances in British Guiana in February 1962*. Colonial No. 354 (London, HMSO), 1962.

Bibliography

Abad, J.R. 1888. *La República Dominicana. Reseña general geográfico-estadística*. Sto. Domingo.

Abel, C. and Torrents, N. eds. 1986. *José Martí: revolutionary democrat.* London.

Adas, M. 'From Avoidance to Confrontation: Peasant Protest in Precolonial and Colonial Asia'. *Comparative Studies in Society and History*. XXIII. pp. 217–247.

Aguilar L. 1972. *Cuba 1933: Prologue to Revolution.* New York.

Alba, Victor 1968. *Politics and the Labor Movement in Latin America.* Stanford, Stanford University Press.

Albert, Bill and Adrian Graves. (eds). 1984. *Crisis and Change in the International Sugar Economy, 1860–1914.* Norwich, ISC Press.

Albuquerque, A. 1961. *Títulos de terrenos comuneros de la República Dominicana.* Ciudad Trujillo.

Alexander, Robert J. 1965. *Organized Labor in Latin America.* New York, Free Press.

Anglade, Georges, Yunén, Rafael Emilio and Audette, Denis, 1982. *Hispaniola: lecturas sobre un mapa mural/les lectures d'une carte murale.* Montréal.

Antonio, Joseph Ph. (et al). 1984. *Haïti briser les chaines.* Lausanne.

Ashdown, Peter. 1978. 'Antonio Soberanis and the disturbances in Belize 1934–1937'. *Caribbean Quarterly*. 24, pp. 61–74.

—— 1979. 'Control or coercion: The motive for Government's nurture of organised labour'. *Journal of Belizean Affairs*. 9, pp. 36–43.

—— 1981. 'Marcus Garvey, the UNIA and the black cause in British Honduras, 1914–1949'. *Journal of Caribbean History*. 15, pp. 41–55.

Asiwaju, A.I. 1976. 'Migrations as Revolt: The Example of the Ivory Coast and the Upper Volta before 1945'. *Journal of African History*. XVII, 4, pp. 577–594.

Auguste, Maurepas. 1974. *Genèse d'une république héréditaire. 25 mai 1957 en Haïti.* Paris.

Baez Evertsz, F. 1978. *Azúcar y dependencia en la República Dominicana.* Santo Domingo, Universidad Autónoma de Santo Domingo.

Balch, Emily Greene (ed.). 1927. *Occupied Haiti.* New York.

Balsac, Jésus. M. n.d. *Apuntes históricos.* (Mayaguez: Imprenta Montalvo, 1906), p. 44 He states that in Mayaguez money donations were collected for striking workers in Ponce. Furthermore, a mass demonstration was organised to protest police brutality in the 16 April incidents at the Ponce public square.

Barbados. 1985. *1980/81 Population Census of the Commonwealth Caribbean: Barbados*. Vol. I, Statistical Service, Barbados.

Barros, Jacques. 1984. *Haïti de 1804 à nos jours. Tome II*. Paris.

Bartra, R. 1975. (et al). *Caciquismo y poder politico en Mexico rural*. Mexico.

Battlefront. 1978. Indentured Labour. 19 May, 7, Vol. 2, Trinidad.

Baud, M. 'Agricultural Transformation in a Caribbean Region'. 1982. Unpublished manuscript, Amsterdam.

—— 1986. 'Ideología y Campesinado: El pensamiento social de José Ramon López'. In *Estudios Sociales*. XIX, 64, April—June, pp. 63—81.

—— 1986. 'Transformación capitalista y regionalización en la República Dominicana. 1875—1920'. In *Investigación y Ciencia*. I, I, Enero-Abril, pp. 17—45.

Beachey, R.W. 1957. *The British West Indian Sugar Industry in the Late Nineteenth Century*. London, Oxford University Press.

Bendix, Reinhard. 1984. *Force, Fate, and Freedom: On Historical Sociology*. Los Angeles, University of California Press.

Benjamin, J.R. 1977. *The United States and Cuba: hegemoney and dependent development, 1880—1934*, Pittsburgh University Press.

Bergad, L.W. 1983. *Coffee and the Growth of Agrarian Capitalism in Nineteenth Century Puerto Rico*. Princeton.

Bolland, O. Nigel. 1977. *The Formation of a Colonial Society: Belize, From Conquest to Crown Colony*. Baltimore, Johns Hopkins University Press.

—— 1979. 'Labour control in post-abolition Belize'. *Journal of Belizean Affairs*. 9, pp. 21—35.

—— 1981. 'Systems of domination after slavery: The control of land and labor in the British West Indies after 1838'. *Comparative Studies in Society and History*. 23, pp. 591—619.

—— 1984a. Reply to William A. Green's 'The perils of comparative history', *Comparative Studies in History and Society*. 26, pp. 120—125.

—— 1984b. 'Labour conditions in Belize: The century after 1838'. *BELCAST Journal of Belizean Affairs*. 1, pp. 48—54.

—— 1986a. *Belize: A New Nation in Central America*. Boulder, Westview Press.

—— 1986b. 'Labour control and resistance in Belize in the century after 1838'. *Slavery and Abolition: A Journal of Comparative Studies*, 7, pp. 175—87.

Bolland, O. Nigel and Shoman, Assad. 1977. *Land in Belize, 1765—1871*. Kingston, Institute of Social and Economic Research.

Bonhomme, Colbert. 1957. *Révolution et contre-révolution en Haïti de 1946 à 1957*. Port-au-Prince.

Bosch, Juan. 1970. *Composición social Dominicana: historia e interpretación*. Santo Domingo.

Boserup, Ester. 1970. *Women's Role in Economic Development*. New York, St Martin's Press.

Brand, Willem. 1965. *Impression of Haiti*. The Hague.

Brea, Ramonina. 1983. *Ensayo sobre la formación del estado capitalista en la República Dominicana y Haití*. Santo Domingo, Editora Taller.

Brenner, Robert. 1976. 'Agrarian Class Structure and Economic Development in Pre-industrial Europe'. *Past and Present*. No. 70, February.

Brizan, George I. 1984. *Grenada: Island of Conflict*. London, Zed Books Ltd.

Brodber, E. 1980. 'Profile of the Jamaican Free Woman'. Paper presented at the Conference of the Caribbean Studies Association, Hoddesdon, Herts.

Brutus, Jacques B. 1963. 'Aperçu historique du mouvement syndical en Haïti'. *Rond Point*. No. 7.

Bryan, Patrick E. 1979. 'La cuestión obrera en la industria azucarera de la República Dominicana a finales del siglo IXX y principios des siglo XX'. *Eme Eme: Estudios Dominicanos*. 4I, marzo-abril.

—— 1979. 'La producción campesina en la República Dominicana a principios de siglo XX'. *Eme Eme Estudios Dominicanos*, VII, 42, Mayo-Junio, pp. 29–62.

Burn, W.L. 1970. *Emancipation and Apprenticeship*. London, pp. 176–177.

Bush, Barbara. 1986. 'Towards Emancipation: Slave Women and Resistance to Coercive Labour Regimes in the British West Indian Colonies, 1790–1838'. In *Abolition and its Aftermath: The historical context, 1790–1916*. Edited by David Richardson. London, Frank Cass, pp. 27–54.

Buvinic, M. and Youssef, N.H. 1978. *Women-headed Households: The Ignored Factor in Development Planning*. Washington, D.C., International Center for Research on Women.

Cabrera, O. 1974. *Antonio Guiteras: su pensamiento revolucionario*. Havana.

Calder, Bruce J. 1978. 'Caudillos and Gavilleros versus the United States Marines: Guerrilla Insurgency during the Dominican Intervention. 1916–1924'. *HAHR*, LVIII, 4, pp. 649–675.

—— 1981. 'The Dominican Turn Toward Sugar'. *Caribbean Review*. 3, Summer.

—— 1984. *The Impact of Intervention: The Dominican Republic during the US Occupation of 1916–1924*, Austin, University of Texas Press.

Carroll, J.J. 1972. 'The Government of Jamaica, 1900–1913, with Special Reference to the Role of Sir Sydney Olivier'. Unpublished Ph.D. thesis, University of London.

Cassá, Roberto. 1980. *'Historia social y económica de la República Dominicana'*. Vol. 2, Santo Domingo, Editora Alfa y Omega.

Castillo, José del. 1981. *Ensavos de sociología Dominicana*. Santo Domingo, Ediciones Siboney.

—— no date. *La inmigración de braceros azucareros en la República Dominicana 1900–1930*. Cuadernos del Centro Dominicano de Investigaciones Antropologicas (CENDIA), CCLXXII, 7, Santo Domingo.

Castor, Suzy. 1971. *La ocupación norteamericana de Haití y sus consecuencias (1915–1934)*. Mexico.

Catrain, Pedro and Oviedo, José. 1981. *Estado y crisis política*. Santo Domingo, Editora Alfa y Omega.

Ceara, H. Miguel, 1984. *Tendencias estructurales y coyuntura de la economía Dominicana, 1968–1983*. Santo Domingo, Editora Nuevas Rutas.

Céspedes, Diógenes. 1984. *Ideas filosóficas. Discurs sindical y mitos cotidianos en Santo Domingo*. Editora Taller, Santo Domingo.

Chapman, C.E. 1927, 1969 reprint. *A History of the Cuban Republic*. New York.

Chase, V. 1986. 'Farming Systems Research in the Eastern Caribbean: An attempt at Intra-Household Dynamics'. Paper presented at the Conference on Gender Issues in Farming Systems Research, University of Florida, Gainesville.

Cheverton, R.L. and Smart, H.P. 1937. *Report of the Committee on Nutrition in the Colony of British Honduras.* Belize, Government Printer.

Clark, Victor S. 'Labor Conditions in Cuba'. *Bulletin of the Department of Labor.* 41 (July 1902), pp. 682–3.

Cohen, Robin, Gutkind, Peter C.W. and Brazier, Phyllis. (eds) 1979. *Peasants and Proletarians: The Struggles of Third World Workers.* London, Hutchinson.

Collier, David. 1979. 'Overview of the Bureaucratic-Authoritarian Model'. In David Collier. (ed). *The New Authoritarianism in Latin America.* Princeton University Press, Princeton.

Craig, Susan. 1977. 'The germs of an idea'. In *Labour in the West Indies* by Arthur Lewis. London, New Beacon Books.

Crassweller, Robert D. Trujillo. 1966. *Life and Times of a Caribbean Dictator.* Macmillan, New York.

Craton, Michael. 1977. *Searching for the Invisible Man: Slavery and Plantation Life in Jamaica.* Cambridge, M.A., Harvard University Press.

—— 1979. (ed). *Roots and Branches.* Toronto.

Craton, Michael and Walvin, James. 1970. *A Jamaican Plantation: The History of Worthy Park. 1670–1970.* London.

Dash, J. Michael. 1981. *Literature and Ideology in Haiti 1915–1961.* London and Basingstoke.

Daumec, Marcel. (n.d.) 'Statistique de travail', in *République d'Haïti.*

Dean, Warren. 1976. *Rio Claro: A Brazilian Plantation System, 1820–1920.* Stanford, Stanford University Press.

Debbasch, Yvan, 1961, 1962. 'Le marronage: Essai sur la desertion de l'esclave antillais'. *L'Année Sociologique.* Vol. 3.

Debien, Gabriel. 1966. 'Le marronage aux Antilles Françaises au XVIIIe siècle'. *Caribbean Studies.* Vol. 3.

—— 1974. *Les esclaves aux Antilles Françaises (XVIIe-XVIIIe siècles).* Basse-Terre and Fort-de-France.

Deive, C.E. 1978. *El Indio, el Negro y la vida tradicional Dominicano.* Sto. Domingo.

Dejean, Pierre, 1963. 'Panorama actuel du syndicalisme Haïtien'. *Rond Point.* No. 7.

De Janvry, A. and Garramon, C. 1976–77. 'The Dynamics of Rural Poverty'. In *Journal of Peasant Studies.* IV.

Denis, Lorimer, and Duvalier, François. 1948. *Le problème du classes à travers l'histoire d'Haïti.* Port-au-Prince.

De Peña Váldez, Julio. 1978. *Breve historia del movimiemto sindical Dominicano.* Santo Domingo, Ediciones Dominicanas Populares.

The Dictionary of National Biography. 1920. London, Oxford University Press.

Diederich, Bernard and Burt, Al. 1972. *Papa Doc, Haiti and Its Dictator.* Harmondsworth.

Disraeli, Benjamin. 1905. *Lord George Bentinck: A Political Biography.* London, Archibald Constable and Company.

Dixon-Mueller, Ruth. 1985. *Women's work in Third World Agriculture.* Geneva, International Labour Office.

Dobson, Narda. 1973. *A History of Belize.* London, Longman Caribbean.

Domínguez, J.I. 1975. *Cuba: Order & Revolution.* Cambridge, Mass.

Doubout, Jean Jacques and Holy, Ulrick. 1974. *Notes sur le développement du mouvement syndical en Haïti.* n.p.

Douglas, Paul H. 1927. 'The American Occupation of Haiti'. *Political Science Quarterly*. Vol. 42.

Drew, Charles B. 1974. 'David Ross and the Oxford Iron Works: A Study in Industrial Slavery in the Early Nineteenth Century'. In *William and Mary Quarterly*. 31, April.

Duarte, Isis and Pérez, José. 1979. 'Consideraciones en torno a la política represiva, y asistencial del Estado Dominicano 1966–1978'. *Realidad Contemporánea*. No. 10–11.

Dunn, Richard S. 1976. 'The Crisis of Subsistence in the British West Indies During and After the American Revolution'. In *William and Mary Quarterly* 33. October.

Duvalier, François. 1967. *Oeuvres essentielles, Volume III. La révolution au pouvoir (première partie)*. Port-au-Prince.

—— 1969. Addresse de Son Excellence le Docteur François Duvalier. Président à Vie de la République a l'occasion du Deuxième Congrès National du Travail. In *République d'Haïti*.

Economic Commission for Latin America (ECLA). 'Statistical Yearbook for Latin America'. United Nations, New York, various years.

Edwards, Bryan. 1801. *The History, Civil and Commercial of the British Colonies in the West Indies*. 3 vols. London.

Edwards, David. 1961. *Report on Economic Study of Small Farming in Jamaica*. ISER, Jamaica, University College of the West Indies.

Edwards, M.R. 1980. *Jamaican Higglers: Their Significance and Potential*. Monograph VII, Swansea, Centre for Development Studies, University College of Wales.

Emmer, M.R. 1986. 'The Great Escape: The Migration of Female Indentured Servants From British India to Surinam 1873–1916'. In *Abolition and its Aftermath: The Historical context. 1790–1916*. David Richardson (Ed.) London, Frank Cass, pp. 245–266.

Engerman, Stanley L. 1984. 'Economic Change and Contract Labour in the British Caribbean: the End of Slavery and the Adjustment to Emancipation'. *Explorations in Economic History*. Vol. 21, pp. 133–150.

Espinal, Rosario R. 1985. 'Classes, Power, and Political Change in the Dominican Republic'. Ph.D. dissertation, Washington University, St Louis.

—— 1986. 'An Interpretation of the Democratic Transition in the Dominican Republic'. In G. di Palma and L. Whitehead (eds.) *The Central American Impasse*. New York, St. Martin's Press.

Farber S. 1976. *Revolution and Reaction in Cuba, 1933–60*. Middletown.

Fermoselle, López. R. 1972 *Black politics in Cuba: The Race War of 1912*. Ph.D. the American University, University Microfilms, Ann Arbor.

Fitzherbert Papers. Derbyshire County Record Office, Matlock, Derbyshire.

Foner, Eric. 1983. *Nothing But Freedom: Emancipation and Its Legacy*. Baton Rouge, Louisiana State University Press.

Ford, Amos A. 1984. *Telling the Truth: The Life and Times of the British Honduran Forestry Unit in Scotland (1914–44)*. London, Karia Press.

Fortune, M. Georges, 1976. *Haïti una nación al servicio del 5%*. Guarenas.

Forum 8: 1983. *La situación laboral en la República Dominicana* (Collection of Papers), Santo Domingo, Editora Amigo del Hogar.

Fouchard, Jean. 1972. *Les marrons de la liberté*. Paris.

Frank, André Gunder. 1969. *Capitalism and Underdevelopment in Latin America. Historical Studies of Chile and Brazil*. Revised edition, New

York and London.

Fraser, Peter. 1981. 'The Fictive Peasantry: Caribbean Rural Groups in the Nineteenth Century'. In Susan Craig (ed), *Contemporary Caribbean.* Vol. 1, pp. 319–347. (Port of Spain, Susan Craig).

Gaillard, R. 1982. *Charlemagne Péralte le caco.* Port-au-Prince.

Galíndez, Jesús de. 1973. *The Era of Trujillo.* University of Arizona Press, Tucson.

Galvin, Miles. 1979. *The Organized Labor Movement in Puerto Rico.* Cranbury and London, Associated University Press.

García, Gervasic and Quintero, Angel. 1982. *Desafío y solidaridad: breve historia del movimiento obrero en Puerto Rico.* Rio Piedras, Ediciones Huracan, p. 40.

Garrido, V. 1970. *En la ruta de mi vida. 1886–1966.* Santo Domingo.

Garrido Puello, E.O. 1963. *Olivorio: un ensayo histórico.* Santo Domingo.

Garvey, M. 1984 *The Marcus Garvey and University Negro Improvement Association Papers.* ed. R. Hill. Vol. III. Berkeley.

Gingras, Jean Pierre O. 1967. *Duvalier Caribbean Cyclone. The History of Haiti and Its Present Government.* New York.

Godio, Julio. 1983. 'El movimiento sindical Latinoamericano: Diagnóstico y perspectivas). (Research Report). Instituto Interamericano de Investigaciones Socialies. Friedrich Ebert Stiftung, Caracas.

Grant, C.H. 1976. *The Making of Modern Belize: Politics, Society and British Colonialism in Central America.* Cambridge, Cambridge University Press.

Great Britain. 1831–2. Parliamentary papers. (Commons) 'Report from the Select Committee on the Extinction of Slavery Throughout the British Dominions'. No. 721, 20.

Green, W.A. 1976. *British Slave Emancipation.* Oxford, Clarendon Press.

—— 1984. 'The perils of comparative history: Belize and the British sugar colonies after slavery'. *Comparative Studies in Society and History.* 26, pp. 112–119.

Grindle, M. 1986. *State and Countryside: Development Policy and Agrarian Politics in Latin America.* Baltimore.

Grunwald, Joseph; Delatour, Leslie and Voltaire, Karl. 1984. 'Offshore Assembly in Haiti'. In Charles R. Foster and Albert Valdman (eds.), *Haiti—Today and Tomorrow. An Interdisciplinary Study.* Lanham, Md.

Guerra y Sánchez, Ramiro. 1976. *Azúcar y población en las Antilles.* Havana, Editorial de Ciencias Sociales.

Guerra y Sánchez, R. 1964. *Sugar and Society in the Caribbean.* New Haven.

Hall, Douglas. 1959. *Free Jamaica, 1838–1865: An Economic History.* New Haven, Yale University Press.

Hamill, Don, 1978. 'Colonialism and the emergence of trade unions in Belize'. *Journal of Belizean Affairs.* 7, pp. 3–20.

Hansen, Bent. 1979. 'Colonial Economic Development with Unlimited Supply of Land'. *Economic Development and Cultural Change.* Vol. 27.

Harrison, J.P. 1952. 'The evolution of the Colombian tobacco trade to 1875'. *HAHR.* XXXII. 2.

—— 1969. *The Colombian Tobacco Industry from government monopoly to free trade. 1778–1876.* Bogota.

Harry, Indra S. 1980. 'Women in Agriculture in Trinidad'. Unpublished M.Sc. thesis, University of Calgary.

Hart, Richard. 1982. 'Trade unionism in the English-speaking Caribbean: The formative years and the Caribbean Labour Congress'. In *Contemporary Caribbean: A Sociological Reader,* edited by Susan Craig, Vol. 2, pp. 59—96, Maracas, College Press.

—— n.d. (c. 1984). *Origin and Development of the Working Class in the English-speaking Caribbean Area—1897 to 1937.* London, Community Education Trust.

Heinl, Robert Debs, Jr. and Heinl, Nancy Gordon. 1978. *Written in Blood. The Story of the Haitian People 1492—1971.* Boston.

Hennessy. A. 1982. 'Cuba' in *The Spanish Civil War, 1936—9: American hemispheric perspectives,* ed. Falcoff. M. and Pike F., Lincoln.

Henry, Frances and Wilson, Pamela. 1975. 'The Status of Women in Caribbean Societies: An Overview of their Social, Economic and Sexual Roles'. In *Social and Economic Studies,* 24, 2, pp. 165—198.

Henshall, J.D. (Momsen). 1981. 'Women and Small Scale Farming in the Caribbean'. In *Papers in Latin American Geography in Honor of Lucia C. Harrison.* O. Horst (ed.), Muncie, Indiana, CLAG pp. 28—43.

—— 1984. 'Gender Versus Ethnic Pluralism in Caribbean Agriculture'. In C. Clarke, D. Ley and C. Peach (eds). *Geography and Ethnic Pluralism.* London, George Allen and Unwin, pp. 173—192.

Higman, B.W. 1976. 'The Slave Population of the British Caribbean: Some Nineteenth Century Valuations'. In S. Proctor (ed.) *Eighteenth Century Florida and the Caribbean.* Gainesville, University Presses of Florida, pp. 60—70.

Higman, B.W. 1976. *Slave Population and Economy in Jamaica 1807—1834.* Cambridge.

Hirschman, Albert O. 1970. *Exit, Voice and Loyalty. Responses to Decline in Firms, Organisations, and States.* Cambridge, Mass. and London.

—— 1981. *Essays in Trespassing. Economics to Politics and Beyond.* Cambridge.

Historia del movimiento obrero cubano, 1985. 2 Vols. Havana, Instituto de Historia del movimiento comunista de la Revolución Socialista de Cuba.

Hoernel, R.B. 1976. 'Sugar and social change in Oriente, Cuba, 1898—1946,' *Journal of Latin American Studies,* viii 2.

Hoetink, H. 1980. 'El Cibao 1844—1900: su Aportación a la Formación Social de la Républica'. *Eme Eme: Estudios Dominicanos.* 48, mayo-junio.

—— 1982. *The Dominican People 1850—1900: Notes for an Historical Sociology* Translated from the Spanish by Stephen Ault. Baltimorel London, Johns Hopkins University Press.

Holt, Thomas. 'The Problem of Freedom: The Political Economy of Jamaica after Slavery'. Unpublished.

Huntington, Samuel. 1968. *Political Order in Changing Societies.* New Haven, Yale University Press.

Hurwitz, S.J. and E.F. 1971. *Jamaica: A Historical Portrait.* London, Pall Mall Press.

Hyam, Ronald. 1979. 'The Colonial Office Mind. 1900—1914'. *Journal of Imperial and Commonwealth History,* vol. 8, No. 1, pp. 30—55.

Hyden, G. 1982. *Beyond Ujamaa in Tanzania: Underdevelopment and an*

Uncaptured Peasantry. London.

Jessop, Bob. 1969. 'Corporatism, Parliamentarianism and Social Democracy'. In Philippe Schmitter and Gerhard Lehmbruch. (eds). *Trends Toward Corporatist Intermediation.* Beverly Hills/London, Sage Publications.

John, N., Elwin, S. Charles and Clarendon, H. 1983. 'The G-Toc Cooperative of Dominica: past and future'. In *Planning for women in Rural Development.* Barbados, WAND, Extra-Mural Department, University of the West Indies, pp. 49–60.

Johnson, Howard. 1977. 'The West Indies and the Conversion of the British Official Classes to the Development Idea'. *Journal of Commonwealth and Comparative Politics.* Vol. XV, pp. 55–83.

Kenny, M. 1961. 'Twentieth-century Spanish expatriates in Cuba: a subculture?' *Anthropological Quarterly,* 34, 2.

Kerkvliet, B.J. 1977. *The Huk Rebellion.* Berkeley.

Kiple, K.F. 1984. *The Caribbean Slave: A Biological History.* Cambridge University Press.

Knight, M.N. 1970. (reprint 1970). *The Americans in Santo Domingo.* New York.

Knox, A.J.G. 1977. 'Opportunities and Opposition, The Rise of Jamaica's Black Peasantry and the Nature of Planter Resistance'. *Canadian Review of Sociology and Anthropology.* 14.

Knudson, Barbara and Yates, Barbara A. 1981. *The Economic Role of Women in Small Scale Agriculture in the Eastern Caribbean—St Lucia.* Barbados, WAND, Extra-Mural Department, University of the West Indies.

Kolchin, Peter. 1977–78. 'The Process of Confrontation: Patterns of Resistance to Bondage in 19th Century Russia and the United States'. *Journal of Social History.* Vol. II.

Korpi, Walter. 1981. 'Conflict, Power and Politics in Industrial Relations'. In Peter Doeringer, (et al.), (eds.) *Industrial Relations in International Perspective: Essays on Research and Policy.* London, Macmillan Press.

Kryzanek, Michael. 1972. 'Diversion, Subversion and Repression: The Strategies of Anti-Opposition Politics in Balaguer's Dominican Republic'. *Caribbean Studies.* Vol. 17, April—July.

Labor Code of the Dominican Republic. 1982. Santo Domingo.

Labor Ministry. Unpublished Documents. Santo Domingo.

Labour and Welfare Department. 1961. *François Duvalier Labour Code.* Port-au-Prince.

Landsberger, H.A. 1969. (ed.) *Latin American Peasant Movements.* Ithaca/London.

Le Franc, E.R. 1980. 'Grenada, St Vincent and St Lucia'. In *Small Farming in the less Developed Countries of the Commonwealth Caribbean.* Barbados, Caribbean Development Bank, pp. 1–143.

Lehmann, Gerard, n.d. *Babydocratie et presse écrite en Haïti. Considérations sur le regne de l'Illustre Heritier du Père de la Nouvelle Haïti de decembre 1980 à juillet 1981.* Odense.

Levy, C. 1980. *Emancipation, Sugar and Federalism: Barbados and the West Indies 1833–1876.* Gainesville, University of Florida Press.

Lewis, Arthur, 1977. *Labour in the West Indies: The Birth of a Workers' Movement* (first published in 1938). London, New Beacon Books.

Lewis, Gordon K. 1968. *The Growth of the Modern West Indies.* London, MacGibbon & Kee.

Leyburn, James G. 1966. *The Haitian People.* (Second Edition), New Haven and London.

Litwack, Leon. 1979. *Been in the Storm So Long: The Aftermath of Slavery.* New York, Random House.

Lobdell, Richard A. 1972. 'Patterns of Investment and Sources of Credit in the British West Indian Sugar Industry, 1838–97'. *Journal of Caribbean History.* Vol. 4, pp. 31–53.

Loveira, C. 1920. *Generales y Doctores,* Havana.

Lowenthal, David. 1972. *West Indian Societies.* London, Oxford University Press.

Lundahl, Mats. 1979. *Peasants and Poverty: A Study of Haiti.* London and New York.

—— 1982. 'A Note on Haitian Migration to Cuba. 1890–1934'. *Cuban Studies.* Vol. 12, 2.

—— 1984. 'Papa Doc: Innovator in the Predatory State'. *Scandia.* Vol. 50.

—— 1985a. 'Government and Inefficiency in the Haitian Economy. The Nineteenth-Century Legacy'. In: Michael B. Connolly and John H. McDermott (eds.) *The Economics of the Caribbean Basin.* New York.

—— 1985b. 'Brain Drain, Illegal Migration and Capital Exports from Less Developed Countries: A Neoclassical Approach'. *Economics Letters.* Vol. 17.

Lundahl, Mats and Vargas, Rosemary. 1983. 'Haitian Migration to the Dominican Republic'. In Mats Lundahl: *The Haitian Economy: Man, Land and Markets.* London, Canberra.

Macmillan, A.A. 1967. *The Development of Market Gardening in Aranguez, Trinidad.* Ph.D. thesis, University of the West Indies, Trinidad.

Macmillan, W.M. 1935. *Warning from the West Indies.* London, Faber and Faber.

Mallon, F.E. 1983. *The Defense of Community in Peru's Central Highlands: Peasant Struggle and Capitalist Transition. 1860–1940.* Princeton.

Manigat, Leslie. 1964. *Haiti of the Sixties. Object of International Concern.* Washington, D.C.

Mariñez, P.A. 1984. *Resistencia Campesina. Imperialismo y reforma agraria en la República Dominica (1899–1978).* Santo Domingo, Ediciones CEPAE.

Marshall, W.K. 1968. 'Notes on Peasant Development in the West Indies Since 1938'. *Social and Economic Studies.* Vol. 17, No. 3, pp. 252–263.

Martínez, L. 1985. 'Palma Sola: Un caso de movimiento social campesino con características mesianisticas'. *Revista Estudios Dominicanos,* 11, 4, April, pp. 9–20.

Mathurin, Lucille. 1975. *The Rebel woman in the British West Indies During Slavery.* Kingston, Institute of Jamaica for the African-Caribbean Institute.

Mericle, Kenneth. 1977. 'Corporatist Control of the Working Class: Authoritarianism in Brazil Since 1964'. In James Malloy (ed.) *Authoritarianism and Corporatism in Latin America.* Pittsburgh, University of Pittsburgh Press.

Meyer, J.A. 1976. *The Cristero Rebellion. The Mexican People between Church and State. 1926–1929.* Cambridge.

Millspaugh, Arthur C. 1931. *Haiti under American Control.* Boston.

Mintz, S.W. 1964., 'Currency Problems in Eighteenth Century Jamaica and Gresham's Law. In *Process and Pattern in Culture: Essays in Honor of*

Julian N. Steward. A. Manners (ed.) Chicago, Aldine Publishing Co.
—— 1974. *Caribbean Transformations.* Chicago, Aldine Publishing Co.
—— 1985. 'From Plantations to Peasantries in the Caribbean'. In S.W. Mintz and S. Price (eds.) *Caribbean Contours.* London, Johns Hopkins University Press, pp. 127–154.
—— 1974. 'The Rural Proletariat and the Problem of Rural Proletarian Consciousness'. *Journal of Peasant Studies.* I, 3.
Monclova, Lidio Cruz. 1970. *Historia de Puerto Rico (Siglo XIX)*, Río Piedras, Editorial Universitaria.
Moore, B. 1966. *Social Origins of Dictatorship and Democracy.* Boston, Beacon Press.
Moore, O. Ernest. 1972. *Haiti: Its Stagnant Society and Shackled Economy: A survey.* New York.
Momsen, J. Henshall. 1969. *The Geography of Land Use and Population in the Caribbean with Special Reference to Barbados and the Windward Islands.* Ph.D. thesis, University of London.
—— 1987. 'Land Settlement as a Solution'. In J. Momsen and J. Besson (eds.) *Land and Development in the Caribbean.* London, Macmillan.
Montserrat. 1984. *1980–81 Population Census of the Commonwealth Caribbean: Montserrat.* Volume I. Jamaica, Statistical Institute.
Moreno Fraginals, Manuel. 1978. *El ingenio: complejo económico social cubano del azúcar.* 3 vols. Havana, Editorial de Ciencias Sociales. Trans. *The Sugar Mill* (1976) abridged, 1 vol. New York.
—— 1983. *La historia como arma y otros estudios sobre esclavos, ingenios y plantaciones.* Barcelona, Editorial Critica.
Moreno Fraginals, Manuel; Moya Pons, Frank, and Engerman, Stanley, (eds.) 1985. *Between Slavery and Free Labour: The Spanish-Speaking Caribbean in the Nineteenth Century.* Baltimore, The Johns Hopkins University Press.
Moreno, José. 1976. 'Class Domination, Repression and Economic Penetration in the Dominican Republic'. *International Studies Series,* University of New York, Buffalo, New York.
Morgan, Philip S. 1982. 'Work and Culture: The Task System and the World of Low Country Blacks 1700–1880'. *William and Mary Quarterly.* 39, October.
Morrisey, M. 1986. 'Women's work. Family Formation and Reproduction Among Caribbean Slaves'. *Review,* IX (3), pp. 339–368.
Morsen, H. 1841. *The Present Conditions of the British West Indies: Their Wants and the Remedy for These.* London, privately published.
Munslow, B. and Finch, H. (eds.) 1984. *Proletarianisation in the Third World: Studies in the Creation of a Labour Force Under Dependent Capitalism.* London, Croom Helm.
Murdoch, G.P. and Provost, C. 1973. 'Factors in the Division of Labour by Sex: A Cross-cultural Analysis'. *Ethnology.* 12, pp. 203–225.
Murray, Gerald, F. 1977. 'The Evolution of Haitian Peasant Land Tenure: A Case Study in Agrarian Adaptation to Population Growth'. Ph.D. Thesis, Columbia University, New York.
Mutto, Paul. 1974. 'La economía de exportación de la República Dominicana 1900–1930'. *Eme Eme: Estudios Dominicanos,* 15, nov-dic.
Nicholls, David. 1979. *From Dessalines to Duvalier. Race, Colour and National Independence in Haiti.* Cambridge.

—— 1984. 'Past and Present in Haitian Politics'. In Charles R. Foster and Albert Valdman (eds.) *Haiti—Today and Tomorrow. An Interdisciplinary Study.* Lanham, Md.

—— 1985. *Haiti in Caribbean Context: Ethnicity, Economy and Revolt.* London.

North, Douglas, C. 1981. *Structure and Change in Economic History.* New York and London.

O'Donnell, Guillermo. 1973. *Modernization and Bureaucratic-Authoritarianism: Studies in South American Politics.* Berkeley, Institute of International Studies, University of California.

Oficina Nacional de Estadisticas. Various years. *República Dominicana en Cifras.* Santo Domingo.

—— Various years. *Estadística Industrial.* Secretaria de Estado de Industria y Comercio, Santo Domingo.

Oficina Nacional de Planificación. 1980. *Hacia una políticsa de empleo en la República Dominicana.* Santo Domingo.

Oficina Nacional del Presumpuesto. Various years. *Ejecución Nacional del Presupuesto.* Santo Domingo.

Olivier, Margaret (ed.) 1948. *Sydney Olivier: Letters and Selected Writings.* London, George Allen and Unwin.

Olivier, Sydney. 1936. *Jamaica: the Blessed Island.* London, Faber and Faber.

Orde Browne, Major G. St. J. 1939. *Labour Conditions in the British West Indies.* London, His Majesty's Stationery Office.

Oviedo, José. 1982. 'Estado y Clases Subalternas: Para una Crítica del Estado Capitalista en la República Dominicana'. *Realidad Contemporanea.* No. 18—19.

Pagan, Ingualdad, Iglesias de. 1973. *El obrerismo en Puerto Rico.* Palencia, Ediciones Juan Ponce de Leon, p. 87.

Pahl, R.E. 1984. *Divisions of Labour.* Oxford, Basil Blackwell.

Paige, J. 1975. *Agrarian Revolution.* New York.

Palmer, E.C. 1976. Land Use and Landscape Change along the Dominican-Haitian Borderlands. Unpublished Ph.D. thesis, University of Florida.

Panitch, Leo. 1981. 'The Limits of State Corporatism: Trade Unions and the Capitalist State'. *New Left Review.* No. 125, Jan—Feb.

The Parliamentary Companion. 1847 and 1850. London, Whittaker & Co.

Patterson, Orlando. 1967. *The Sociology of Slavery.* London, MacGibbon & Kee.

Pérez, L.A. 1976. *Army Politics in Cuba, 1898—1958.* Pittsburgh University Press.

1978. *Intervention, Revolution and Politics in Cuba, 1913—21* Pittsburgh.

1983. *Cuba Between Empires 1878—1907.* Pittsburgh.

1986. 'The pursuit of pacification: banditry and the United States occupation of Cuba, 1899—1902'. *Journal of Latin American Studies,* 18, 2.

Pérez de la Riva, J. 1979. Cuba y la migración antillana, 1900—1932. *Anuario de Estudios Cubanos.*

Phelps, O.W. 1960. 'Rise of the labour movement in Jamaica'. *Social and Economic Studies.* 9, pp. 427—468.

Pierre-Charles, Gerard. 1969. *Radiografía de una dictadura—Haití bajo el régimen del doctor Duvalier.* Mexico.

—— n.d. *Haiti: la crisis ininterrumpida 1930—1975.* n.p.

Piven, Frances Fox and Cloward, Richard A. 1971. *Regulating the Poor: The Functions of Public Welfare.* New York, Pantheon Books.

Plasencia Moro, A. 1984. 'El movimiento obrero cubano'. In González Casanova, *Historia del movimiento obrero en América Latina,* Mexico.

Plummer, Brenda Gayle. 1981. 'Black and White in the Caribbean: Haitian-American Relations. 1902–1934'. Ph.D. thesis, Cornell University, Ithaca, New York.

Pollitt, B. Agrarian reform and the agricultural proletariat in Cuba. 1958–66. Further notes and some second thoughts. *Occasional Papers 27 and 30.* University of Glasgow. I.L.A.S.

Post, Ken. 1978. *Arise ye Starvelings: The Jamaican Labour Rebellion of 1938 and its Aftermath.* The Hague, Martinus Nijhoff.

—— 1981. *Strike the Iron: A Colony at War—Jamaica, 1939–1945.* 2 vols. Atlantic Highlands, Humanities Press.

Problems of the New Cuba. 1935. New York, Foreign Policy Association.

Queiroz, M.I.P. de. 1965. 'Messiahs in Brazil'. *Past and Present.* 31 July. pp. 62–86.

Ramos Mattei, Andrés A. 1982. *Azúcar y esclavitud.* San Juan, Puerto Rico, Universidad do Puerto Rico.

Ransom, Roger L. and Sutch, Richard. 1977. *One kind of Freedom: The Economic Consequences of Emancipation.* Cambridge, England, Cambridge University Press.

Reddock, Rhoda. 1985a. 'Women and Slavery in the Caribbean: A Feminist Perspective'. *Latin American Perspectives.* 12(1), pp. 63–80.

—— 1985b. 'Freedoms Denied: Indian Women and Indentureship in Trinidad and Tobago. 1845–1917'. *Economic and Political Weekly.* XX (43), 26 October, pp. 79–87.

Regini, Marino. 1979. 'Labor Unions. Industrial Action and Politics'. West European Politics, 2, No. 3 October.

Reidy, Joseph P. 1980. 'Sugar and Freedom: Emancipation in Louisiana's Sugar Parishes'. Presented at the American Historical Association Annual Meetings, (December).

—— 1982. 'The Development of Central Factories and the Rise of Tenancy in Louisiana's Sugar Economy. 1880–1910'. Prepared for the Social Science History Association Annual Meeting. (November).

Report on Cuba, 1951. Washington D.C., International Bank for Reconstruction and Development.

République d'Haïti. Department du Travail et du Bien-etre Social. n.d. *Actes du Premier Congres National du Travail. I er mai 1949.* Port-au-Prince.

République d'Haïti. Secrétairerie d'Etat des Affaires Sociales. 1969a. *Actes du Deuxième Congrès National du travail. 21–30 avril 1969. Tome I* Port-au-Prince.

—— 1969b. *Actes du Deuxieme Congrès national du travail, 21–30 avril 1969. Tome II.* Port-au-Prince.

Rivero Muñiz, J. 1961. *El movimiento obrero durante la primera intervención.* Universidad Central de las Villas.

Roberts, G.W. 1957. *The Population of Jamaica.* Cambridge, Cambridge University Press.

Rodney, Walter. 1981. *History of the Guyanese Working People 1881–1905.* London, Johns Hopkins University Press.

Rodríguez Demorizi, E. (ed.) 1939. *Hostos en Santo Domingo*. Ciudad Trujillo.
—— 1964. *Papeles de Pedro F. Bono*. Santo Domingo. 1980 ed. was published Barcelona, M. Pareja.
—— 1975. *Lengua y folklore de Santo Domingo*. Santiago.
Roig de Leuchsenring, E. 1954. *Cuba libre: Juan Gualberto Gómez*. Havana.
Roseberry, W. 1983. *Coffee and Capitalism in the Venezuelan Andes*. Austin.
Rotberg, Robert I. with Clague, Christopher K. 1971. *Haiti. The Politics of Squalor*. Boston.
Roughley, T. 1823. *The Jamaica Planter's Guide*. London.
Sánchez, Juan J. 1893. *La caña en Santo Domingo*. Santo Domingo.
—— 1893. *La caña en Santo Domingo*. Santo Domingo, (reprint 1972).
Scarborough, Wm. K. 1966. *The Overseer*. Baton Rouge, Louisiana State University Press.
Schmidt, Hans, 1971. *The United States Occupation of Haiti, 1915–1934*. New Brunswick, N.J.
Schmitter, Philippe C. 1979. 'Still a Century of Corporatism?'. In Philippe Schmitter and Gerhard Lehmbruch (eds.) *Trends Toward Corporatist Intermediation*. Sage Publications, Beverley-Hills/London.
Scott, J.C. and Kerkvliet, B.J. 1973. 'How Traditional Rural Patrons Lose Legitimacy'. *Cultures et développement*. Summer, pp. 501–540.
Scott, J.C. 1976. *The Moral Economy of the Peasant. Rebellion and Subsistence in South East Asia*. New Haven, London.
—— 1985. *Weapons of the Weak: Everyday Forms of Peasant Resistance*. New Haven/London.
Scott, Rebecca J. 1985. *Slave Emancipation in Cuba: The Transition to Free Labour. 1860–1899*. Princeton University Press.
—— 1985. 'Class Relations in Sugar and Political Mobilization in Cuba'. *Cuban Studies/Estudios Cubanos*. 15 (Winter), pp. 15–28.
—— 1983. 'Gradual Abolition and the Dynamics of Slave Emancipation in Cuba'. *Hispanic American Historical Review*. 63 (August), pp. 449–477.
—— 1984. 'Explaining Abolition: Contradiction, Adpatation and Challenge in Cuban Slave Society. 1860–1886'. *Comparative Studies in Society and History*. 26 (January), pp. 83–111.
Sheridan, R.B. 1974. *Sugar and Slavery: An Economic History of the British West Indies, 1623–1775*. Barbados.
Shoman, Assad. 1973 'The birth of the nationalist movement in Belize, 1950–1954'. *Journal of Belizean Affairs*, 2, pp. 3–40.
Sitterton, J. Carlyle. 1953. *Sugar Country: The Cane Sugar Industry in the South. 1753–1950*. Lexington, The University of Kentucky Press.
Snell, K.D.M. 1980. 'Agricultural Seasonal Unemployment, the Standards of Living and Women's Work in the South and East 1690–1860'. *Economic History Review*. pp. 407–437.
Soberanis, Antonio and Kemp, L.D. 1949. *The Third Side of the Anglo-Guatemala Dispute*. Belize City, Commercial Press.
Spector, Robert Melvyn. 1961. 'W. Cameroon Forbes and the Hoover Commissions to Haiti'. Ph.D. thesis, Boston University, Boston.
Stubbs, J. 1985. *Tobacco in the periphery: a case study in Cuban labour, 1860–1958*. Cambridge University Press.
Thomas, H, *Cuba or the pursuit of freedom*. London.
Tiebout, Charles. 1956. 'A Pure Theory of Local Expenditures'. *Journal of*

Political Economy. Vol. 64.

Tullock, Gordon. 1967. *The Social Dilemma. The Economics of War and Revolution*. Blacksburg, Va.

Turton, P. 1986. *José Martí: architect of Cuba's freedom*. London.

US War Department. 1900. *Report on the Census of Cuba, 1899*. Washington, Government Printing Office.

Useem, B. 'Peasant involvement in the Cuban Revolution'. *Journal of Peasant Studies*. I.

Valenzuela, Samuel, 1983. 'Movimientos obreros y sistemas políticos: Un análisis conceptual y tipológico'. *Desarrollo Economico*. 23, No. 91, Oct—Dec.

Vedovato, Claudio. 1986. *Politics, Foreign Trade & Economic Development: A Study of the Dominican Republic*. New York, St Martin's Press.

Waddell, D.A.G. 1961. *British Honduras: A Historical and Contemporary Survey*. London, Oxford University Press.

Weinstein, Brian and Segal, Aaron. 1984. *Haiti, Political Failures, Cultural Sucesses*. New York.

Wiarda, Howard and Kryzanek, Michael. 1982. *The Dominican Republic: A Caribbean Crucible*. Boulder, Westview Press.

Wiener, Jonathan. 1979. 'Class Structure and Economic Development in the American South. 1865–1955'. *The American Historical Review*. 84, (October), pp. 970–992.

Will, H.A. 1970. *Constitutional Change in the British West Indies, 1880–1903*. Oxford, Clarendon Press.

Williams, Eric. 1970. *From Columbus to Castro*. London, Andre Deutsch.

Woodman, Harold D. 1970. 'Sequel to Slavery: The New History Views the Postbellum South'. *Journal of Southern History*. (November), pp. 523–554.

—— 1971. *The Negro in the Caribbean*. Westport, Connecticut, Negro Universities Press. (Reprint of the 1942 edition).

Wolf, E.R. 1969. *Peasant Wars of the Twentieth Century*. New York.

—— 1982. *Europe and the People Without History*. Cambridge.

Wood, E.F.L. 1922. *West Indies and British Guiana*. London, His Majesty's Stationery Office.

Young, Dennis R. 1976. 'Consolidation of Diversity: Choices in the Structure of Urban Governance'. *American Economic Review*. Vol. 66.

Zeitlin, M. 1967. *Revolutionary politics and the Cuban working class*. Princeton.

Index